"Creation is important for far more t[illegible] Dennis Hollinger shows us how this foundational doctrine is vital for discerning how to navigate the complexities of life in the world God created. Hollinger makes a clear connection between doctrine and ethics, and his depth of study and insight will help Christians walk with conviction, wisdom, humility, and generosity."

—**Vincent Bacote**, Center for Applied Christian Ethics, Wheaton College

"Hollinger is a wise ethicist who has given us a book that is full of wisdom. He argues convincingly—and eloquently—that a biblical ethics that is genuinely biblical must be firmly grounded in the knowledge of God's creating purposes in designing the marvelous world where he calls us to do his will. I learned much from this book, and I plan to return to it frequently to learn even more."

—**Richard J. Mouw**, Fuller Theological Seminary (emeritus)

"Hollinger's fundamental instinct—which he consistently and ably applies throughout the book and across various subjects—is to make sure our ethics begin with the goodness of creation. It sounds easier than it often proves to be in practice: some downplay the goodness of creation because of a hyper-emphasis on the fall, while others ignore creation by giving the spirit of this age too much unquestioned influence. I'm glad to see him push us toward the goodness and the faithful trajectory of God's creation in the way he does."

—**Kelly M. Kapic**, Covenant College

"If the resurrection vindicates creation, then understanding the significance of creation in its biblical and trinitarian foundation alongside the teachings of Jesus, the kingdom, and eschatology is paramount for Christian ethics. *Creation and Christian Ethics* reclaims the centrality of this doctrine for understanding our creatureliness and social responsibility regarding an array of critical topics facing the contemporary church. Timely and comprehensive, this book is an essential read for discerning faithful witness and ethical practice in our day."

—**Autumn Alcott Ridenour**, Gordon-Conwell Theological Seminary

"Hollinger is one of the most respected evangelical Protestant ethicists of our generation. This much-needed book is clear, cogent, and impressively comprehensive. This outstanding work of contemporary moral reflection is biblically rich, philosophically astute, and contextually engaged."

—**Jeffrey P. Greenman**, Regent College

"A masterful examination of creation and its implications for contemporary Christian ethics. Hollinger carefully navigates the theory-praxis tension so often present in the field by offering a refreshingly robust biblical and theological account of creation and its practical application to many of the most challenging ethical issues of our day."

—**Michael J. Sleasman**, Trinity Evangelical Divinity School

"As we've come to expect from Hollinger, *Creation and Christian Ethics* is another first-rate work in the area of Christian ethics. It is thorough and well documented and will be a rich resource for those thinking hard about questions at the intersection of Christian faith and culture. The evangelical tradition has not always given the doctrine of creation sufficient weight—Hollinger corrects that neglect well in this important work."

—**Scott B. Rae**, Talbot School of Theology, Biola University

CREATION AND CHRISTIAN ETHICS

CREATION AND CHRISTIAN ETHICS

UNDERSTANDING GOD'S DESIGNS FOR HUMANITY AND THE WORLD

DENNIS P. HOLLINGER

Baker Academic
a division of Baker Publishing Group
Grand Rapids, Michigan

Published by Baker Academic
a division of Baker Publishing Group
Grand Rapids, Michigan
www.bakeracademic.com

Printed in the United States of America

Library of Congress Cataloging-in-Publication Data
Names: Hollinger, Dennis P., 1948– author.
Title: Creation and Christian ethics : understanding God's designs for humanity and the world / Dennis P. Hollinger.
Description: Grand Rapids, Michigan : Baker Academic, a division of Baker Publishing Group, [2023] | Includes bibliographical references and index.
Identifiers: LCCN 2023016629 | ISBN 9781540967176 (paperback) | ISBN 9781540967282 (casebound) | ISBN 9781493444311 (ebook) | ISBN 9781493444328 (pdf)
Subjects: LCSH: Theological anthropology—Christianity. | Creation—Religious aspects—Christianity. | Christian ethics.
Classification: LCC BT701.3 .H65 2023 | DDC 241—dc23/eng/20230629
LC record available at https://lccn.loc.gov/2023016629

Baker Publishing Group publications use paper produced from sustainable forestry practices and post-consumer waste whenever possible.

23 24 25 26 27 28 29 7 6 5 4 3 2 1

Contents

Introduction

Why Creation for Ethics?

What has creation to do with ethics? That's the puzzled question I'm frequently asked by people who hear about this project. The prophets and ethics? Yes. Jesus and ethics? Certainly. Paul and ethics? Without a doubt. The kingdom and ethics? Absolutely. But creation?

After all, when many Christian people hear the word *creation*, their mind immediately goes to the controversies: When did God create the world and humans? How did God bring about this creation? And to what extent did God use natural processes in the unfolding of creation? These questions have engendered intense divisions among Christians, and it is only natural that we ask them. But in Scripture these are not the primary issues, and they tend to mask the most salient biblical teachings about creation. Our actual response to these when and how questions will likely have little direct bearing on ethics.

Some, upon hearing the tandem of creation and ethics, might assume that this book is about creation care, our alertness to and stewardship of God's good creation. And indeed, we will devote a whole chapter to that important topic. But creation care by no means exhausts the ethical implications of creation. As we will see, creation provides paradigms for crucial and complex issues, such as racial justice, economic justice, bioethics, sexual ethics, artificial intelligence (AI), and even political thought. Creation provides moral frameworks, sets boundaries, specifies directions, and even reveals something of the nature and actions of God, the source of all ethical norms. In creation we see the moral designs of God that impact our thought, actions, and character.

Other readers might assume that this is a book about natural law. That is, God has ordered the world in such a way that his designs are not only embedded in creation but can be discerned by all human beings through reason, observation, history, or experience. There is, of course, a long tradition of natural law ethics, most visible in the Roman Catholic tradition and perhaps best expressed in the thinking of Thomas Aquinas in the thirteenth century. Creation has played a role in this tradition with the assumption that God has designed the world in such a way that much of God's law is accessible outside of special revelation and saving grace in Christ. Because humans are the product of God's good creation and bear God's image, all have access to the essentials of God's moral designs. This book will give some modified credence to natural law, for after all the apostle Paul argues, "What may be known about God is plain to [people], because God has made it plain to them. For since the creation of the world God's invisible qualities—his eternal power and divine nature—have been clearly seen, being understood from what has been made, so that people are without excuse" (Rom. 1:19–20). But the biblical story of creation encompasses far more than a natural law implanted in all humans. Moreover, today natural law ethics faces as much an uphill battle for approval as biblical ethics. The hardness of human hearts and the acceptance of larger narratives about the world and human nature preclude many from accepting a natural law framework for ethical thought and living. Thus, my argument is not a natural law defense, for creation, as we will see, is a theological precept, comprehended primarily through divine revelation and God's grace in Christ.

Still others might think that a book on creation and ethics is harkening back to a concept prevalent among some of the Reformers and then later thinkers in the Reformed tradition—creation ordinances, orders, or mandates. Luther, Calvin, and various thinkers in modern times have spoken of God at creation ordaining or mandating particular spheres of reality with specified ethical guidance in those spheres, including temporal authorities ordained by God for those realms. Among the suggested creation ordinances have been marriage, work, culture, and the state. Some of what follows in this book will have similarities with that tradition, but there will be substantial differences. The whole notion of creation ordinances has been highly critiqued among ethicists and theologians in the past century, and to some degree rightly so. Dietrich Bonhoeffer, preferring the term *mandates* over *ordinances*, notes "the danger of directing attention rather towards the actual state of the institution than towards its foundation, which lies solely in the divine warrant, legitimation and authorization." The result, he notes, "can all too easily be the assumption of a divine sanction for all existing orders and institutions in general and a romantic conservatism which is entirely at variance with the Christian doctrine of the . . . divine mandates."[1] While creation provides ethical frameworks and mandates that are timeless, this does not mean an acceptance and blessing of current, fallen realities that originated in creation.

The argument of this book is very simply that in and through creation our loving, triune God has designed and spoken in such a way that essential

1. Dietrich Bonhoeffer, *Ethics*, ed. Eberhard Bethge (New York: Macmillan, 1949), 288.

paradigms are put in place for humans to follow. These paradigms, frameworks, and moral directives are affirmed throughout the rest of Scripture and by Jesus, and further revelation deepens the understanding. Further revelation, however, does not overturn what God has disclosed in the creation story or other biblical teachings about creation. In other words, creation is an essential theological component for the Christian faith and for the everyday life of a believer traversing the moral landscape of today's complex world. As Bruce Riley Ashford and Craig Bartholomew put it, "Approaching our world through the lens of creation is radical in our late modern context and provides fresh perspectives on area after area of life."[2] This by no means sets aside the Decalogue, Wisdom literature, the Prophets, Jesus and the Gospels, Paul's Letters, or any of the other canonical writings. But these core elements of biblical-ethical thought reinforce what the triune God was up to in creation and what was revealed in the creation narratives and the rest of Scripture concerning creation.

And what do I mean by creation? As will become clear, much will be drawn from Genesis 1–2, but with reinforcement from many other biblical texts on creation. My focus in this book is not the physical creation or nature, though that is included, but primarily theological and ethical themes embedded in God's creation design. "Creation isn't simply a teaching about the beginning of things. More importantly, it is about the character of the world and its proper orientation, alerting us to the meaning, value, and purpose of everything that is."[3] As we will see shortly, creation is essential to understanding the biblical story in its entirety, and in the creation paradigms, we are drawing together the reality of a triune God whose persons cannot be pitted against each other. God the Creator and God the Redeemer are one, and thus what we find in God's gracious giving of the Decalogue and what is found in the biblical poets, prophets, Jesus, Paul, and John's Apocalypse are in continuity with creation designs. Thus, in creation we find as the subtitle of this book puts it, an ethic of "God's Designs for Humanity and the World." And in the end, we find the great gathering around the throne in which "the living creatures" give glory, honor, and thanks to the God of creation: "You are worthy, our Lord and God, to receive glory and honor and power, for you created all things, and by your will they were created and have their being" (Rev. 4:11). Creation and eschaton are never pulled apart.

But why creation for ethics? In the remainder of this chapter, we explore five primary reasons for creation being the starting point of Christian ethics: the biblical story (metanarrative) is incomplete without creation; creation is

2. Bruce Riley Ashford and Craig G. Bartholomew, *The Doctrine of Creation: A Constructive Kuyperian Approach* (Downers Grove, IL: IVP Academic, 2020), 3.

3. Norman Wirzba, "Creation *through* Christ," in *Christ and the Created Order: Perspectives from Theology, Philosophy, and Science*, ed. Andrew B. Torrance and Thomas H. McCall (Grand Rapids: Zondervan, 2018), 40.

a major theme throughout the whole of Scripture; the doctrine of the Trinity is at stake; the final consummation is not a starting over of creation but a renewal or restoration of what God created in the beginning; and creation is full of salient ethical themes.

The Biblical Story (Metanarrative) Is Incomplete without Creation

As is frequently noted, the biblical narrative has four main components: creation, fall, redemption, and consummation (or restoration). Pull out one component of the story, and the whole narrative falls apart. The various parts of Scripture and the theological reflections implied in God's written Word only make sense in light of the whole. But it is precisely the isolation of one part of the story to the exclusion of the other parts that has been the norm in ethical discourse in the past century or two.

Reinhold Niebuhr has been deemed by many the most significant ethical voice of the mid-twentieth century. Niebuhr was quite clear that one dimension of the biblical story was most salient for understanding our world and finding our way ethically—namely, the fall. His Christian social realism was built upon the fallenness of humanity, which permeated society and its major social institutions. It's doubtful that Niebuhr understood the fall as a real historical event; rather, he saw it as a mythical construct that enables us to see ourselves, others, and the world. There was minimal space for creation in his view, and Jesus simply embodied the "impossible possibility," judging all human and societal endeavors but providing no guidance for the complexities of social life.[4]

John Howard Yoder, the Anabaptist theologian, strongly castigates the Niebuhrian realist tradition in his *Politics of Jesus*. However, his own ethic makes an opposite error by isolating the redemptive component of the biblical story. In contrast to constructing an ethic from the way things are in the fallen world, Yoder argues that Jesus is "not only relevant but also normative for a contemporary Christian social ethic."[5] For Yoder, this Jesus-centered social ethic will not be found in the powers of government or other social institutions but will be lodged in the church. Redemptive ethics centered in Jesus was reinforced by Stanley Hauerwas in his claim that the church does not have a social ethic; it is a social ethic, embodying the teachings and actions of Jesus in its life together. Creation is virtually missing in Yoder's rendition and plays a minimal role in Hauerwas's construal.[6]

4. See Reinhold Niebuhr, *An Interpretation of Christian Ethics* (London: SCM, 1936), esp. 47–74; and Niebuhr, *Moral Man and Immoral Society: A Study in Ethics and Politics* (New York: Scribner's Sons, 1960).

5. John Howard Yoder, *The Politics of Jesus: Vicit Agnus Noster*, 2nd ed. (Grand Rapids: Eerdmans, 1994), 11.

6. See, for example, Stanley Hauerwas, *Approaching the End: Eschatological Reflections on Church, Politics, and Life* (Grand Rapids: Eerdmans, 2013). See particularly pp. 3–21, where

Going back to the nineteenth century, the Social Gospel movement argued that the kingdom of God was the heart of social ethics. The kingdom was the major theme of Jesus, and while it was an eschatological term, it had immediate relevance for transforming the structures of society, particularly economics, in accordance with kingdom ideals. But creation was missing in the Social Gospel movement. In more recent times, various authors have seen the kingdom theme as the central motif in Christian ethics, sometimes with an explicit rejection of creation having ethical significance. Writing on sexual ethics, David Gushee argues that we should not look back to "God's purported design in creation" but rather look forward to Jesus and the kingdom. He writes, "I am suggesting the idea that Christian theology does better leaning forward toward Jesus Christ, his person and his work, his way of doing ministry and advancing God's coming kingdom, the new creation he brings forth, rather than leaning backward to the primeval creation narratives, where we so often run into trouble." He then adds, "Instead of relying just on Genesis 1–2, we should consider more seriously the implications for sexual ethics of living in a Genesis 3 world,"[7] but always with an eye toward the kingdom. Here creation is not merely missing; it is explicitly rejected for ethics and thus divorced from an understanding of the coming new creation, which I will contend is in continuity with creation.

Each of the above construals fails to hold together the whole of the biblical story and the Christian theological metanarrative, a failure that comes about by focusing on one dimension and leaving aside creation. But pulling out creation renders the other parts incoherent. We only understand the meaning and nature of the fall by first grasping the meaning of creation. The fall is a rejection of what God the Creator designed and commanded, and its effects are only evident in relation to God's creational intentions. In the story of the fall in Genesis 3, the one who created Adam and Eve has a claim upon their lives precisely because he made them. With the tree of life and the tree of the knowledge of good and evil in the middle of the garden, God commands them not to eat of the latter: "You must not eat from the tree of the knowledge of good and evil, for when you eat from it you will certainly die" (2:17). Adam and Eve give into the tempter with the deluded promise that they will now be like the one who made them, hence knowing good and evil (3:5). This is not failing to uphold an abstract law of God but is trampling on the designs of the loving, personal God who made them. It matters precisely because God is their Creator. Thus, the subsequent fall of humanity and the entire

---

he argues that we can only understand creation from an eschatological perspective, meaning through Christ. Here and in other works by Hauerwas, creation provides no substantive ethical guidance.

7. David Gushee, *Changing Our Mind: A Call from America's Leading Evangelical Ethics Scholar for Full Acceptance of LGBT Christians in the Church* (Canton, MI: Read the Spirit Books, 2014), Kindle loc. 1418, 1440–48.

cosmos is only understood with reference to creation. The fall leads to an alienation from God (vv. 8–10), self (vv. 10, 13), others (vv. 12, 16), and even nature (vv. 17–19).

After the fall God begins a process of redemption to restore the broken relationships and all the other effects of the fall. This process begins already with a promise in Genesis 3, where the Creator says to the serpent, the vehicle of Satan, "I will put enmity between you and the woman, and between your offspring and hers; he will strike your head, and you will strike his heel" (v. 15 NRSV). A further promise is given to Abraham that through his descendants (linked to Jesus of Nazareth), a salvific blessing will come for the whole world. God calls out a people to himself, liberates them from bondage, gives them his law (a reflection of creation designs), and promises them a Savior who will come to restore and heal the breach. Christ, the Redeemer, Savior, and Lord, comes into the world to redeem humanity from their sin and alienation, but also to display to his followers a new way to live—a way already patterned in the creation of which he was a part. A generation ago Oliver O'Donovan wisely argued that the resurrection of Christ and creation are deeply interwoven and, thus, that the kingdom-creation divide in Christian ethics is unacceptable. "We are driven to concentrate on the resurrection as our starting point because it tells us of God's vindication of his creation, and so of our created life." Moreover, he contends, "A kingdom ethics which was set up in opposition to creation could not possibly be interested in the eschatological kingdom as that which the New Testament proclaims. . . . A creation ethics, on the other hand, which was set up in opposition to the kingdom, could not possibly be evangelical ethics, since it would fail to take note of the good news that God acted to bring all that he had made to its fulfilment."[8]

Christopher Watkin argues that "if God made everything, then he owns it and is in charge of it. Conversely, if God didn't create the universe, if he is just one of its many inhabitants like you and me, then the idea of sin as an offence against God does not make sense. And if sin does not make sense, then salvation does not make sense either."[9] And as Brent Waters writes, "Christ's redemptive work refers to a created order because it 'suggests the recovery of something given and lost'—namely, the properly ordered relationship among the creator, creation, and its creatures."[10] Without creation both sin and redemption become incoherent.

8. Oliver O'Donovan, *Resurrection and Moral Order: An Outline for Evangelical Ethics* (Grand Rapids: Eerdmans, 1986), 13, 15.

9. Christopher Watkin, *Biblical Critical Theory: How the Bible's Unfolding Story Makes Sense of Modern Life and Culture* (Grand Rapids: Zondervan Academic, 2022), 53.

10. Brent Waters, *Common Callings and Ordinary Virtues: Christian Ethics for Everyday Life* (Grand Rapids: Baker Academic, 2022), 7; Waters quotes O'Donovan, *Resurrection and Moral Order*, 54.

But, of course, that's not the end of the story. Jesus leaves this world to return to the Father and sends the Spirit in fullness to enable his people, the church, to live in accordance with his Word, which reflects the designs of his creation. Before leaving this world, Jesus, echoing the prophets of the Old Testament, reminds his followers that though the work of redemption has been fully accomplished on the cross, the working out of that redemption awaits the eschaton, the fullness of his kingdom. But as we will see, the final consummation is not a destruction of God's good creation but a restoration of what was intended in creation. The eschaton, the fullness of the kingdom, can only be understood as being in continuity with what God intended in the first place, before sin wreaked havoc in the world and the lives of humans.

From all of this, we deduce that without creation the rest of the biblical story is not only incomplete but incoherent. As Luke Timothy Johnson puts it, "The designation of God as creator, or as the 'one who makes' . . . , grounds all other statements of the creed. It is because God, the one, all-powerful Father, is the source of all things that God can be revealer, savior, sanctifier, and judge of all."[11] Thus, creation, fall, redemption, and consummation (ultimate restoration) stand together. The only discontinuity is the fall, which distorts and mars God's designs from creation. Creation cannot be removed from the grand narrative that informs and guides our Christian ethic.

Creation: A Central Theme throughout Scripture

Not only is creation central to the big-picture story of biblical faith, but it is also a major theme throughout all of the Scriptures. An analysis of all pertinent texts dealing with creation could span another book by itself, and others have already published analyses of that kind. But let me highlight a few significant texts, reflecting various parts of Scripture and multiple biblical genres. Seeing how central a theme creation is in the canon of God's written Word grounds its corresponding centrality to belief, worship, spiritual formation, Christian community, and yes, ethical living.

The Decalogue

In the Exodus account of the Ten Commandments, there is one explicit reference to creation but several inferred or indirect references. The explicit is the rationale for keeping the Sabbath: "Remember the Sabbath day by keeping it holy. Six days you shall labor and do all your work, but the seventh day

11. Luke Timothy Johnson, *The Creed: What Christians Believe and Why It Matters* (New York: Doubleday, 2005), 93.

is a sabbath to the LORD your God. On it you shall not do any work, neither you, nor your son or daughter, nor your male or female servant, nor your animals, nor any foreigner residing in your towns. For in six days the LORD made the heavens and the earth . . . , but he rested on the seventh day. Therefore the LORD blessed the Sabbath day and made it holy" (20:8–11). In this text the Sabbath (and all it entails—i.e., worship of God, self-care, and justice; see chap. 8) is to be obeyed because it mirrors the very work of the Creator. In the Deuteronomy account, the rationale is God's liberating activity in the Exodus: "Remember that you were slaves in Egypt and that the LORD your God brought you out of there with a mighty hand and an outstretched arm. Therefore the LORD your God has commanded you to observe the Sabbath day" (5:15). It is significant, however, that in the preceding chapter, as the people are about to hear the Decalogue, the Lord calls them back to faithfulness with an appeal to creation: "Ask now about former ages . . . , ever since the day that God created human beings on the earth; ask from one end of heaven to the other" (4:32 NRSV).

In the Decalogue there are also inferred or indirect references to divine creation. The first three commands (prohibiting other gods, images of God, and the misuse of God's name) all assume the priority of a God who has a claim upon them. This correlates with the opening lines of Scripture, "In the beginning God . . ." (Gen. 1:1). The eternal God exists before the world, humanity, and the revelation of divine designs within the world; thus, it only makes sense that the law of God begins with the priority and exclusivity of God. The sixth commandment, prohibiting murder (Exod. 20:13), reflects God's creation of humans in his own image (Gen. 1:26–27), and Genesis 9:6 makes an explicit tie between protecting human life and being made in God's image. The fifth and seventh commandments, regarding honoring father and mother (Exod. 20:12) and prohibiting adultery (v. 14), have their roots in God's creation establishment of marriage, sex, and family, with the man and the woman becoming "one flesh" (Gen. 2:24).

The eighth commandment, prohibiting stealing (Exod. 20:15), and the tenth commandment, against coveting a neighbor's house, wife, servant, animals, or anything else belonging to him (v. 17), reflect several dimensions of creation. They assume that material realities are good, as clearly referenced throughout Genesis 1, and they also assume God's mandate to both properly steward God's good creation (vv. 28–30) and work (2:15). The ninth commandment, "You shall not give false testimony against your neighbor" (Exod. 20:16), is not only a command to protect the dignity of a neighbor, stemming from creation in God's image, but a generalized protection of truth that is essential for humans living together in this world as created, relational beings. As Gil Meilaender puts it, "The Creator has so ordered human life that our societies cannot easily survive without at least a general commitment to truthful speech. Were lying a common and expected practice, it would easily turn out to be self-defeating; we could never trust each other."[12] Our created relationality would be impossible.

God's moral law in the Decalogue is frequently thought to be one of the major summaries of human moral obligation. It is summarized by Jesus as love of God and love of neighbor (Matt. 22:37–40). But we must also understand that the Decalogue and Jesus's summary of it point back to God's creation, his designs from the beginning.

Job

The book of Job is not only a story of suffering and the attempt to make sense of it; it is a story climaxing in the memory of God's creation. After Job's suffering and three rounds of the friends' accusation of guilt and Job's defense of his innocence, God intervenes and takes him on a journey through creation. "Job 38:1–42:6 sets out what is unquestionably the most comprehensive understanding of God as creator to be found in the Old Testament, stressing the role of God as creator and sustainer of the world."[13] Just a few samplings of the beauty and glory of this poetry will have to suffice:

> Where were you when I laid the earth's foundation?
> Tell me, if you understand.
> Who marked off its dimensions? Surely you know!
> Who stretched a measuring line across it?
> On what were its footings set,
> or who laid its cornerstone—
> while the morning stars sang together
> and all the angels shouted for joy? (38:4–7)
>
> Can you bring forth the constellations in their seasons
> or lead out the Bear with its cubs?
> Do you know the laws of the heavens?
> Can you set up God's dominion over the earth?
> Can you raise your voice to the clouds
> and cover yourself with a flood of water?
> Do you send the lightning bolts on their way?
> Do they report to you, "Here we are"? (vv. 32–35)

After the grand tour of creation and the rhetorical questions from the Creator, Job replies to the Lord, "I know that you can do all things; no purpose of yours can be thwarted. . . . My ears had heard of you but now my eyes have seen you. Therefore I despise myself and repent in dust and ashes" (42:2,

12. Gilbert Meilaender, *Thy Will Be Done: The Ten Commandments and the Christian Life* (Grand Rapids: Baker Academic, 2020), 98.

13. Alister E. McGrath, *Christian Theology: An Introduction*, 5th ed. (Oxford: Wiley-Blackwell, 2011), 216.

5–6). Reflecting on divine creation leads Job to a place of understanding, repentance, renewal, and then restoration.

The Psalms

The Psalms, a primary source of worship and liturgy for both the Hebrew people and the Christian church, frequently appeal to creation as a foundation for worship and guidance. Below is just a small sampling of creation themes in the Psalms. In Psalm 8 we see a link between the majesty of God's creation and the value of human beings, who have been given the task of caring for that creation:

> LORD, our Lord,
> how majestic is your name in all the earth! . . .
>
> When I consider your heavens,
> the work of your fingers,
> the moon and the stars,
> which you have set in place,
> what is [humankind] that you are mindful of them,
> human beings that you care for them?
>
> You have made them a little lower than the angels
> and crowned them with glory and honor.
> You made them rulers over the works of your hands;
> you put everything under their feet. . . .
>
> LORD, our Lord,
> how majestic is your name in all the earth! (Ps. 8:1, 3–6, 9)

Psalm 19 portrays what has sometimes been called the two books of God, through which he speaks: the created world of nature and the law of God (or written Word). It begins with creation: "The heavens declare the glory of God; the skies proclaim the work of his hands. Day after day they pour forth speech; night after night they reveal knowledge" (vv. 1–2). The second half of the psalm turns to God's written law: "The law of the LORD is perfect, refreshing the soul. The statutes of the LORD are trustworthy, making wise the simple. The precepts of the LORD are right, giving joy to the heart. The commands of the LORD are radiant, giving light to the eyes" (vv. 7–8). As a result of both forms of revelation and divine activity (including creation), there is a call to righteous living: "Keep your servant also from willful sins; may they not rule over me. Then I will be blameless, innocent of great transgression" (v. 13).

Psalm 33 ties divine righteousness, justice, and love to creation: "He loves righteousness and justice; the earth is full of the steadfast love of the LORD. By the word of the LORD the heavens were made, and all their host by the breath of his mouth. . . . For he spoke, and it came to be; he commanded, and it stood firm" (vv. 5–6, 9 NRSV). Here God's moral designs for humans, reflecting his own righteousness, justice, and love, are linked to God's speaking in creation. The physical designs of creation are not separated from the moral designs. As a result the following verses indicate that the Lord frustrates human plans and brings to nothing the counsel of nations, whereas his own counsel stands forever (vv. 10–11).

Wisdom Literature

Wisdom is a significant moral category in Scripture, for it involves not only clear, right paths to follow in life but also discernment in the more complex circumstances of life, in which the right path might not be immediately clear. While wisdom is a significant theme throughout the entire Bible, some segments are designated Wisdom literature and come to us in a very particularized genre, most notably the book of Proverbs with its proverbial-style statements. Proverbs 8 is one of the great wisdom texts in the book, with its personification of wisdom, which is seen not only as part of creation but even as predating creation because it is rooted in the eternal Godhead. The chapter, like others surrounding it, begins with the significance of wisdom for understanding, truth, justice, and uprightness of life. Then the text turns to wisdom's relationship to divine creation:

> The LORD brought me [wisdom] forth as the first of his works,
> before his deeds of old;
> I was formed long ages ago,
> at the very beginning, when the world came to be.
> When there were no watery depths, I was given birth, . . .
> before he made the world or its fields
> or any of the dust of the earth.
> I was there when he set the heavens in place,
> when he marked out the horizon on the face of the deep, . . .
> when he gave the sea its boundary
> so the waters would not overstep his command,
> and when he marked out the foundations of the earth.
> Then I was constantly at his side.
> I was filled with delight day after day,
> rejoicing always in his presence,
> rejoicing in his whole world
> and delighting in [humankind]. (vv. 22–24, 26–27, 29–31)

The chapter then closes with this promise: "For those who find me [wisdom] find life and receive favor from the LORD. But those who fail to find me harm themselves; all who hate me love death" (vv. 35–36).

In the book of James, the moral appeal of wisdom is evident, and some see it as a creational application for ethical living, along with the appeal to kingdom principles.[14] James utilizes various dimensions of nature to make his appeal that faith needs works to demonstrate its genuineness: wild flowers and the sun (1:9–11); animals, the tongue, water, and a fig tree (3:1–12). For "who is wise and understanding among you? Show by your good life that your works are done with gentleness born of wisdom" (v. 13 NRSV). James seems to be harkening back to the creational wisdom seen in the Proverbs. And as an Old Testament scholar once put it, "Wisdom is ethical conformity to God's creation."[15]

The Prophets

The prophets of the Old Testament make many references to creation in calling God's people back to fidelity, righteousness, and justice. Hosea writes, "Israel has forgotten their Maker and built palaces; Judah has fortified many towns. But I will send fire on their cities that will consume their fortresses" (Hosea 8:14). Malachi speaks of the loss of God's favor because the people have broken a covenant relationship with God and with their spouses. Why are there tears? "It is because the Lord is the witness between you and the wife of your youth. You have been unfaithful to her, though she is your partner, the wife of your marriage covenant. Has not the one God made you? You belong to him in body and spirit" (Mal. 2:14–15). God has a claim upon their lives and marriages precisely because he is their Maker and Designer. As the people of God exhibit apathy, injustice, and idolatry, the prophet Amos reminds them of God's intentions for their lives, for it is their Maker "who forms the mountains, who creates the wind, and who reveals his thoughts to [humankind], who turns dawn to darkness, and treads on the heights of the earth—the Lord God Almighty is his name" (Amos 4:13). And when the prophet Jeremiah is struggling with his prophetic calling, the Lord assures him based on creation: "Thus says the Lord who made the earth, the Lord who formed it to establish it—the Lord is his name: Call to me and I will answer you, and will tell you great and hidden things that you have not known" (Jer. 33:2–3 NRSV).

The prophet Isaiah exhibits the greatest appeal and linkage to creation themes. "Isaiah holds both creation and redemption in tension throughout the book, and then the discourse as a whole climaxes with Israel's new creation as ideal servants who tremble at the word of God and live in obedience to the covenant."[16] Isaiah 40, one of the great messianic-prophecy texts, begins

14. My thanks go to Justin Zahraee and his paper "The Epistle of James as a Way Forward in the Ethics of Creation versus Ethics of the Kingdom Theological Debate" (presented at the Annual Meeting of the Evangelical Theological Society, Denver, CO, November 2018). Zahraee notes the similarities between James's use of created, natural phenomena and the use of such phenomena in ancient Jewish Wisdom literature.

15. James Fleming, *Personalities of the Old Testament* (New York: Scribner's Sons, 1939), 302.

16. Terrance R. Wardlaw Jr., "The Significance of Creation in the Book of Isaiah," *Journal of the Evangelical Theological Society* 59, no. 3 (2016): 466.

with the words "Comfort, comfort my people, says your God" (v. 1). Part of the comfort for the people is that the God who will tend "his flock like a shepherd" (v. 11) is God the Creator:

> Who has measured the waters in the hollow of his hand,
> or with the breadth of his hand marked off the heavens?
> Who has held the dust of the earth in a basket,
> or weighed the mountains on the scales
> and the hills in a balance? . . .
>
> Do you not know?
> Have you not heard?
> Has it not been told you from the beginning?
> Have you not understood since the earth was founded?
> [God] sits enthroned above the circle of the earth,
> and its people are like grasshoppers.
> He stretches out the heavens like a canopy,
> and spreads them out like a tent to live in. (vv. 12, 21–22)

The prophecy closes with divine restoration, which is in continuity with what God originally intended in creation. "See, I will create new heavens and a new earth. The former things will not be remembered, nor will they come to mind" (65:17; cf. 66:22). In that day of final renewal and consummation, "the wolf and the lamb will feed together, and the lion will eat straw like the ox, and dust will be the serpent's food. They will neither harm nor destroy on all my holy mountain" (65:25).

The Gospels

In the Gospels we find Jesus appealing to creation regarding a moral issue, acts of Jesus with allusion to creation, and descriptions of our Lord as Creator. In Matthew 19 (cf. Mark 10), Jesus responds to the Pharisees' question about divorce by quoting from the creation paradigm on marriage: "Have you not read that he who created them from the beginning made them male and female, and said, 'Therefore a man shall leave his father and his mother and hold fast to his wife, and the two shall become one flesh'? So they are no longer two but one flesh. What therefore God has joined together, let [no one] separate" (vv. 4–6 ESV). Here Jesus is quoting from both Genesis 1 and Genesis 2 in affirming the permanence of marriage, with an exception noted (v. 9).[17] Commenting on Jesus's statement, Wesley Hill writes, "Jesus . . . reads

17. While adultery is noted here as a grounds for divorce, Paul also includes abandonment by an unbelieving spouse as grounds (1 Cor. 7:12–16). Many, including myself, would by extension also see other grounds, such as spouse abuse, as a grounds for divorce because the covenant has been broken by abusive actions.

the sexual difference of humanity in Genesis 1:26–27—the creation of humanity as male and female—alongside the affirmation of a bond of faithful union in Genesis 2:24. With that fusion of the two texts, sexual difference and the meaning of marriage are pulled together and intertwined."[18] Jesus here then affirms a marriage paradigm for humanity, despite the fact that the fall and sin will wreak havoc and bring challenges to the creational design.

Along with direct quoting of creation paradigms, at least two actions of Jesus are portrayed in the Gospel of Mark as having indirect allusions to creation: Jesus calming the storm (4:35–41) and Jesus walking on the water (6:45–56). In each story the language and metaphors used would evoke in the Jewish mind the Creator's work in Genesis 1. For example, when Jesus calms the storm, the disciples respond, "Who is this? Even the wind and the waves obey him!" (Mark 4:41). Thus, "Mark's narrative presents Jesus as ruler over the realm of creation, and therefore, Creator of the realm he rules."[19]

In John 1 we find the most explicit portrayal of Christ as the Creator. Being one with the Father, the Word became flesh, and through him we see the glory of God. But this incarnate one was Creator and thus bound up with all that the act of creation encompassed.

> In the beginning was the Word, and the Word was with God, and the Word was God. He was with God in the beginning. Through him all things were made; without him nothing was made that has been made. In him was life, and that life was the light of all [humankind]. The light shines in the darkness, and the darkness has not overcome it. . . . He was in the world, and though the world was made through him, the world did not recognize him. . . . Yet to all who did receive him, to those who believed in his name, he gave the right to become children of God. (vv. 1–5, 10, 12)

Here not only is the Word identified as Creator, but his taking on human flesh in the midst of this world affirms the significance and goodness of his creation. N. T. Wright and Michael Bird describe it this way: "John was writing a new Genesis. His whole book, opening with the words 'in the beginning,' which echo Genesis 1:1, is about how the world's creator has come at last to remake his world."[20] The reference to the Word bringing life and light amid darkness portrays not only themes of redemption but moral designs enabling humans

18. Wesley Hill, "How Should Gay Christians Love?," in *Beauty, Order, and Mystery: A Christian Vision of Human Sexuality*, ed. Gerald Hiestand and Todd Wilson (Downers Grove, IL: IVP Academic, 2017), 39.

19. Darrin Snyder Belousek, "Who Then Is This? Jesus the Creator in the Gospel of Mark," in *The Earth Is the Lord's: Essays on Creation and the Bible in Honor of Ben C. Ollenburger*, ed. Ryan D. Harker and Heather L. Bunce (University Park: Pennsylvania State University Press, 2019), 106.

20. N. T. Wright and Michael F. Bird, *The New Testament in Its World: An Introduction to the History, Literature, and Theology of the First Christians* (Grand Rapids: Zondervan, 2019), 650.

to find their way in this world. What the triune God established at creation is affirmed by Jesus the Creator, the one who entered this world full of grace and truth (vv. 14, 17), a model for our own lives.

Acts and the Epistles

Themes of creation resound throughout the rest of the New Testament. In the book of Acts, after Peter and John are released by the Sanhedrin following accusations of disturbance for preaching the gospel, they return to the early believers. When these early followers of Christ hear what God is doing through their ministry, they respond with a prayer that rehearses God's revelation and history, starting with creation: "Sovereign Lord, who made the heaven and the earth and the sea and everything in them" (Acts 4:24 ESV). In Acts 10, after Cornelius, a gentile, summons Peter to learn more about the faith, God gives Peter a vision. In the vision Peter sees a sheet being let down from heaven and containing all kinds of four-footed animals, along with reptiles and birds. He hears a voice command him to eat the animals, but Peter replies that he has never eaten anything impure or unclean. Peter then hears a voice echoing the "It is good" refrain of creation in Genesis 1: "Do not call anything impure that God has made clean" (Acts 10:15). It is through a creation appeal that Peter overcomes his ethnocentricity and goes to the gentiles.

In Acts 17 Paul appears before the Areopagus in Athens and makes a presentation, following their inquiry about his new teaching (v. 19). In his apologetic Paul eventually gets to Christ and the resurrection, but he begins by noting their own gods and religious symbols, and then he turns to creation. "The God who made the world and everything in it is the Lord of heaven and earth and does not live in temples built by human hands. And he is not served by human hands, as if he needed anything. Rather, he himself gives everyone life and breath and everything else" (vv. 24–25). For Paul, the story of Christ and his resurrection is a story that begins with creation.

Paul frequently utilizes creational themes in his epistles, such as in the already-noted Romans 1:20: "For since the creation of the world God's invisible qualities—his eternal power and divine nature—have been clearly seen, being understood from what has been made, so that people are without excuse." In Ephesians 5:31 he quotes from the one-flesh text of Genesis 2 in describing the mutual responsibilities of husband and wife as a sign of the mystery of Christ's love for his church. In Colossians 1 Paul makes the case for Christ being the head of the church by appealing to his work in creation: "He is the image of the invisible God, the firstborn of all creation. For by him all things were created, in heaven and on earth, visible and invisible, whether thrones or dominions or rulers or authorities—all things were created through him. . . . And in him all things hold together" (vv. 15–17 ESV). And in 1 Timothy 4, Paul debunks ascetic false teachers who "forbid people to marry and order them to abstain from certain foods" (v. 3a) by appealing to the goodness of creation. The false-teaching ascetics were rejecting gifts that "God created to be received with thanksgiving by those who believe and who know the truth. For everything God created is good, and nothing is to be rejected if it is received with thanksgiving" (vv. 3b–4). Creation is used as an ethical foundation.

The book of Hebrews begins with the supremacy of God's Son by linking him to creation. "In these last days [God] has spoken to us by his Son, whom he appointed the heir of all things, through whom also he created the world" (1:2 ESV). In the great faith chapter of Hebrews, we are told, "By faith we understand that the universe was created by the word of God, so that what is seen was not made out of things that are visible" (11:3 ESV). The word translated "created" here refers to an ordering and establishing on the basis of God's command, and this refers to ethical paradigms as well as physical realities. Though Romans 1 indicates that through creation humans can know something of God's intentions and designs and, therefore, are without excuse, here in Hebrews it is clear that a fuller understanding of creation and its implications for Christian living comes through faith in Christ, not a natural law.[21]

The book of Revelation is filled with creation motifs, but we will focus on that reality shortly in terms of God's restoration, which affirms original creation designs. What we have seen in the foregoing section is that creation is a major theme throughout the Bible and should therefore play a role in ethics.

Creation, Ethics, and the Doctrine of the Trinity

A third main reason that creation should be a salient foundation for Christian ethics is that the doctrine of the Trinity is at stake. Though the word does not appear in Scripture, *Trinity* is the best designation for understanding the mysterious oneness of God as three persons—Father, Son, and Holy Spirit. Trinitarian theology has historically been at the core of all branches of the Christian church. But as H. Richard Niebuhr many years ago noted, Christian bodies and particularly Christian ethics have exhibited a functional tendency toward unitarianism. Though "Christianity has often been accused of being a polytheism with three Gods . . . , it seems nearer the truth to say that Christianity as a whole is more likely to be an association . . . of three Unitarian religions."[22] Despite the creedal affirmations, various movements and thinkers have tended to accentuate one person of the Trinity over the others, and this has been particularly evident in ethics. Some, in their ethical

21. For more on this, see Ashford and Bartholomew, *Doctrine of Creation*, 12–14.

22. H. Richard Niebuhr, "The Doctrine of the Trinity and the Unity of the Church," *Theology Today* 3 (1946): 372. See also Richard J. Mouw, *The God Who Commands: A Study in Divine Command Ethics* (Notre Dame, IN: University of Notre Dame Press, 1990), 150–61.

framework, have focused primarily on the Father, while neglecting the Son and the Spirit. Others have had an ethic of the Son, while neglecting the Father and the Spirit, and still others have had an ethic of the Spirit, while neglecting the Father and the Son.

As we noted earlier, there has been a significant emphasis in some quarters on Jesus and the kingdom, while neglecting creation. In so doing not only do we pull apart the overarching biblical narrative (creation, fall, redemption, re-creation), but we pull asunder the unity of the divine Trinity. As Karl Barth states, "God is one and indivisible in His working. That He is Creator, Reconciler and Redeemer does not imply the existence of separate divine departments and branches of authority." This is most significant when we reflect on the command of God, for "if we consider it in its different spheres, and therefore if we here ask particularly about the command of God the Creator, this cannot and must not mean that beside the first there is a second and separate command, that of God the Reconciler, and then a third, that of God the Redeemer."[23] That is, in the command of God, we cannot separate God the Creator from God the Reconciler-Redeemer without distorting the unity of the Holy Trinity.

We should recognize that the entire Trinity is involved in creation, redemption, and the final restoration. Creation is not just the work of the Father and the Son but is also the work of the Holy Spirit. In Genesis 1:2, "The Spirit of God was hovering over the waters,"[24] and in the great creation psalm, Psalm 104, we read, "When you [LORD] send your Spirit, [all creatures] are created, and you renew the face of the ground" (v. 30). In John 6:63 Jesus refers to the Spirit as the giver of life, no doubt meaning both spiritual life and physical life. It is possible to affirm the trinitarian work of creation but simply to neglect it in ethics. But if we intentionally set the words and work of Jesus in ethics over against creation, we really are pulling apart the divine Trinity and their wholistic work of creation, redemption, sanctification, and final restoration. If the Godhead is one, then the commands (or paradigms, as I'm terming them) of God the Creator and God the Redeemer must be one. Otherwise, we fall prey to a unitarian ethic.

In formulating a Christian ethic, Barth was right to insist that "the God who meets man[25] as Creator in His commandment is the God who is gracious

23. Karl Barth, *Church Dogmatics*, vol. III/4, *The Doctrine of Creation*, trans. Geoffrey Bromiley, ed. T. F. Torrance (Edinburgh: T&T Clark, 1961), 32–33.

24. I recognize that we must be careful in reading a full trinitarian doctrine into this verse and that some feel this is not an explicit reference to the Holy Spirit but simply to God's spirit. However, it is possible that in the providence of God there is an implicit reference here to the Holy Spirit, even though the writer did not have full knowledge of the distinctions between Father, Son, and Holy Spirit.

25. Though I am personally committed to inclusive human language, for the sake of clarity and brevity, I have retained the original language of authors in quotations.

to him in Jesus Christ. He is not then a new and strange God who could require from man as his Commander something new and strange and even perhaps in conflict with what is asked of him by the God who is gracious to him in Jesus Christ."[26] This means that an ethic that focuses on creation but does not include Christ and the Spirit is negligent, just as an ethic that focuses on Christ or the Spirit but does not include creation is negligent. Both the unity and diversity of the Holy Trinity are at stake, for just as we hold creation, redemption, and final restoration together and in continuity, so we must hold together the Father, Son, and Holy Spirit in all their works in this world.[27]

The Final Restoration Is a Renewing of What God Created in the Beginning

There has long been a tendency to see creation and eschatology in discontinuity. It can take one of two forms. For some progressive Christians, the eschaton is a utopian dream on this earth enabled by human pursuits of justice, love, and human flourishing. In this construal we will reach a glorious future without reference to the past, including creation. Indeed, the past is often perceived to be shrouded in ignorance and injustices, from which we have now been liberated by a new narrative that will lead us to the promised land. In a different vein, for some fundamentalist Christians (particularly those in the strict dispensationalist camp), our hope for the future resides entirely with the return of Christ, which is an escape from the perils of this world. The portrayed scenario is one in which this physical world is ultimately destroyed and replaced by "a new heaven and a new earth," without reference to either the original creation or God's providential work over creation now. Both accounts bring with them an ethic, but in both accounts creation as a theological foundation is missing.

Increasingly, theologians and biblical scholars, including those from my own evangelical tradition, are seeing continuity between the first creation and God's final restoration. The late Colin Gunton describes it this way: "The realization of the end is anticipated in the present as the rule of Christ, inaugurated in his ministry, continues in the present, moving forward the project of creation." This does not mean a totally new work of God, for "the general point is that it is when we look at the nature of what God achieves through the Son and the Spirit that we are better able to develop an eschatology which is concerned with the completing of that which was once established in the

26. Barth, *Church Dogmatics* III/4, 35.

27. For a helpful theological work on the unity of the Trinity in all of its operations, see Adonis Vidu, *The Same God Who Works All Things: Inseparable Operations in Trinitarian Theology* (Grand Rapids: Eerdmans, 2021).

beginning."[28] In this understanding, creation, redemption through Christ's death and resurrection, and the kingdom or final eschaton are in continuity with each other, thus calling for a commensurate ethical framework. What is the biblical support for such a claim?

We have already noted Isaiah 65:17 and its vision of "new heavens and a new earth," with various texts throughout the prophecy linking the prophetic vision back to creation. The Old Testament prophecies envisioning something radically new "inspire us to expect a new world order in which the redeemed will live in peace and righteousness on the earth."[29] Chapter 66 of Isaiah at first glance appears to teach a dissolution of this created world with its language of fire and sword (vv. 15–16), but such a depiction portrays judgment, which is necessary in God's accomplishment of redemption. It is best, in light of other Isaiah texts, to read this chapter as a restoration of what God has made: "'As the new heavens and the new earth that I make will endure before me,' declares the LORD, 'so will your name and descendants endure'" (v. 22). The "new" is best understood as renewed in accordance with God's creational purposes, rather than something totally new without continuity.

In the New Testament eschaton texts, one can make a strong case for a restoration of God's creational designs in the coming kingdom. Jesus speaks of "the renewal of all things, when the Son of Man sits on his glorious throne" (Matt. 19:28). Peter, giving one of his early sermons to fellow Israelites in Acts 3, reminds them of the messianic foretelling and calls them to "repent, then, and turn to God, so that your sins may be wiped out, that times of refreshing may come from the Lord, and that he may send the Messiah, who has been appointed for you—even Jesus. Heaven must receive him until the time comes for God to restore everything, as he promised long ago through his holy prophets" (Acts 3:19–21). Here restoration language is utilized, emphasizing a reestablishment of what once was. In Ephesians 1:10 Paul speaks of the fulfillment through Christ "to bring unity to all things in heaven and on earth under Christ." In Colossians 1:19–20 he writes, "For God was pleased to have all his fullness dwell in him, and through him to reconcile to himself all things, whether things on earth or things in heaven, by making peace through his blood, shed on the cross." And in Romans 8:21, in the midst of discussing present sufferings, Paul asserts that "the creation itself will be liberated from its bondage to decay and brought into the freedom and glory of the children of God." Though all of creation has been "groaning" in this present world, we have a future hope, the future redemption of our bodies (vv. 22–23). Here creation is not destroyed, but the fullness of redemption in Christ brings even created, bodily restoration.

28. Colin E. Gunton, *The Triune Creator: A Historical and Systematic Study*, Edinburgh Studies in Constructive Theology (Grand Rapids: Eerdmans, 1998), 220–21, 222.

29. J. Richard Middleton, *A New Heaven and a New Earth: Reclaiming Biblical Eschatology* (Grand Rapids: Baker Academic, 2014), 109.

The book of Revelation has numerous references to God as Creator (4:11; 5:13; 10:5–6; 14:7) and metaphors pointing to the eschaton as a restoration and culmination of what God originally designed. God and the Lamb are worshiped as Creator around the throne, and the Lamb gives the promise, "I am making all things new" (21:5 ESV). "He does not proclaim 'I am making new things.' The language here suggests renewal, not destruction."[30] Of course, many take verse 1 of that chapter to portray a destruction of the current world: "Then I saw a new heaven and a new earth, for the first heaven and the first earth had passed away, and the sea was no more" (ESV). But in these and similar texts, the metaphors of fire and destruction are used to describe divine judgment. Douglas Moo points out that the language of passing away "could also suggest that it is the sinful 'form' of this world which is to pass away rather than the world itself. And there are other pointers in this context to the idea of renovation."[31]

Among these pointers are at least three images from Genesis 1–2 that are utilized to describe the fullness of the kingdom, the eschaton, in the closing chapters of Revelation.[32] First, there is reference to light needing no sun in the new Jerusalem: "The city does not need the sun or the moon to shine on it, for the glory of God gives it light, and the Lamb is its light. The nations will walk by its light" (Rev. 21:23–24). And we read in the next chapter, "There will be no more night. [God's servants] will not need the light of a lamp or the light of the sun, for the Lord God will give them light" (22:5). This clearly parallels and harkens back to the first day of creation, in which, after a description of darkness being "over the surface of the deep," God says, "'Let there be light,' and there was light. God saw that the light was good, and he separated the light from the darkness" (Gen. 1:2, 3–4). Light is present as God's first act, though the sun, moon, and stars do not appear until the fourth day (vv. 14–19). This, of course, is not a scientific rendition but a theological statement that light is central to God's work in the world, seen in creation, redemption, and consummation.

Second, there is "the river of the water of life, as clear as crystal, flowing from the throne of God and of the Lamb down the middle of the great street of the city" (Rev. 22:1–2a; cf. 21:6). This no doubt harkens back to the river flowing through the garden of Eden: "Streams came up from the earth and watered

30. Douglas J. Moo, "Nature in the New Creation: New Testament Eschatology and the Environment," *Journal of the Evangelical Theological Society* 49, no. 3 (2006): 466.

31. Moo, "Nature in the New Creation," 466. Certainly there are texts that at first glance seem to teach a destruction of this earth, such as Matt. 24:29 or 2 Pet. 3:10–12. For an explanation of these texts from a restorationist perspective, see Moo's whole article (449–88) and Middleton, *A New Heaven and a New Earth*, 179–210. These and other scholars see the graphic language, which at first glance seems to show destruction, as really constituting metaphors for divine judgment.

32. See, for example, Gregory Stevenson, "The Theology of Creation in the Book of Revelation," *Leaven* 21, no. 3 (2013): 139–42.

the whole surface of the ground" (Gen. 2:6), and "a river watering the garden flowed from Eden; from there it was separated into four headwaters" (v. 10).

And then, third, there is the imagery of the tree of life appearing at creation and in the eschaton. For "on each side of the river stood the tree of life, bearing twelve crops of fruit, yielding its fruit every month. And the leaves of the tree are for the healing of the nations" (Rev. 22:2b). This clearly references that "in the middle of the garden were the tree of life and the tree of the knowledge of good and evil" (Gen. 2:9).

That these images from the creation account are found in the scenes of the new Jerusalem in the eschaton provides evidence for a restoration of creation, not a destruction of it. What God began at creation—and what is now fallen—is being redeemed and will be consummated in the fullness of his kingdom. And one final piece of evidence for a renewal of creation and its designs, as opposed to a discontinuity model, is the image of the new Jerusalem coming down out of heaven from God to earth (Rev. 21:2, 10), not humans being taken up from this earth to a nonphysical heaven.

If the fullness of the kingdom is linked to creation, this affirms that all of God's creational designs are paradigmatic now, as we live in "the already but not yet." An ethic of the kingdom of God can never be set over against an ethic of creation, for the kingdom is bringing God's creation designs to their fullness and affirming that what God established in creation is normative throughout human history. When King Jesus fully establishes his kingdom, all of the good ethical designs of creation will become reality on earth, a truth captured powerfully in a hymn by C. Sylvester Horner, "Sing We the King Who Is Coming to Reign":

> Sing we the king who is coming to reign,
> Glory to Jesus, the Lamb that was slain,
> Life and salvation his empire shall bring
> Joy to the nations when Jesus is King.
>
> *Refrain:*
> Come let us sing: Praise to our King,
> Jesus our King, Jesus our King;
> This is our song, who to Jesus belong:
> Glory to Jesus, to Jesus our King.
>
> All men shall dwell in his marvelous light,
> Races long severed his love shall unite,
> Justice and truth from his sceptre shall spring,
> Wrong shall be ended when Jesus is King.
>
> All shall be well in his Kingdom of peace,
> Freedom shall flourish and wisdom increase,
> Foe shall be friend when his triumph we sing,
> Sword shall be sickle when Jesus is King.

> Souls shall be saved from the burden of sin,
> Doubt shall not darken his witness within,
> Hell hath no terrors, and death hath no sting;
> Love is victorious when Jesus is King.
>
> Kingdom of Christ, for thy coming we pray,
> Hasten, O Father, the dawn of the day
> When this new song thy creation shall sing,
> Satan is vanquished and Jesus is King.[33]

In that glorious day, the divine intentions of creation will be fully realized on earth. As Sandra Richter writes, "God's original intent is his final intent. Eden was the perfect plan, and God has never had any other."[34]

Creation Is Full of Salient Ethical Themes

In the rest of this book, we will explore numerous ethical themes that serve as paradigms for our journey in this world. The creation accounts and often the rest of Scripture do not provide us with the strategies for implementing these paradigms amid a broken and complex world, but they do provide God's designs as we live in the "already but not yet" kingdom that will renew God's good creational foundations.

In chapter 1 we will explore the ultimate foundation that a loving, triune God designed not only the physical world but the moral world and has self-disclosed those designs in special revelation. In chapter 2 we find that this creation is good—a unique perspective in ancient creation narratives—and we will see its contrast with various forms of ethical asceticism. This will be applied to the good but fallen gifts down through history of money, sex, and power. Chapter 3 explores the theme of human dignity stemming from our creation in God's image, with application to caring for the most vulnerable from womb to end of life—and to all humanity, with relevance to racism, tribalism, and ethnocentrism. Chapter 4 examines God's call to care for his good creation, showing how the stewardship mandate differs from other worldview frameworks for our interactions with the earth and its resources. Chapter 5 shows that we were created as relational beings with implications for sexuality, marriage, sex, and family. Chapter 6 continues the relational theme but focuses on other social institutions, including the state. In chapter 7 we find that we were created to work, and we also see the implications of this reality for human identity and human provision in this world.

33. C. Sylvester Horner, "Sing We the King Who Is Coming to Reign," in *The Song Book of the Salvation Army* (St. Albans, UK: Salvation Army, 1986), no. 166, https://hymnary.org/hymn/SBSA1986/166.

34. Sandra L. Richter, *The Epic of Eden: A Christian Entry into the Old Testament* (Downers Grove, IL: IVP Academic, 2008), 129.

Chapter 8 explores God's creational institution of the Sabbath as not only a mandate to worship the Creator and care for oneself but also a mandate to pursue justice. In chapter 9 we explore the important creational theme of human finitude and its ethical implications for eugenics—the possibilities of changing human nature through genetic engineering—as well as its significance for engaging various political utopianisms. In chapter 10 we find that we were created as embodied souls (or ensouled bodies), and we see the implications of this phenomenon for a number of issues: commitment to both evangelism and social concern, our use of artificial intelligence, and an acceptance of our mortality at the end of life. In the conclusion, we will discuss how we live out a creation ethic amid a fallen, complex world. Throughout all of these chapters, we will see that embedded in the creation narratives and other creation texts of Scripture is much to guide us in our thinking, character, and actions.

Conclusion

So why creation for ethics? Why not just stick with the Decalogue, the Prophets, Jesus, Paul, or the kingdom? As we have seen in this chapter, creation is integral to the overarching biblical narrative: creation, fall, redemption, and restoration. Detaching creation from the story leads to incoherence. The whole of Scripture appeals to creation for the purposes of worship, spiritual formation, theological thinking, and ethical living. The doctrine of the Trinity is at stake, for if we leave out creation, we separate the commands of Father, Son, and Holy Spirit and, hence, pull apart the unity of the Godhead. The final eschaton is a restoration of creation, not a destruction, and thus creation and kingdom must be held together. As we are about to explore, embedded in the creation narrative of Genesis and in creation teaching throughout Scripture are numerous rich themes and paradigms to guide us amid a complex, fallen world. It is to that world that God calls us to live out the designs of Christ, our Creator and Redeemer.

1

In the Beginning God

A Loving, Designing, Self-Disclosing Maker

"In the beginning God created the heavens and the earth" (Gen. 1:1). This is one of the simplest yet most profound statements of Holy Scripture. All of reality begins with God, and from the rest of Scripture we see that this God is clearly the triune God: Father, Son, and Holy Spirit. God creates from nothing—ex nihilo, as theologians and philosophers term it—therefore, all that exists comes ultimately from the hand of God, either by direct creation or providential guiding. "Beginnings and endings reveal a lot about the scope and significance of a story. So it matters that the story of the Bible begins and ends with creation." Moreover, "the Bible begins by centering us on the only one who in his very being is life and love, the uncreated one who is the source of all goodness."[1]

God designed the world, and in that design are contours and directions for how humans, the apex of divine creation, should live and orient their lives. The material world comes from the hand of God, and so does the immaterial world—hence, parts seen and unseen. And in those unseen dimensions (and in some of the seen dimensions), which God has designed, are clear guidelines to enable humans to love God and others and to flourish as God's creatures. We are not made to live unto ourselves or by ourselves but to live unto God and in relation to his creatures, including fellow humans made in his image and the rest of nature, for which we are called to care. But all of the cosmos and all

1. Douglas J. Moo and Jonathan A. Moo, *Creation Care: A Biblical Theology of the Natural World*, Biblical Theology for Life (Grand Rapids: Zondervan, 2018), 45, 46.

of life in this world starts with the Creator. As a eucharistic prayer from the Book of Common Prayer beautifully describes it, "Holy and Gracious Father: in your infinite love you have made us for yourself."[2] And as his creatures, we find ourselves and our pathway to true and integral living in our Creator.

This creation narrative and worldview stands in stark contrast to portrayals such as that by Richard Dawkins, one of the well-known secular scientists of the modern world. He states, "The universe we observe has precisely the properties we should expect if there is, at bottom, no design, no purpose, no evil and no good, nothing but blind, pitiless indifference. . . . DNA neither knows nor cares. DNA just is. And we dance to its music."[3] The biblical narrative, though, portrays not a story of random, uncaring indifference but one of design and purpose. Moreover, the creation story shows a speaking God who reveals himself in both actions and words and does so as a reflection of love.

The focus of this chapter is threefold. First, we consider God's creation as an act of love, reflecting the very nature of God. The love that inheres in the Holy Trinity, between the Father, the Son, and the Holy Spirit, is the same love that creates; and it is the same love that would eventually redeem a broken, fallen humanity through the death and resurrection of Jesus Christ. It is the same love that will one day consummate his kingdom, restoring his world back to its creational intentions. Athanasius is certainly right when he argues, "The first fact you must grasp is this: the renewal of the creation has been wrought by the Self-same Word Who made it in the beginning. There is thus no inconsistency between creation and salvation; for the One Father has employed the same Agent for both works, effecting salvation of the world through the same Word Who made it in the first place."[4] The love that created and redeemed is also the love that guides our ethical path in this world.

Second, in the creation narrative we see design evidenced in the structure of the story and most specifically through the structure of the days of creation. But beyond the linguistic, narrative structural elements, we find design in human life and the moral contours that enable human life to best flourish and fulfill God's purposes on earth. These designs of our Maker are also evidenced in the key ethical guidelines from the Decalogue and the prophetic utterances to the life and teaching of Jesus and the teaching of the Epistles. This design gives definition to the divine love that created and norms our ethical lives.

Third, we see in the creation story that God is a speaking God, who speaks the world and its elements into being. This reflects the self-disclosing nature of God, a God of revelation. Creation is the first scene of the revelatory drama, which then unfolds following the fall through God's calling a people to himself,

2. *The Book of Common Prayer* (New York: Seabury, 1979), 362.

3. Richard Dawkins, *River out of Eden: A Darwinian View of Life*, Science Masters Series (London: Basic Books, 1995), 133.

4. Athanasius, *On the Incarnation*, trans. Penelope Lawson (Crestwood, NY: St. Vladimir's Orthodox Theological Seminary, 1953), 1.1.

revealing himself in his written Word and in the incarnate Word. It is the revelatory nature of God and creation that provides guidance for every domain of life and serves as our ultimate authority for belief, character, and actions.

This chapter, then, is central to the other chapters of the book in that it portrays a God of love who provides both physical and moral designs and reveals those designs in both Scripture and Christ. These are presuppositions for the paradigms that guide our ethical thinking, living, and being in a wide range of issues with which we will grapple throughout this book.

A Loving, Triune God Loves the World into Being

The word "love" does not appear in the Genesis creation narrative, but it is implicit as a logical, theological, and biblical foundation for creation. Creation as an act of love is ultimately rooted in the eternal love of the three persons of the Godhead, and thus love serves as a major ethical norm for God's image bearers in this world. As Colin Gunton puts it, "Because [the doctrine of the Trinity] holds that God is already, 'in advance' of creation, a communion of persons existing in loving relations, it becomes possible to say that he does not need the world, and so is able to will the existence of something else simply for its own sake. Creation is the outcome of God's love indeed, but of his unconstrained love."[5]

That creation is an act of love flowing from the divine love between Father, Son, and Holy Spirit is a logical outcome of the biblical affirmation that "God is love" (1 John 4:8). "God did not have to create, nor did God create within a context of constraining conditions. That God creates at all is, therefore, a sign of a divine, hospitable intention for others to be. God creates *ex amore*, from love, because love is the only reason at work in God's creating action." And this is the work of the Holy Trinity, reflecting the love the divine persons have shared from eternity. Thus, "the loving power that Jesus models in his feeding the hungry, healing the sick, exorcising the demon-possessed, and befriending the stranger and outcast is the same divine power that brings all creatures into being and that daily sustains and nurtures them."[6] This stands in stark contrast to the stories of creation from the ancient Near East, in which the world and humans frequently emerge from conflict and animosity among warring gods or to serve the self-centered purposes of the gods.[7] In contrast

5. Colin E. Gunton, *The Triune Creator: A Historical and Systematic Study*, Edinburgh Studies in Constructive Theology (Grand Rapids: Eerdmans, 1998), 9.

6. Norman Wirzba, "Creation *through* Christ," in *Christ and the Created Order: Perspectives from Theology, Philosophy, and Science*, ed. Andrew B. Torrance and Thomas H. McCall (Grand Rapids: Zondervan, 2018), 38, 39.

7. See, for example, Bryan Windle, "Three Ancient Near Eastern Creation Myths," *Bible Archaeology Report* (blog), February 22, 2019, https://biblearchaeologyreport.com/2019/02/22/three-ancient-near-eastern-creation-myths/.

to these portrayals, in his *Paradise* Dante completes his journey by beholding the loving Creator full of light, saying, "My will and my desire were turned by love, the love that moves the sun and other stars."[8]

The understanding of creation as flowing from trinitarian, divine love was a significant emphasis among patristic writers, especially in the Eastern church. Summarizing the early church thinkers, Donald Fairbairn states, "Christian monotheism affirms the presence of three eternal, divine persons who are united in such a way as to be a single God and whose love for one another is the basis for all of human life."[9] Many of the defenders in the trinitarian controversies of the fourth century describe the profound intimacy shared by the persons of the Trinity. Basil the Great describes the attributes shared by Father, Son, and Holy Spirit, such as holiness, goodness, truth, uprightness, and love. He writes, "The Spirit shares titles held in common by the Father and the Son; He receives these titles due to his natural and intimate relationship with them."[10] And on the Western side of the church, Saint Augustine writes, "Just as Father and Son are one not only by equality of substance but also by identity of will, so also [humans are] . . . being bound in the fellowship of the same love."[11]

The theme of creation stemming from love and hence serving as a guide for believers gets picked up by other thinkers throughout the history of the church. In the eighteenth century, Jonathan Edwards, the noted philosopher, revivalist, theologian, and pastor, was convinced that the creation of the world flowed from God's eternal attributes. In *The Nature of True Virtue*, he writes, "It is evident that the divine virtue . . . must consist primarily in love to himself, or in the mutual love and friendship which subsists eternally and necessarily between the several persons in the Godhead." Thus, "God's goodness and love to created beings is derived from, and subordinate to his love to himself." Love between humans will then of necessity be derived from this ultimate love; it will "arise from the temper of mind wherein consists a disposition to love God supremely."[12]

While Edwards believes that all humans have some capacity for the virtue of love because they come from the hand of God in creation, he asserts that "the most proper evidence of love to a created being arising from the temper

8. Dante Alighieri, *The Divine Comedy*, vol. 3, *Paradise*, trans. Dorothy L. Sayers and Barbara Reynolds (Middlesex, UK: Penguin Books, 1962), 347.

9. Donald Fairbairn, *Life in the Trinity: An Introduction to Theology with the Help of the Church Fathers* (Downers Grove, IL: IVP Academic, 2009), 54.

10. Basil the Great, *On the Holy Spirit*, trans. David Anderson, Popular Patristics Series (Crestwood, NY: St. Vladimir's Seminary Press, 1980), par. 48, p. 76.

11. Augustine, *On the Trinity*, trans Edmund Hill, The Works of St. Augustine I/5 (New York: New City, 1991), 4.9.12, p. 161.

12. Jonathan Edwards, *The Nature of True Virtue* (Ann Arbor: University of Michigan Press, 1969), 23.

of mind wherein consists a supreme propensity of heart to God, seems to be the agreeableness of the kind and degree of our love to God's end in our creation, and in the creation of all things."[13] And what is that end for which we were created? "A truly virtuous mind, being as it were under the sovereign dominion of love to God, above all things, seeks the glory of God, and makes this his supreme, governing and ultimate end." Moral agents thus are to seek the ultimate end of God's glory, for it is "the last end for which God made all things." And it is in seeking this ultimate end that humans are most capable of reflecting the love of the triune God, both in their love of God and in their love of others. "And so far as a virtuous mind exercises true virtue in benevolence to created beings, it chiefly seeks the good of the creature; consisting in its knowledge or view of God's glory and beauty, its union with God, conformity and love to him, and joy in him."[14] For Edwards creation plays a significant role in the design of the virtuous or moral life, with redemption through God's saving grace in Christ enabling a person's enactment in this world.

When we come to the twentieth century, Karl Barth also sees creation flowing from God's love; this then forms the basis for all human love. "The creature is not self-existent" and does not exist by itself or for itself. "It is not the creature itself but its Creator who exists and thinks and speaks and cares for the creature."[15] But why did God will this creation? It is because of divine love. "He wills and posits the creature neither out of caprice nor necessity, but because He has loved it from eternity, because He wills to demonstrate His love for it." All of this flows from "the love with which God loves himself—the Father the Son and Son the Father in the Holy Spirit. . . . The existence and being of the creature willed and constituted by God are the object and to that extent the presupposition of this love."[16]

This, then, is the framework in which God bestows his grace upon human beings, but it is also the foundation for humans loving God as the recipients of God's grace. But the eternal divine life does not stop there for Barth; it is the foundation for our love toward all of God's creatures made in his image. "Divine love is perfect love, the inaccessible prototype and true basis of all creaturely love."[17]

These theological and philosophical reflections on creation flowing from the divine love of the triune Godhead and thus serving as the ultimate source for human love are rooted in biblical teaching about love. While there is no explicit reference grounding creation in love and thus serving as a foundation

13. Edwards, *Nature of True Virtue*, 24.

14. Edwards, *Nature of True Virtue*, 25.

15. Karl Barth, *Church Dogmatics*, vol. III/1, *The Doctrine of Creation*, trans. Geoffrey Bromiley, ed. T. F. Torrance (Edinburgh: T&T Clark, 1958), 94.

16. Barth, *Church Dogmatics* III/1, 95, 97.

17. Barth, *Church Dogmatics* III/1, 96.

for human love, these assertions flow logically from various biblical teachings about love. To make this point, we will draw on two biblical texts, John 13–17 (Jesus's Upper Room Discourse) and 1 John 3–4, exploring five major themes on love.

First, these texts portray the divine love in the Holy Trinity:

> I do as the Father has commanded me, so that the world may know that I love the Father. (John 14:31 ESV)

> As the Father has loved me, so have I loved you. (15:9 ESV)

> You loved me before the foundation of the world. . . . I made known to them your name . . . , that the love with which you have loved me may be in them, and I in them. (17:24, 26 ESV)

All of this, of course, flows from God's nature and attributes as a God of love and grace, as evidenced in 1 John:

> Beloved, let us love one another, because love is from God. . . . God is love. (4:7, 8 NRSV)

> God is love, and those who abide in love abide in God. (v. 16 NRSV)

Second, implied in these texts is the assertion that God created this world and human beings on the basis of love. As noted earlier in this chapter, there are no biblical texts that explicitly say God created on this basis. The notion simply flows logically from the fact that God is love and that love is expressed in the Godhead from before creation. God did not have to create to complete anything within himself, but his creation is a manifestation of his eternal love. There is one passage that might link love to creation—namely, 1 John 3:11: "This is the message you have heard from the beginning, that we should love one another" (NRSV). This is sometimes taken to mean that from the beginning of Jesus's ministry, his followers had heard the message of love. But John frequently in his writings uses "the beginning" to harken back to creation. He begins his first epistle with these words: "That which was from the beginning, which we have heard, which we have seen with our eyes, . . . we proclaim concerning the Word of life" (1 John 1:1). This reference to Christ as both incarnate and eternal is, of course, proclaimed in even more depth in John's Gospel: "In the beginning was the Word, and the Word was with God, and the Word was God. He was in the beginning with God. All things were made through him, and without him was not any thing made that was made" (John 1:1–3 ESV). If the triune God is love, then it only follows that this world, including planet Earth with all its inhabitants, was created on the basis of love, the same love that would redeem a fallen world and serve as its most pronounced moral norm.

Third, these texts teach God's love for us as his special creation, made in his image:

> A new commandment I give to you, that you love one another: just as I have loved you, you also are to love one another. (John 13:34 ESV)[18]
>
> The one who loves me will be loved by my Father, and I too will love them and show myself to them. (14:21)
>
> Love each other as I have loved you. (15:12)
>
> I . . . will continue to make you known in order that the love you have for me may be in them. (17:26)
>
> Beloved, since God loved us so much, we also ought to love one another. (1 John 4:11 NRSV)

The fourth theme is our love for God, which interestingly, in both the Gospel and the epistle, focuses not on inner or emotive love but on keeping God's commands or Jesus's teachings as evidence of our love:

> If you love me, you will keep my commandments. (John 14:15 NRSV)
>
> They who have my commandments and keep them are those who love me. (v. 21 NRSV)
>
> Anyone who loves me will obey my teaching. . . . Anyone who does not love me will not obey my teaching. (vv. 23, 24)
>
> If you keep my commandments, you will abide in my love. (15:10 ESV)
>
> By this we know that we love the children of God, when we love God and obey his commandments. . . . And his commandments are not burdensome. (1 John 5:2, 3 ESV)

The fifth theme is our love for others as evidence that we know the eternal God of love. While the "one another" language appears to focus on love for fellow believers, the commands and teachings of Jesus clearly point toward

18. Of course, this does not mean that love in the world is new, for it was at the core of God's creation and manifested continually to the Hebrew people. What was new was the radical manifestation of love in the incarnation, the eternal God taking on human flesh. It was also new in its extent—inclusive of all humanity, including one's enemies.

loving all humans, even those different from ourselves and those perceived as enemies. Some of the following texts we have already seen, for they are intertwined with the other dimensions of love:

> Love one another. By this all people will know that you are my disciples, if you have love for one another. (John 13:34–35 ESV)

> This is my commandment, that you love one another as I have loved you. . . . I am giving you these commands so that you may love one another. (15:12, 17 NRSV)

> For this is the message you have heard from the beginning, that we should love one another. . . . We know that we have passed from death to life, because we love one other. (1 John 3:11, 14 NRSV)

> And this is his commandment, that we should believe in the name of his Son Jesus Christ and love one another, just as he has commanded us. (v. 23 NRSV)

> Beloved, let us love one another, because love is from God; everyone who loves is born of God and knows God. (4:7 NRSV)

> Dear friends, since God so loved us, we also ought to love one another. . . . If we love one another, God lives in us and his love is made complete in us. (vv. 11, 12)

When we look at these two Johannine passages, there is much on God's love but also much on the life that flows from such love, humanity's love for each other. As N. T. Wright and Michael Bird put it, "Christian faith grows out of this confession about God's love and how the one true God has revealed himself through the Son as love incarnate. Accordingly, love incarnate must be the badge worn by the members of the community, the sign not only of who they are but of who their God is."[19] And that loving God is both Creator and Redeemer, for God created on the basis of love.

God's Design in Creation

When we explore the creation account in Genesis 1–2, one of the major takeaways is the intricate design in creation. Genesis is not a scientific rendition of creation but a theological one in which we see design in the narrative, including moral design, which flows from key elements in the creation process. The picture of the physical design of the universe in Genesis 1–2 is not set forth in our contemporary scientific understandings of the world but rather in the pictures that were familiar to ancient cultures. The reference to

19. N. T. Wright and Michael F. Bird, *The New Testament in Its World: An Introduction to the History, Literature, and Theology of the First Christians* (Grand Rapids: Zondervan, 2019), 800.

"a vault between the waters to separate water from water" (1:6) was familiar language to people in the ancient world. "If we ask why God didn't reveal a modern picture of the cosmos to these ancient peoples, the answer is obvious: no one in the ancient audience would have believed it (or even understood it)."[20] Rather, God began where the people were so they could begin to sense the intricate design of his world, both physically and morally, even if their picture of the physical world was different from ours today.

The concept of design is implied in the Hebrews 11:3 statement on creation, "By faith we understand that the universe was created by the word of God" (ESV). The word used for "created" here carries the idea of forming with a proper order and sometimes implies a sense of moral order and rightness.[21] Noting the way in which this stands over against modern historicism and its reduction of ethics to historical factors, Oliver O'Donovan writes, "Classical Christian thought proceeded from a universal order of meaning and value, an order given in creation and fulfilled in the kingdom of God, an order, therefore, which forms a framework for all action and history."[22]

Design in the universe is seen not only in the biblical account but by observation of the universe. William Newsome, a neuroscientist at Stanford, describes it this way:

> An increasing cadre of scientists is recognizing that the laws and constants that make up the fundamental physical reality of our universe are improbably hospitable to the emergence of life. These critical constants determine, among other things, the rate of expansion of the universe, the strength of interaction of subatomic particles within the nucleus, and the unique chemical-bonding properties of carbon, oxygen, nitrogen, and hydrogen—the fundamental atomic constituents of organic life. If any of these physical constants had been different by an infinitesimally small amount, the emergence of life in our universe would have been impossible. . . . The fundamental nature of our physical universe is peculiarly well suited to the emergence of intelligent life.[23]

With such physical design in the universe to enable its existence, it only follows that there are spiritual and moral designs as well, if indeed God is the Creator.

20. Terence Nichols, *Death and Afterlife: A Theological Introduction* (Grand Rapids: Brazos, 2010), 82.

21. See Gerhard Delling, "ἄρτιος [*artios*]," in *Theological Dictionary of the New Testament*, ed. Gerhard Kittel, trans. Geoffrey W. Bromiley (Grand Rapids: Eerdmans, 1964), 1:476; William L. Lane, *Hebrews 9–13*, Word Biblical Commentary 47B (Dallas: Word, 1991), 331.

22. Oliver O'Donovan, *Resurrection and Moral Order: An Outline for Evangelical Ethics* (Grand Rapids: Eerdmans, 1986), 67.

23. William Newsome, "Life of Science, Life of Faith," in *Visions of Discovery: New Light on Physics, Cosmology, and Consciousness*, ed. Raymond Y. Chiao, Marvin L. Cohen, Anthony J. Leggett, William D. Phillips, and Charles L. Harper Jr. (Cambridge: Cambridge University Press, 2010), 731.

Various biblical scholars have noted the intricate design of Genesis 1, which is based not on a chronological schema but a literary one. There is a correspondence between days one and four, two and five, and three and six: light on day one (vv. 3–5) corresponds to the creation of the sun, moon, and stars on day four (vv. 14–19); the separation of the waters from the sky on day two (vv. 6–8) parallels the creation of birds and fish on day five (vv. 20–23); the creation of dry land with various forms of vegetation on day three (vv. 9–13) corresponds to the creation of various forms of animal life and then humans on day six (vv. 24–27). The Creator then sets humans, both male and female, apart from the rest of creation with the stamp of his image upon them and grants them unique roles and responsibilities (vv. 28–31). God then designs a rhythm of life on the seventh day, setting it apart as a guide for humans to follow in honoring both God and their fellow humans (2:1–3; Exod. 20:8–11) as they carry out the mandates God has designed for them. Chapter 1 of Genesis involves "creative activities, but all in relation to the way that the ancient world thought about creation and existence: by naming, separating and assigning functions and roles in an ordered system."[24]

In the creation narrative, it is clear that "the creator has a purpose and a will for creation. . . . The creator continues to address the creation, calling it to faithful response and glad obedience to his will. The creation has not been turned loose on its own."[25] Purposeful design is pervasive throughout the creation story. "The opening expression, *In the beginning*, is more than a bare note of time. The variations on this theme in Isaiah 40ff. show that the beginning is pregnant with the end, and the whole process present to God who is First and Last."[26] Genesis 1:2 then states, "The earth was without form and void, and darkness was over the face of the deep. And the Spirit of God was hovering over the face of the waters" (ESV). God then begins the process of bringing order and design out of what has been created but is "without form and void." *Bara'*, the Hebrew term for creation in the Old Testament, invariably points to God doing the work of creation and frequently carries with it the idea of formation or design.

The very first element in creation design is light: "God said, 'Let there be light,' and there was light. And God saw that the light was good" (1:3–4 ESV). This is a highly significant theological and ethical statement. Peter Leithart in an Epiphany meditation notes, "Light is the beginning of creation, and by creating light God gives everything else. Without light, things are invisible, not recognizable things at all. A world without light is a world . . . formless

24. John H. Walton, *The Lost World of Genesis One: Ancient Cosmology and the Origins Debate* (Downers Grove, IL: IVP Academic, 2009), 46.

25. Walter Brueggemann, *Genesis*, Interpretation: A Bible Commentary for Teaching and Preaching (Atlanta: John Knox, 1982), 13.

26. Derek Kidner, *Genesis: An Introduction and Commentary*, Tyndale Old Testament Commentaries (Downers Grove, IL: InterVarsity, 1972), 43.

and empty (Gen. 1:2). Light is good, the first created good, the good without which nothing else could be, or be good. Nothing can live without light."[27] Leithart goes on to assert that because of the initial design of light, "the whole creation gleams with the refracted light of God." Moreover, "light exposes what's hidden, and so makes judgment possible. Exposure is judgment. God is light also because he is the Judge whose burning eyes see every secret. Light repels those who want to hide their evil deeds; light attracts those who practice the truth. . . . Light conquers darkness." All of this then guides our spiritual and moral life, for through redemption in Christ we encounter anew the light of lights who was there at creation. "In the light of Jesus, we shine with tomorrow's light, so the light of the last day may illumine the way. We become ourselves the epiphany of the God of light."[28]

When John wrote the prologue of his Gospel, clearly he had Genesis 1 in mind, for light is a central theme in introducing the Creator Logos:

> In the beginning was the Word, and the Word was with God, and the Word was God. He was in the beginning with God. All things were made through him, and without him was not any thing made that was made. In him was life, and the life was the light of [humans]. The light shines in the darkness, and the darkness has not overcome it. . . . The true light, which enlightens everyone, was coming into the world. He was in the world, and the world was made through him, yet the world did not know him. . . . But to all who did receive him, who believed in his name, he gave the right to become children of God. (John 1:1–5, 9–10, 12 ESV)

Even before the fall in Genesis 3, light was essential, not only physically but also spiritually and ethically. But this created good was even more essential once spiritual and moral darkness entered the world. Nyctophobia is a severe fear of the dark, accompanied by physiological symptoms such as nausea, shaking, and palpitations of the heart. Even a common fear of the dark can be unsettling. It is precisely why we need the brightness of sunshine. And it is surely this reality that led God in his wisdom to make light as the first act of creation, both because of the physiological need but also to illuminate our path toward righteousness, justice, mercy, goodness, and integrity. "For God, who said, 'Let light shine out of darkness,' made his light shine in our hearts to give us the light of the knowledge of God's glory displayed in the face of Christ" (2 Cor. 4:6). And it is through this divine act of creation and redemption that God calls those who have embraced his grace and forgiveness in Christ to be the light of the world (Matt. 5:14–16). As such, those who in Christ are the light of the world live in light of an eschaton in which "there

27. Peter J. Leithart, "God Is Light," *First Things*, January 3, 2020, https://www.firstthings.com/web-exclusives/2020/01/god-is-light.

28. Leithart, "God Is Light."

will be no more night. They will not need the light of a lamp or the light of the sun, for the Lord God will give them light. And they will reign for ever and ever" (Rev. 22:5). And in the words of Revelation 21:23–25, "The city has no need of sun or moon to shine on it, for the glory of God is its light, and its lamp is the Lamb. The nations will walk by its light, and the kings of the earth will bring their glory into it. Its gates will never be shut by day—and there will be no night there" (NSRV). Clearly creation, redemption, and the final restoration are in continuity with each other, theologically and ethically; and light is significant in the whole biblical drama.

When humans think and live contrary to the designs of God, it is as though there is an undoing of creation. The prophet Jeremiah uses the language and metaphors of Genesis 1 to describe people who are "skilled in doing evil" and who "know not how to do good" (Jer. 4:22).

> I looked at the earth,
> and it was formless and empty;
> and at the heavens,
> and their light was gone.
> I looked at the mountains,
> and they were quaking;
> all the hills were swaying.
> I looked, and there were no people;
> every bird in the sky had flown away.
> I looked, and the fruitful land was a desert;
> all its towns lay in ruins
> before the LORD, before his fierce anger. (vv. 23–26)

Jeremiah is making a direct reference to the created order in Genesis 1, where the light comes immediately after the statement that the earth "was formless and empty" and precedes all the other parts of God's creation. The people's moral and spiritual evils had metaphorically rendered the earth formless and void, and the light was gone. When the divine designs of creation are negated, consequences follow. This is part of the meaning of divine judgment.

Throughout Genesis 1 and 2, the designs of God flow from light. This is what the rest of this book will unpack. They include designs such as the goodness of the created world; human dignity and value based on creation in God's image; the caring and stewarding of God's good creation; the relational realities of marriage, sex, and reproduction; other relational realities that point to social institutions; the establishment of work to provide for human need and creativity; the Sabbath, which prioritizes both honoring God and honoring humans with self-care and justice; our finitude, reminding us we are limited and dependent in our human endeavors within God's good creation; and the embodied-soul wholeness of human beings. These are not happenstance. They are not socially constructed. They are not the results of

Dawkins's "blind, pitiless indifference."[29] They are the designs of God who created out of love. As Norman Wirzba writes concerning creation, "More importantly, it is about the character of the world and its proper orientation, alerting us to the meaning, values, and purpose of everything that is."[30]

It is important to grasp the designs of creation in relation to the rest of God's revelation. As one Old Testament scholar puts it, "The order of this creation will undergird God's later revelations regarding humanity's social order. His law (the teachings of Scripture) is in harmony with the created order. Thus, to flout his revealed moral order is to contradict creation, his created reality."[31] The link between creation designs and the law of God is explicit in Psalm 19. It begins with the glories of creation: "The heavens declare the glory of God, and the sky above proclaims his handwork. Day to day pours out speech, and night to night reveals knowledge. There is no speech, nor are there words, whose voice is not heard. Their voice goes out through all the earth, and their words to the end of the world" (vv. 1–4 ESV). The psalm then turns to the law of God, demonstrating the link between creation and God's designs or law: "The law of the Lord is perfect, reviving the soul; the testimony of the Lord is sure, making wise the simple; the precepts of the Lord are right, rejoicing the heart" (vv. 7–8 ESV).

The loving, triune God created a world of design—physically, spiritually, and morally. And the designs of creation are designs and paradigms for our lives today. They are reiterated throughout the rest of God's self-disclosure, divine revelation.

A Speaking God: Divine Revelation

In the Genesis creation story, God speaks realities into existence. The phrase "And God said" occurs nine times in Genesis 1. "Creation comes into existence as God speaks, and it comes to pass. God's word is both powerful and effective, for at his word the creation comes into being."[32] The theme of God speaking as the modality of creation occurs again in the Psalms: "By the word of the Lord the heavens were made, their starry host by the breath of his mouth. . . . For he spoke, and it came to be; he commanded, and it stood firm" (Ps. 33:6, 9). In the New Testament, we find the same theme: "By faith we understand that the universe was created by the word of God, so that what is seen was not made out of things that are visible" (Heb. 11:3 ESV).

29. Dawkins, *River out of Eden*, 133.

30. Wirzba, "Creation *through* Christ," 40.

31. Bruce K. Waltke, *Genesis: A Commentary*, with Cathi J. Fredricks (Grand Rapids: Zondervan, 2001), 55.

32. Carol M. Kaminski, *Casket Empty: God's Plan of Redemption through History* (N.p.: Casket Empty Media, 2012), 3.

The word translated "'word' here is not *logos* (as in John 1:1ff.) but *rhēma*, referring to the utterance by which God summoned into existence what had no existence before."[33] Moreover, from this text we see that "faith, then, must embrace creation as well as re-creation; hence the affirmation here that it is by faith that we understand that the world was created by the word of God."[34] And 2 Peter 3:5 says, "By God's word the heavens came into being and the earth was formed."

This oral means of creating makes clear that God is a speaking God. Commenting on the Genesis creation account, J. I. Packer notes various categories of God's speaking:

> God's first word to Adam and Eve is a word of *command*, summoning them to fulfill humankind's vocation of ruling the created order. ("Be fruitful . . . and have dominion . . . ," v. 28.) Then follows a word of *testimony* ("Behold . . . ," v. 29) in which God explains that green plants, crops and fruit have been made for humans and animals to eat. Next we meet a *prohibition*, with sanction appended: "but you must not eat from the tree of the knowledge of good and evil, for when you eat of it you will surely die" (2:17). Finally, after the Fall, God comes near to Adam and Eve and speaks to them again, and this time his words are words of *promise*, both favorable and unfavorable. . . . Here, within the compass of these three short chapters, we see the word of God in all the relations in which it stands to the world, and to [humans] within it.[35]

God doesn't act remotely or without definition; rather, consistent with his being, God's self-revelation is an integral dimension of both the nature and actions of God. As Bonhoeffer writes, "That God creates by the word means that creation is God's order or command, and that this command is free." Furthermore, "The term *word* means a spoken word, not a symbol, a meaning, or an idea, but just what it designates. That God creates by speaking means that in God the thought, the name, and the work are in their created reality one."[36] The Word of God that created the world is commensurate with the Word of God we hold in our hands, and with the very incarnate Word of God who in the flesh visibly revealed God's ways and paths for humanity and brought salvation. God's revelation encompasses, then, both act and word, and creation is clearly an act but is accomplished through the word of the triune Creator and embodies that word in the creation paradigms.

33. F. F. Bruce, *The Epistle to the Hebrews*, New International Commentary on the New Testament (Grand Rapids: Eerdmans, 1973), 280.

34. Philip E. Hughes, *A Commentary on the Epistle to the Hebrews* (Grand Rapids: Eerdmans, 1977), 442.

35. J. I. Packer, *Knowing God*, 20th anniv. ed. (Downers Grove, IL: InterVarsity, 1993), 111.

36. Dietrich Bonhoeffer, *Creation and Fall: A Theological Exposition of Genesis 1–3*, ed. John W. de Gruchy, trans. Douglas Stephen Bax, Dietrich Bonhoeffer Works 3 (Minneapolis: Fortress, 1997), 41, 42.

The purpose of God's speaking to us is so that we can both know the Creator experientially and have knowledge of our loving Creator's designs for belief, character, and action. Part of that knowledge is revealed in what God has created—that is, natural revelation or natural law (Ps. 19:1–6; Rom. 1:18–31). Thus, a number of early modern scientists said God has two books: the book of God's works seen in nature and the book of God's words in the Bible. Though significant, the book of natural knowledge is incomplete in the sense that we do not see the whole grand picture of God's designs and the biblical story. Oliver O'Donovan describes it this way:

> What, then, must such knowledge of created order be, if it is really to be available to us? It must be an apprehensive knowledge of the whole of things, yet which does not pretend to a transcendence over the universe, but reaches out to understand the whole from a central point within it. It must be a human knowledge that is coordinated with the true performance of the human task in worship of God and obedience to the moral law. . . . Such knowledge, according to the Christian gospel, is given to us as we participate in the life of Jesus Christ.[37]

If God has truly put designs in place for our moral lives, it only follows that God would reveal them to us. The uniqueness and power of this special revelation is that it came to humanity in concrete historical contexts as believers struggled to know and live out the divine designs. Both the written Word and the incarnate Word have a concreteness that requires hermeneutical acuteness and yet ensures truthful applicability for all contexts and all times.[38] This revelation is also a progressive revelation, in that God starts where humans are in their comprehension of his creational designs. God doesn't dump out the whole story at once, for his sense of time and ours are quite different. As John Calvin puts it, "For who even of slight intelligence does not understand that, as nurses commonly do with infants, God is wont in a measure to 'lisp' in speaking to us? Thus such forms of speaking do not so much express clearly what God is like as accommodate the knowledge of him to our slight capacity."[39] There is a progressive revelation in God's Word, harkening back to creation paradigms and foreseeing the inbreaking of God's kingdom in our Redeemer and in the final consummation of all things.

Despite the historical and human writing dimension of this revelation, "no prophecy of scripture is a matter of one's own interpretation, because no prophecy ever came by human will, but men and women moved by the Holy

37. O'Donovan, *Resurrection and Moral Order*, 85.

38. For helpful insight into the way our reading of Scripture is influenced by our own setting but not limited by or subordinate to our context, see Esau McCaulley, *Reading While Black: African American Biblical Interpretation as an Exercise in Hope* (Downers Grove, IL: IVP Academic, 2020).

39. John Calvin, *Institutes of the Christian Religion*, ed. John T. McNeill, trans. Ford Lewis Battles, Library of Christian Classics 20 (Philadelphia: Westminster, 1960), 1.13.1.

Spirit spoke from God" (2 Pet. 1:20–21 NRSV). As a result of the Spirit's work, "all Scripture is God-breathed and is useful for teaching, rebuking, correcting and training in righteousness, so that the servant of God may be thoroughly equipped for every good work" (2 Tim. 3:16–17). While the preceding verse indicates that the inspired (i.e., God-breathed) "Holy Scriptures . . . are able to make you wise for salvation through faith in Christ Jesus" (v. 15), this Word is also the ultimate, authoritative, and truthful guide and direction for Christian action and character.

Psalm 119, the longest chapter in the Bible, utilizes numerous terms for God's Word written: "law," "word," "statutes," "commands," "precepts," all of which point to "the transformative power of the Word of God."[40] The psalmist shows a love for God's Word because it is from God and is the vehicle to lead us to loving our Maker and carrying out his creation designs, declaring, "Your word is a lamp to my feet and a light to my path. I have sworn an oath and confirmed it, to observe your righteous ordinances" (Ps. 119:105–6 NRSV). In a fallen world, it is precisely a covenant with God through faith in God's provisions (Christ's death and resurrection) and the enabling power of the Holy Spirit that personally actuate the moral lamp for our feet and light for our path. Thus, as Alan Torrance reminds us, "The imperatives of grace precede and sustain the imperatives of law."[41] Creation was first an act of love and grace, and then from it God's designs (or law) flow forth.

Believers find wisdom for life in this world through reason, experience, and tradition, but Holy Scripture is our ultimate authority. It has authority not because of its existential power but because it is the Word from God. "The phrase 'the authority of Scripture' is commonly used in a prescriptive sense, namely that the Scriptures tell us what we must believe and what we must and must not do. They have an authority over our minds and our actions because they come from the one who is Lord of both."[42]

The authority of Scripture for belief and ethics has been the orthodox position down through the ages for Protestantism, Roman Catholicism, and Eastern Orthodoxy, despite their differences surrounding Scripture, including the canon. It was only with the emergence of liberalism and progressive versions of Christianity that the Word ceased to be the norm for ethics. This new view held that "the Bible 'norms us' rather than being our primary source and norm for belief. . . . It means that the Bible gives us certain symbols and images that shape our Christian character but is not the supreme

40. W. Ross Hastings, *Theological Ethics: The Moral Life of the Gospel in Contemporary Context* (Grand Rapids: Zondervan Academic, 2021), 56.

41. Alan J. Torrance, "On Deriving 'Ought' from 'Is': Christology, Covenant and *Koinonia*," in *The Doctrine of God and Theological Ethics*, ed. Alan J. Torrance and Michael Banner (London: T&T Clark, 2006), 172.

42. Christopher J. H. Wright, *Walking in the Ways of the Lord: The Ethical Authority of the Old Testament* (Downers Grove, IL: InterVarsity, 1995), 47.

authority."[43] Within the context of late modernity (or postmodernity), where truth is questioned and moral relativism reigns, it is difficult to accept this authority. Christopher Wright puts it this way: "From the pop culture's 'If it feels OK and nobody gets hurt, who can say it's wrong?' to the more sophisticated forms of subjectivism, existentialism, situationism and utilitarian consequentialism, the common dogma is that there is no transcendent authority by which absolute right or wrong, good or evil, can be determined *a priori*."[44] Wright goes on to note the logical contradiction of such relativism: "Those who assert that morality is historically and culturally relative *per se* . . . themselves absolutize that which is relative (the historical process), and relativize that which is absolute (the order of creation)." This stands in direct contrast to biblical morality, which "is preconditioned by the given shape of creation, which underlies and precedes the relativity of cultural responses to it within history."[45]

The link between creation, divine revelation, and ethics is further noted by Albert Wolters in his work *Creation Regained*. He writes, "In the Scriptures there is a close connection between God's 'Word' and his law. The word of the Sovereign is law, and it is often quite appropriate to translate the Hebrew *dabar* ('word') as 'command' when it refers to God's speaking."[46] These commands do not come to us just as imperatives but frequently as ordinances or paradigms related to all spheres of reality, including business, government, education, art, and agriculture. "An implication of the revelation of God in creation is that the creation order is knowable."[47] This does not mean that God has spelled out in his Word or law every detail of what we should do in these spheres, but it does provide a framework for making sense of these domains and seeking the ethically good, even amid fallenness and complexities. Creation as "Word" provides the essential understanding of who God is, who we are, and the most essential dimensions for life in this world, most of which receive fuller understanding in the rest of Scripture. But the contours and frameworks are set at creation, and the rest of revelation does not contradict the creation paradigms.

Just as creation and redemption are in continuity with each other, so, too, the written Word of Scripture and the incarnate Word in Christ are in continuity as well. There is a tendency in some circles to develop a red-letter Bible canon, in which the words of Jesus are set over against the rest of the written Word. But if the Word (prior to the incarnation) was at work in the

43. Roger E. Olson, *Against Liberal Theology: Putting the Brakes on Progressive Christianity* (Grand Rapids: Zondervan Reflective, 2022), 36.

44. Wright, *Walking in the Ways of the Lord*, 48.

45. Wright, *Walking in the Ways of the Lord*, 54.

46. Albert M. Wolters, *Creation Regained: Biblical Basics for a Reformational Worldview*, 2nd ed. (Grand Rapids: Eerdmans, 2005), 20.

47. Wolters, *Creation Regained*, 33.

designs of creation, and if the written Word builds on creation, then the written Word and the incarnate Word must be seen as unified. In the incarnation we have a revelation from God in which divine designs are exemplified and made concrete in the realities of history. Christ's own taking on human flesh and then exemplifying creation-kingdom patterns constitute the incarnate Word of God. In the great incarnation passage, John writes, "The Word became flesh and lived among us, and we have seen his glory, the glory as of a father's only son, full of grace and truth. . . . The law indeed was given through Moses; grace and truth came through Jesus Christ" (John 1:14, 17 NRSV). In Christ's coming into our broken, sinful world, he models something significant for his followers: not a removal from this world but an entrance into its very brokenness, demonstrating truth and grace. Throughout his life and ministry, he continually demonstrates the truth of God and the grace and love of God. Thus, on the night before his death, Jesus washes his disciples' feet, embodying a service model for his followers in a power-hungry world, and he adds, "So if I, your Lord and Teacher, have washed your feet, you also ought to wash one another's feet. For I have set you an example, that you also should do as I have done to you" (John 13:14–15 NRSV). And Peter, speaking of Jesus's moral example, writes, "If you endure when you are beaten for doing wrong, what credit is that? But if you endure when you do right and suffer for it, you have God's approval. For to this you have been called, because Christ also suffered for you, leaving you an example, so that you should follow in his steps" (1 Pet. 2:20–21 NRSV).

The incarnation is part of divine revelation precisely because Christ is the full and perfect image of God. Though humans are made in God's image, Christ in the incarnation has revealed to humanity the fullness of what it means to be human. "He is the image of the invisible God, the firstborn of all creation; for in him all things in heaven and on earth were created. . . . In him all things hold together" (Col. 1:15–17 NRSV). And as the writer to the Hebrews puts it, "In these last days [God] has spoken to us by his Son, whom he appointed heir of all things, and through whom also he made the universe. The Son is the radiance of God's glory and the exact representation of his being, sustaining all things by his powerful word" (Heb. 1:2–3). It is only natural, then, that we look to Christ incarnate as the concrete expression of God's revelation through which he calls us to his designs. Thus, "we grow by looking away from ourselves to the Christ whom we imitate (2 Cor. 3:18), whom we imitate not as an impossible and cruel quest but as those in union with him."[48]

The other dimension of the incarnation as revelation is the teachings of Jesus. As I have already noted, some are tempted to set the teachings of Jesus over against other parts of the canon of Holy Scripture, such as judgment

48. Hastings, *Theological Ethics*, 128.

texts or certain parts of the Old Testament. There are, of course, elements of the Old Testament law or historical narratives, such as the treatment of women or violent wars, that give us great pause and call for wise hermeneutical analysis. This is not the place to grapple with those troubling texts, not least because others have already done so.[49] But many are tempted to say, as David Lamb puts it, "How did the mean Old Testament God morph into a nice guy like Jesus?"[50] First, we should note that Jesus is clear that he did not come "to abolish the law or the prophets"; he came "not to abolish but to fulfill" (Matt. 5:17 NRSV). Second, we should affirm that the teachings of Jesus are binding on all believers, for "everyone then who hears these words of mine and acts on them will be like a wise man who built his house on rock" (Matt. 7:24 NRSV). But third, we must observe when we are tempted to adopt a red-letter version of the Bible, setting Jesus over against the parts that don't fit our presuppositions, that "God in the Old Testament is consistently described as slow to anger and abounding in steadfast love, but Jesus speaks about hell more than anyone else in Scripture."[51] Thus, it is problematic to take a selective approach to the canon of Scripture, legitimizing those passages that fit the mood of our time, our personal temperaments, or our ideological biases, and rejecting the rest.[52]

Jesus's incarnation and teachings are all part of divine revelation, a revelation that both comforts and confronts. But this divine revelation goes back to what the triune God was doing in creation, when God spoke, and it came to be. At creation God discloses his nature as a speaking God, and in the incarnation, we see God's Word exemplified and taught. But the incarnate Word and the written Word are unified, for God the Creator, the Revealer, and the Redeemer are one. "Though God is a great king, it is not his wish to live at a distance from his subjects. Rather the reverse: He made us with the intention that he and we might walk together forever in a love relationship. But such a relationship can exist only when the parties involved know something of each other."[53] Thus, God has spoken through Holy Scripture, his Word. And this is our ultimate, truthful, and unfailing authority in ethical decisions and character—a Word that comes to us in a broad array of genres, from laws and principles to narratives (with both positive and negative moral

49. See, for example, William J. Webb and Gordon K. Oeste, *Bloody, Brutal, and Barbaric? Wrestling with Troubling War Texts* (Downers Grove, IL: IVP Academic, 2019); and Paul Copan, *Is God a Vindictive Bully? Reconciling Portrayals of God in the Old and New Testaments* (Grand Rapids: Baker Academic, 2022).

50. David T. Lamb, *God Behaving Badly: Is the God of the Old Testament Angry, Sexist and Racist?* (Downers Grove, IL: IVP Books, 2011), Kindle loc. 42.

51. Lamb, *God Behaving Badly*, Kindle loc. 42.

52. This was the error of Marcion in the second century AD; he set the God of Jesus and Paul over against the God of the Old Testament. As a result Marcion was declared a heretic and excommunicated from the church.

53. Packer, *Knowing God*, 110.

examples) and broad paradigms.[54] We may have questions about this revelation and struggle with how best to interpret it. But it makes all the difference in the world to put ourselves under the Word's authority, rather than over it as if we were the ultimate arbiters. To put ourselves under this gracious Word, written and incarnate, is to put ourselves under the reign of God, our Creator and Redeemer.

Divine revelation reflects something of the very nature of God. Just as God creates out of the love inherent within the divine Trinity, so God reveals himself in the written Word and incarnate Word from the same love. The God who designs loves humanity so much that it was in the nature of that love to reveal his designs to a lost humanity and to bring them back to himself in redemption through the death and resurrection of our Savior. Without divine revelation humanity resides in darkness, a darkness dispelled by the first act of creation. "And God said, 'Let there be light'" (Gen. 1:3), and it is that same light in which God reveals to humanity his path to salvation and his path to living the designs of creation, which are the designs of Christ, our Savior and Lord. The triune God is a speaking God.

Conclusion

In this chapter we have explored themes that are central to the specific ethical paradigms covered in the rest of this book. God creates the world out of love, the love that inheres in the eternal relationship of the triune God. Because God creates on the basis of love, love becomes the major (though not only) ethical norm in our relationship to God, others, and the world. But this love takes form and definition in the designs of God from creation. God not only designs the world and humans but designs spheres of activity and moral direction for those spheres, all of which begin to be laid out in the creation narrative. Furthermore, in the creation story God speaks reality into being, demonstrating that he is a self-disclosing God. Divine revelation, both written and incarnate, is our ultimate authority for discerning those creation designs, providing wisdom for how we implement them in a complex, broken world.

Indeed, "in the beginning God created," and in that creation we see a loving, designing, self-disclosing God.

54. For a more detailed analysis of the forms of ethical guidance in Scripture, see Dennis P. Hollinger, *Choosing the Good: Christian Ethics in a Complex World* (Grand Rapids: Baker Academic, 2002), 162–73.

2

It's a Good World After All

Money, Sex, and Power

In the creational account of Genesis, a remarkable phrase occurs throughout creation—"And God saw that it was good." The phrase occurs either in that exact form or in a variation in verses 4, 10, 12, 18, 21, and 25 of chapter 1. After God completes creation, including the creation of humans in the image of God, and gives them mandates for procreation, stewardship of the earth, and cultural development, he looks at all he has made and sees that "it was very good" (v. 31 NRSV). Along with these observations of goodness are three blessings: of birds and sea creatures (v. 22), of humans (v. 28), and then of the seventh day (2:3). "It is significant that God sees things as 'good' long before humans come onto the scene, and that God's blessing is not restricted to humanity."[1]

And what is pronounced good in this narrative? Not what we commonly think of as spiritual realities, but rather physical and material realities: light, dry ground, vegetation, the heavenly bodies, birds, creatures of the sea, other animals, and then human beings. There is nothing quite like this in the other creation stories of the ancient world. The Hebrew word for "good" here, *tov*, like our English word, connotes various meanings of goodness, ranging from moral qualities ("She's a good person") to aesthetic qualities ("It's a good painting"), even to functional qualities ("It's a good house structurally"). Perhaps the Creator's judgment embodies all of those, but it's important to

1. Andrew Sloane, *At Home in a Strange Land: Using the Old Testament in Christian Ethics* (Peabody, MA: Hendrickson, 2008), 150.

understand that the good of these physical, material realities is an intrinsic goodness and a goodness that, though impacted by the fall, remains in our broken world. It is a metaphysical or ontological goodness, so that while money, sex, and power (the three ethical case studies of this chapter) have been impacted significantly by the fall, they remain intrinsically good gifts of God. It is indeed a good world after all. These physical gifts of God to adorn this world and bring beauty, love, functionality, new life, creativity, and majesty reflect the intrinsic goodness of God and serve as ethical paradigms that can bring glory to our Maker, even amid fallen, idolatrous human proclivities. No wonder John Calvin could write, "There is no portion of the world, however minute, that does not exhibit at least some sparks of beauty; while it is impossible to contemplate the vast and beautiful fabric as it extends around, without being overwhelmed by the immense weight of glory."[2]

The goodness of divine creation is at the heart of Archbishop William Temple's judgment that "Christianity . . . is the most avowedly materialistic of all the great religions."[3] By "materialistic" he did not mean love of money, but rather an affirmation of the material, embodied realities of this world. The goodness of the physical is upheld by three cardinal doctrines of the Christian faith: creation, incarnation, and the resurrection of the body. Some would add the Eucharist or Lord's Supper to this list. In creation God pronounces good that which is material, physical, and embodied. In the incarnation God takes on human flesh and dwells among us, much to the suspicion of some who have been influenced by Platonic dualisms, which deem the physical suspect. Some theologians of the past even argue that the incarnation was necessary aside from the fall and our need for redemption, as an affirmation of creation and God's uniting of the entire cosmos under himself.[4] And in the future eschaton, there is a physical resurrection not of our souls but of our bodies. In the Lord's Supper or Eucharist, using physical bread and wine, we celebrate the death of Christ through either an affirmation of some kind of real presence or a symbolic remembrance of the literal, physical death of Christ.

Through and through, biblical faith affirms the material realm, thus confirming the metaphysical goodness of this world. "This is a world in which God delights and in which God invites humans to share in God's pleasure. This reinforces, of course, the intrinsic value of the creation in God's eyes. It is not just good for us, God's purposes, and so on; it is good, period."[5] All of this implies that God calls us to live out his designs in this world. The call

2. John Calvin, *The Institutes of the Christian Religion*, trans. Henry Beveridge, rev. ed. (Peabody, MA: Hendrickson, 2008), 1.5.1.

3. William Temple, *Nature, Man and God* (London: Macmillan, 1949), 478.

4. For a helpful overview of this debate, see Marilyn McCord Adams, "For Better for Worse Solidarity," in *Christ and the Created Order: Perspectives from Theology, Philosophy, and Science*, ed. Andrew B. Torrance and Thomas H. McCall (Grand Rapids: Zondervan, 2018), 167–78.

5. Sloane, *At Home in a Strange Land*, 155.

of God is not to the monastery or some spiritualized reality apart from the material realities of this world. When I was growing up, I sometimes heard an old gospel song that went, "This world is not my home, I'm just a passing through. My treasures are laid up, somewhere beyond the blue. The angels beckon me from heaven's open door, and I can't feel at home in this world any more."[6] These types of spiritualities have led critics of Christianity like Ludwig Feuerbach to argue, "Nature, the world, has no value, no interest, for Christians. The Christian thinks only of himself and the salvation of his soul."[7]

Sadly, various Christian spiritualities and ethical frameworks fed into Feuerbach's judgment. But in this work, in accordance with many theologians from the past and the present, I am seeking to portray an ethic that says, "This world is my home; but we are rooted in the transcendent as we live in our good, though now fallen, earthly home." Yes, much in this world is blatantly sinful, unjust, coercive, sensual, deceptive, power hungry, and idolatrous. To those proclivities of our sinful, broken world the follower of Christ says no. But we recognize that this world belongs to our loving Creator, who continues to stamp the mark of goodness on it. This is the world to which God has called us, precisely because the Creator-Savior Jesus Christ entered into it to redeem it. One day God will restore this world back to its creational beauty, wholeness, and holiness; but in the meantime, we live in this good but broken world in light of creational, incarnational, and eschatological realities, which are one. The call to this good world is affirmed by Scripture's holding creation and redemption together. For example, Paul, writing to the church at Colossae, with its struggle over heretical impulses, states, "He is the image of the invisible God, the firstborn of all creation; for in him all things in heaven and on earth were created. . . . All things have been created through him and for him. He himself is before all things, and in him all things hold together" (Col. 1:15–17 NRSV). But Paul then turns to the church and redemption: "He is the head of the body, the church. . . . For in him all the fullness of God was pleased to dwell, and through him God was pleased to reconcile to himself all things . . . , by making peace through the blood of his cross" (vv. 18–20 NRSV). Bill Edgar rightly points out that from this emerges a world engagement, for "the rest of the Colossian letter spells out various ways in which cultural transformation can take place, including physical freedom (Col 2:16–23); racial reconciliation (Col 3:11); compassion, kindness, and the like (Col 3:12–13); music (Col 3:16); family (Col 3:18–21); the workplace (Col 3:22–4:1); missions (Col 4:2–4); and relations with unbelievers (Col 4:5–6)."[8]

6. "This World Is Not My Home," attributed to A. P. Carter, Hymnary.org, accessed March 24, 2023, https://hymnary.org/text/this_world_is_not_my_home_im_just_a.

7. Ludwig Feuerbach, *The Essence of Christianity*, trans. Georg Eliot (New York: Harper & Brothers, 1957), 287.

8. William Edgar, *Created and Creating: A Biblical Theology of Culture* (Downers Grove, IL: IVP Academic, 2016), 150.

The goodness of God's created physical world is powerfully portrayed in the great creation psalm, Psalm 104. The psalm begins with the splendor and majesty of God (v. 1) and the priority of light (v. 2), as we noted in the last chapter. It then beautifully and poetically rehearses the grandeur and majesty of the created heavens and earth. In the middle of the psalm, the goodness of creation is affirmed:

> From your lofty abode you water the mountains;
> the earth is satisfied with the fruit of your work.
>
> You cause the grass to grow for the cattle,
> and plants for people to use,
> to bring forth food from the earth,
> and wine to gladden the human heart,
> oil to make the face shine,
> and bread to strengthen the human heart. . . .
>
> [Your creatures] all look to you
> to give them their food in due season;
> when you give to them, they gather it up;
> when you open your hand, they are filled with good things.
> (vv. 13–15, 27–28 NRSV)

The significance of the goodness of creation for ethics is the focus of this chapter. First, we will examine the uneven history of the Christian church on matters physical and bodily, exploring various forms of Gnosticism and milder dualisms found in asceticism. In this section we will also note theologians and movements that resisted these heresies and affirmed a strong biblical theology of the physical creation. We will then explore three ethical issues that are often viewed through the lens of Gnostic and ascetic tendencies: money, sex, and power. Some would contend that the most potent ethical problems we face in this world are related to at least one of these three issues. I will seek to show that money, sex, and power are really good gifts of creation and are best dealt with by discerning the goodness and ends (i.e., purposes) that God intends for them. We best understand the aberrations of each by first affirming the good for which God created them, and we best find paths to moral goodness through a theology and spirituality clearly affirming the goodness of the material, embodied life.

Historic Tensions on the Goodness of Creation

Because Christian faith is rooted in a vertical relationship with a transcendent God, it is likely inevitable that in accentuating the vertical, life in this world would be minimized or even suspect. From the earliest days of Christianity, antiphysical impulses began to be a threat, so that John in his First Epistle had to affirm the bodily dimension of Jesus: "That which was from the beginning, which we have heard, which we have seen with our eyes, which we looked upon and have touched with our hands, concerning the word of life . . ." (1 John 1:1 ESV). Later denials of Jesus's full humanity would circulate under the name of docetism, a heresy that said Jesus appeared to have a physical body but it wasn't genuinely human flesh. Why the heresy? Because of a suspicion and then an overt rejection of the material and bodily realms of life. This came to be most evident in a broad array of movements generally called Gnosticism, which usually made a distinction between the god who redeemed humans away from this world and an inferior god who created the world. But an error about creation leads to errors in just about everything else in theology, and so Gnosticism was wayward on divine revelation, sin and evil, salvation, Christ, and the essence of Christian living—spirituality and ethics.

It was the denial of the goodness of creation, with its material-physical affirmations, that led Gnosticism astray. Creation was typically seen not as ex nihilo but as a construction from problematic preexistent matter. As a result, as Alister McGrath notes, "The existence of evil in the world was thus to be explained on the basis of the intractability of this pre-existent matter. God's options in creating the world were limited by the poor quality of the material available."[9] The roots of Gnosticism lie in the Platonic tradition, with its adulation of the ideal realm over material realms. The most real realities in this world are not physical realities but soulish, ideal realities in the minds of humans. This would lead the Gnostics to very different versions of salvation, spirituality, and ethics. Salvation was achieved through an esoteric knowledge of the divine, which led to a spirituality focused totally on soulish elements, with minimal relationship to everyday life.

The Gnostics' radical dualism led, as Irenaeus in the second century pointed out, to two contradictory approaches to ethics. One approach was rigid asceticism, with its strident suppression of bodily impulses, and the other was moral license on the grounds that since the body is unimportant, what we do in and with it doesn't really matter.[10] As Colin Gunton observes, "Both moralities derive from the same underestimation of the goodness of the creation." Furthermore, he writes, "Gnosticism was—and indeed, remains—a Christian heresy which fed upon Greek philosophical suspicions of the goodness and reality of the material world. Like many heresies, however, it provided the spur . . . to counter it, and in the process gave the church one of its greatest theological achievements"[11]—namely, the biblical doctrine of creation, as articulated by Irenaeus and those who followed him.

9. Alister E. McGrath, *Christian Theology: An Introduction*, 2nd ed. (Oxford: Blackwell, 1997), 268.

10. Irenaeus, *Against Heresies* 1.28.1–2.

11. Colin E. Gunton, *The Triune Creator: A Historical and Systematic Study*, Edinburgh Studies in Constructive Theology (Grand Rapids: Eerdmans, 1998), 49–50.

Gnosticism in the second century AD had many variations and never constituted a unified movement. Elaine Pagels, seeking partly to legitimize the various forms, including a whole array of works found at Nag Hammadi, describes Gnosticism "as a sort of umbrella term to cover the people that the leaders of the church don't like. It covers probably a huge variety of points of view. And yet there is a theme; . . . the divine is to be discovered by some kind of interior search, and not simply by a savior who is outside of you."[12] This interior search led to a spiritualized knowledge that only the elite could achieve. But in addition to this knowledge, "what the many exponents [had] in common [was] an attempt to escape from evil by denying the material world."[13] Some, like the Manicheans, members of a particular Gnostic movement, asserted a radical dualism between body and soul and emphasized a struggle between the spiritual world of light and the material world of darkness.

One of the major figures of Gnosticism was Valentinus, a second-century Alexandrian teacher whom we know primarily through those who rebutted his theology. At the heart of his thinking is a variant view of creation centered in the rebellion of *Sophia*, Wisdom. Peter Brown, in his description of the myth, describes it this way: "Rebellious Wisdom became a frenetic power of mere proliferation. Driven to create out of despair at her separation from God, *Sophia* formed a redundant universe. Matter came into being, and with matter, the sad sense . . . that the material world was an abortive attempt to imitate an infinitely distant, invisible, and ever-elusive model." The human being with physical form was distorted, for "the body was deeply alien to the true self."[14] Valentinus set forth a form of redemption in which the physical would be left behind and spiritual union would supplant it, leading even to the eradication of the sexes. The Gnostic Gospel of Thomas reflects this framework: "They said to Him: 'Shall we then, as children, enter the Kingdom?' Jesus said to them: 'When you make the two one . . . and when you make the male and the female into one and the same, so that the male shall not be male nor the female female, . . . then you shall enter the Kingdom.'"[15] The physical sexes are repudiated, and sex itself is renounced, for in baptism the spiritual elite enter the company of the angels.

Another movement similar to Gnosticism was *Encratism*, the word literally meaning "abstain." Irenaeus and Eusebius, the church historian, attribute the founding of the movement to Tatian, a second-century Assyrian writer. The

12. Elaine H. Pagels, "Gnostics and Other Heretics," FRONTLINE, Public Broadcasting Service, accessed April 26, 2021, www.pbs.org/wgbh/pages/frontline/shows/religion/story/heretics.html.

13. Edgar, *Created and Creating*, 148.

14. Peter Brown, *The Body and Society: Men, Women and Sexual Renunciation in Early Christianity* (New York: Columbia University Press, 1988), 108, 109.

15. April D. Deconick, *The Original Gospel of Thomas in Translation: With a Commentary and New English Translation of the Complete Gospel* (London: T&T Clark, 2007), 22:1–7, p. 115.

Encratites abstained from meat and wine, deplored marriage, and even substituted milk or water for wine in the Eucharist. One part of the group, like Marcion, came to reject certain parts of Scripture, and some even declared women the work of Satan. Tatian himself reinterpreted the Genesis text on marriage (i.e., 2:24): "For Tatian, once Adam had willfully decided to 'leave' his Father and Mother, God and His Spirit, he became subject to death and so was forced to 'cleave,' through physical intercourse to a woman by marrying Eve."[16] Thus, to experience the Spirit of God, one must abandon marriage and sex. One variation of this idea was spiritual marriage, in which couples married but abstained from sexual intercourse, and if they were really spiritual, they shared the same bed chastely. Underlying the Encratites' theology was a radical rejection of the goodness of creation.

While these movements flourished in the second and third centuries, evidently there were already forms of this kind of thinking in first-century Christianity, for 1 Timothy 4 describes false teachers who "forbid marriage and require abstinence from foods that God created to be received with thanksgiving by those who believe and know the truth" (v. 3 ESV). The text then appeals to creation to repudiate the heresies: "For everything created by God is good, and nothing is to be rejected if it is received with thanksgiving" (v. 4 ESV).

While Gnosticism in its various forms reflected the most radical rejections of the goodness of creation, there were milder rejections that we can simply term *asceticism*—a strong suspicion of bodily, material forms in this world. While most of these people were theologically orthodox, embracing the Trinity and the full humanity and deity of Christ, they struggled most visibly in coming to terms with physical intimacy in marriage. Sex was a stumbling block.

Jerome is a key figure in the history of the Christian church, for he translated the Bible into Latin, a translation that was essentially the authorized version of the church for more than a millennium. Living in the fourth and fifth centuries, with part of his time in Bethlehem, Jerome had a mixed pedigree regarding the goodness of creation. On the one hand, he believed, contrary to the sentiments of many church leaders, that women were able to study Scripture and theology, copy and translate texts, and identify heresies. At the same time, "the human body remained for Jerome a darkened forest, filled with the roaring of wild beasts, that could be controlled only by rigid codes of diet and by strict avoidance of occasions for sexual attraction."[17] In all of this, Jerome reflected the kind of asceticism advocated by the desert fathers who fled to the desert to avoid the temptations of this world, with the hope of freeing their bodies for a bodiless eternity.

Jerome believed not that marriage was evil but rather that it was inferior and thus a barrier to true spirituality and holy living. Virginity was highly

16. Brown, *Body and Society*, 92.
17. Brown, *Body and Society*, 376.

esteemed, for "he who . . . in the married state renders his wife her due cannot so pray. Either we pray always and are virgins or we cease to pray that we may fulfill the claims of marriage."[18] Thus, his advice to husbands seeking to be both married and spiritual was this: "If I grieve that I have not shared in Christ's body it does help me to avoid for a little while my wife's embraces, and to prefer to wedded love the love of Christ."[19] For Jerome this was not merely a spiritual discipline to more fully know the reality of Christ in one's life, but was an asceticism fueled by suspicions concerning the physical, bodily realms—God's good creation.

When we come to Saint Augustine, the greatest theologian of the early church, we find a very different outlook on creation, and yet remnants of asceticism remain in his thinking. He was writing and preaching in a difficult time, for "the ascetic movements had placed marriage under a cloud. Stories of dramatic renunciations of sex were in the air. Couples were praised for having entered into vows of perpetual chastity on their wedding night."[20] For the most part, Augustine challenged this. He affirmed the human being as a mix of body and soul, though the latter was clearly the most significant theologically and experientially. He wrote extensively on creation, and unlike many other church leaders and theologians, he affirmed the body as part of God's good creation. In his own philosophical and spiritual journey, Augustine had drunk deeply from the waters of radical dualism in Neoplatonism and Manicheanism. He eventually found them wanting, though, and after his conversion, he was clear that marriage and physical intimacy were not results of the fall or simply suspect because they were bodily. Augustine clearly affirmed that the body is not intrinsically evil, for "it was not the corruptible flesh that made the soul sinful, but the sinful soul that made the flesh corruptible."[21]

Augustine affirms marriage and sex as gifts of God from creation, to which Jesus himself gives confirmation. Marriage and its accompanying physical intimacy are given primarily for procreation, though Augustine also sees companionship as a complementary dimension. But he asserts that something radical happened in the fall to our physical bodies, our desires, and most notably our will. Since the fall and its impact on the will, humans have inevitably experienced physical intimacy with lust and unbridled passion, which seems, then, to bring suspicion to the physical-material realms—a tinge of asceticism. Augustine writes the following:

18. Jerome, "Letter 22," in *Select Library of Nicene and Post-Nicene Fathers of the Christian Church*, 2nd series, ed. Philip Schaff and Henry Wace (Grand Rapids: Eerdmans, 1979), 6:30.

19. Jerome, "Letter 48," in Schaff, *Select Library of Nicene and Post-Nicene Fathers*, 6:75.

20. Peter Brown, *Augustine of Hippo: A Biography*, 45th anniv. ed. (Berkeley: University of California Press, 2000), 451.

21. Saint Augustine, *The City of God*, trans. Marcus Dods (New York: Random House, 1950), 444 (14.4).

> This lust not only takes possession of the whole body and outward members, but also makes itself felt within, and moves the whole man with a passion in which mental emotion is mingled with bodily appetite, so that the pleasure which results is the greatest of all bodily pleasures. So possessing indeed is this pleasure, that at the moment of time in which it is consummated, all mental activity is suspended. What friend of wisdom . . . would not prefer, if this were possible, to beget children without this lust . . . but . . . be actuated by his volition . . . ?[22]

Augustine believed the moral ideal in sexual intercourse was to be controlled not by physical passion but entirely by the rational will. In the garden of Eden before the fall, "the man, then, would have sown the seed, and the woman received it, as need required, the generative organs being moved by the will, not excited by lust."[23] Nonetheless, even with suspect passions, marriage and physical intimacy are good because they produce children, a necessity for society to endure. It was particularly in his sermons that "what married couples heard from Augustine the preacher was economical and deliberately banal. They should be careful. Ideally, they should not have sex except to conceive children."[24] In these cautions Augustine is a long way from Jerome, the desert fathers, and certainly the various forms of Gnosticism. Nonetheless, the tint of asceticism in one of the greatest theological thinkers of all time was to unfortunately have a long-term impact upon the Christian church. The true goodness of creation is tinged by suspicions that the body, material realities, and the various dimensions of human culture are intrinsically problematic for Christian living—and not just because of the fall.

When we come to the medieval period, the highest good was viewed as leaving the world of money, marriage, and societal power and heading to the monastery or nunnery. There was a twofold way of being a Christian: a lower way lived in the world with money, marriage, and power, contrasted with a higher way involving vows of poverty, chastity, and obedience. Monasticism was fueled not merely by forms of positive spirituality, though some leading monastics left us with treasured spiritual insights. But its withdrawal and day-to-day existence was fueled by an asceticism that was suspicious of the physical, material world. A good creation was rarely part of one's language and thinking. Even the great medieval theologian Thomas Aquinas, while affirming creation as significant, still finds ways to prioritize the life of chastity or virginity, because it avoids bodily pleasure and therefore best facilitates a focus on God. Thomas affirmed marriage as instituted by God, but "marriage is allowed in the state of infirmity by indulgence. . . . Therefore, it needs to be excused by certain goods"—most notably, procreation and a sacrament pointing to Christ's union with his church. The most problematic element

22. Augustine, *City of God*, 464 (14.16).
23. Augustine, *City of God*, 472 (14.24).
24. Brown, *Augustine of Hippo*, 502.

in sex is "a loss of reason incidental to the union of man and woman, both because the reason is carried away entirely on account of the vehemence of the pleasure . . . and again because of the tribulation of the flesh."[25] The ascetic tendencies in Aquinas and the medieval church led to a truncated view of spirituality and ethics. And those tendencies have at times surfaced even in the modern Christian world.

Fortunately, some theologians throughout history clearly affirmed what Genesis 1 so eloquently teaches about creation and its physical, bodily dimensions: "It was good," and "It was very good" (e.g., vv. 10, 31). One of the early theological voices was Irenaeus, a second-century church leader from Asia Minor (present-day Turkey) who ministered for most of his life in Lyons (in present-day France). In *Against Heresies* Irenaeus gives an in-depth overview and theological critique of Gnosticism that, until the Nag Hammadi discoveries in 1945, was our primary lens into the various Gnostic movements. "Irenaeus countered these Gnostic theologies by asserting creation as an act of divine love from a triune God and thus the nonhierarchical goodness of all creation."[26] He held to the unity of Holy Scripture and thereby saw continuity between creation and the incarnation, thus also affirming the physical realm in God's world. As for creation he writes, "The rule of truth which we hold, is, that there is one God Almighty, who made all things by His Word, and fashioned and formed, out of that which had no existence, all things which exist."[27] But this creation doesn't stand alone theologically. "The basis of Irenaeus' affirmative attitude to the whole created order is christological. If God in his Son takes to himself the reality of human flesh, then nothing created, and certainly nothing material, can be downgraded to unreality, semi-reality or treated as fundamentally evil, as in the Manichaean version of Gnosticism."[28]

During the Reformation years, John Calvin had a most positive view of the created world and all of the gifts of culture emanating from God's good creation. Despite a radical fall into sin and humanity's need of God's grace in Christ alone for redemption, a created goodness remains available to all human beings, which later Reformed theologians would term "common grace." Linking human activity and God's good gifts of creation, Calvin writes,

> It becomes man seriously to employ his eyes considering the works of God, since a place has been assigned him in this most glorious theatre that he may be a spectator of them. . . . Sculpture and painting are gifts of God. . . . Intelligence

25. Thomas Aquinas, *Summa Theologica*, trans. Fathers of the English Dominican Province, 2nd ed. (New York: Benziger Brothers, 1948), 2736, 2737 (III.49).

26. Bruce Riley Ashford and Craig G. Bartholomew, *The Doctrine of Creation: A Constructive Kuyperian Approach* (Downers Grove, IL: IVP Academic, 2020), 47.

27. Irenaeus, *Against Heresies*, in *The Ante-Nicene Fathers*, ed. Alexander Roberts and James Donaldson (Grand Rapids: Eerdmans, 1979), 1:347 (1.22.1).

28. Gunton, *Triune Creator*, 52.

> in some particular art [is] a special gift of God. . . . In reading profane authors, the admirable light of truth displayed should remind us that the human mind . . . is still adorned and invested with admirable gifts. . . . We will be careful . . . not to reject truth wherever it appears. In despising the gifts we insult the Giver.[29]

Whereas the Eastern church is often thought to have an otherworldly outlook that undermines physical life in this world, certain representatives have strongly affirmed creational goodness, such as the twentieth-century Orthodox theologian Alexander Schmemann. Schmemann believed that the goodness of creation was affirmed through the incarnation, resurrection, and the sacraments. He writes, "I realized that theologically I have one idea—the eschatological content of Christianity, and of the Church as the presence in this world of the Kingdom . . . —this presence as the salvation of the world and not escape from it. . . . Once you love [the Kingdom], you cannot avoid loving all creation."[30]

Dietrich Bonhoeffer, the twentieth-century theologian-ethicist martyred by the Nazis, wrote an exposition of the opening chapters of Genesis that affirms that the goodness of creation continues after the fall. "Because the world is God's world, it is good. God, the Creator and Lord of the world, wills a good world, a good work. The flight from the created work to bodiless spirit, or to the internal spiritual disposition . . . , is prohibited."[31] In seeking to overcome the secular-sacred division, Bonhoeffer insists that we must be in and engage with this good world, for the world belongs to Christ. In his *Ethics* he writes, "In Christ we are offered the possibility of partaking in the reality of God and in the reality of the world, but not in the one without the other." At creation God instituted mandates through which we engage this good world—labor, marriage, government, and the church—and "this means that there can be no retreating from a 'secular' into the 'spiritual' sphere."[32]

Many other theologians could be added to the list of either those who failed to affirm the goodness of creation or those who embraced it. The Christian church and its thinkers have clearly had an uneven history in embracing Genesis's refrain "And God saw that it was good." But what are the implications of this biblical teaching? We turn now to three issues in which the starting point must be the refrain "It is good." Yes, money, sex, and power are fallen, and badly so. They have been turned into idols, utilized to oppress others, and pursued with self-centeredness. Unrighteousness and

29. Calvin, *Institutes*, 1.6.2, 1.11.12, 2.2.14, quoted in R. E. O. White, *Christian Ethics: The Historical Development* (Atlanta: John Knox, 1981), 184.

30. Alexander Schmemann, *The Journals of Father Alexander Schmemann, 1973–1983* (Crestwood, NY: St. Vladimir's Seminary Press, 2000), 174.

31. Dietrich Bonhoeffer, *Creation and Fall: A Theological Exposition of Genesis 1–3*, ed. John W. de Gruchy, trans. Douglas Stephen Bax, Dietrich Bonhoeffer Works 3 (Minneapolis: Fortress, 1997), 46.

32. Dietrich Bonhoeffer, *Ethics* (New York: Macmillan, 1965), 195, 207.

injustice pervade them in this broken world. But the starting point in an ethic of money, sex, and power must be the verdict of creation and the verdict of Christ our Creator-Redeemer, "It is good." Only then do we have a compass to guide us in the use of these good gifts and a framework for avoiding their abuse.

The Goodness of Money

Money is a medium of exchange that allows us to purchase or provide goods and services. Wealth is a measure of value for various assets owned by a person, community, company, or society; it includes money, property, goods, and other mediums of exchange and value, such as stocks and bonds. No, the words "money" and "wealth" do not appear in the Genesis creation story, but the *stuff* of money and wealth are there; and they are pronounced good. Many ethical evaluations of money, wealth, and economic realities start with a negative assumption due to their many abuses in a fallen world. Indeed, "Christian moral theology has never been entirely comfortable with the topic of riches and possessions. This discomfort is extended to economics, given its association with the creation and distribution of wealth."[33] But I want to suggest that the starting point in creation ethics is not the fallen realities surrounding material realms, but rather an affirmation of those material realities as good gifts of God. We don't adequately get to the many abuses of money and wealth unless we first start with their positive goodness and value.

As we have noted already in this book, the goodness pronounced over creation includes land, various forms of vegetation, waters to nurture the vegetation, the mechanisms of seasons that regulate growth and harvest, and various forms of animal life. God creates humans in his image "so that they may rule over the fish in the sea and the birds in the sky, over the livestock and all the wild animals, and over all the creatures that move along the ground" (Gen. 1:26). God goes on to tell his image bearers, "I have given you every plant yielding seed that is on the face of all the earth, and every tree with seed in its fruit. You shall have them for food" (v. 29 ESV). And then God grants to all of the animals green plants for food (v. 30). Early hunting and gathering and then agricultural societies were fairly self-sufficient with the very basics of natural life, but it didn't take long till humans, with these good natural resources, began to barter and trade with their wealth. And eventually all these resources would be traded, using various kinds of market mechanisms, through the medium we call money. And God's verdict on all of this? "It was very good" (1:31 ESV).

33. Brent Waters, *Just Capitalism: A Christian Ethic of Economic Globalization* (Louisville: Westminster John Knox, 2016), 19.

All of the created, material goods at creation constitute what would be at the heart of traditional economic life. This is not the place to provide a full-scale ethical evaluation of economic realities but rather to simply postulate that the starting point for any ethical evaluation must be a fundamental affirmation of wealth and money, which enable the exchange of goods, services, and investments that further economic flourishing. The realities of Genesis 1 are very earthy, but they form the heart of what humans and all of nature need in order to survive and flourish. Amid this good creation, God creates the man and the woman as responsible beings who are expected to make wise choices not only in meeting their own needs and the needs of others but also in being judicious stewards over these good gifts for the glory of God and the ongoing flourishing of fellow image bearers and the natural world. The British economist Sir Brian Griffiths puts it this way: "Man has been created with an urge to control and harness the resources of nature in the interests of the common good, but he is subject to his accountability to God as a trustee to preserve and care for it. This process is precisely what an economist would refer to as *responsible wealth creation*."[34]

The responsibilities that were given to humans to tend, nurture, and develop this world have a built-in assumption that humans would be creative in their stewardship. They would build buildings, towns, and modes of transportation. They would develop machinery and technologies to aid in the process of working with these created goods. They would find new ways to creatively carry out the work mandate, engaging all the wealth resources God created. All of this would mean not just a utilization of existing wealth but an actual creation of new wealth through new jobs, goods, and services, an exploration of new resources, and not only technology to harness the earth's resources but even new technologies and information that would one day help protect and wisely steward these resources, like renewable energy. This stands in contrast to zero-sum assumptions, which some bring to the world of money and wealth. In this fallacious perception, there is a set amount of wealth in the world, and thus a plan of controlled redistribution is the primary mechanism for meeting human need, as opposed to the understanding that God's image bearers, in their creative utilization and stewardship of creation, should create new forms of wealth, which in turn have the potential for creating new jobs and meeting human need.[35]

But, of course, like all of God's good creation gifts, wealth and money are deeply fallen and thus misused. Scripture is clear on the many sins associated with the misuse of money and wealth, and they generally fall along three lines: idolatry, injustices, and failure to respond to the needs of others. Because

34. Brian Griffiths, *The Creation of Wealth: The Christian's Case for Capitalism* (Downers Grove, IL: InterVarsity, 1984), 52–53.

35. See, for example, "The Zero-Sum Fallacy," PovertyCure, accessed May 12, 2021, https://www.povertycure.org/learn/issues/charity-hurts/zero-sum-fallacy.

money is good, it seems inevitable that fallen humanity would elevate this good to the ultimate good and turn it into a god. This is at the heart of Jesus's parable of the rich fool in Luke 12. One day someone comes to Jesus asking him to settle a dispute over inheritance. Sensing his idolatrous propensities, Jesus warns him strongly, "Be on your guard against all kinds of greed; for one's life does not consist in the abundance of possessions" (v. 15 NRSV). He then goes on to tell the parable of a rich farmer who had an abundant harvest. In response the farmer says, "I will do this: I will pull down my barns and build larger ones, and there I will store all my grain and my goods. And I will say to my soul, 'Soul, you have ample goods laid up for many years; relax, eat, drink, and be merry'" (vv. 18–19 NRSV). But God's response to the man's idolatry is stern: "You fool! This very night your life is being demanded of you" (12:20 NRSV). In a similar vein, the apostle Paul writes:

> Now there is great gain in godliness with contentment, for we brought nothing into the world, and we cannot take anything out of the world. But if we have food and clothing, with these we will be content. But those who desire to be rich fall into temptation, into a snare, into many senseless and harmful desires that plunge people into ruin and destruction. For the love of money is a root of all kinds of evil. It is through this craving that some have wandered away from the faith and pierced themselves with many pangs. (1 Tim. 6:6–10 ESV)

Idolatry takes God's good gift and turns it into something God never intended: the ultimate source of satisfaction and identity. Idolatry is frequently accompanied by greed, the persistent desire to acquire more and more, believing it will bring happiness and fulfillment.

The second set of biblical teachings on the misuse of God's good gifts focuses on injustices, and such texts are found throughout Scripture, calling into question the exploitation of others, unfairness in pay, and bribery. The psalmist describes the Maker of heaven and earth as one who "executes justice for the oppressed, who gives food to the hungry" (Ps. 146:7 ESV). The prophets continually rail against the economic injustices of God's people:

> For if you truly amend your ways and your doings, if you truly act justly one with another, if you do not oppress the alien, the orphan, and the widow, . . . then I will dwell with you in this place, in the land that I gave of old to your ancestors forever and ever. (Jer. 7:5–7 NRSV)

> You levy a straw tax on the poor
>   and impose a tax on their grain. . . .
> For I know how many are your offenses
>   and how great your sins.
>
> There are those who oppress the innocent and take bribes
>   and deprive the poor of justice in the courts. (Amos 5:11–12)

> They covet fields, and seize them;
> houses, and take them away;
> they oppress householder and house,
> people and their inheritance. (Mic. 2:2 NRSV)

Jesus, in his first sermon in his hometown of Nazareth, quotes the prophet Isaiah, indicating that the Scripture is now being fulfilled: "The Spirit of the Lord is upon me, because he has anointed me to bring good news to the poor. He has sent me to proclaim release to the captives and recovery of sight to the blind, to let the oppressed go free" (Luke 4:18 NRSV). And Mary in her Magnificat says, "He has filled the hungry with good things, and sent the rich away empty" (1:53 NRSV).

The third set of biblical texts on misusing God's good gifts concentrates on a failure to respond to the material needs of others. While individual responsibility is noted in various texts about poverty and wealth (Prov. 6:6–11; 19:15; 28:19; Luke 10:7; 1 Tim. 5:18), far more texts focus on our explicit responsibility to respond to poverty and need, such as the following:

> For six years you shall sow your land and gather in its yield; but the seventh year you shall let it rest and lie fallow, so that the poor of your people may eat; and what they leave the wild animals may eat. (Exod. 23:10–11 NRSV)

> The Lord secures justice for the poor
> and upholds the cause of the needy. (Ps. 140:12)

> I was hungry and you gave me food, I was thirsty and you gave me something to drink. . . . Just as you did it to one of the least of these who are members of my family, you did it to me. (Matt. 25:35, 40 NRSV)

> If a brother or sister is naked and lacks daily food, and one of you says to them, "Go in peace; keep warm and eat your fill," and yet you do not supply their bodily needs, what is the good of that? So faith by itself, if it has no works, is dead. (James 2:15–17 NRSV)

The sins of idolatry, injustice, and apathy toward poverty exist precisely because money and wealth are good gifts of God. If they were not an intrinsic good, there would be no reason to guard against their misuse. Their goodness is affirmed by the eighth command, for "by saying, 'you shall not steal,' God indicated that people have a right to ownership. Otherwise, the whole concept of stealing would fail to make any sense."[36] Goodness is implicit in the proverb "Do not withhold good from those to whom it is due, when it is in your power to do it. Do not say to your neighbor, 'Go, and come again,

36. Craig L. Blomberg, *Christians in an Age of Wealth: A Biblical Theology of Stewardship*, Biblical Theology for Life (Grand Rapids: Zondervan, 2013), 44.

tomorrow I will give it'—when you have it with you" (Prov. 3:27–28 NRSV). And in the story of the good Samaritan, Jesus gives a positive view of money when the Samaritan takes the man who has been robbed and beaten to an inn for care. He gives the innkeeper two days' wages to take care of the beaten man (Luke 10:35). I'm certain that on this day, Jesus the Creator-Redeemer looked at all he had made, including the Samaritan's resources, and said, "It is very good."

Indeed, through money and wealth, families are cared for, the poor are fed, educational institutions are built, the arts are performed, athletes compete, nonprofits are formed to pursue justice, people enjoy a night out at a restaurant, missionaries go to the unreached, churches are established, the gospel is preached, and people become self-sufficient to participate in God's sufficiency for all humanity. And it is very good.

The Goodness of Sex

God's very first command to the male and female he creates is to have physical intimacy and enjoy it, for "it was very good." Sex stories are prevalent in the creation myths of the ancient Near East, but they are riddled with incest, conflict, and hostility. "The Mesopotamian religions abounded with both male and female deities, and their myths often described creation and continuing fertility as occurring by means of sex among the deities. . . . In Sumerian mythology there was a whole pantheon of gods and goddesses, often paired as male and female partners. . . . The fertility of the land is set in motion by sexual action."[37] And in those Sumerian myths, "the complicated sexual interactions between deities was shown to involve trickery, deception and disguise."[38] The biblical creation narrative and many other texts in the Old Testament are written over against the sexual patterns found in rival cultures. While boundless pleasure is present in their myths, there is nothing like the verdict in Genesis 1:31: "God saw everything that he had made, and indeed, it was very good" (NRSV). But as the rest of the creation story and the rest of Scripture makes clear, this good gift for humans has purpose and meaning, and its goodness is found in relationships embodying the ends for which God created sex.

The first reference to sex in the Genesis story is with reference to animals and, more particularly, to the birds and creatures of the sea. After pronouncing their creation good, "God blessed them and said, 'Be fruitful and increase in

37. Richard M. Davidson, *The Flame of Yahweh: Sexuality in the Old Testament* (Peabody, MA: Hendrickson, 2007), 85, 87.

38. Louise Pryke, "In Ancient Mesopotamia, Sex among the Gods Shook Heaven and Earth," The Conversation, April 22, 2018, https://theconversation.com/in-ancient-mesopotamia-sex-among-the-gods-shook-heaven-and-earth-87858.

number and fill the water in the seas, and let the birds increase on the earth'" (Gen. 1:22). God gives the very same command to humans in verse 28, with the additional responsibility to rule over the other portions of creation and steward them. The fact that God gives the command to have sex and be fruitful to animals reminds us that sexuality and sex are pervasive throughout the natural world. "The dawn of sexual reproduction has always been a puzzle for scientists. Today on Earth 99% of multicellular creatures—the big organisms we can see—reproduce sexually. . . . Even with all this mesmeric diversity, all sexually reproducing organisms follow the same base route to make new offspring—two members of the same species combine their DNA to produce a new genome."[39] And in doing so, they bring genetic diversity into the new organism, which enables it to adapt to stresses from the environment. And yes, sex is found even in plants, so that "even the perfume produced by a flower is simply a clever trick to attract insects that will pick up pollen and then make a beeline to neighboring plants, fertilizing them in the process."[40] The whole world is filled with sexuality and sex, as created by God and pronounced good by our Creator.

After God creates the animal world with the mandate to reproduce, we come to a most majestic moment in the narrative, as humans are created in God's image and created male and female. As Old Testament scholar Richard Davidson describes it, "The first two chapters of the Bible deal directly and extensively with human sexuality. Not only is human sexuality presented as a basic fact of creation; an elucidation of the nature and theology of sexuality receives central, climactic placement in the Genesis creation accounts."[41]

> So God created humankind in his image,
> in the image of God he created them;
> male and female he created them.
>
> God blessed them, and God said to them, "Be fruitful and multiply, and fill the earth and subdue it." . . . God saw everything that he had made, and indeed, it was very good. (Gen. 1:27–28, 31 NRSV)

At this point in the story, several things stand out as part of the proclamation of goodness. First is the creation of humans as male and female—hence created with sexuality. Though the fall would at times play havoc with this twofold way of being human, the moral paradigm is the goodness of human

39. Vivien Cumming, "The Real Reasons We Have Sex," BBC Earth, British Broadcasting Corporation, accessed May 14, 2021, http://www.bbc.com/earth/story/20160704-the-real-reasons-why-we-have-sex (the page has since been taken down).

40. Cumming, "Real Reasons We Have Sex." See also "The Secret Sex Life of Plants," University of Tasmania, April 10, 2017, https://www.utas.edu.au/news/2017/4/10/260-the-secret-sex-life-of-plants/.

41. Davidson, *Flame of Yahweh*, 15.

sexuality as male and female. Moreover, the creation story points not to hierarchy or distinctive roles but to an ontological and physical distinction that leads to a further dimension of the good gift—procreation. Children are eventually born to the man and the woman precisely because God forms them with physiological characteristics enabling new life to begin. They are incapable of engendering new life without the other and are given the command to "be fruitful and multiply," a command that occurs five times in the first nine chapters of Genesis (Gen. 1:22, 28; 8:17; 9:1, 7). And when God sees all that he has made, he notices that "it was very good" (1:31 NRSV). "The Hebrew expression [*tov me'od*] ('very good') connotes the quintessence of goodness, wholesomeness, appropriateness, beauty. It is that which is both morally and aesthetically pleasing."[42]

As we move on to Genesis 2, the goodness of sexuality and sex is further developed. Among the animals that Adam names, none can function as an appropriate covenant partner for life or through which new life can emerge. Thus, the Lord makes the woman and brings her to Adam, and he is ecstatic: "This is now bone of my bones and flesh of my flesh" (v. 23). Then comes the climactic definition of this new relationship: "That is why a man leaves his father and mother and is united to his wife, and they become one flesh" (v. 24). We will unpack this basic definition of marriage further in chapter 5, but for now we simply focus on the goodness of the gift of sex. The term "one flesh" clearly includes the sexual union, for in 1 Corinthians 6:16 Paul refers to a man going to a prostitute and becoming "one flesh" with her, referring back to Genesis 1. The sexual intimacy of becoming "one flesh" not only has the capacity to create new human life, but it consummates their marriage, setting it apart from all other relationships.

Then comes another statement on the beauty and goodness of this gift: "The man and his wife were both naked, and were not ashamed" (v. 25 NRSV). Thus, Genesis 2 "breathes an atmosphere of unabashed sensuality. There is no puritanical or ascetic disparagement of sexuality. The story contains not the slightest hint of moral or cultic impurity. . . . The coming together of the couple is the healthy fulfilling of the Creator's intention, without shadow or qualification."[43] The portrayal of beauty, goodness, and divine purpose is a long way off from the erotic frolicking of the Near Eastern gods' creation, from the Baal fertility cults of numerous ancient cultures, and from the Gnosticism and asceticism that rendered sex and the human body suspect.

The goodness of sex is found in other places in Scripture as well, with one whole book extolling the beauty and joys of physical, marital love—the Song of Songs.

42. Davidson, *Flame of Yahweh*, 50.

43. Samuel Terrien, *Till the Heart Sings: A Biblical Theology of Manhood and Womanhood* (Philadelphia: Fortress, 1985), 16.

> As an apple tree among the trees of the forest,
> so is my beloved among the young men.
> With great delight I sat in his shadow,
> and his fruit was sweet to my taste.
> He brought me to the banqueting house,
> and his banner over me was love.
> Sustain me with raisins,
> refresh me with apples,
> for I am sick with love.
> His left hand is under my head,
> and his right hand embraces me! (2:3–6 ESV)

The man to his bride says,

> How beautiful is your love, my sister, my bride!
> How much better is your love than wine,
> and the fragrance of your oils than any spice!
> Your lips drop nectar, my bride;
> honey and milk are under your tongue;
> the fragrance of your garments is like the fragrance of Lebanon.
> A garden locked is my sister, my bride,
> a spring locked, a fountain sealed. (4:10–12 ESV)

In a similar vein, in the middle of a Proverbs chapter warning against adultery, we find this powerful evoking of goodness:

> Let your fountain be blessed,
> and rejoice in the wife of your youth,
> a lovely deer, a graceful doe.
> Let her breasts fill you at all times with delight;
> be intoxicated always in her love. (5:18–19 ESV)

The warning against breaking covenant vows through adultery is best understood in light of the goodness and delight of marital sex.

When we come to the New Testament, Jesus himself affirms the creation paradigm by quoting from the Genesis 1 and 2 texts on sex and marriage in his discussion of divorce in Matthew 19:4–6. In the descriptions of the new heavens and new earth in Revelation, marital bliss is used to describe the joys and grandeur of the eschaton. "I saw the Holy City, the new Jerusalem, coming down out of heaven from God, prepared as a bride beautifully dressed for her husband" (Rev. 21:2). The apostle Paul confirms the goodness of the gift when he writes, "The husband should fulfill his marital duty to his wife, and likewise the wife to her husband. The wife does not have authority over her own body but yields it to her husband. In the same way, the husband does not have authority over his own body but yields it to his wife" (1 Cor. 7:3–4).

And the writer to the Hebrews asserts, "Let marriage be held in honor by all, and let the marriage bed be kept undefiled" (13:4 NRSV).

But, of course, Scripture is filled with warnings about sexual sins, for in our fallen state humans seek to follow cultural norms and misplaced inner passions. The several Hebrew and Greek terms for sexual immorality have been typically translated in English as "fornication" and "adultery." "Fornication" (or "sexual immorality," as it's translated in modern versions) is the broad term for all sexual immorality, meaning any sexual relations outside of a marriage between a man and a woman. Ezekiel, prophesying during the exile in the sixth century BC, describes the many sins that led to the people's captivity, including a broad array of sexual sins: "But thou didst trust in thine own beauty, and playedst the harlot because of thy renown, and pouredst out thy fornications on every one that passed by. . . . Thou hast also committed fornication with the Egyptians thy neighbours . . . and hast increased thy whoredoms, to provoke me to anger" (Ezek. 16:15, 26 KJV). And in the New Testament, Paul writes, "Do not be deceived: Neither the sexually immoral ["fornicators" in the KJV] nor idolaters nor adulterers nor men who have sex with men . . . will inherit the kingdom of God" (1 Cor. 6:9–10).

The words in Hebrew and Greek translated "adultery" refer specifically to breaking the covenant bond of a marriage by one partner having sex with someone who is not their spouse. Thus, the seventh command, "You shall not commit adultery" (Exod. 20:14 NRSV), is clear, and the psalmist, describing the sinful proclivities of the Hebrew people, says, "When you see a thief, you join with him; you throw in your lot with adulterers" (Ps. 50:18). Jesus states that adultery stems from the heart of humans (Mark 7:21–22) and warns, "Everyone who looks at a woman with lustful intent has already committed adultery with her in his heart" (Matt. 5:28 ESV). Sexual sin is not limited to rape or unwanted advances but rather is taking God's good gift and turning it into something our Creator never intended. Sexual sin negates the "It is good" dimension of sex, and the best way to maintain sexual purity and fidelity is to start with its goodness and the purposes for which God created physical intimacy.

The Goodness of Power

Upon hearing the word *power*, most people think it is negative. Frequently, the oft-quoted words of Lord Acton come to mind: "Power tends to corrupt and absolute power corrupts absolutely."[44] Or we think of Marx's verdict in the context of imagining a utopian world without class distinctions: "Political

44. "Acton-Creighton Correspondence (1887)," Online Library of Liberty, Liberty Fund Network, accessed May 24, 2021, https://oll.libertyfund.org/page/acton-creighton-correspon dence-1887.

power, properly so called, is merely the organized power of one class for oppressing another."[45] For many, power of any type is equated with coercion, manipulation, domination, injustice, violence, and triumphalism. So it may come as a surprise to hear that power is part of God's pronouncement at creation, "It is good."

Power is best understood simply as the capacity to make things happen or to exert influence in various spheres of life. Reflecting theologically on creation and the whole of Scripture, Andy Crouch says, "Power is the ability to make something of the world."[46] Christian sociologist James Davison Hunter defines it this way: "Power is not a substance or a property but a facility that is exercised in relation to others as well as . . . to the natural world. This facility manifests itself through individuals, through social groups of every size, shape and kind, through social structures . . . , and through our own subjectivity." He further states, "Because human beings are by nature social in constitution and habits of life, everyone possesses at least some power. . . . Power, then, is inescapable."[47] These definitions of power stand in stark contrast to the cynical definitions of philosophers Friedrich Nietzsche and Michel Foucault, who see every human endeavor as filled with a power that seeks to control and exert one's will over others.

To rightly understand power ethically, we must start with power as a good gift of God, one that goes back to creation, which is filled with power at every turn. Creation begins with God, who speaks the world into being with great power: "'Let there be . . .' And it was so" (see, e.g., Gen. 1:6–7). Because God created humans in his image, it is only natural that the Creator would grant them power in relation to the creation. It is manifest in the divine mandate to "be fruitful and multiply and fill the earth and subdue it" (v. 28 ESV). Bringing new life into the world and nurturing that life to maturity carries with it great facility in making something of God's created world (i.e., power). When the Creator gives to humanity the tasks of ruling over animal life and stewarding all nature (vv. 28–30), these are tasks filled with the ability to make things happen and to influence the created world, including cultural artifacts that derive from the natural creation. Great power is demonstrated when God brings the animals "to the man to see what he would name them; and whatever the man called each living creature, that was its name" (2:19). "To be made in the image of God and to be charged with the task of working in and cultivating, preserving, and protecting the creation is to possess power. The creation mandate, then, is a mandate to use that power in the world in

45. Karl Marx and Friedrich Engels, *Basic Writings on Politics and Philosophy*, ed. Lewis Feuer (Garden City, NY: Anchor Books, 1959), 29.

46. Andy Crouch, *Playing God: Redeeming the Gift of Power* (Downers Grove, IL: IVP Books, 2013), 17.

47. James Davison Hunter, *To Change the World: The Irony, Tragedy, and Possibility of Christianity in the Late Modern World* (New York: Oxford University Press, 2010), 179.

ways that reflect God's intentions."[48] Power is a good gift of God, for "God saw everything that he had made, and behold, it was very good" (1:31 ESV).

But, of course, that's not the end of the story, for "on the very next page of our Bible is a tragic twist to the story. The original image bearers flaunt their freedom in the garden and abandon their original vocation. The result is diminishing, rather than flourishing, their own and the whole created orders, as dominion and delight turn to domination and exploitation."[49] The whole of the fall in Genesis 3 can be viewed from the standpoint of an unwillingness to accept God's designs for the appropriate use of power. Satan tempts with the false lure that "God knows that when you eat of it your eyes will be opened, and you will be like God, knowing good and evil" (Gen. 3:5 ESV). Adam and Eve give into the temptation, and power that was meant to serve, nurture, create, and enable now turns to idolatry, injustice, and a false sense of one's role in God's world. It doesn't take long to see the insidious consequences of power gone awry in the Genesis story: Cain kills his brother Abel (chap. 4), God sends judgment in a flood for the wickedness of humanity (chaps. 6–7), and Noah's son betrays the proper boundaries of power between son and father (9:20–25). And then, when we get to Genesis 11, the people in the plain of Shinar get power hungry and say, "Come, let us build ourselves a city and a tower with its top in the heavens, and let us make a name for ourselves" (v. 4 ESV). The tower of Babel, with the judgment that follows, is a continual reminder of what happens when humans seek power beyond God's designs or when power becomes an idol and turns into injustice, coercion, and unwarranted violence.

Given the many abuses of power in our broken world, it is understandable that some Christians have opted for an antipower stance. The neo-Anabaptist movement, following the lead of the late John Howard Yoder, argues that the mark of faithful discipleship and hence Christian ethics is "accepting powerlessness."[50] But such a stance is not only sociologically naive; it is contrary to the creation paradigm, the broad teachings of Scripture, and the example and teachings of our Creator-Redeemer, Jesus Christ. The real Christian ethics issue is not abandoning all power but redefining power as service to others and as making things happen in the various spheres of life in accordance with God's overall designs. It is true that when Israel asks to have a king in order to be like all the nations around them, the Lord says to Samuel, "Listen to all that the people are saying to you; it is not you they have rejected, but they

48. Hunter, *To Change the World*, 183.

49. Crouch, *Playing God*, 36.

50. John Howard Yoder, *The Politics of Jesus: Vicit Agnus Noster*, 2nd ed. (Grand Rapids: Eerdmans, 1994), 237. In the context Yoder is defending pacificism and rejecting the "prevailing assumption from the time of Constantine . . . that the fundamental responsibility of the church for society is to manage it" (240). This is at the heart of what he means by accepting powerlessness.

have rejected me as their king . . . , forsaking me and serving other gods" (1 Sam. 8:7–8). But the issue here is not God calling the people to powerlessness in their journey in this world, but to a different form of power that would lead to righteousness and justice. Even if they had not opted to have a king like the rest of the world, they still would have experienced power in work, agriculture, building projects, the temple ministries, local leaders, and the family.

It is in Jesus that we see the most explicit redefinition of power in accordance with creational designs. In Philippians 2 Paul calls believers away from "selfish ambition or conceit" (v. 3 NRSV) to a life of humility and seeking the interests of others by pointing to Christ's example. In this great kenosis hymn, we see a model for how to use power: Jesus, "being in very nature God, did not consider equality with God something to be used to his own advantage; rather, he made himself nothing by taking the very nature of a servant, being made in human likeness. And being found in appearance as a man, he humbled himself by becoming obedient to death—even death on a cross" (vv. 6–8). Many translations rightly give a more literal rendering of verse 7 when they translate "he emptied himself" (see, e.g., NASB, NRSV) rather than "he made himself nothing." Jesus, of course, did not empty himself of his deity but rather emptied himself of all the prerogatives and privileges he had with the Father in heaven, by coming into our broken world, not to glory in his power but to employ it in a life of servitude, leading to the cross. The result of his proper use of his almighty, eternal power as our incarnate Creator-Redeemer was that "God also highly exalted him and gave him the name that is above every name" (v. 9 NRSV). The incarnation—God taking on human flesh to serve and redeem the world—is the greatest act in history of using power to enable others. It is a model for all humans with power, and all have some.

Jesus also teaches a proper use of power when the brothers James and John request special privilege: "Grant us to sit, one at your right and one at your left, in your glory" (Mark 10:37 NRSV). The request, which according to Matthew involves their mother, is met with the usual response to humans' quest for privilege with their power: their fellow apostles begin "to be angry with James and John" (v. 41 NRSV)—likely because they want the same. Jesus then gathers the apostles together and gives them what is no doubt the greatest statement in human history on leadership and power: "You know that among the Gentiles those whom they recognize as their rulers lord it over them, and their great ones are tyrants over them. But it is not so among you; but whoever wishes to become great among you must be your servant, and whoever wishes to be first among you must be slave of all. For the Son of Man came not to be served but to serve, and to give his life a ransom for many" (vv. 42–45 NRSV). Jesus here is not negating power. He is portraying it as service to others rather than as hoarding privileged power for self-centeredness.

God looks at all that he has made and sees that it is "very good" (Gen. 1:31 NRSV). And that includes power, the capacity to make things happen for God's glory in the various spheres of life. For fifteen years I served as a seminary president. It would have been foolish and dangerous to believe that my task was to become powerless. It is often in negating the power God places into our hands that power is most misused, as we deceive ourselves about the realities set before us. Every day as a seminary president, I reminded myself that the power I had in the position to which God and my school's board of trustees called me was to be used to serve others and ultimately to serve the kingdom of God, a notion consonant with what God designed in creation. As Andy Crouch puts it, "When human beings do what they were created to do, the latent possibilities in creation come to fruition, a flourishing reality that would never exist without the application of human intelligence and intentionality. That is what image bearing is for."[51] In the midst of a proper utilization of power, we must recall that successes in various arenas of responsibility are frequently the triggers leading to a self-deception that can easily result in the misuse of this good gift.

Conclusion

Money, sex, and power. In recent years numerous well-known, successful, and influential church leaders have fallen prey to scandals precisely over these big three. They are clearly among the greatest sources of temptation. It is precisely because they are good gifts of God from creation that their misuse is so disastrous and shameful. But the ethical answer to money, sex, and power is not some form of Gnosticism, asceticism, or withdrawal from the world. The ethical answer is to affirm their created goodness, experience their redemption through Christ, and live according to the designs of each through the power of the Holy Spirit.

Money, sex, and power are good gifts of God. The creation pronouncement "It was very good" reverberates throughout all of God's material, created world and is foundational for Christian ethics. It's a good world after all—even in its fallen, rebellious state.

51. Crouch, *Playing God*, 105.

3

Made in the Image of God

Human Dignity in All Humans and the Whole of Human Life

In the creation story, there is both continuity and discontinuity between humans and the rest of the created world. On the continuity side, we find that humans, along with livestock and various other animals, are created on the sixth day (Gen. 1:24–27). Moreover, both humans and the animals are formed from the dust of the ground or the land (v. 24; 2:7).[1] In addition "humans are created things, like all the rest of creation. The 'living creature' language applied to humans in Genesis 2:7 is the same as that applied to all creatures in Genesis 1."[2] And both humans and the rest of creation are pronounced good. All of these commonalities point to some degree of continuity between humans and the rest of creation, a notion that also finds support in the world of science. From the human genome project, we now know that all humans, no matter their nationality, race, or ethnicity, not only share 99.9 percent of the same DNA but also share substantial DNA or genetic sequencing with

1. A number of other texts speak of the same: Gen. 3:19; Ps. 103:14; Eccles. 3:20; 1 Cor. 15:47.

2. Robert C. Bishop, Larry L. Funck, Raymond J. Lewis, Stephen O. Moshier, and John H. Walton, *Understanding Scientific Theories of Origins: Cosmology, Geology, and Biology in Christian Perspective*, BioLogos Books on Science and Christianity (Downers Grove, IL: IVP Academic, 2018), 604. While a number of translations render the Hebrew term *nephesh* as "soul" in 2:7, it is the same word used of animals in 1:20, 21, 24, and 30 and is usually translated "life" or "creatures" relative to the animals.

the rest of creation: 98 percent with chimpanzees, 85 percent with mice, and even 60 percent with bananas.[3]

Despite the continuities there is one major difference, from which other discontinuities come—only humans are made in the image of God. "Then God said, 'Let us make humankind in our image, according to our likeness; and let them have dominion over the fish of the sea, and over the birds of the air, and over the cattle, and over all the wild animals of the earth, and over every creeping thing that creeps upon the earth.' So God created humankind in his image, in the image of God he created them; male and female he created them" (Gen. 1:26–27 NRSV). As the Genesis narrative moves along, it travels toward a crescendo in the creation of *'adam*—humankind. Throughout the creation of the vegetative world and animal world, there is the continued reference to things being created "according to their kinds" (vv. 21, 24). "When the time comes to describe the act of creating humankind, the author makes sure the reader understands the uniqueness of this act by omitting altogether the earlier repeated affirmation." In its place comes the language of "Let us make humankind in our image" and the accompanying poetic parallelism—"So God created humanity in his own image, in the image of God he created them"—which "is the clearest indicator that this act of creation is itself unparalleled in the rest of the liturgy of creation."[4] Some have taken the "let us" language to be a plural of grandeur, and others have seen at least a veiled reference to the Holy Trinity. What is clear in the creation story is that "Genesis 1 draws a sharp distinction between humanity (male and female) and the other created beings; . . . just as the plants and animals were created according to their own type, humanity was made according to *God's kind*, metaphorically speaking."[5]

The fact that *'adam* is used to describe humankind as a whole stands in significant contrast to the other creation stories of the ancient Near East, in which only the king is viewed as the image of god.[6] "Many translations obscure the fact that the first reference to this 'humankind' in verse 27 employs a singular pronoun, by which the Hebrew text indicates that in some sense it is the single entity, humanity as a whole, that is associated with God's image." Thus, "in the Bible not merely the king is involved in God's image, but even

3. Bishop et al., *Understanding Scientific Theories of Origins*, 585; and Deborah Meister, "What Is the Haploid and Diploid Cell Number for a Monkey?," Sciencing, accessed June 4, 2021, https://sciencing.com/what-is-the-haploid-diploid-cell-number-for-a-monkey-12732203.html.

4. Richard Lints, *Identity and Idolatry: The Image of God and Its Inversion*, New Studies in Biblical Theology 36 (Downers Grove, IL: InterVarsity, 2015), 58.

5. Catherine McDowell, "'In the Image of God He Created Them': How Genesis 1:26–27 Defines the Divine-Human Relationship and Why It Matters," in *The Image of God in an Image Driven Age: Explorations in Theological Anthropology*, ed. Beth Felker Jones and Jeffrey W. Barbeau (Downers Grove, IL: IVP Academic, 2016), 38.

6. McDowell, "'In the Image of God He Created Them,'" 34.

the lowliest of people are involved as well."[7] This will become a salient point as we explore human dignity in all people and in all phases of human life later in this chapter. This stands in direct contradiction to the anti-Semitism heresy of Adolf Hitler, who writes, "The Jew is the creature of another god, the anti-man. . . . He is a creature outside nature and alien to nature."[8] In contrast Paul at Mars Hill says, "From one man [God] made all the nations, that they should inhabit the whole earth" (Acts 17:26). And from the one made in God's image, all humanity shares that unique status.

But not only is all humanity created in the image of God. For John Kilner notes that "being in God's image has to do with people as entire beings. . . . There is no suggestion that being in the image is constituted only by current human 'attributes' (i.e., abilities, traits, capacities, and other things that people have, are, do, etc.)."[9] God creates humanity as embodied beings, but clearly also with dimensions that transcend the body, so that humanity can relate to God, others, and creation in ways that are distinct from the natural world. We are whole persons made in the image of God. This, too, is significant relative to human dignity, for it is not a functional dignity but an intrinsic dignity, residing in the whole of the person and in all persons. As Martin Luther King Jr. writes, "There are no gradations in the image of God."[10]

Along these lines, we also note that both men and women are created in the image of God (Gen. 1:27). This does not mean that men and women are biologically and ontologically identical but that both bear this unique status and intrinsic value, which flows from their mutual creation in God's image. It has long been debated whether this relational dimension, male and female, constitutes the image or is a result of creation in God's image, but what is clear is that both male and female are made in God's likeness. Historically, societies and the church have frequently treated women in ways that are contrary to this biblical-theological affirmation. But because "demeaning women is an affront to people in God's image, it is an offense against God."[11]

In the creation story, there is one other element that we must note related to the image of God. While humanity and the rest of creation share some continuity, humans are given a special role in relation to the rest of creation—namely, a task of stewardship. Here again, exegetes and theologians have debated whether this role over the rest of creation is the essence of the *imago Dei* or a result of it. In the next chapter, we will unpack in detail the meaning,

7. John F. Kilner, *Dignity and Destiny: Humanity in the Image of God* (Grand Rapids: Eerdmans, 2015), 86, 88.

8. Quoted in Leni Yahil, *The Holocaust* (New York: Oxford University Press, 1990), 44.

9. Kilner, *Dignity and Destiny*, 95.

10. Martin Luther King Jr., "The American Dream" (speech, Ebenezer Baptist Church, Atlanta, GA, July 4, 1965), https://www.rev.com/blog/transcripts/the-american-dream-july-4th-speech-transcript-martin-luther-king-jr.

11. Kilner, *Dignity and Destiny*, 322.

significance, and misinterpretations of this text relative to creation care, but humans made in God's image are distinct from the rest of creation and yet have a vital role in stewarding and caring for nature, which God has blessed and pronounced good. This distinction between humans and the rest of nature and the human stewardship over nature stands in contrast to animistic worldviews and some forms of deep ecology, with their radical ecophilosophies, seeing little value distinction between humans and the rest of nature.

Other Biblical Texts on the Image of God

The image-of-God language does not appear frequently throughout Scripture and is used more broadly than the creational image. This, however, does not undermine the significance of the creational *imago Dei*, for it underlies much biblical and theological teaching. The term has three primary uses throughout the Bible: the creational image, Christ as the image, and humanity's renewal in the image.

The Creational Image

First, there are several texts that clearly harken back to God's creation, and all of them occur after the fall of humanity into sin in Genesis 3. This is significant because some have attempted to argue that the image was either lost at the fall or so badly damaged that the creational image is no longer relevant. Genesis 5 gives an account of Adam's family line and begins with reference to the image of God: "When God created humankind, he made them in the likeness of God. Male and female he created them, and he blessed them and named them 'Humankind' when they were created. When Adam had lived one hundred thirty years, he became the father of a son in his likeness, according to his image, and named him Seth" (vv. 1–3 NRSV). Several observations can be made about this text. First, the use of the terms "likeness" and "image" here parallels Genesis 1:26, where both terms are used. Some have tried to differentiate "likeness" from "image," but in both texts this close placement of terms is an example of Hebrew parallelism, in which the second term simply mirrors the first. Second, the fact that Seth is in his father's likeness would seem to underline the fact that he, too, is made in God's image, like Adam. Seth, even after the fall, is made in God's image because he is made in the likeness of his father.

In Genesis 9:5–6 we read, "And from each human being, too, I will demand an accounting for the life of another human being. Whoever sheds human blood, by humans shall their blood be shed; for in the image of God has God made [humankind]." Why is murder wrong and an act of justice required as recompense? Because humans bear the image of God. When one willingly and unjustly takes the life of another, they have made an attack on God, because that person bears his image. By implication this would have broader application than murder, for as David Gushee notes, "Just as I cannot murder you because you are one made in God's image, so also I cannot assault you for the very same reason. An assault may violate or even desecrate another human being without taking her life."[12] However we define the image of God in humans, it is clear that a major result is human dignity and value, which are to be protected in all spheres of human life and among all human beings.

James 3:9 also appeals to the creational image of God, in a passage on the power of the tongue for good or ill: "With the tongue we praise our Lord and Father, and with it we curse human beings, who have been made in God's likeness." This text has broad creational significance, because it "is one of the only two direct New Testament statements that humanity in general is in God's image. In verse 7, James notes the role that human beings have played in taming all kinds of land, air, and sea animals. That observation is reminiscent of the role God gave to human beings regarding . . . creatures in Genesis 1:28."[13] This passage is highly significant "because, like Genesis 9:6, it indicates that even unbelievers are made in and still remain in God's likeness. For this reason, James explains, it is the height of inconsistency to praise God and curse any human being."[14] To harm a human being made in God's image with our tongues amounts to an attack upon our Maker.

The other New Testament text on the creational image of God is the difficult and much-discussed Pauline text in 1 Corinthians 11. In context Paul is discussing propriety in worship and here, more specifically, head coverings for women and no head coverings for men, as well as hair lengths. This discussion no doubt relates to cultural patterns that were associated with immorality. In his argument Paul then says, "A man ought not to cover his head, since he is the image and glory of God; but woman is the glory of man. For man did not come from woman, but woman from man; neither was man created for woman, but woman for man" (vv. 7–9). Some will, of course, sweep this text away by saying Paul was a male chauvinist and the text has no bearing on us today, and others will attempt to argue for male headship because the man was created first. Historically, the whole of 1 Corinthians 11:1–16 has been a notoriously difficult passage with a wide scope of interpretations.[15] But relevant to our discussion of the *imago Dei*, Marc Cortez has wisely stated

12. David P. Gushee, *The Sacredness of Human Life: Why an Ancient Biblical Vision Is Key to the World's Future* (Grand Rapids: Eerdmans, 2013), 51.

13. Kilner, *Dignity and Destiny*, 138.

14. Craig L. Blomberg, "'True Righteousness and Holiness': The Image of God in the New Testament," in Jones and Barbeau, *Image of God in an Image Driven Age*, 75.

15. For a helpful overview of interpretations, see Lucy Peppiatt, "Man as the Image and Glory of God, and Woman as the Glory of Man: Perspicuity or Ambiguity?," *Priscilla Papers* 33, no. 3 (2019): 12–18. See also Amy Peeler, "Imaging Glory: 1 Corinthians 11, Gender, and Bodies at Worship," in *Beauty, Order, and Mystery: A Christian Vision of Human Sexuality*, ed. Gerald Hiestand and Todd Wilson (Downers Grove, IL: IVP Academic, 2017), 151–63.

that "to see Paul as limiting the image only to men in 1 Corinthians 11:7, we would have to contend that he is doing so in direct contrast to every other image passage in the Bible."[16] It is important to note that Paul does not deny that women are made in God's image. "More likely, given the clear allusion to the creation stories in 1 Corinthians 11:8–9, is that woman appears as man's glory in contrast to the animals that man named but that could not serve as his helpers."[17] Moreover, we cannot overlook Paul's statement of mutuality in the next verses: "In the Lord woman is not independent of man or man independent of woman. For just as woman came from man, so man comes through woman; but all things come from God" (vv. 11–12 NRSV). This very difficult passage should not undermine the universality of God's image, nor should it undermine women.

Christ as the Image of God

While exploring the doctrine of the image as a whole, we must note several texts that refer to Christ as the image of God. Second Corinthians 4:4 says, "The god of this world has blinded the minds of the unbelievers, to keep them from seeing the light of the gospel of the glory of Christ, who is the image of God" (NRSV). In Colossians 1:15 Paul writes that the Son "is the image of the invisible God, the firstborn of all creation" (ESV). Though image language is not used, Hebrews 1:3 portrays a similar concept: "The Son is the radiance of God's glory and the exact representation of his being, sustaining all things by his powerful word. After he had provided purification for sins, he sat down at the right hand of the Majesty in heaven." What are we to make of these texts in relation to the creation account of the *imago Dei*? Several observations can be made.

First, it is helpful to note that these texts say that Jesus *is* the image of God, whereas most of the creational texts (with the exception of 1 Cor. 11:7) say humans are made *in* the image of God. The distinction is significant, for indeed Christ is in essence God, the "exact representation of his being." Humans, on the other hand, bear some type of unique or potential relationship with but are not themselves part of the Godhead. Second, these texts imply that it is the incarnational Christ who is the image of God. If this is true, then third, "we should understand the *imago Dei* in the New Testament as primarily an anthropological claim identifying Jesus as the perfect expression of what it means to be human."[18] Because Christ is God and we are not, we cannot experience divine attributes that belong to God alone, but Christ, in his life and teachings, points most fully to what authentic humanness looks

16. Marc Cortez, *ReSourcing Theological Anthropology: A Constructive Account of Humanity in the Light of Christ* (Grand Rapids: Zondervan, 2017), 193.

17. Blomberg, "'True Righteousness and Holiness,'" 82.

18. Cortez, *ReSourcing Theological Anthropology*, 116.

like. However we end up defining the image of God, Jesus as the image and humans made in the image point in a direction of, as John Kilner puts it, "a special connection with God and the intended reflection of God."[19] That leads us to the third use of the term "image of God" in Scripture: humanity's renewal in the image of God or in the image of the Son.

Humanity's Renewal in the Image of God or the Son

A number of texts speak of believers being transformed or renewed in the image of God or of the Son, through the work of Christ and the Holy Spirit. Romans 8:29 states, "For those God foreknew he also predestined to be conformed to the image of his Son, that he might be the firstborn among many brothers and sisters." Second Corinthians 3:18 puts it this way: "And we all, who with unveiled faces contemplate the Lord's glory, are being transformed into his image with ever-increasing glory, which comes from the Lord, who is the Spirit." Paul encourages believers to put off sinful practices of the old self, for they are now a people who "have put on the new self, which is being renewed in knowledge after the image of its creator" (Col. 3:10 ESV). In a similar text, with likeness language, Paul admonishes believers "to put on the new self, created after the likeness of God in true righteousness and holiness" (Eph. 4:24 ESV).

At first glance we might think these New Testament passages indicate that the creation in God's image has been lost or so badly damaged that it is only renewed through Christ and the Holy Spirit. This, however, would contradict the clear creational-image texts we have noted, which occur after the fall (i.e., Gen. 5:1–3; 9:5–6; James 3:9). Arguing that "creation in God's image entails a special connection with God and an intended reflection of God" (even if the offer is rejected), Kilner states, "Renewal in God's image entails a more intimate connection with God through Christ and an increasingly actual reflection of God in Christ, to God's glory. This connection with God is the basis of human dignity."[20] Attempting to understand these New Testament passages in relation to Genesis, he notes that in the fall "God's image did not change, people did. God's image, including God's intentions and standards, remains as constant as God is over time. Humanity, though, changes, first for the worse and later, in Christ, for the better."[21] Even if one does not buy Kilner's definition of the image, we can understand that God created humans in his image and that his image is still intact in some way. Because we are fallen image-bearing creatures, Christ comes into the world

19. Kilner, *Dignity and Destiny*, 288.

20. Kilner, *Dignity and Destiny*, xi. It should be noted that in this statement Kilner is not implying that all humans will accept the offer of God's grace; rather, "all of humanity participates in human dignity."

21. Kilner, *Dignity and Destiny*, 257.

not only as Savior but as model of what it truly means to be human, so that "the *imago Dei* attains a unique status in the person of Jesus Christ . . . as the perfect image of God."[22] Through redemption in Christ, we can be conformed to his image so that we become more fully what God intended us to be at creation as his image bearers.

The Meaning of God's Image in Humans

Given the various texts in Scripture, how are we to define the *imago Dei* from creation? We should note that nowhere does the Bible explicitly define the image. That, however, has not prevented many attempted definitions, and there are varying proposals by both biblical scholars and theologians. Catherine McDowell describes four historic definitions of the image. First, she describes an interpretation of "spiritual and mental similarity to God," in which there is reason and an ability to comprehend moral and religious truths. Second is a material interpretation that emphasizes the form and embodiment of humans, a view found in some rabbinic theologies. Third is the image as relationship, for "in being created male and female, humanity is both plural and differentiated and thus reflects relationship within the godhead"—the view of Karl Barth. And fourth is the royal-representative view, in which humans have a privileged status amid and over the rest of creation.[23] McDowell rejects each of these views, arguing that many of the noted characteristics are results of the image but not the essence of the image. In their place she opts for an understanding of the image in which "humanity is defined both as God's royal 'son' and as living 'statuettes' representing God and his rule in his macro-temple, the world."[24]

Carl Henry argues that the image of God in humans can be understood through two dimensions: a formal dimension focusing on human personality (including moral responsibility and intelligence) and a material dimension focusing on knowledge of God and God's will.[25] Millard Erickson describes three major interpretations of the image: a substantive view focusing on psychological and spiritual qualities, including reason; a relational view; and a functional view emphasizing human dominion in the world. He favors the substantive interpretation.[26] Nonna Harrison, drawing particularly on patris-

22. Lints, *Identity and Idolatry*, 120.

23. McDowell, "'In the Image of God He Created Them,'" 31–34.

24. McDowell, "'In the Image of God He Created Them,'" 42. For a detailed analysis of McDowell's view and arguments, see Catherine L. McDowell, *The Image of God in the Garden of Eden: The Creation of Humankind in Genesis 2:5–3:24 in Light of* mīs pî pīt pî *and* wpt-r *Rituals of Mesopotamia and Ancient Egypt*, Siphrut 15 (Winona Lake, IN: Eisenbrauns, 2015).

25. Carl F. H. Henry, "Image of God," in *Evangelical Dictionary of Theology*, ed. Walter Elwell (Grand Rapids: Baker, 1984), 547.

26. Millard J. Erickson, *Christian Theology*, 3rd ed. (Grand Rapids: Baker Academic, 2013), 471.

tic thinkers in the Eastern church, argues that the image is multifaceted with capacities for freedom and responsibility, connection to God, spiritual perception, and the potential for moral excellence (i.e., the virtues).[27] And Kilner sees four major historic interpretations of the image: reason, righteousness, rulership, and relationships—all of which he sees as results of the *imago Dei* but not the essence, which he believes "entails a special connection with God and an intended reflection of God."[28]

From this very brief overview, it is clear that the image of God has elicited varying and conflicting definitions. As a result we might be wise to affirm with Christopher Wright that "since the Bible nowhere defines the term, it is probably futile to attempt to do so very precisely."[29] What we can say is that the image in humans means a uniqueness in the created world, for humans alone are created in the image of God. Human beings therefore enjoy a grandeur and splendor in their set-apart status. Also, we should affirm that the image is not dependent on functional characteristics like reason or rationality, for if we buy into that understanding, when humans are deficient in these functional characteristics, they are then deemed inferior, lacking the full *imago Dei*. These functional characteristics, including a stewardship over the rest of creation (Gen. 1:26, 28), certainly are linked to the image of God, but only in terms of being a result of creation in God's image, not the essence of the image. While there may be difficulty in finding a precise definition, one thing is clear: because humans have this unique status, they have a value and dignity that must be protected in all humans and in every phase of life.

The Value and Dignity of God's Image Bearers

The value and dignity of humanity is evident, as already noted, in several biblical texts focusing on the *imago Dei*. In Genesis 9:6 shedding the blood of another human being is deemed wrong because "in his own image God made humankind" (NRSV). And in James 3:9, we are told that when we harm an image bearer with words, it is an afront to God, thus implying human dignity in the person. Human dignity means that every human being has an intrinsic dignity that is to be respected in all spheres of life. Or to put it another way, "Human life is sacred: this means that each and every human being has been set apart for designation as a being of elevated status and dignity. Each human being must therefore be viewed with reverence and treated with due respect

27. Nonna Verna Harrison, *God's Many-Splendored Image: Theological Anthropology for Christian Formation* (Grand Rapids: Baker Academic, 2010), 7.

28. Kilner, *Dignity and Destiny*, 1.

29. Christopher J. H. Wright, *Old Testament Ethics for the People of God* (Downers Grove, IL: IVP Academic, 2004), 119.

and care."[30] The value and sacredness of humans is not dependent on their functionality (such as reasoning or relationality), status, or being valued by others. It is intrinsic within the human person simply because they are *Homo sapiens*, a member of the human family. Though this dignity is intrinsic, inhering within the person, it is also an alien dignity, coming not from the person's self-perception or perception by others but from the unique, set-apart creation of humanity by God. Thus, in the memorable words of C. S. Lewis, "There are no ordinary people. You have never talked to a mere mortal."[31]

Biblical texts do not have to explicitly speak of the *imago Dei* to affirm human dignity and value. For example, though Psalm 8 does not utilize the language, the *imago Dei* is clearly in view as the psalmist portrays the grandeur, glory, and value of human beings. It begins with what should be the starting point for comprehending human dignity, the worship of God: "O LORD, our Sovereign, how majestic is your name in all the earth! You have set your glory above the heavens" (v. 1 NRSV). The psalm then moves from God to the significance of his image bearers:

> When I look at your heavens, the work of your fingers,
> the moon and the stars that you have established;
> what are human beings that you are mindful of them,
> mortals that you care for them?
>
> Yet you have made them a little lower than God,
> and crowned them with glory and honor. (vv. 3–5 NRSV)

Like Genesis 1, following creation in the image of God, humans are given a royal task:

> You have given them dominion over the works of your hands;
> you have put all things under their feet,
> all sheep and oxen,
> and also the beasts of the field,
> the birds of the air, and the fish of the sea,
> whatever passes along the paths of the seas. (Ps. 8:8 NRSV)

The psalm then fittingly concludes with adoration of the source of it all:

> O LORD, our Sovereign,
> how majestic is your name in all the earth! (v. 9 NRSV)

Psalm 8 is quoted in Hebrews 2:6–8, with the verses that follow noting that Christ, the incarnate one, is greater than and above humanity.

30. Gushee, *Sacredness of Human Life*, 33.
31. C. S. Lewis, *The Weight of Glory, and Other Essays* (New York: Macmillan, 1949), 19.

Psalm 144 echoes the language of Psalm 8: "O Lord, what are human beings that you regard them, or mortals that you think of them? They are like a breath; their days are like a passing shadow" (144:3–4 NRSV). Though human beings are finite and fallen—"like a breath; . . . like a passing shadow"—they nonetheless are valued deeply by their Maker.

The incarnation of Christ further affirms the dignity and value of human beings. Though he was one with the Father in creation, "the Word became flesh and dwelt among us" (John 1:14 ESV). If human beings did not have an intrinsic value and worth, why would the Son of God come into the world, making "himself nothing by taking the very nature of a servant, being made in human likeness" (Phil. 2:7)? Christ's own suffering and death on the cross for human sin demonstrates how much the triune God values and loves those made in his image, despite their waywardness.

Jesus also teaches the uniqueness and set-apartness of humans in creation. On one occasion, when he is challenged by the religious leaders for healing on the Sabbath, Jesus says to them, "Suppose one of you has only one sheep and it falls into a pit on the sabbath; will you not lay hold of it and lift it out? How much more valuable is a human being than a sheep!" (Matt. 12:11–12 NRSV). And in similar language, as he teaches his disciples to trust in God rather than worry, Jesus says, "Look at the birds of the air; they neither sow nor reap nor gather into barns, and yet your heavenly Father feeds them. Are you not of more value than they?" (Matt. 6:26 NRSV). Again, in Matthew 10:29–31 Jesus says, "Are not two sparrows sold for a penny? Yet not one of them will fall to the ground apart from your Father. And even the hairs of your head are all counted. So do not be afraid; you are of more value than many sparrows" (NRSV). In making these statements about human worth, Jesus is not denigrating the rest of creation but echoing Genesis 1, where humans are created in God's image. Our Lord's incarnation, teaching, death, and resurrection all affirm the dignity, value, and grandeur of humanity, even in a fallen state.

When we look at various parts of the Old Testament, certain actions and even commands appear to run contrary to human dignity and worth. The wars, mass killings, and treatment of women give us pause in ethical analysis and are, of course, ammunition for critics of biblical faith. One such critic is atheist Richard Dawkins, who writes, "The God of the Old Testament is arguably the most unpleasant character in all fiction: jealous and proud of it; a petty, unjust, unforgiving control-freak; a vindictive, bloodthirsty ethnic cleanser; a misogynistic, homophobic, racist, infanticidal, genocidal, . . . malevolent bully."[32] Dawkins clearly exaggerates and makes no attempt to probe behind the alleged events or compare the Bible's theological descriptions with those of other ancient Near Eastern societies. Nonetheless, certain texts

32. Richard Dawkins, *The God Delusion* (New York: Mariner, 2008), 51.

are ethically unsettling, and there have been various attempts to understand them. Attempting to analyze what initially appears to be the very opposite of human dignity could comprise another book, and others have already done that. I personally find the work of William Webb and Gordon Oeste, *Bloody, Brutal, and Barbaric: Wrestling with Troubling War Texts*, to be helpful. They argue for "an incremental redemptive-movement ethic," which "means that God often brings his people along in at least incremental steps relative to the world around them (foreign movement) or relative to earlier stages in the redemptive story line (canonical movement)."[33] And I would suggest that such a progressive revelation with an "incremental redemptive-movement" is always harkening back to the creation design, which is made possible in redemption and fulfilled in the eschaton.

Despite the challenging texts, many Old Testament commands and actions clearly affirm the dignity flowing from human creation in God's image. For example, Numbers 5:6–7 states, "When a man or a woman wrongs another, breaking faith with the Lord, that person incurs guilt and shall confess the sin that has been committed. The person shall make full restitution for the wrong, adding one-fifth to it, and giving it to the one who was wronged" (NRSV). This statement and command embody a clear sense of human dignity and worth, for "the text implies . . . that no human interaction is merely a human interaction. There is always something more than meets the eye when human beings harm and help, love and hate, one another."[34] Human dignity also underlies most of the commandments of the Decalogue (Exod. 20), which begins with a proper allegiance to God but then moves to our allegiance to and protection of fellow humans: the Sabbath command protects fellow workers; honoring father and mother and not committing adultery protect marriage and family bonds; the command to not murder is built upon the image of God in persons; the commands to neither steal nor covet protect the property of a fellow human; and the command to not give false testimony against one's neighbor protects the integrity of

33. William J. Webb and Gordon K. Oeste, *Bloody, Brutal, and Barbaric? Wrestling with Troubling War Texts* (Downers Grove, IL: IVP Academic, 2019), 17. There are various other attempts to wrestle with the troubling texts; see, for example, Paul Copan, *Is God a Vindictive Bully? Reconciling Portrayals of God in the Old and New Testaments* (Grand Rapids: Baker Academic, 2022); C. S. Cowles, Eugene H. Merrill, Daniel L. Gard, and Tremper Longman III, *Show Them No Mercy: Four Views on God and Canaanite Genocide*, Counterpoints (Grand Rapids: Zondervan, 2003); David T. Lamb, *God Behaving Badly: Is the God of the Old Testament Angry, Sexist and Racist?* (Downers Grove, IL: IVP Books, 2011); Christopher J. H. Wright, *The God I Don't Understand: Reflections on Tough Questions of Faith* (Grand Rapids: Zondervan, 2008); and, with a lower view of biblical authority, Eric A. Seibert, *Disturbing Divine Behavior: Troubling Old Testament Images of God* (Minneapolis: Fortress, 2009); and Seibert, *The Violence of Scripture: Overcoming the Old Testament's Troubling Legacy* (Minneapolis: Fortress, 2012).

34. Gushee, *Sacredness of Human Life*, 37.

another.[35] Underlying all of these commands is a guarding of human dignity and sacredness.

The commands to treat foreigners and immigrants with justice and dignity are pivotal in comprehending the value of all humans. Leviticus 19:33–34 reads, "When a stranger sojourns with you in your land, you shall not do him wrong. You shall treat the stranger who sojourns with you as the native among you, and you shall love him as yourself, for you were strangers in the land of Egypt: I am the LORD your God" (ESV). Deuteronomy 24:17 states, "You shall not pervert the justice due to the sojourner or to the fatherless, . . . but you shall remember that you were a slave in Egypt [as immigrants] and the LORD your God redeemed you from there" (ESV). These directives are then echoed by Jesus in Matthew 25: "I was a stranger and you welcomed me, I was naked and you clothed me. . . . Truly, I say to you, as you did it to one of the least of these my brothers, you did it to me" (vv. 35, 40 ESV). And it is human dignity that underlies the many prophetic injunctions to justice: "And what does the LORD require of you but to do justice, and to love kindness, and to walk humbly with your God?" (Mic. 6:8 NRSV); "This is what the LORD Almighty said: 'Administer true justice; show mercy and compassion to one another. Do not oppress the widow or the fatherless, the foreigner or the poor'" (Zech. 7:9–10). And Jesus affirms these commitments when he chastises the Pharisees: "But woe to you Pharisees! For you tithe mint and rue and every herb, and neglect justice and the love of God. These you ought to have done, without neglecting the others" (Luke 11:42 ESV).

Though human dignity ultimately resides in the creation of men and women in God's image and is known explicitly through divine revelation, human beings have an intuitive and experiential sense of human worth, often termed *natural law*. One evidence of this is that, following the tragedies and atrocities of World War II, the General Assembly of the United Nations (UN) issued a document called "Universal Declaration of Human Rights," in which the theme of dignity is highly visible. The document starts with "recognition of the inherent dignity and of the equal and inalienable rights of all members of the human family" as the foundation of "freedom, justice and peace in the world." In article 1 of the declaration, the theme emerges again: "All human beings are born free and equal in dignity and rights."[36] The various human rights enunciated in the document flow from the dignity of all human beings. Interestingly, during the writing of the declaration, the UN brought together a group of philosophers to explore the theoretical

35. For a helpful overview of the Decalogue and the relevance of the commands for today, see Gilbert Meilaender, *Thy Will Be Done: The Ten Commandments and the Christian Life* (Grand Rapids: Baker Academic, 2020).

36. United Nations General Assembly, "Universal Declaration of Human Rights," United Nations, adopted December 10, 1948, https://www.un.org/en/about-us/universal-declaration-of-human-rights; quotations from "Preamble" and "Article 1."

foundation for dignity and human rights. Reflecting on that deliberation, Jacques Maritain, a noted Roman Catholic philosopher, states, "At one of the meetings . . . where human rights were being discussed, someone expressed astonishment that certain champions of violently opposed ideologies had agreed on a list of those rights. 'Yes,' they said, 'We agree about the rights but on condition that no one asks us why.'"[37] They could agree, though without acknowledgment of their agreement's source, because all humans are made in the image of God and thus have a sense of the dignity that flows from it, thereby intuitively wanting to be treated with the dignity endowed by their Creator.

The great ethical significance of humanity's creation in God's image is the dignity and worth of all people and all peoples, in every phase of a person's life, from beginning to end. Yes, humans are badly fallen and fail to think and live in accordance with this dignity. Moreover, their dignity does not cover over sinful patterns and choices that they make in this world. Our great value and worth does not imply that every human disposition, behavior, and lifestyle is to be morally legitimized. What it does mean is that even the vilest of sinners still bears the mark of God's image and, hence, a dignity and sacredness that is to be protected, even amid their regrettable patterns of life and in the civil, retributive justice that may be meted out. As God's set-apart creation, we are indeed wonderfully made and terribly fallen. And the understanding that we are wonderfully made in the image of God has made a powerful ethical impact in our world. "It has fostered respect and protection for those who have been wrongly oppressed, including impoverished, ill, and disabled people, as well as Native Americans, enslaved Africans and their descendants, and women."[38] In what follows we will see the ethical relevance of this view for key issues, with still much work to be done in embodying and espousing that dignity and human worth.

Dignity for All Peoples: Ethical Application to Racism and Ethnocentrism

Among the most troubling ethical issues in today's world are various forms of racism and ethnocentrism, both of which are an affront to intrinsic dignity. *Ethnocentrism*, the broader category, "is a term applied to the cultural or ethnic bias—whether conscious or unconscious—in which an individual views the world from the perspective of his or her own group, establishing the in-group as archetypal and rating all other groups with reference to this ideal." The result is "an inability to adequately understand cultures that are different from one's own and value judgments that preference the in-group

37. Jacques Maritain, introduction to *Human Rights: Comments and Interpretations; A Symposium*, ed. UNESCO (New York: Columbia University Press, 1949), 9.

38. Kilner, *Dignity and Destiny*, 17.

and assert its inherent superiority."[39] From a Christian perspective, rejecting ethnocentrism should not lead to an ethical relativism that says all value judgments and ethical foundations are relative to given times and places and there are no moral constants. Rather, image-based human dignity means that no particular society, culture, nation, tribe, or race has an inherent superiority. Our cultures are good gifts of God serving as a kind of mental map by which we view the world. They provide us with language, customs, values, traditions, and sentiments. All cultures are fallen, and thus ethical judgments can be made about cultures and societies, but always with the caveat that our own is also fallen and not superior. We thus hold in creative tension the goodness of cultures, with their unique gifts, and the fallenness of cultures, always asserting the dignity of humanity therein.

Racism, a specific form of ethnocentrism, is "the belief that humans may be divided into separate and exclusive biological entities called 'races'; that there is a causal link between inherited physical traits and traits of personality, intellect, morality, and other cultural and behavioral features; and that some races are innately superior to others." Futher, "the term is also applied to political, economic, or legal institutions and systems that engage in or perpetuate discrimination on the basis of race or otherwise reinforce racial inequalities in wealth and income, education, health care, civil rights, and other areas."[40] All humans are made in the image of God, but "racism declares, explicitly or implicitly, that the full expression of this image is found only in certain races. Racism thus usurps God's rightful position in creation."[41] It usually accepts a particular color as normative, and in the Western world whiteness has been the norm.

Ethnocentrism and racism involve several dimensions that distort human dignity. First, they involve a set of beliefs and attitudes held by a given individual or group, which traditionally have gone under the label "prejudice." In his classic work on the subject, Gordon Allport defines it this way: "Ethnic prejudice is an antipathy based upon a faulty and inflexible generalization. It may be felt or expressed. It may be directed toward a group as a whole, or toward an individual because he is a member of that group."[42] Frequently, individuals are unaware of their prejudices, and "people who reject one out-group will tend to reject other out-groups."[43] This understanding of racism

39. Elizabeth Baylor, "Ethnocentrism," Oxford Bibliographies, last modified January 11, 2012, https://www.oxfordbibliographies.com/view/document/obo-9780199766567/obo-9780199766567-0045.xml.

40. Audrey Smedley, "Racism," Britannica, last modified January 5, 2023, https://www.britannica.com/topic/racism.

41. Soong-Chan Rah, "The Sin of Racism: Racialization of the Image of God," in Jones and Barbeau, *Image of God in an Image Driven Age*, 207.

42. Gordon Allport, *The Nature of Prejudice* (Garden City, NY: Doubleday Anchor, 1958), 10.

43. Allport, *Nature of Prejudice*, 66.

has been castigated by some in favor of a purely structural one, but this either-or thinking fails to address racism at the individual level.[44]

The second dimension of ethnocentrism and racism is human action toward another individual or group. This is usually a manifestation of the first dimension—beliefs and attitudes. We frequently see reality through the lens of our own culture or place in society and fail to see the way in which our actions and even language are hurtful to people of other races and ethnic groups. Thus, it is not just the pernicious and violent actions of white supremacist groups that fall into this category, but all of us are frequently culpable in ways we do not see. Christians who believe that conversion should change one's patterns of thinking and actions should seek to affirm that these dimensions are significant, but we dare not overlook the next dimension.

The third dimension is structural or systemic racism and ethnocentrism. Here we focus on policies, laws, procedures, and societal or institutional arrangements that work against justice for particular racial or ethnic groups. This dimension is often the most controversial and hard to define, but it is important, for we often fail to see the way in which explicit patterns from the past, such as segregation, are now manifest in other ways that discriminate and harm, thus denigrating human dignity and leading to severe inequalities in society. We refer to this as *structural sin*, and there are numerous biblical texts to support this understanding. When the psalmist speaks of misery by decrees and laws (Ps. 94:20) or Isaiah speaks of unjust laws and oppressive decrees depriving the poor of their rights (Isa. 10:1–2), they are speaking of structural sin. And John points to the same when he writes, "Do not love the world or the things in the world" (1 John 2:15 ESV), for the Greek word *kosmos* is speaking here not of the inhabitants of the world but of patterns and values deeply embedded in culture and societal structures. Frequently, Americans fail to grasp the structural, systemic dimension because of our individualism, in which we look at the world only through individual categories.

At the heart of racism and ethnocentrism is a disposition of otherness toward people outside our circle, perceiving those unlike us as "the other." In a fallen world, the other is frequently viewed with suspicion, prejudice,

44. See, for example, John McWhorter, "The Dictionary Definition of *Racism* Has to Change," *The Atlantic*, June 22, 2020, https://www.theatlantic.com/ideas/archive/2020/06/dictionary-definition-racism-has-change/613324/. McWhorter gives an excellent overview of the history of the definition of *racism* and believes, contrary to many, that individual prejudice and structural elements can and should go together. For an example of a definition of *racism* that prioritizes the structural, with a particular focus on inequity, see Ibram X. Kendi, *How to Be an Antiracist* (New York: One World, 2019). Kendi argues with regard to racism and antiracism that "the defining question is whether the discrimination is creating equity or inequity. If discrimination is creating equity, then it is antiracist. If discrimination is creating inequity, then it is racist" (19).

hatred—and human dignity is denied. Through Christ the Creator-Redeemer, believers are called to a reconciliation with the other precisely because God created the other in his image and the other is thus a fellow human; we are also called to such reconciliation because through the cross we can be brought together, reconciled, as brothers and sisters in Christ, in his church. Miroslav Volf, wrestling with identity and otherness in the wake of the conflicts in his native Croatia, writes, "The practice of 'embrace,' with its concomitant struggle against deception, injustice, and violence, is intelligible only against the backdrop of a powerful, contagious, and destructive evil I call 'exclusion' . . . and is for Christians possible only if, in the name of God's crucified Messiah, we distance ourselves from ourselves and our cultures in order to create a space for the other."[45] This does not mean a rejection of self-identity and cultures that have given us identity, language, habits, and traditions, but it means they are subservient to Christ's kingdom and the path of love and justice. Missiologist Paul Hiebert, describing the biblical worldview of others and otherness, puts it this way: "First, it affirms the common humanity of all people. The Scriptures lead us to a startling conclusion: at the deepest level of identity as humans, there are no others—there is only us." And the second conclusion is that "in the church all are members of one new people,"[46] coming from every tribe and nation.

Unfortunately, history is replete with examples of otherness fed by ethnocentrism and racism, and the Christian church is not exempt from that sordid history. Throughout the centuries and around the world tribalism and ethnocentrism have led to bloody warfare and slavery between groups. Slavery took on different forms: indentured servitude to pay off debts, slave kidnapping between tribes, slavery of prisoners taken in war, punishment for crime, people sold into slavery by parents or relatives to meet economic needs, and others born into slavery. And then, of course, there was chattel slavery in which Africans were rounded up, sometimes with the aid of neighboring tribes, boarded into crates on ships, and sold as merchandise to support an economic system, particularly in the Americas and Europe. In all of this history, human dignity was denied through a devaluing of the other—usually deemed an enemy at worst or an object at best.

Massacres between ancient native civilizations were common, but then came the Western explorers seeking wealth and new territories. Despite the brutality between native groups, their treatment by Europeans coming to their shores, usually under the banner of Christianity and civilization, is a sad history in both the West and in the Christian church. Land was taken, treaties were either broken or often written without the native inhabitants'

45. Miroslav Volf, *Exclusion and Embrace: A Theological Exploration of Identity, Otherness, and Reconciliation* (Nashville: Abingdon, 1996), 22.

46. Paul G. Hiebert, *Transforming Worldviews: An Anthropological Understanding of How People Change* (Grand Rapids: Baker Academic, 2008), 289.

understanding, and basic rights were simply denied. The sense of otherness emerged because these so-called Christian Europeans failed to affirm the dignity of all humans made in God's image.

For example, in the Spanish invasions into Native American populations, the theologian Juan Ginés de Sepúlveda in the mid-sixteenth century argued that native populations were not fully human or at least not as human or of the same inherent value as his own people. He argued they were barbarians, incapable of learning and unable to govern themselves—hence the legitimacy of enslavement and conquering their lands by "moral superiors."[47] Native American children in both the United States and Canada were frequently taken from their families and placed in schools with the stated purpose of undermining their native culture. In the late 1800s, a Roman Catholic bishop in Manitoba, Canada, stated that the goal of these schools was to "instill in [the children] a profound distaste for native life that they should feel humiliated when reminded of their origin." It is noted that "over 150,000 children, some as young as 4 or 5, were forcibly taken from their parents to the 130 schools across the country [i.e., Canada]. Many were physically and sexually abused, and an estimated 6,000 are believed to have died in the schools due to illness and poor living conditions."[48] Similar abuses occurred in the United States as well.

Though slavery had existed throughout history, including on the continent of Africa, the greatest tragedy and moral culpability lay with the chattel slavery from Africa to Europe and the Americas, by people purporting to be Christians, or at least Americans who believed in "life and liberty for all." Human dignity was denied at every turn as, in a period of roughly three hundred years, ten million Africans were transported to the Americas in the transatlantic slave trade, and two million of them died in the inhumane conditions of the voyage.[49] Humans were then sold on the auction block like pieces of merchandise, families were often split apart, and "as many as one-third of African slaves died within their first three years in the Americas."[50] From the beginning of this intrinsically unjust institution, African American slaves were viewed as the other, not counted as being fully human. Already in 1667 the question emerged in the Virginia Colony as to whether baptism of enslaved people would confer freedom. The Virginia General Assembly decided against

47. Gushee, *Sacredness of Human Life*, 192–93. For detailed analysis see Lewis Hanke, *All Mankind Is One: A Study of the Disputation between Bartolomé de Las Casas and Juan Ginés de Sepúlveda in 1550 on the Intellectual and Religious Capacity of the American Indians* (DeKalb: Northern Illinois University Press, 1974).

48. John Longhurst, "Mennonites Respond to Discovery of Graves at Canadian Residential School," *Anabaptist World*, July 30, 2021, https://anabaptistworld.org/mennonites-respond-to-discovery-of-graves-at-canadian-residential-school/.

49. Jemar Tisby, *The Color of Compromise: The Truth about the American Church's Complicity in Racism* (Grand Rapids: Zondervan, 2019), 29.

50. Tisby, *Color of Compromise*, 32.

this: "It is enacted and declared by this Grand Assembly, and the authority thereof, that the conferring of baptism does not alter the condition of the person as to his bondage or freedom."[51] On the floor of the United States Senate in 1860, Mississippi senator Jefferson Davis, the future president of the Confederacy, made this statement: "This Government was not founded by negroes nor for negroes" but "by white men for white men."[52]

In those years, Christian churches frequently set aside the ultimate questions of freedom, justice, and dignity, arguing that enslaved persons could and should become Christians, but their conversion had no bearing on their status as human beings created in the image of God. Even in the First Great Awakening, many slaves made professions of faith, but as historian Mark Noll notes, "as a revival movement, . . . evangelicalism transformed people within their inherited social setting, but worked only partial and selective transformation on the social settings themselves."[53] Slavery and racism would eventually divide the nation in a civil war, split churches apart, and manifest themselves in new ways, such as with Jim Crow laws—and the racial issues are still with us in new forms. Throughout this sad history, Christian churches have been complicit not just in support of slavery but in the inability to work eagerly at both justice and racial reconciliation.[54]

Fortunately, some Christian leaders truly believed that all humans have an inherent dignity flowing from their creation in the image of God and worked to overturn ethnocentrism, racism, and slavery. In the sixteenth century, a strong voice against the Spanish conquests and massacres was Bartolomé de Las Casas, who argued that God deeply loves all humans, for they are "formed in his image and likeness."[55] Though Las Casas initially supported slavery, he eventually came to reject it on the grounds of human dignity from the *imago Dei*. And the British slave trade and eventually British slavery itself came to an end in large part because of Christians like William Wilberforce, who staunchly believed oppression and cruelty against humans was contrary to human worth and dignity.

51. Quoted in Tisby, *Color of Compromise*, 25.

52. Senator Jefferson Davis, 36th Cong., 1st session, *Congressional Globe*, April 12, 1860, 1682, https://memory.loc.gov/cgi-bin/ampage?collId=llcg&fileName=052/llcg052.db&recNum=739.

53. Mark A. Noll, *The Rise of Evangelicalism: The Age of Edwards, Whitefield and the Wesleys*, A History of Evangelicalism 1 (Downers Grove, IL: IVP Academic, 2018), 254.

54. For a helpful overview of the history of churches' complicity, see Tisby's excellent and convicting *The Color of Compromise*. For a helpful work in thinking through how we deal with racial issues today, see George Yancey, *Beyond Racial Division: A Unifying Alternative to Colorblindness and Antiracism* (Downers Grove, IL: InterVarsity, 2022).

55. Bartolome de Las Casas, "Tratado Comprobatorio del Imperio Soberano y Principado universal que los Reyes de Castilla y Leon Tienen sobre las Indias," in *Obras Escogidas*, ed. Juan Perez de Tudela Bueso (Madrid: Atlas, 1958), 5:357, quoted in Kilner, *Dignity and Destiny*, 10.

Dignity in the Whole of Life: Ethical Application to Abortion and Euthanasia

Human dignity extends not only to all people but to humans in every phase of life. This reality particularly calls into question attempts to define *human value* and *worth* based on certain functions or capacities, and thus it has relevance for issues at the beginning of life and the end of life: abortion and euthanasia (or its more common expression today, "medical assistance in dying").

When dealing with abortion, we must first of all note that there are no direct references to abortion in the Bible. Moreover, some attempts to utilize certain biblical texts in demonstrating full humanness or personhood of the life in the womb are based on faulty interpretations. For example, David's great confession psalm says, "Surely I was sinful at birth, sinful from the time my mother conceived me. Yet you desired faithfulness even in the womb; you taught me wisdom in that secret place" (Ps. 51:5–6). In this confession David is expressing utter sorrow for his sin, utilizing metaphorical terms to convey it, not making a metaphysical statement about when human life begins. The second verse regarding faithfulness and wisdom in the womb clearly does convey that God is at work in nascent life and that we should not regard the life in the womb as a mere appendage or tissue. Similarly, Jeremiah recounts the Lord's call on him to be a prophet: "Before I formed you in the womb I knew you, and before you were born I consecrated you; I appointed you a prophet to the nations" (Jer. 1:5 NRSV). If we take this text to affirm definitive human life or personhood in the womb, we also have to conclude from it a preexistence of the human soul, which the Christian church has always rejected.

One of the contested texts regarding abortion is Exodus 21:22–25, which deals with compensation for injury related to a child in the womb. Both sides of the abortion debate have used this text to support their stance, with the pro-life side arguing that there is a premature birth with compensation for the early birth, while the pro-choice side argues that there is a miscarriage in which the child is dead, but the compensation is not the same as if it were a human being outside the womb. The debate centers around the Hebrew term *yatsa*, with some arguing it simply means coming out (and hence refers here to a premature birth with the child surviving) and others arguing that it means a miscarriage in which the child is dead. I personally concur with John Makujina, who argues that in the Pentateuch *yatsa* describes a natural delivery of a child.[56] Under this interpretation, the compensation does not differ whether it is harm to the child or to the mother.

56. John Majujina, "The Semantics of *Yatsa* in Exodus 21:22: Reassessing the Variables that Determine Meaning," *Bulletin for Biblical Research* 23, no. 3 (2013): 305–21. See also Jeanette Hagen Pifer, "Made in God's Image: Personhood according to Scripture," in *Choose Life: Answering Key Claims of Abortion Defenders with Compassion*, ed. Jeanette Hagen Pifer and John K. Goodrich (Chicago: Moody, 2022), 94–98.

Certain biblical texts portray God as the author of life in the womb and at work in a human being's development, even if they lack clear indication that human life begins at conception. Psalm 139 is one of the best examples: "For it was you who formed my inward parts; you knit me together in my mother's womb. . . . I am fearfully and wonderfully made. . . . My frame was not hidden from you, when I was being made in secret, intricately woven in the depths of the earth. Your eyes beheld my unformed substance" (vv. 13–16 NRSV). Luke 1:44 is frequently used to affirm a person in the womb, but I think for the wrong reasons: "As soon as I heard the sound of your greeting, the child in my womb leaped for joy" (NRSV). The significance here lies not in baby John's recognition of the Messiah and his response in Elizabeth's womb, but rather in the term that is used for the life in the womb—*brephos*. It is a term used not just for an unborn child but also for a child that is born and recognized as a human being—as in Luke 2:12, Acts 7:19, and 2 Timothy 3:15, as well as in other ancient writings.[57]

Beyond the biblical texts, contemporary science points to the fact that from the moment of conception the being in the womb is genetically complete, though it will grow in interaction with the environment. The being is a member of the species *Homo sapiens* and will not grow to be something other than a human. Stephen Schwarz helpfully describes four differences between an unborn and born human: size, level of development, environment, and degree of dependency. He then notes, "I remain myself through the various changes, phases of growth and development, phases of relative dependency or independence, that pertain to my body. I am not any less me because my body may be in a state of greater dependency than at another time."[58]

Some have tried to argue that there is a difference between being a biological human and being a person, with a person so designated by stipulated functions. But as theologian Thomas Torrance notes, "If . . . we want to think of the human embryo as 'potentially person,' that must be taken to mean, not that the embryo is in the process of becoming something else, but rather that the embryo continues to become what he or she already is."[59] As the American College of Pediatricians puts it, "The predominance of human biological research confirms that human life begins at conception. . . . At fertilization, the human being emerges as a whole, genetically distinct, individuated zygotic living human organism, a member of the

57. W. Bauer, F. W. Danker, W. F. Arndt, and F. W. Gingrich, *Greek-English Lexicon of the New Testament and Other Early Christian Literature*, 3rd ed. (Chicago: University of Chicago Press, 2000), 183.

58. Stephen D. Schwarz, *The Moral Question of Abortion* (Chicago: Loyola University Press, 1990), 17.

59. Thomas F. Torrance, *Test-Tube Babies: Morals, Science and the Law* (Edinburgh: Scottish Academic, 1984), 11.

species Homo sapiens."[60] In a study of 5,502 academic biologists, 95 percent affirmed the descriptive view that a human's life begins at fertilization, even though many scientists and average Americans do not affirm the normative view that human fetuses deserve the same moral and legal protection as those humans outside the womb.[61] And interestingly, a growing number of secularists are affirming human dignity for the life in the womb, with a 2022 Gallup poll finding that 21 percent of religious "nones" believe that abortion is unethical.[62]

At the heart of many normative pro-choice sentiments is a functional view of human dignity and worth. As long as the fetus is in the mother's womb, her right to control her own body has ascendency over the human life growing in her womb, even if one believes that life is human. Thus, as Peter Singer and Helga Kuhse argue, "We must abandon the idea that all human life is of equal worth."[63] This abandonment not only makes abortion allowable, but Singer and Kuhse insist it applies to infanticide of deformed infants: such humans do not have an intrinsic dignity; rather, their value is based on degrees of functionality. In a classic and broadly circulated essay published a number of decades ago, philosopher Judith Jarvis Thomson argues that "having a right to life does not guarantee having either a right to be given the use of or a right to be allowed continued use of another person's body—even if one needs it for life itself."[64] Here the value of the life in the womb is subject to the autonomy and desires of the mother.

These arguments have several major fallacies. First, they negate the procreative nature of sex, which all of human history has understood until moderns negated it by arguing that a "consent-to-sex is a distinct act from consenting to pregnancy."[65] If one voluntarily engages in a sexual act, they must be willing to assume the potential consequences of that act, even if unintended; otherwise, personal responsibility and part of the very nature of sex are negated. Second, these arguments are determining the value of a human on the basis of the degree of their being wanted. As Sidney Callahan has pointed out, this establishes the worth of the powerless by the powerful. "The powerful (including parents) cannot be allowed to want and unwant

60. Fred de Miranda, "When Human Life Begins," ed. Patricia Lee June, American College of Pediatricians, March 2017, https://acpeds.org/position-statements/when-human-life-begins.

61. Steven Andrew Jacobs, "Biologists' Consensus on 'When Life Begins,'" SSRN, Elsevier, July 25, 2018, https://papers.ssrn.com/sol3/papers.cfm?abstract_id=3211703.

62. "When Nones Choose Life," *Christianity Today*, December 2022, 21.

63. Peter Singer and Helen Kuhse, "On Letting Handicapped Infants Die," in *The Right Thing to Do: Basic Readings in Moral Philosophy*, ed. James Rachels (New York: Random House, 1989), 146.

64. Judith Jarvis Thomson, "A Defense of Abortion," in *The Problem of Abortion*, ed. Joel Feinberg, 2nd ed. (Belmont, CA: Wadsworth, 1984), 180.

65. Francis J. Beckwith, *Defending Life: A Moral and Legal Case against Abortion Choice* (Cambridge: Cambridge University Press, 2007), 179.

people at will. . . . It's destructive of family life for parents even to think in these categories of wanted and unwanted children."[66] For both above arguments, the worth of a human is determined by an attributed value—how they function or how much they are wanted. The negation of intrinsic dignity is not far removed from the kinds of arguments we saw relative to racism and ethnocentrism. We fall into a moral abyss when we decide who counts as a human or who has intrinsic value to be protected. With the prevalence of prenatal genetic screening, many have aborted children diagnosed with Down syndrome, with the result that in Iceland very few are now born with this condition,[67] and the numbers are declining rapidly in the United States.

The arguments in favor of pro-choice are not limited to secular ones. For example, New Testament scholar Max Turner argues that the call to be children of God presupposes "bodily existence for authentic human personhood" and "an individual who is publicly identifiable as a distinct, continuous and integrated social location, . . . whence communication may originate and to which it may be directed."[68] A zygote in the womb, he contends, does not meet these criteria. In a different vein, Margaret Kamitsuka argues against a developmental-markers approach in assessing the fetus, proposing "that the status of the fetus is best understood in terms of a tensive, dual claim: a fetus is not a nonperson without value, but neither is a fetus a person whom a woman is morally obligated always to gestate." Though having value, "the being in her womb . . . does not overrule her maternal authority to decide its gestational fate and her own."[69] When she wants to have it both ways (not a nonperson and not a person) and when she contends that "the fetus is a kind of human being,"[70] Kamitsuka falls prey to the very same kinds of arguments that were used to subjugate Native Americans and slaves from Africa—assuming a fetus is a kind of human being but not a full human. Moreover, her "mothering authority" once again fails to adequately deal with the reality that a voluntary sex act carries with it the possibility of children.

66. Sidney Callahan, "Talk of 'Wanted Child' Makes for Doll Objects," *National Catholic Reporter*, December 3, 1971, 7.

67. Julian Quinones and Arijeta Lajka, "'What Kind of Society Do You Want to Live In?': Inside the Country Where Down Syndrome Is Disappearing," CBS News, last updated August 15, 2017, https://www.cbsnews.com/news/down-syndrome-iceland/. Iceland has responded back to this report of the disappearance of Down syndrome, saying it was misleading, but the facts are still quite clear. See "Fact Check: No, Iceland Is NOT Systematically Eradicating Down Syndrome," *Iceland Magazine*, August 17, 2017, https://icelandmag.is/article/fact-check-no-iceland-not-systematically-eradicating-down-syndrome.

68. Max Turner, "Approaching Personhood in the New Testament, with Special Reference to Ephesians," *Evangelical Quarterly* 77, no. 3 (2005): 218, 221, 230.

69. Margaret D. Kamitsuka, *Abortion and the Christian Tradition: A Pro-Choice Theological Ethic* (Louisville: Westminster John Knox, 2019), 122.

70. Kamitsuka, *Abortion and the Christian Tradition*, 152.

Abortion is perhaps the most vivid example of the self-deception that accompanies the fall (Gen. 3:13). Changing the language to "reproductive rights" or "reproductive health" when babies' bodies are torn apart, suctioned out, or chemically evacuated from the womb because they are not wanted is hardly descriptive of reality. Moreover, to attribute life-preserving dignity to one only when he or she is wanted, often on the grounds of personal autonomy,[71] is not only logically inconsistent but an example of defacing dignity, which then has implications for other unwanted humans. Allowances must be made when carrying the child to term threatens the life of the mother, and I believe a strong case can be made for allowances in the case of rape, in which there has been an invasion into the life of the mother.[72]

Whereas abortion has been a highly contentious issue throughout the world, it is perhaps being matched by medical assistance in dying. I have long found it fascinating that the nomenclature for ethical issues is frequently changed to make them more palatable—thus the linguistic move from "euthanasia" to "physician-assisted suicide" to "medical assistance in dying." Now legal and practiced in a number of countries and states or provinces, euthanasia is the active taking of a person's life when that life is deemed no longer worth living or involves excruciating pain. The most widely heralded form is voluntary euthanasia, which occurs through the request of the person being killed and is usually a form of suicide with the aid of a doctor—hence *physician-assisted suicide* or *medical assistance in dying*. It is often labeled "death with dignity," because the person believes it is not dignified to experience a life of pain or feelings of worthlessness. It is important to understand that this act is distinct from death by treatment termination, for in treatment termination the disease takes the life, whereas in euthanasia a person (oneself or one's doctor) takes the life.

Historically, the majority of the Christian church has allowed the taking of a human life only under the framework of just war theory, which permits "the killing of those who are actively engaged in perpetrating unjust aggression" and presumes "the innocence of all who are not."[73] The church has rejected suicide and all forms of euthanasia on the grounds of intrinsic human dignity flowing from creation in the image of God. Moreover, "because human life is not simply our property, but a gift or loan from God, we have no right to damage or destroy it."[74] When one looks at the vast array of writings in sup-

71. For a helpful critique of the way radical autonomy is employed in medicine today, see Farr Curlin and Christopher Tollefsen, *The Way of Medicine: Ethics and the Healing Profession*, Notre Dame Studies in Medical Ethics and Bioethics (Notre Dame, IN: University of Notre Dame Press, 2021), 65–78.

72. One way of thinking about this might be to use analogies to just war theory, in which taking a life is warranted on the grounds of invasion or threat. This is a subject that needs further work.

73. Nigel Biggar, *Aiming to Kill: The Ethics of Suicide and Euthanasia* (London: Darton, Longman & Todd, 2004), 10.

74. Biggar, *Aiming to Kill*, 18.

port of medical assistance in dying (whether legal, ethical, or popular), the arguments in favor usually boil down to four primary ones: autonomy, compassion for the suffering, the desire to not be a burden to family and friends, and the contention that there is no difference between assisted suicide and treatment termination.[75] We will note a few responses to these arguments but then turn to the dignity issues.

While autonomy has been a major principle in contemporary bioethics, we do well to remember that we are never autonomous beings, and both the patient and the doctor are intimately connected to others, all of whom will be affected by the act of killing. While Christians are always called to show compassion, compassion should never be the moral trump card. Moreover, because our faith hinges on a suffering Savior, we will have a whole different perspective on suffering, while also contending that most suffering today can be alleviated through pain medicine or palliative sedation. As to the desire to not be a burden, we should note that humans are always called to walk with others in their deepest moments of trial and that much of this sentiment is likely fueled by depression amid suffering.[76] And as already noted, allowing a person to die when further treatment is futile and burdensome is vastly different from actively inducing death in assisted suicide.

But at the heart of many of these arguments is the assumption that human dignity and worth depend on the ability to perform certain functions and to ward off pain, as opposed to the Christian view that human life has intrinsic dignity. For example, Marjorie Pabst Battin contends that "if the life one is given [by God] is an unsatisfactory one—involving a diseased or deformed body, severe poverty, desperate political repression, terrifying insanity, unbearable grief or deprivation—we would be very much less likely . . . to claim that one is obliged to be grateful for it" and thus legitimately opt for suicide.[77] Similarly, Nancy Duff, retired ethics professor at Princeton Seminary, supports assisted suicide by arguing, "We . . . have to recognize that some people who are dying reach a point where life has ceased to have value *for them*—no matter what others think. For some people, losing the capacity to work in the garden, or interact with children or grandchildren, or enjoy a meal, will make life lose its value."[78]

75. See, for example, Alejandro Gutierrez-Castillo, Javier Gutierrez-Castillo, Francisco Guadarrama-Conzuelo, Amado Jimenez-Ruiz, and Jose Luis Ruiz-Sandoval, "Euthanasia and Physician-Assisted Suicide: A Systematic Review of Medical Students' Attitudes in the Last 10 Years," *Journal of Medical Ethics and the History of Medicine* 13, no. 22 (2020): 13–22.

76. Marije L. van der Lee, Johanna G. van der Bom, Nikkie B. Swarte, A. Peter M. Heintz, Alexander de Graeff, and Jan van den Bout, "Euthanasia and Depression: A Prospective Cohort Study among Terminally Ill Cancer Patients," *Journal of Clinical Oncology* 23, no. 27 (2005): 6607–12.

77. Marjorie Pabst Battin, *The Least Worst Death: Essays in Bioethics on the End of Life* (New York: Oxford University Press, 1994), 218.

78. Nancy J. Duff, *Making Faithful Decisions at the End of Life* (Louisville: Westminster John Knox, 2018), 64.

If human dignity flows from humanity's creation in God's image, it is intrinsic and not dependent on our capacities, such as rationality, relationality, or the recognition of others. As bioethicist Daniel Sulmasy and his coauthors put it, "Human dignity ultimately rests not on a person's interests, but on the value of the person . . . ; and the value of the person is infinite."[79] This does not mean that we must do everything possible to fight off impending death, for that, too, can be playing God. But it does mean that we ought not to take a life, even amid one's suffering and feelings of abandonment. In such contexts we share the compassion of Christ through our mercy, presence, and prayers. We would do well to heed the words of John Donne, the seventeenth-century English poet and clergyman: "No man is an island, entire of itself; every man is a piece of the continent, a part of the main. If a clod be washed away by the sea, Europe is the less. . . . Any man's death diminishes me because I am involved in mankind, and therefore never send to know for whom the bell tolls; it tolls for thee."[80]

Conclusion

All of creation is good, but within that creation only human beings are set apart as made in the image of God. The primary ethical significance of this doctrine is the intrinsic dignity of all human beings in all phases of life. Human worth and dignity are not based on one's attributes, functions, or assessments by others. They inhere within the person simply because they are a member of the human race, not because they are a member of a particular race, tribe, ethnic group, or nation.

While ethnocentrism and racism, on the one hand, and abortion and euthanasia, on the other, might appear to be very different kinds of ethical matters, they share in common an estimation of value and dignity based on functions, performance, conditions, and the attribution of others. But the Christian ethical foundation for these issues (and many others) is the unique creation of humans in God's image, which tells us that even in a sinful, broken world, all humans in all phases of life are wonderfully made, possessing an inherent dignity granted not by society but by our Maker.

79. Daniel P. Sulmasy, John M. Travaline, Louise A. Mitchell, and E. Wesley Ely, "Non-Faith-Based Arguments against Physician-Assisted Suicide and Euthanasia," *Linacre Quarterly* 83, no. 3 (2016): 248, https://www.ncbi.nlm.nih.gov/pmc/articles/PMC5102187/.

80. John Donne, "Meditations XVII," in *Norton Anthology of English Literature*, ed. M. H. Abrams (New York: Norton, 1968), 528.

4

Creation Care

Stewarding God's Good Creation

After creating the universe and then planet Earth, God begins to fill it. God provides vegetation and water, sea creatures, birds, and various creatures that move along the ground, including livestock and wild animals. The Creator pronounces all of it good. At the apex of creation, God creates humanity in his own image and as a result gives to humans a responsibility with the rest of creation:

> Then God said, "Let us make humankind in our image, according to our likeness; and let them have dominion over the fish of the sea, and over the birds of the air, and over the cattle, and over all the wild animals of the earth, and over every creeping thing that creeps upon the earth."
>
> So God created humankind in his image,
> in the image of God he created them;
> male and female he created them.
>
> God blessed them, and God said to them, "Be fruitful and multiply, and fill the earth and subdue it; and have dominion over the fish of the sea and over the birds of the air and over every living thing that moves upon the earth." God said, "See, I have given you every plant yielding seed that is upon the face of all the earth, and every tree with seed in its fruit; you shall have them for food." (Gen. 1:26–29 NRSV)

It is precisely this, other biblical texts, and some Christian doctrines that critics have used to say Christian faith is incompatible with a healthy environmental ethic that cares for the physical world. In fact, some have laid the blame for our current crisis at the feet of Christianity.

In a widely distributed and much-discussed article from 1967, historian Lynn White rightly writes, "What people do about their ecology depends on what they think about themselves in relation to things around them"—meaning "nature." But from there White goes on to say, "Christianity is the most anthropocentric religion the world has seen," and this is the primary cause of our raging environmental crisis. While recognizing that Christianity is complex, "Christianity bears a huge burden of guilt," he says. Why? Because "Christianity, in absolute contrast to ancient paganism and Asia's religions . . . , not only established a dualism of man and nature but also insisted that it is God's will that man exploit nature for his proper ends." The Christian worldview gave impetus not only to the rise of modern science and its subsequent technology to exploit nature, but the Genesis account of dominion fueled the fires: "Man named all the animals, thus establishing his dominance over them."[1] White held out little hope, despite being an active churchman, that Christian faith could provide an ethical foundation for the care of the natural world around us.

Many others have added to the various critiques of biblical faith.[2] One critique is that monotheism contributes to the abuse of our environment. In monotheism there is one transcendent God, distinct from creation; thus, there is, so goes the charge, an exclusivist approach to reality and apathy toward the physical world around us. Historian Arnold Toynbee, for example, claims that "some of the major maladies of the present-day world—for instance the recklessly extravagant consumption of nature's irreplaceable treasures, and the pollution of those . . . that man has not already devoured—can be traced back in the last analysis to a religious cause, and . . . this cause is the rise of monotheism." Toynbee believes the solution to the exploitation of nature "lies in reverting from the *Weltanschauung* [worldview] of monotheism to the *Weltanschauung* of pantheism."[3] In this critique pantheism is preferable to monotheism because God and nature are one and not distinct from each other.

A second critique of Christianity highlights the "dominion" and "rule" language in the Genesis creation story. This was part of the critique of Lynn White and is also evident in the work of historian Roderick Nash, who believes that "the harsh imagery of absolute domination" has led Christians to

1. Lynn White Jr., "The Historic Roots of Our Ecological Crisis," *Science* 155 (1967): 1205, 1206.

2. For a helpful overview of complaints against Christianity as the cause of the ecological crisis, see Steven Bouma-Prediger, *For the Beauty of the Earth: A Christian Vision for Creation Care*, 2nd ed., Engaging Culture (Grand Rapids: Baker Academic, 2010), 59–80. Much of my following analysis of the critiques is drawn from this excellent work.

3. Arnold Toynbee, "The Religious Background of the Present Environmental Crisis," in *Ecology and Religion in History*, ed. David Spring and Eileen Spring (New York: Harper & Row, 1974), 146, 148.

"understand Genesis 1:28 as a divine commandment to conquer every part of nature and make it humankind's slave." This, he argues, has provided "intellectual lubrication for the exploitation of nature."[4] In this critique humanity is set "over against nature," and this "encourages humans to conquer and exploit the natural world."[5]

A third critique underscores the various perceived dualisms found in historic Christianity, which then undercut any serious and positive engagement with the material, natural world. This, too, was part of White's critique, but others have noted and contended that the dualisms of soul and body, spirit and matter, grace and nature, male and female, Creator and creature are all the culprits. One philosopher charges that the "dualism between God and nature" inevitably leads to exploitation of the latter, for "Christianity has encouraged man to think of himself as nature's absolute master, for whom everything that exists was designed."[6] Ecofeminism has asserted that dualisms are at the heart of oppressing both nature and women, and they are linked together. Ecofeminist theologian Rosemary Radford Ruether argues, "Male domination of women and domination of nature are interconnected, both in cultural ideology and in social structures."[7]

A fourth critique of Christianity centers on its eschatology, at least in some quarters of the church. In one version of eschatology, Christ returns and raptures believers out of this sinful world, and in the end God destroys it. In the future eschaton, this earth will have no place, for it will be burned up and eradicated. God will then, in the language of Revelation 21, build a new heavens and a new earth, discarding the old and starting anew. And so, as journalist Bill Moyers quips, "Why care about the earth when the droughts, floods, famine, and pestilence brought by ecological collapse are signs of the apocalypse foretold in the Bible? Why care about global climate change when you and yours will be rescued in the rapture?"[8] Essentially, then, "this argument contends that because Christians believe the world will ultimately be destroyed, they feel no need to care for it."[9]

We can respond to these critiques in two ways. One is to challenge the biblical and theological misperceptions and counter with different interpretations.

4. Roderick Frazier Nash, *The Rights of Nature: A History of Environmental Ethics*, History of American Thought and Culture (Madison: University of Wisconsin Press, 1989), 90.

5. Bouma-Prediger, *For the Beauty of the Earth*, 60.

6. John Passmore, *Man's Responsibility for Nature: Ecological Problems and Western Traditions* (New York: Scribner's Sons, 1974), 12, 13.

7. Rosemary Radford Ruether, *Gaia and God: An Ecofeminist Theology of Earth Healing* (San Francisco: Harper, 1992), 2. See also Ruether's *Integrating Ecofeminism, Globalization, and World Religions*, Nature's Meaning (New York: Rowman & Littlefield, 2004).

8. Bill Moyers, "On Receiving Harvard Medical School's Global Environment Citizen Award," Common Dreams, December 6, 2004, https://www.commondreams.org/views/2004/12/06/receiving-harvard-medical-schools-global-environment-citizen-award.

9. Bouma-Prediger, *For the Beauty of the Earth*, 63.

That is what this chapter seeks to do while exploring Genesis 1–2 and other salient creation texts in the Bible. We attempt to provide a reading of Scripture and theology that gives significant foundations for creation care and an environmental ethic. The second response to the critiques is a different reading of history and therefore seeing other causes of our sad degradation of God's good creation. Richard Bauckham, for example, puts the blame on the Baconian vision of science and technology conquering nature. In seventeenth-century England Francis Bacon "created the vision that inspired the great scientific-technological project that has in large part made the modern world. . . . He foresaw only the benefits and none of the downsides." While Bacon alluded to Genesis 1–2 as a license for exploiting natural resources, he was essentially a materialist in his worldview, and that is what propelled his vision. Bauckham writes, "His view of the value of the natural world was purely utilitarian: the natural world was . . . a resource from which humans could fashion things of much more benefit to human life." Technology that is developed through modern science enables humans "to conquer nature and force her under torture to work for human benefit."[10] This is what led us to the rape of the earth's resources.

A number of writers put the blame on modern materialism and consumerism, treating creation as a storehouse of goods to satiate our greed. Norman Wirzba sees the primary factor in the environmental crisis as "the steady erosion of the practical and theoretical conditions necessary for the experience of the world as creation." That erosion is fueled by our "naturalist, materialist, and consumer assumptions, that the world has little purpose other than the instrumental purposes humans ascribe to it."[11] As a result human interests are set over against the natural world and are a license to exploit it. In similar fashion Steven Bouma-Prediger believes that "we must renounce the idols to which we have pledged our allegiance—the false gods of scientism, technicism, and materialism, among others—and return to a faith refined of hubris and marked instead by humility. . . . We must call the church out of its captivity to Western culture and into a faithful obedience to Jesus."[12]

Worldviews Underlying Environmental Ethics

When we probe different stances toward an environmental ethic, it quickly becomes clear that there are larger worldviews underlying the various stances. At

10. Richard Bauckham, "Being Human in the Community of Creation: A Biblical Perspective," in *Ecotheology: A Christian Conversation*, ed. Kiara A. Jorgenson and Alan G. Padgett (Grand Rapids: Eerdmans, 2020), 17, 18.

11. Norman Wirzba, *The Paradise of God: Renewing Religion in an Ecological Age* (New York: Oxford University Press, 2003), 61, 62.

12. Bouma-Prediger, *For the Beauty of the Earth*, 80.

the heart of these worldviews are understandings of the relationship between God or the gods, nature, and human beings. These worldview assumptions powerfully impact one's approach to the environment. We could no doubt examine numerous worldviews here, but for the sake of simplicity, we will explore three types that have been at the heart of contemporary discussions: anthropocentrism, biocentrism, and theocentrism. It is the latter that I am seeking to defend in this chapter. As we explore these worldviews, it is helpful to remember that this analysis is a typology, and thus no one movement or individual fits perfectly into a given type, and there are variations within each type. It is a broad construal to help us make sense of a vast array of approaches to environmental ethics.

Anthropocentrism

By *anthropocentrism* we mean a worldview in which human beings are at the center of creation, which was made primarily for humanity's sake. Most in this approach are theists who truly believe in God and affirm Scripture, but they emphasize that God gave us the task of ruling and having dominion, which are taken to mean that the creation is primarily for our good and serves us. "The natural world is envisaged and spoken of as a 'natural resource' to be managed as prudently as possible by humans for human good. Nonhuman creatures do not have intrinsic value. Their value is derived exclusively for their usefulness for humans—trees are for lumber, water for human consumption, the prairie for grazing cattle." In this framework, "the natural world is valuable, but only as a means of serving human interests."[13]

A prominent voice in this paradigm is Thomas Derr, former professor of religion at Smith College. Derr reluctantly accepts the anthropocentric label but prefers to label himself a Christian humanist—"meaning that my priority in matters ecological is humankind."[14] Derr is concerned that many modern environmentalists distort reality by submerging human life into nature, rather than recognizing humans' appropriate power over it. He believes that environmental degradation is not just a modern problem fueled by technology, for historically overgrazing and deforestation caused civilizations to fall, as with the Egyptians, Persians, Romans, Aztecs, and Native Americans. Westerners who romanticize other cultures are blind to these realities.[15] As we look at our modern situation, "there seems to be no reasonable, morally defensible way to proceed except by using human welfare as our compass heading. Yes, this is an anthropocentric prescription. It is inescapable." Derr goes on to say,

13. Bouma-Prediger, *For the Beauty of the Earth*, 120.

14. Thomas Sieger Derr, *Environmental Ethics and Christian Humanism*, with James A. Nash and Richard John Neuhaus, Abingdon Press Studies in Christian Ethics and Economic Life (Nashville: Abingdon, 1996), 18.

15. Derr, *Environmental Ethics and Christian Humanism*, 20.

"When it comes to practice, to policy public and private, I would refrain from destruction, favor restoration, practice preservation, and in cases of conflict unapologetically give priority to human need."[16]

Another voice in the anthropocentric camp is Calvin Beisner, who interprets Genesis 1–2 to mean that "man's cultivating the earth is designed . . . to cause the earth to serve man."[17] Beisner does not accept the anthropocentric label and contends he is theocentric, but in his critique of others and in his own views, he has anthropocentric proclivities. He contends, "As man was not made for the sabbath, but the sabbath for man (Mark 2:27), so also man was not made for the earth, but the earth for man."[18] Beisner is a strong defender of laissez-faire capitalism, meaning there should be few interventions or interferences in the production and distribution of resources. The dominion mandate in Genesis "clearly means that the earth, with everything in it—though it all belongs to God (Ps. 24:1)—was intended by God to serve man's needs. Man was not made for the earth; the earth was made for man." In addition, "the dominion mandate does not tell us what particular uses of the earth are best suited to man's service." As a result, "within the limits of God's moral Law, the best policy of resource management is to permit every individual to use what belongs to him as he pleases."[19] His anthropocentrism is also evident when he argues, "Human beings can and should be viewed not as enemies but friends of endangered species. One of the most important ways to ensure that this friendship occurs is to seek ways to turn protection of species to people's advantage."[20]

There are other writers who, while not being anthropocentric in worldview, land in a similar outlook in terms of downgrading the significance of the created world. The twentieth-century Swiss theologian Emil Brunner once wrote, "The cosmic element in the Bible is never anything more than the scenery in which the history of mankind takes place."[21] Numerous Christians, both scholarly and lay, have taken similar stances toward the natural world.

How should we assess anthropocentrism as a framework for environmental ethics? On a positive note, it is right to see human beings as distinct from the rest of the created world because God created us in his image. But its major fallacies are to both misinterpret the dominion texts of Scripture and to place

16. Derr, *Environmental Ethics and Christian Humanism*, 100, 140.

17. E. Calvin Beisner, *Where Garden Meets Wilderness: Evangelical Entry into the Environmental Debate* (Grand Rapids: Eerdmans, 1997), 14.

18. E. Calvin Beisner, *Prospects for Growth: A Biblical View of Population, Resources, and the Future* (1990; repr., Eugene, OR: Wipf & Stock, 2004), 24.

19. Beisner, *Prospects for Growth*, 163, 156.

20. Beisner, *Where Garden Meets Wilderness*, 145.

21. Emil Brunner, *Revelation and Reason: The Christian Doctrine of Faith and Knowledge*, trans. Olive Wyon (Philadelphia: Westminster, 1946), 33. For another analysis of anthropocentric ethics, particularly in virtue ethics, see Dominika Dzwonkowska, "Is Environmental Virtue Ethics Anthropocentric?," *Journal of Agricultural and Environmental Ethics* 31 (2018): 723–38.

humans, rather than God, at the center of this whole earth. Alister McGrath, taking issue with Lynn White's assessment that Christianity is the cause of our environmental crisis, writes, "The most self-centered religion in history is the secular creed of . . . Western culture, whose roots lie in the Enlightenment of the eighteenth century and whose foundation belief is that humanity is the arbiter of all ideas and values."[22] While Derr and Beisner both give lip service to God's ownership of the world, they appear to imbibe too readily at the waters of the Enlightenment notions of freedom and carry this over into their view of God's creation. Humanity is given too much ascendency, and while freedom is vital for God's image bearers, it always entails limits for the glory of God, love of neighbor, and stewardship of God's creation. "This is not our world, over which we have sovereignty: it is God's, and we are his stewards, appointed and called to tend his world as something that has been entrusted to us."[23] And as Francis Schaeffer writes, "We shall continue to have a worsening ecologic crisis until we reject the . . . axiom that nature has no reason for existence save to serve man."[24]

Biocentrism

Biocentrism is a worldview encompassing a broad variety of adherents with varied emphases but accentuating an inherent value to all living things. Thus, it calls for strong measures to curb human behaviors in favor of the natural world. The biocentric outlook stands stridently against any form of anthropocentrism on the grounds that humans should not have a favored space on planet Earth, over against the rest of nature. Many biocentrists have made the claim that the natural world has rights, just as humans have rights. The biocentric outlook on nature has both religious adherents, such as Jainists, Buddhists, pantheists, and some ecofeminists, and secular adherents, such as Peter Singer, deep ecologists, and the followers of the Gaia hypothesis, which is a mix of religious and secular perspectives.

Peter Singer, a Princeton philosopher originally from Australia, is a secular utilitarian, meaning that he thinks ethical decisions should be based on the greatest interests for the greatest number of beings. But to limit "beings" to humans, argues Singer, is speciesism, elevating the inherent value of the human species over all others. This doesn't mean all of nature should be treated

22. Alister McGrath, *The Reenchantment of Nature: The Denial of Religion and the Ecological Crisis* (New York: Doubleday, 2002), 54.

23. Alister McGrath, "The Doctrine of Creation: Some Theological Reflections," in *As Long as the Earth Endures: The Bible, Creation and the Environment*, ed. Jonathan Moo and Robin Routledge (Nottingham: Apollos, 2014), 40.

24. Francis Schaeffer, *Pollution and the Death of Man: The Christian View of Ecology* (Wheaton: Tyndale, 1970), 114. Schaeffer was one of the first evangelical Christians to respond to both White and the ecological crisis, and his book contains rich wisdom for thinking about God's creation. This was before his unfortunate turn to more ideological stances in the 1980s.

equally, as he appeals to sentience, the capacity for sensations and feelings as an ethical marker. He draws "the boundary of moral consideration around all sentient creatures but leaves other living things outside that boundary. This means that if a valley is to be flooded, we should give weight to the interests of human beings . . . and to the interests of wallabies, possums, . . . and birds living there; but the drowning of the ancient forests . . . [and other destructions] are factors to be taken into account only insofar as they adversely affect sentient creatures."[25] Singer is one of the world's best-known animal activists; he contends that the human tyranny over animals "caused and today is still causing an amount of pain and suffering that can only be compared with that which resulted from the centuries of tyranny by white humans over black humans."[26] Singer's biocentrism, then, is not a complete one, in that only sentient members of the natural world have the same value as humans and a certain form of rights.

Deep ecology is a movement that extends those rights even further. In this view, "all things—humans, animals, plants, bacteria, mountains, rivers, lakes—have an equal right to exist. In other words deep ecology acknowledges the intrinsic value of the natural world and affirms that nonhuman organisms not only count morally but count equally."[27] Arne Naess, the founder of the movement, distinguishes between shallow and deep perspectives on the environment and clearly opts for the latter. He even contends that "if [human] vital needs come in conflict with the vital needs of nonhumans, then humans should defer to the latter."[28]

In terms of religious dimensions in the biocentric movement, there is a tendency to laud either pantheism or some form of animism, in that both hold nature, humans, and the transcendent close together. In pantheism everything is in essence one; therefore, to harm nature is to harm god. And in animism all of nature is animated by spirits, gods, or some spiritual qualities and hence needs to be protected. These sentiments have led some Western biocentric supporters to ethically romanticize indigenous cultures, overlooking deforestation by groups such as the Mayans[29] or the human sacrifices of the Aztecs.[30] Another biocentric movement, which in some quarters has religious

25. Peter Singer, *Writings on an Ethical Life* (New York: HarperCollins, 2000), 97.

26. Singer, *Writings on an Ethical Life*, 21.

27. Bouma-Prediger, *For the Beauty of the Earth*, 125.

28. Arne Naess, "The Deep Ecological Movement: Some Philosophical Aspects," in *Environmental Philosophy: From Animal Rights to Radical Ecology*, ed. Michael Zimmerman (Englewood Cliffs, NJ: Prentice-Hall, 1993), 203.

29. Michelle Werts, "A Lesson from the Past," American Forests, August 27, 2012, www.americanforests.org/blog/a-lesson-from-the-past/. Werts notes that recent research is now showing that the Mayan civilization declined not because of European conquest but likely because of deforestation, which contributed to drought.

30. Dave Roos, "Human Sacrifice: Why the Aztecs Practiced the Gory Ritual," History, October 11, 2018, https://www.history.com/news/aztec-human-sacrifice-religion. Initially, these

overtones as well as secular adherents, is the Gaia hypothesis, which first emerged in the 1970s. Scientific adherents argued that the earth is a living organism in which the parts interact, including their inorganic parts, to form a synergistic and self-regulating system. Gaia was an ancient Greek goddess, and it was only natural that some adherents, including some scientists, new age followers, and ecofeminists, could coalesce around the theme that the universe is sacred because all is one.[31]

As Christians, how should we view biocentrism, given its many variations? On a positive note, Doug and Jonathan Moo write, "If, then, some radical environmentalists have exaggerated the degree to which humans are simply a part of creation, it seems to be the case that many people in the West, including many Christians, have neglected to see the degree to which we are bound up with creation." But they also write, "From the standpoint of Christian theology, humans are created beings. We owe our existence to a Creator, and we exist as part of—not apart from—the thing we call creation. At the same time, humans, uniquely, have been created in the image of God," which "give[s] us a distinct place within that created world."[32] In a similar tone, Bouma-Prediger gives this critique: "Any position that puts life at the center of things must, from a theocentric point of view, be judged inadequate. God lies at the center of things, not life. Despite these problems, biocentrism . . . possesses the not inconsiderable virtue of expanding our moral imagination to include more than merely the human."[33] I would also add to the critique the tendency of some biocentrists to exaggerate environmental realities to shore up their advocacy. In the late 1960s and early '70s, when I was in college, my fellow students and I all had to read Paul Ehrlich's *Population Bomb*, which argues that if we don't curb population growth, environmental disasters are very soon on the horizon, and mass starvation around the world will occur in the 1970s.[34] The end of planet Earth is near, he says. Many of Ehrlich's predictions never came to pass, and unfortunately those kinds of biocentric exaggerations have often kept people from taking seriously the environmental challenges we face. Moreover, in biocentrism the attempt to grant nature rights is problematic in that rights entail responsibilities, and it's hard to imagine how plants and animals demonstrate some sort of responsibility in relation to granted rights.

---

reports from the Spanish conquistadors were dismissed as justification for their mistreatment of the Aztecs, but in excavations in 2015 and 2018, archaeologists found clear evidence of human sacrifices, including skull towers and skull racks.

31. For a helpful overview, see Loren Wilkinson, "Gaia Spirituality: A Christian Critique," *Themelios* 18, no. 3 (1993): 4–8.

32. Douglas J. Moo and Jonathan A. Moo, *Creation Care: A Biblical Theology of the Natural World*, Biblical Theology for Life (Grand Rapids: Zondervan, 2018), 181.

33. Bouma-Prediger, *For the Beauty of the Earth*, 123.

34. Paul R. Ehrlich, *The Population Bomb: Population Control or Race to Oblivion?* (New York: Ballantine Books, 1968).

Theocentrism

In contrast to both anthropocentrism and biocentrism, theocentrism views God as the center of all reality and the defining point of our relationship to the world. God, not humans or nature, is the alpha and the omega, the beginning and the end, the foundation of our life and actions. The Creator is distinct from his creation, and within the good gift of creation, he distinguishes between nature and humans, for only humans are created in God's image. As a result they have a significant role in stewarding God's good world, which has intrinsic value, beauty, and bountiful riches. While human beings live from those bountiful riches, the environment that provides them is not valued merely for its usefulness to humans. It is this theocentric model that we now turn to as the foundation for creation care and environmental ethics. It emerges from Genesis 1–2, numerous other biblical texts, and implied theological affirmations.

A Theocentric Foundation: The Creation Story—Genesis 1–2

"In the beginning, God created the heavens and the earth" (Gen. 1:1 ESV). That is the foundation for creation care. As we have been contending in this book, the creation story is central to a Christian ethic, and nothing in the rest of Scripture overturns or supersedes the creation paradigms. The rest of God's unfolding revelation, including the incarnate Christ, extends and gives greater depth and understanding to the creation story, especially in light of the fall, but creation is the starting point. So we begin there, and then we turn to other creation texts in both the Old and New Testaments to explore our responsibility of stewardship in God's magnificent and varied creation.

The Distinction between Creator and the Created

The first thing we observe in the creation story is a distinction between Creator and the created world. The created world is good, has beauty, brings pleasure, points to God, and in some creation texts actually praises God, but the created world has no divine qualities in essence—not even humans made in God's image. "The affirmation that God created the heavens and the earth implies a fundamental ontological distinction between God as creator and everything created. This duality is essential to all biblical thought and to a Christian worldview. It should not be confused with other kinds of unbiblical dualism (e.g. between body and soul). It stands against both monism and pantheism."[35] The triune God who creates is both sovereign and one, unlike

35. Christopher J. H. Wright, *Walking in the Ways of the Lord: The Ethical Authority of the Old Testament* (Downers Grove, IL: InterVarsity, 1995), 182.

the finite, multiple gods of Israel's neighbors, who divinized natural forces around them.

God creates the sun and the moon on day four, but unlike some religions that revere them as deity, in Genesis there is a clear demarcation between Creator and created, even though "God set them in the expanse of the heavens to give light on the earth, to rule over the day and over the night, and to separate the light from the darkness" (1:17–18 ESV). In similar fashion God creates land, trees, and vegetation, but unlike animism, in which these creational realities are viewed as animated with gods or spirits, and unlike monism, in which they are deemed one with the gods and humans, Genesis provides a clear demarcation.

This distinction is particularly pertinent in environmental ethics, for as we've already noted, some who follow biocentric approaches today are drawn to new age religions, pagan religions, pantheism, and a veneration of indigenous religions in which the distinction between Creator and created is blurred. Thus, needlessly and intentionally cutting down trees in the woods may be poor stewardship of God's creation, but it is not killing the gods or offending evil spirits. The Creator-creation distinction is not license to do with creation as we please, but it is a recognition that the Creator is the one who gives value to the natural world, not humans or even nature itself. Such a distinction prevents idolatry and serves as a broad framework for a Christian approach to creation care. Moreover, Scripture teaches that God continues a providential rule over his created world, for the world belongs to God, not to humans, nor to nature. "This is not to deny that God has built into the earth an incredible capacity for renewal, recovery, balance and adaptation. But the way in which all these systems work and interrelate is itself planned and sustained by God."[36]

The Goodness of God's Creation

As we discussed in chapter 2, after each day of creation God looks at his divine handiwork and pronounces it good. At the end of Genesis 1, after God has created each part of the world and after creating humans in his image, the text reads, "God saw everything that he had made, and behold, it was very good" (Gen. 1:31 ESV). Contrary to the Gnostic beliefs in early Christianity, the materiality of the created world in its entirety is intrinsically good and retains that goodness even after the fall, in its groaning state (Rom. 8:22). The goodness of the created world is announced by God even before humans enter the scene, and its goodness is therefore not dependent on human usage of it. The anthropocentric, utilitarian ideas that the natural earth exists primarily to serve humans and that it is good for that reason

36. Wright, *Walking in the Ways of the Lord*, 182.

are precluded by creation's intrinsic goodness, which God recognized before human beings even existed.

In creation's goodness there is a form of power within the natural processes themselves, demonstrating their grandeur and glory. This is demonstrated when God says, "'Let the land produce vegetation: seed-bearing plants and trees on the land that bear fruit with seed in it, according to their various kinds.' . . . The land produced [i.e., brought forth] vegetation: plants bearing seed according to their kinds and trees bearing fruit with seed in it according to their kinds. And God saw that it was good" (Gen. 1:11–12). In verses 20–21 the waters are said to bring forth living creatures, and the living creatures, including the birds, are given the same procreative mandate later given to human beings: "God blessed them, saying, 'Be fruitful and multiply and fill the waters in the seas, and let birds multiply on the earth'" (v. 22 ESV). In the following verses, the land is to produce creatures that move along the ground, livestock (presumably domestic animals), and even wild animals. "And God saw that it was good" (v. 25 ESV).

The goodness and order of God's creation stands in significant contrast to the creation stories of other ancient Near Eastern myths. In the Enuma Elish, the Babylonian myth of creation portrays heaven and earth coming into being when the god Marduk violently kills the goddess Tiamat.

> Tiāmat and Marduk, the sage of the gods, came together,
> Joining in strife, drawing near to battle. . . .
> Her inwards were distended and she opened her mouth wide.
> He let fly an arrow and pierced her belly,
> He tore open her entrails and slit her inwards,
> He bound her and extinguished her life.

Marduk then cuts her in half and forms earth and heaven from the two severed parts of her body.[37] It is hard to imagine a good earth stewarded with care coming from such a hostile and violent creation, in contrast to the Genesis account of goodness.

There is, then, a goodness that reverberates throughout God's marvelous creation, that is independent of human activity and pronouncement. When humans have a strong sense that all of God's earth, organic and nonorganic, is good, they will treat it with respect and humility, not because it is a god but because it is a gift of God, expressing God's own grandeur and glory. Yes, humans and animals eat from the ground of God's good earth (Gen. 1:29–30), and after the flood humans are granted the right to eat meat from animals, but the goodness remains and calls for a treatment befitting the earth's status as good but not divine. It is a goodness filled with beauty, variety, and bountifulness.

37. W. G. Lambert, *Babylonian Creation Myths*, ed. Jerrold S. Cooper, Mesopotamian Civilizations 16 (Winona Lake, IN: Eisenbrauns, 2013), 91, 93.

Humans a Part of Nature

In the Genesis story, as we discussed in chapter 3, several elements clearly indicate a certain linkage between humanity and the rest of the natural world, which calls forth a deep respect for those elements of creation. First, both land animals and humans are created on the sixth day, and the land animals include "the livestock, the creatures that move along the ground, and the wild animals, each according to its kind" (1:24). While there is a clear distinction between the animals and humans, the fact that both come forth on the same day shows some commonality between the two. After all, we share 98 percent of DNA with chimpanzees, suggesting that God may have utilized natural processes in creation.

A second indication that humans are part of nature is that we are portrayed as being formed from the dust of the ground: "Then the Lord God formed man from the dust of the ground" (2:7 NRSV). This means that "the human earth-creature (*ʾādām*) is made from the earth (*ʾădāmâ*). . . . To carry the Hebrew wordplay into Latin, we are human because we are from the humus. We, too, are earthly and earthy creatures."[38] Thus, as other biblical texts note, "he knows how we were made; he remembers that we are dust. As for mortals, their days are like grass; they flourish like a flower of the field; for the wind passes over it, and it is gone" (Ps. 103:14–16 NRSV). And as Peter, quoting Isaiah, puts it, "All flesh is like grass and all its glory like the flower of grass. The grass withers, and the flower falls, but the word of the Lord endures forever" (1 Pet. 1:24–25 NRSV). This clearly means that all elements of the created world, both humans and the rest of nature, are finite.

And third, on that sixth day when God creates humans from the dust of the ground, the text tells us that the Lord God "breathed into [the man's] nostrils the breath of life; and the man [*'adam*] became a living being" (2:7 NRSV). The word for "living being" is the Hebrew *nephesh*, and it is used four times in Genesis 1 with reference to the creation of animals: sea life (v. 20), great creatures of the sea (v. 21), land creatures (v. 24), and all creatures (v. 30). While the word is sometimes translated "living soul" with reference to humans, this does not imply that animals have a soul or are a living soul, as the term can take on various connotations in different contexts. But the fact that the term is used in Genesis 1–2 for both animal life and humans demonstrates that we are part of nature.

Beyond the Genesis texts, Doug and Jonathan Moo contend that because both humans and creation suffer from human sin and God's judgment, this also demonstrates an interrelatedness between the two. "That the earth should suffer from God's judgment through no fault of its own ('not of its own will,' Paul says) may raise questions for us. Yet this is

38. Bouma-Prediger, *For the Beauty of the Earth*, 64.

finally but an extension of the interrelatedness of humankind and the rest of creation."[39]

Humans are described in the creation story as being part of the natural world, and thus our connection calls for respect, humility, and care for all of God's good creation. But there's more to the story, for humans are also distinct from the rest of nature.

Humans Distinct from the Rest of Nature

Though humans are part of the natural world, in the creation story they are clearly demarcated from the rest of creation. After the creation of the world—heavenly bodies, earth, and all the living elements of the earth—comes a building crescendo in the story: "Then God said, 'Let us make humankind in our image, according to our likeness'" (1:26 NRSV). No other elements of God's good creation are given this designation, and thus humans are set apart in ways that make them distinct and thus with a different value. This in no way devalues the rest of God's creation or gives license to unbounded human freedom and exploitation of creation, but it clearly elevates humanity and its role in the created order, in contrast to biocentric views.

After the flood story in Genesis 6–9, God makes a covenant with Noah, and various elements of creation care from Genesis 1–2 are reiterated. But so, too, is the distinction between human beings and the animal world, which has been preserved by Noah's obedience to God in building the ark. In Genesis 9, "even after the tragedy of the fall, the image of God that Adam bears will continue in Adam's offspring. . . . The image of God serves to distinguish human beings from other creatures. Other animals may be killed and eaten (v. 3), but human blood may not be shed." Moreover, "a certain respect for the life of other creatures is still engendered by the proscription against eating 'meat that has its lifeblood still on it' (v. 4). . . . But human beings are unique and distinct in bearing God's image, and so murder is strictly forbidden. The distinctive value of human life is such that an accounting will be demanded even from animals that kill human beings (v. 5)."[40]

The distinctiveness of humanity in the theocentric approach to creation is significantly different from certain biocentric versions, in which humans and the natural world are essentially the same in value and rights. A theocentric version does not deify nature; does not see nature, humans, and God as one; and does not equate humans and salamanders. At the apex of God's good creation, in which humans and nature share some things in common, God creates humans in his image. This sets them apart, and they are given a task relative to the rest of creation.

39. Moo and Moo, *Creation Care*, 110.
40. Moo and Moo, *Creation Care*, 73.

Humanity's Stewardship of the Natural World

God creates humankind in his image and as a result gives them a significant and set-apart role within creation:

> Then God said, "Let us make humankind in our image, according to our likeness; and let them have dominion over the fish of the sea, and over the birds of the air, and over the cattle, and over all the wild animals of the earth. . . . Be fruitful and multiply, and fill the earth and subdue it; and have dominion over the fish of the sea and over the birds of the air and over every living thing that moves upon the earth." God said, "See, I have given you every plant yielding seed that is upon the face of all the earth, and every tree with seed in its fruit; you shall have them for food. And to every beast of the earth, and to every bird of the air, and to everything that creeps on the earth, everything that has the breath of life, I have given every green plant for food." (Gen. 1:26, 28–30 NRSV)

Then, as Genesis 2:15 tells us, "the Lord God took the man and put him in the Garden of Eden to work it and take care of it." Reflecting on the creation account, Colin Gunton writes, "Our continuity with the rest of the world maintains a due measure of our finite and limited state, but our difference from it is a witness to our high calling under God to exercise a right dominion over the rest of the created world."[41] And many have rightly argued that the best way to understand that dominion is through the language of stewardship.

At the heart of interpreting the above texts is our understanding of the words "rule" or "have dominion" (*radah*) and "subdue" (*kavash*). The best way to understand these terms is through various Old Testament texts admonishing kings to rule with justice and righteousness (Deut. 17:18–20; 1 Kings 10:9; Ps. 72:1–6). "If we look to the description of God's ideal king in the Old Testament as our guide, we find that the king is meant to rule [*radah*] as a first among equals, and as one whose rule is first and foremost for the benefit of those under his care. He is not to use his position selfishly to accumulate things for himself." Such an understanding, then, "makes impossible any interpretation of *dominion* in Genesis 1:26–28 as *domination* . . . , that we may use [creatures] or the rest of creation however we like."[42] The word "subdue" (*kavash*) carries the notion of bringing something under control through significant effort and thus "indicates that hard work will be required if human beings are to rule in the earth as God intends."[43] This understanding of a stewardly care is reinforced in Genesis 2, where the man and (later) the woman are placed "in the Garden of Eden to work it and take care of it" (v. 15). This admonition for the care of Eden is symbolic of the care of the whole

41. Colin E. Gunton, *The Triune Creator: A Historical and Systematic Study*, Edinburgh Studies in Constructive Theology (Grand Rapids: Eerdmans, 1998), 211.

42. Moo and Moo, *Creation Care*, 78, 79.

43. Moo and Moo, *Creation Care*, 77.

earth. Sandra Richter summarizes this stewardly care this way: "Whereas the ongoing flourishing of the created order is dependent on the sovereignty of the Creator, it is the privilege and responsibility of the Creator's stewards . . . to facilitate this ideal plan by ruling in his stead. . . . Like any vassal who has been offered a land grant by his suzerain, humanity is commanded to 'take possession' of this vast universe per the instruction of his sovereign Lord." As a result, Richter argues, "We rule as he would rule. We are stewards, not kings."[44]

This stewardship and care of creation is further reinforced by several other biblical teachings. In the Genesis account, after the Creator gives humans the privilege to use "every seed-bearing plant" and "fruit with seed" for food (1:29), he reminds them of his provision for animals (v. 30). Thus, God provides through his creation resources for both humans and creatures, implying that human stewardship should not destroy the divine resources for the rest of nature, which have built-in mechanisms of reproduction (i.e., seeds). In addition to this, we must remember in our stewardship that the earth does not belong to us, is not only for our use, and is never for our selfish use. Numerous texts reiterate God's ultimate ownership, implying that human rule is a stewardship, not an ultimate ownership.

> All the earth is mine. (Exod. 19:5 ESV)
>
> The earth is the LORD's and all that is in it,
> the world, and those who live in it. (Ps. 24:1 NRSV)
>
> Every animal of the forest is mine,
> and the cattle on a thousand hills.
> I know every bird in the mountains,
> and the insects in the fields are mine. . . .
> For the world is mine, and all that is in it. (Ps. 50:10–12)
>
> The earth is the Lord's, and everything in it. (1 Cor. 10:26)

The Mandate to Procreate

Along with the stewardship of God's good earth, humanity is given a divine mandate to procreate and bring children into the world: "God blessed them, and God said to them, 'Be fruitful and multiply, and fill the earth'" (Gen. 1:28 NRSV). A few verses earlier, the very same reproductive mandate is given to the animal world (v. 22). This raises an interesting quandary when discussing creation care, because many environmentalists see population control as a necessary vehicle to an environmental ethic. Some radical environmentalists stigmatize bringing children into the world, and some seek mandatory

44. Sandra L. Richter, *Stewards of Eden: What Scripture Says about the Environment and Why It Matters* (Downers Grove, IL: IVP Academic, 2020), 11.

controls or highly incentivized methods, ranging from more accessible contraceptives to abortion to overbearing governmental regulations. This was attempted in China's one-child policy, which was enforced by steep taxation and has now been rescinded. Population control is sought because increased populations require greater natural resources and inevitably impact global warming through increased technology and fossil-fuel utilization.

How should we respond to this dilemma? Here is an example of a need to hold in creative tension two ethical mandates: the procreation mandate and the stewardship of the earth's resources. The procreation mandate does not mean we should have as many children as possible, and the mandate is compatible with family planning, which I believe can include ethical uses of contraceptives.[45] The motivation for such family planning can never be a negative view toward children, but rather a stewardship of the couple's personal resources and a stewardship of God's good creation. It must always uphold the biblical teaching that children are a marvelous gift of God (see, e.g., Ps. 127:3; Matt. 19:13–14). When it comes to population control, too often the debates are driven by ideologies, with significant exaggeration on both sides. Biocentrists, with radical views on population control, frequently overlook the creative human initiatives that can find ways to grow more food without adverse effects on the environment and new forms of technology that can mitigate pollution and global warming. Meanwhile, anthropocentrists frequently overlook the realities of population growth's impact on the environment and overaccentuate human freedom. Amid the debates, numerous developed countries in the world are facing a potential economic crisis regarding underpopulation, in that they are not producing enough children for employment needs or for funding pension or retirement programs. Hence, both the procreation mandate and the creation-care mandate must be affirmed, with great wisdom for living them out.

A Theocentric Foundation for Creation Care: The Rest of Scripture

As we have seen frequently in our journey so far, creation themes are pervasive throughout the Bible. The same stewardship care we find in the Genesis creation story is affirmed in various places and contexts, either directly or by implication.

Creation Care in Old Testament Laws

Following the exodus, God leads his people into a promised land and gives them his law, and therein are clear mandates for protecting God's good

45. See Dennis P. Hollinger, "The Ethics of Contraception: A Theological Assessment," *Journal of the Evangelical Theological Society* 56, no. 4 (2013): 683–96.

creation. Part of the law's stipulation is the protection of the land, for the land belongs to God. "It is a land the LORD your God cares for; the eyes of the LORD your God are continually on it from the beginning of the year to its end" (Deut. 11:12). As a result, "Canaan was a land grant, distributed to the tribes,"[46] so that if they kept the Lord's commands, they would flourish in the land; but if they violated the commands, they would be uprooted from it and experience judgment (11:16–17; 28:38–42). The law has built-in mechanisms for sustainable agriculture, as the Sabbath laws protect the land and provide for the poor:

> For six years you shall sow your fields, and for six years you shall prune your vineyard and gather in its fruits, but in the seventh year there shall be a Sabbath of solemn rest for the land, a Sabbath to the LORD. You shall not sow your field or prune your vineyard. You shall not reap what grows of itself in your harvest, or gather the grapes of your undressed vine. It shall be a year of solemn rest for the land. The Sabbath of the land shall provide food for you, for yourself and for your male and female slaves and for your hired servant and the sojourner who lives with you, and for your cattle and for the wild animals that are in your land. (Lev. 25:3–7 ESV)

The Exodus version adds, "Then the poor among your people may get food from [the land], and the wild animals may eat what is left" (23:11). The Deuteronomic law even lays forth a prohibition of cutting down an enemy's trees in warfare: "When you besiege a city for a long time, making war against it in order to take it, you shall not destroy its trees by wielding an ax against them. . . . You shall not cut them down" (Deut. 20:19 ESV). The next verse makes clear that such trees were fruit trees, which take significant time to grow in the Middle East.

But not only did the law protect fields and organic life; there were protections of animal life. The Sabbath rest (Exod. 20:8), patterned after God's own rest at creation, is extended not only to humans but to their animals. Deuteronomy 22:6 says, "If you come across a bird's nest beside the road, either in a tree or on the ground, and the mother is sitting on the young or on the eggs, do not take the mother with the young. You may take the young, but be sure to let the mother go, so that it may go well with you and you may have a long life." Richter notes, "God's people were certainly allowed to slaughter and eat the animals they raised, but any domestic animal had to be taken before the priest first. According to Leviticus 17, this practice ensured that the animal's *nephesh* (its life) had been considered. . . . Deuteronomic law required that even the wild gazelle be slaughtered with due care (Deut. 12:15, 22; 14:5; 15:22)."[47] And the Moos summarize how the

46. Richter, *Stewards of Eden*, 15.
47. Richter, *Stewards of Eden*, 41.

blood of slain animals is to be handled: "The blood is never to be consumed, and the blood of slain animals is to be poured out and covered with earth, because it represents the life of the animal (Lev. 17:10–14; Deut. 12:23–25). So significant was this stipulation . . . that it remained in force for the early church . . . (Acts 15:19–20, 29)."[48]

Clearly, the laws given to the Hebrew people have protections for the care of God's good earth. Unfortunately, the principles undergirding these specific laws have been ignored by most Christians in the world today. The strategies for stewardship may change according to context, but the underlying principles are still normative.

The Grandeur and Beauty of God's Creation

Scripture frequently points to the grandeur and beauty of creation as reflecting the glory of God, "for whom and through whom everything exists" (Heb. 2:10). This stands in contrast to the anthropocentric model, which states that the earth exists to serve humanity. Isaiah the prophet echoes great praise with his words "Holy, holy, holy is the LORD Almighty; the whole earth is full of his glory" (Isa. 6:3), though one scholar suggests on the basis of the grammar a translation of "The fulness of all the earth is his glory."[49] Psalm 104 eloquently portrays the grandeur and beauty of creation, so that human response must be simultaneous praise to God and care for its beauty and grandeur. A few verses will have to suffice:

> Praise the LORD, my soul.
>
> LORD my God, you are very great;
> you are clothed with splendor and majesty.
>
> The LORD wraps himself in light as with a garment;
> he stretches out the heavens like a tent
> and lays the beams of his upper chamber on their waters.
> He makes the clouds his chariot
> and rides on the wings of the wind. . . .
>
> He makes grass grow for the cattle,
> and plants for people to cultivate—
> bringing forth food from the earth:
> wine that gladdens human hearts,
> oil to make their faces shine,
> and bread that sustains their hearts.
> The trees of the LORD are well watered,
> the cedars of Lebanon that he planted.

48. Moo and Moo, *Creation Care*, 93.

49. Hilary F. Marlow, *Biblical Prophets and Contemporary Environmental Ethics: Re-reading Amos, Hosea, and First Isaiah* (Oxford: Oxford University Press, 2009), 237.

> There the birds make their nests;
> the stork has its home in the junipers.
> The high mountains belong to the wild goats;
> the crags are a refuge for the hyrax. . . .
>
> How many are your works, LORD!
> In wisdom you made them all;
> the earth is full of your creatures. (vv. 1–3, 14–18, 24)

In similar fashion Job 38–41 is a magnificent tour of God's majestic creation, after Job's rounds with his friends, including his own attempt to justify himself. It begins with the Lord questioning Job:

> Where were you when I laid the earth's foundation?
> Tell me, if you understand.
> Who marked off its dimension? Surely you know!
> Who stretched a measuring line across it? . . .
>
> Who shut up the sea behind doors
> when it burst forth from the womb,
> when I made the clouds its garment
> and wrapped it in thick darkness,
> when I fixed limits for it
> and set its doors and bars in place. . . .
>
> Have you entered the storehouses of the snow
> or seen the storehouses of the hail,
> which I reserve for times of trouble,
> for days of war and battle? . . .
> Who cuts a channel for the torrents of rain,
> and a path for the thunderstorm,
> to water a land where no one lives,
> an uninhabited desert,
> to satisfy a desolate wasteland
> and make it sprout with grass? (38:4–5, 8–10, 22–23, 25–27)

The beauty and grandeur of God's good creation call for its care.

Jesus and the Created World

As noted earlier, Jesus affirms this good world by entering it in the incarnation, the very reality that so troubled Gnosticism. The incarnation is one of the most salient dimensions of a theocentric approach to creation care. Some scholars have also taken Jesus's experience of temptation in the wilderness as an affirmation of what is to come regarding nature in the eschaton. "And the Spirit immediately drove him out into the wilderness. He was in the wilderness forty days, tempted by Satan; and he was with the wild beasts;

and the angels waited on him" (Mark 1:12–13 NRSV). Richard Bauckham suggests that this brief allusion to the wild animals is likely pointing to the peaceable kingdom foreseen by the prophet Isaiah, in which "the wolf will live with the lamb, the leopard will lie down with the goat, the calf and the lion and the yearling together; and a little child will lead them" (Isa. 11:6; cf. 65:25).[50] Though parts of nature in this fallen world are ferocious and threatening to each other and humanity,[51] this good creation will one day be restored and renewed; and our care for God's creation now points to that eschatological reality.

Jesus also affirms creation stewardship in his teaching about the natural world. In his guidance about the futility of anxiety, Jesus says, "Look at the birds of the air; they neither sow nor reap nor gather into barns, and yet your heavenly Father feeds them. Are you not of more value than they?" (Matt. 6:26 NRSV). Here Jesus, in contrast to some biocentrists, clearly affirms that humanity has greater value than nature, and yet God cares for nature, and we learn from his created world. He then adds, "Consider the lilies of the field, how they grow; they neither toil nor spin, yet I tell you, even Solomon in all his glory was not clothed like one of these" (6:28–29 NRSV). "Followers of Jesus are here told to look at the natural world, to appreciate its beauty, and to draw conclusions from it—about the nature of the God who created it and what our response should be."[52] Thus, Jesus's love for his own magnificent creation calls us to be stewards of it.

Eschatological Texts

Clearly all of nature groans deeply amid this fallen world, but from both the Old and New Testaments, we are taught that a healing restoration of that groaning world is coming. As the apostle Paul puts it, "For the creation waits in eager expectation for the children of God to be revealed. . . . The creation itself will be liberated from its bondage to decay and brought into the freedom and glory of the children of God. We know that the whole creation has been groaning as in the pains of childbirth right up to the present time" (Rom. 8:19, 21–22). But as Paul says in the following verses, "If we hope for what we do not yet have, we wait for it patiently" (v. 25). The hope is for "a new heaven and a new earth" (Rev. 21:1 NRSV), which is best understood as a renewed heaven and earth, based on the meaning of the word "new" that is used here. Thus, in Revelation 21:5—"I am making all things new" (NRSV)—the meaning is

50. Richard Bauckham, *The Bible and Ecology: Rediscovering the Community of Creation*, Sarum Theological Lectures (Waco: Baylor University Press, 2010), 126–28.

51. This does not preclude the fact that prehistoric animals were ferocious and threatening to each other, but the fall evidently exacerbated the threats, which will be ameliorated in some fashion in the final, peaceable kingdom.

52. Moo and Moo, *Creation Care*, 121.

not "I am making new things. Making everything new rather suggests the renewal of what exists, not its replacement with something else."[53]

There are, of course, interpretations of the eschaton that expect an eradication of this earth, based on texts such as 2 Peter 3:10–11: "But the day of the Lord will come like a thief. The heavens will disappear with a roar; the elements will be destroyed by fire, and the earth and everything done in it will be laid bare. Since everything will be destroyed in this way, what kind of people ought you to be? You ought to live holy and godly lives." If one takes this text as teaching an annihilation of this created world, we might easily ask, "Why should we care for it?" Needless to say, this text has engendered numerous interpretations and much controversy. But a good case can be made that Peter is utilizing language of judgment rather than annihilation with his terms "destroyed," "fire," and "laid bare." Earlier in the same chapter, Peter refers to Noah and the flood using similar terms. Thus, as Doug and Jonathan Moo contend, "as the parallel with the flood suggests, Peter is predicting that God will 'destroy' this world by judging evil, establishing justice and peace, and radically transforming the creation into a place where 'righteousness makes its home,' reflecting God's original intentions for it from the beginning."[54] Thus, Rikk Watts writes, "the final goal is not the destruction of creation but rather the unification of heaven and earth such that the renewed earth itself becomes Yahweh's throne room. We are not going to heaven. Heaven is coming here."[55]

If God created this good world, has given us the mandate of stewardship, and is one day going to restore this groaning world back to his intended creation, we are called, as Peter says, "to live holy and godly lives" (2 Pet. 3:11), and part of that holiness is a stewardship of all he places in our hands. And that includes care for his creation.

Caring for God's Creation: Strategies for Stewardship

Facing the many environmental issues of our world today calls for personal strategies, institutional strategies, and public policy strategies. It is important to recognize that the strategies employed are not the moral absolutes and have not been given to us in Holy Scripture. Ethical norms are absolutes, but strategies are relative. Part of how we respond to the crises of our age will depend on empirical readings of the situation at hand, and frequently, empirical readings are unfortunately motivated more by social or political

53. Moo and Moo, *Creation Care*, 163.

54. Moo and Moo, *Creation Care*, 161.

55. Rikk E. Watts, "The New Exodus/New Creational Restoration of the Image of God: A Biblical-Theological Perspective on Salvation," in *What Does It Mean to Be Saved? Broadening Evangelical Horizons of Salvation*, ed. John G. Stackhouse Jr. (Grand Rapids: Baker Academic, 2002), 36.

ideology than by objectivity. As Christians committed to truth, we ought to seek the truth about environmental realities, recognizing, of course, that there are competing readings of the various issues. Few of us are experts in the respective fields, so it calls for wisdom and for humility.

When it comes to creation care and ethics in general, new legalisms can easily develop that can be every bit as deceptive as the old legalisms in Christianity a couple of generations ago. For example, some Christians and others have made purchasing and drinking fair-trade coffee an absolute and the only ethical pattern for coffee consumers. Even though one usually pays more for the fair-trade certification, the contention is that fair-trade coffees are more environmentally friendly and provide more just and adequate pay for poorer coffee growers and workers than the coffees produced by larger corporations. However, while the concept of fair trade is a laudable one, various studies have demonstrated that the impact is not what many consumers think. One major study out of London concludes, "What did surprise us is how wages are typically lower, and on the whole conditions worse, for workers in areas with Fairtrade organisations than for those in other areas."[56] I mention this not to degrade fair-trade coffee but to guard against legalisms that easily develop and can mislead.

Today numerous environmental issues call for wise and caring responses. Frequently the issues are interrelated or have impacts on other dimensions of the environment. Here are just some of the issues:

- *Pollution* of air, water, and land (e.g., hazardous waste, oil spills) can cause serious health concerns and destruction of nonhuman life.
- *Nonrenewable resources* are resources we only get once, such as fossil fuels (petroleum, coal, and natural gas) and land minerals. We cannot renew these natural resources, and thus the development of new technologies (e.g., hybrid and electric cars, solar and wind energy) is an important step in stewarding these resources and protecting the environment.
- *Renewable resources* are things that can be used repeatedly and are naturally replaced. This can involve the destruction of land and forests, which can be renewed; but this takes significant time. The destruction of these resources negatively impacts other environmentally significant areas and can contribute to greater poverty.
- *Species depletion*, which can impact the ecosystems and destroy the beauty of God's creation, has been exacerbated by humans. Similarly, humans have engaged in overly harsh treatment of animals in

56. Christopher Cramer, "Harsh Truths Are Necessary If Fairtrade Is to Change the Lives of the Very Poor," The Guardian, May 24, 2014, https://www.theguardian.com/global-development/2014/may/24/harsh-truths-are-necessary-fairtrade.

preparation for their slaughter and then human consumption. Included here is also the significant loss of fish in the oceans in recent years due to overfishing and the pollution of the oceans.

- *Global warming* involves the warming of the earth, with various dire consequences caused by greenhouse gases that trap heat in the lower atmosphere. The gases come in part from the carbon dioxide that emanates from fossil fuels humans use in industry and automobiles. The warming contributes to deleterious weather patterns, flooding, and forest fires, causing significant economic and human loss. It has the potential to wipe out portions of countries and millions of people. While climate instability has been the norm throughout the earth's long history, "science shows with reasonable certainty that increased greenhouse gas emissions along with several other anthropogenic factors are the primary causes of the global warming trend."[57]
- *Ecosystem destruction* involves damage to the intricate link between the various parts of our environment: land, water, animals, and plants. When ecobalance is damaged, other parts severely suffer.

This is a much-too-brief overview of just some of the issues faced today in God's good creation.

Our response to the issues is not motivated just by environmental need or human impact, but rather by the facts that this is God's good world and that he has given us the task of stewarding it well for the Creator's glory. Creation care is also a way of loving our neighbors, for environmental damage has significant impact on fellow humans. "It is obvious that a person's surroundings will have a huge impact on their well-being. The polluted air that plagues so many of our modern cities has an obvious, negative [effect] on the people who have to breathe it every day. The harsh realities of the ecological crisis we now face force us to recognize that it is impossible truly to love others without caring for the environment in which they live."[58]

Our response to the crises will involve several levels. First, it will involve personal responses that include our own habits, such as wise consumption, eating, purchasing, and recycling. We frequently may feel that our own personal responses don't make much difference, but they reflect our own faithfulness to God, and when large numbers practice creation care, it makes a difference. Second are institutional responses from churches, Christian institutions, and businesses. Wise utilization of energy and adoption of new energy forms, such as solar energy, are not only good stewardship practices;

57. Hugh Ross, *Weathering Climate Change: A Fresh Approach* (Covina, CA: Reasons to Believe, 2020), 42. In this work Ross, an astrophysicist in background, shows that there have been patterns of global warming and cooling throughout the earth's history, but clearly in our contemporary situations, human factors have resulted in a critical situation.

58. Moo and Moo, *Creation Care*, 186.

they also send a significant sign to members and constituents of what creation care can look like.

And then finally are the public policy approaches in various levels of government, from local to state or provincial to federal. Christians should advocate for wise and just policies that are not primarily defined by political party or ideology but seek to bring together people from across the political spectrum. Public policy judgments often involve complexity and even conflicting moral goods, such as a conflict between economic flourishing and environmental health. Policy measures that focus only or even primarily on economic realities can do great damage to the environment, but policies that focus only or primarily on environmental realities can have negative impacts on people's jobs and engender greater poverty. We will always need great discernment based on objective renderings of the situations and options, with clear ethical commitments to keep both economic flourishing and environmental flourishing in a healthy tension. In addition we should be open to newly emerging technologies that have potential for improving the environmental challenges before us. For example, some have lauded the potential of thorium nuclear reactors, which would be safer and pose less risk than traditional uranium and plutonium nuclear reactors.[59]

Conclusion

Creation care is not an ancillary dimension of our Christian faith. We are called to stewardship in many spheres of life, including material goods, money, personal gifts, and the environment. Our stewardship of God's good world arises from the creation story and is reinforced by other biblical texts and theological reflection. A theocentric approach to creation care emphasizes that the earth is the Lord's, that humans are part of nature and yet distinct from it, that the physical world is a good world, and that we are to steward the natural world to meet human need and give glory to its Maker. This stands in contrast to anthropocentric models, which emphasize the natural world as primarily a resource to serve humans, with a "dominion" perspective that frequently leads to dominance. But it also stands in contrast to biocentric models, which frequently see little difference between human beings and the rest of nature.

Creation care is part of the ethical responsibility of Christians. It is rooted in the creation paradigms, considers the fallenness of this world, and is reaffirmed by both redemption and the final restoration. To neglect our stewardship of creation has the potential to imperil our world and ourselves. But more importantly, such neglect is an affront to our Maker, who calls us to care for his good world.

59. Vincent Roose, "Thorium—a Gamechanger for Future Energy Supply?," Warp News, November 30, 2021, https://www.warpnews.org/energy/thorium-a-gamechanger-for-future-energy-supply/.

5

Created for Relationship (1)

Sexuality, Marriage, Sex, and Family

From the beginning the triune God creates humans for relationship, both with himself and with others. The first time something in the creation story is said to not be good occurs in Genesis 2:18: "It is not good that the man should be alone; I will make him a helper as his partner" (NRSV). God does not create a self-sufficient, autonomous humanity; rather, he creates humans to emerge, develop, and flourish in specific forms and with particular designs given by the Creator. Relationship with God is essential, but to be truly human, one also needs human relationships. As we see in both Genesis 1 and 2, God institutes sexuality, marriage, physical intimacy, and family as the means through which humans are born and then develop to carry out the God-given cultural mandates (such as creation care and work) and hopefully come to know the God who creates and redeems. God creates his creatures as male and female, and the very first command given to them is to have sex: "God blessed them, and God said to them, 'Be fruitful and multiply, and fill the earth'" (1:28 NRSV).

The paradigms for these themes emerge clearly in the Genesis story and then are affirmed throughout the rest of Holy Scripture, including by Jesus. Though marriage and family have been expressed in various forms throughout different cultures, and though male and female roles will take on different patterns throughout history, God ordains from the beginning paradigms that both honor the Creator and enable the best possible way for humans to live. The pertinent Genesis texts for this chapter are as follows:

> So God created humankind in his image,
> in the image of God he created them;
> male and female he created them.
>
> God blessed them, and God said to them, "Be fruitful and multiply, and fill the earth." (1:27–28 NRSV)
>
> It is not good that the man should be alone. (2:18 NRSV)
>
> And the rib that the LORD God had taken from the man he made into a woman and brought her to the man. Then the man said,
> "This at last is bone of my bones
> and flesh of my flesh;
> this one shall be called Woman,
> for out of Man this one was taken."
> Therefore a man leaves his father and his mother and clings to his wife, and they become one flesh. And the man and his wife were both naked, and were not ashamed. (vv. 22–25 NRSV)

Yes, the fall will play havoc with these designs, which will then call for love and pastoral care when the paradigms are broken. But creation's norms are not eradicated by cultural norms or human desires, drives, or self-defined identities. We also recognize that marriage and family are not the only institutions designed by God, and though all humans come from a gamete union of a man and a woman, not all will enter into marriage, thus forming a new family. But all are relational and will need interaction with others in family settings, friendships, and, yes, the church.[1] Singleness is compatible with God's specific designs. Moreover, as we will see in the next chapter, our relationality or sociality requires other institutions in society to enable human flourishing. These include economic institutions, educational institutions, associations, and even the state. These are implied forms of relationality in Genesis 1 and 2 and should not supplant the first forms of relationality, which are explicit and to which we now turn. Marriage and family form the most foundational and important institutions in societies, for from them come new human life, socialization, and support for navigating the challenging terrains of life.

When we dealt with humans being created in the image of God and hence having intrinsic dignity, the focus tended to be a bit more on the individualized side of human life, though we did note the relational dimension to the image. But now we focus more explicitly on humans being intrinsically relational in nature, thus finding their greatest fulfillments and ethical obligations in

1. For a helpful analysis of the importance and role of friendship, see Wesley Hill, *Spiritual Friendship: Finding Love in the Church as a Celibate Gay Christian* (Grand Rapids: Brazos, 2015).

relationship. This becomes increasingly difficult in atomized Western cultures, in which the human self is understood and operates from an "expressive individualism," as various cultural analysts have dubbed it. Such an understanding "begins with the premise that the fundamental unit of human reality is the individual person, considered as separate and distinct from the manner in which he is or is not embedded in a web of social relations." With expressive individualism, the "vision of personhood understands human flourishing as the pursuit of projects of one's own invention and choosing."[2] Ethics and foundational relationships are defined by an "unencumbered self,"[3] in which there are no intrinsic norms, essences, or obligations, only the atomized human will standing alone. Self-actualization becomes the ethical norm as many turn from an external moral authority to an internal, therapeutic one.

What follows in the next two chapters stands in stark contrast to this individualism, which, of course, has a long history, particularly in American culture but also in other Western cultures. The commitment to a relational self does not absolutize or deify all institutions, including marriage and family. Indeed, the fall has impacted all of them. Some have at times become deeply oppressive. But if a Christian ethic is inherently creational, then redemption and kingdom are not abdications of those foundational relationships but a strengthening and enabling of them to accomplish the purposes for which God created them.

Created with Sexuality: Male and Female

"In the image of God he created them; male and female he created them" (Gen. 1:27 NRSV). When Jesus is questioned by the religious leaders of his day about divorce, he quotes this creational paradigm: "Have you not read that the one who made them at the beginning 'made them male and female' . . . ?" (Matt. 19:4 NRSV). Thus, in the creational design, "all human community is centered around the community of man and woman. This is described in two phrases which look first only to the community of man and woman, and then in a broader sense to all human community."[4] Sexuality is pervasive in some form throughout God's creation—from animals to plant life—for the seed-bearing plants and fruit-bearing trees imply the sexual and reproductive nature of plant life (Gen. 1:11–12). Moreover, the command to "be fruitful

2. O. Carter Snead, *What It Means to Be Human: The Case for the Body in Public Bioethics* (Cambridge, MA: Harvard University Press, 2020), 69, 79. Expressive individualism is analyzed by a group of scholars and cultural analysts, including Robert Bellah, Charles Taylor, Alasdair MacIntyre, Michael Sandel, and Carter Snead.

3. Michael J. Sandel, "The Procedural Republic and the Unencumbered Self," *Political Theory* 12, no. 1 (1984): 86.

4. Claus Westermann, *Genesis 1–11: A Commentary*, trans. John J. Scullion, Continental Commentaries (Minneapolis: Augsburg, 1984), 227.

and multiply" (v. 22 NRSV) is given to animals before it is given to humans. The sexuality of animal life is reaffirmed in the flood story, as male and female "came to Noah and entered the ark, as God had commanded" (7:9). The animals enter the ark two by two in conjunction with their sexuality, and following the flood, God commands, "Bring out every kind of living creature that is with you—the birds, the animals, and all the creatures that move along the ground—so they can multiply on the earth and be fruitful and increase in number on it" (8:17)—a clear reference back to Genesis 1.

Though we know from science that there are varying forms of sexuality in the natural world, including the plant world,[5] the creation paradigm is a twofold way of being human—male and female. While particular relational roles, beyond the reproductive role, will vary over time, the ontological distinction of male and female remains. The human reproductive system "is the only bodily system that requires two people (no more, no less) to fulfill its natural function. They are not just any two people, but a male and a female."[6] This twofold, relational way of being human is reaffirmed in the Old Testament law, for in Deuteronomy 22:5 we read that "a woman shall not wear a man's apparel, nor shall a man put on a woman's garment; for whoever does such things is abhorrent to the LORD your God" (NRSV). This law does not tell us what constitutes male or female clothing, for that is highly dependent on given cultures. Rather, it is a stipulation that the twofold ontological reality of male and female is to be upheld. It is the paradigm of God's design, and the "abhorrent" language sets it apart from other laws, such as those dealing with mixed seed or mixed types of cloth.

In the creational paradigm of Genesis 1–2, we do not find specific roles for the male and female other than their reproductive roles. Moreover, there is no hint in these chapters of one sex being subservient to the other, for power differentials only come in the broken relational alienation of the fall: "Your desire shall be for your husband, and he shall rule over you" (3:16 NRSV). Rather, we have implied physiological differences that enable life to continue, and we know from science that there are other differences that are salient in medicine, education, and mutual understanding between the sexes.

> We know that, biologically speaking, women and men have different chromosomal make-ups, different hormones (or more accurately, different amounts of the same gender-related hormones), and secondary sex characteristics that chromosomes and hormones produce. We also know that major illnesses such

5. See, for example, W. P. Armstrong, "Plant Sexuality and Political Correctness," Wayne's Word, last modified May 7, 2015, http://www.waynesword.net/ww0404.htm. We also know that a small number of animals reproduce without the introduction of a male sperm—a process called *parthenogenesis*.

6. Keith D. Stanglin, *Ethics beyond Rules: How Christ's Call to Love Informs Our Moral Choices* (Grand Rapids: Zondervan Reflective, 2021), 86.

> as lung cancer, osteoporosis, and heart disease require different medical treatments for women and for men. We know that brain-imaging technologies show differences in the responses of women and men to external stimulations of all sorts, even though brain responses along gender lines frequently do not seem to represent gender differences in behavior.[7]

Recent studies also reveal that "women are twice as likely as men to experience clinical depression in their lifetimes. . . . Men are twice as likely to become alcoholic or drug-dependent, and 40 percent more likely to develop schizophrenia. Boys' dyslexia rate is perhaps 10 times that of girls, and they're four or five times as likely to get a diagnosis of autism spectrum disorder." During the past two decades, "there's been a sea change as new technologies have generated a growing pile of evidence that there are inherent differences in how men's and women's brains are wired and how they work. Not how well they work, mind you. Our differences don't mean one sex or the other is better or smarter or more deserving."[8] These broad differences between the sexes can help us more fully experience the kinds of relationships God intends in marriages, friendships, the church, and societal life together. And they do evidence distinctions between male and female, for "God created male and female in the image of God—and God intended male and female to work together as the image of God in the service of God."[9]

In this fallen world, the male-female paradigm as the twofold way of being faces some challenges. On the one hand, in a small number of cases some people experience an intersex condition in which there are either chromosomal, hormonal, genital, or gonad anomalies. Intersex includes over forty different conditions, such as Klinefelter's syndrome, Turner's syndrome, congenital adrenal hyperplasia, and various forms of ambiguous genitalia. For example, in Klinefelter's syndrome a male is born with an extra X chromosome resulting in an XXY arrangement that can lead to low levels of testosterone and delayed puberty. It is difficult to give an exact number of persons with intersex conditions because there is not always agreement as to what is truly "intersex," and some advocacy groups tend to exaggerate the numbers. One recent study finds that the number of births with ambiguous genitalia is about one per one thousand.[10] There has also been controversy over the

7. Margaret A. Farley, *Just Love: A Framework for Christian Sexual Ethics* (New York: Continuum, 2006), 146.

8. Bruce Goldman, "Two Minds: The Cognitive Differences between Men and Women," *Stanford Medicine Magazine*, May 22, 2017, https://stanmed.stanford.edu/2017spring/how-mens-and-womens-brains-are-different.html.

9. Darrin W. Snyder Belousek, *Marriage, Scripture, and the Church: Theological Discernment on the Question of Same-Sex Union* (Grand Rapids: Baker Academic, 2021), 36.

10. Robert Preidt, "About 1 in 1,000 Babies Born 'Intersex,' Study Finds," HealthDay, May 3, 2019, https://consumer.healthday.com/women-s-health-information-34/birth-health-news-61/about-1-in-1-000-babies-born-intersex-study-finds-745441.html.

best medical response to these conditions, and some advocates argue against binary (male-female) sexuality with an appeal to intersex conditions. But as Emi Koyama, the founder of the Intersex Initiative in Portland, Oregon, notes, "most people born with intersex conditions do view themselves as belonging to one binary sex or another. They simply see themselves as a man (or a woman) with a birth condition like any other."[11]

The second challenge to the male-female binary has been gender dysphoria and the transgender movement. According to the American Psychiatric Association (APA), *transgender* is viewed by some as an outdated term, but the APA defines it as "an umbrella term for persons whose gender identity, gender expression or behavior does not conform to that typically associated with the sex to which they were assigned at birth."[12] The clinical term is *gender dysphoria*, and the APA's *Diagnostic and Statistical Manual of Mental Disorders* (*DSM-5*) defines "gender dysphoria in adolescents and adults as a marked incongruence between one's experienced/expressed gender and their assigned gender, lasting at least 6 months, as manifested by at least two [conditions]"—with a list of characteristics that focus primarily on the distress one feels as a result of the incongruence.[13] The clinical definitions distinguish *gender identity* and *gender expression* and emphasize that not all transgender persons experience gender dysphoria. There have been various forms of intervention for transgender persons, ranging from counseling (to cope with one's dysphoria); social transition (coming out and sometimes taking on a new name, wardrobe, etc.); puberty blockers (to prevent the normal process of maturation and development); cross-sex hormones (to develop certain gender characteristics); and sex-reassignment surgery (a removal or augmentation of certain sex-related body parts). *DSM-5*, from 2013, estimates that somewhere between 0.005 and 0.014 percent of adult males, and between 0.002 and 0.003 percent of adult females experience gender dysphoria,[14] but because this data is based on those seeking treatment, others believe the numbers are higher.

11. Emi Koyama, "From 'Intersex' to 'DSD': Toward a Queer Disability Politics of Gender," Intersex Initiative, accessed September 29, 2021, http://www.intersexinitiative.org/articles/intersextodsd.html. Part of my overview and analysis is drawn from James K. Beilby and Paul Rhodes Eddy, eds., *Understanding Transgender Identities: Four Views* (Grand Rapids: Baker Academic, 2019), 16–17. For a Christian advocate who tends to deconstruct the normative male-female binary because of intersex conditions, see Megan K. DeFranza, *Sex Difference in Christian Theology: Male, Female, and Intersex in the Image of God* (Grand Rapids: Eerdmans, 2015).

12. "Transgender People, Gender Identity and Gender Expression," American Psychological Association, accessed December 20, 2021, www.apa.org/topics/lgbtq/transgender.

13. "What Is Gender Dysphoria?," American Psychiatric Association, accessed December 20, 2021, www.psychiatry.org/patients-families/gender-dysphoria/what-is-gender-dysphoria.

14. American Psychiatric Association, *Diagnostic and Statistical Manual of Mental Disorders*, 5th ed. (Washington, DC: American Psychiatric Association, 2013), 454.

There have been a wide range of terms employed related to the transgender movement and experience, such as the following:

- *Bigender*—a person's identity is a combination of male and female
- *Gender diverse*—those who do not adhere to societal expectations regarding gender identity
- *Gender fluid*—those who view their experience as shifting and thus manifest it in various ways
- *Gender queer*—a person's gender identity that is neither male nor female, and thus a combination of various genders
- *Transsexual*—one who seeks to change their primary or secondary sex characteristics through medical interventions[15]

With all of these variations, it seems clear, as Mark Yarhouse and Julia Sadusky describe it, that "the West in recent years has witnessed a remarkable shift from viewing such experiences in terms of mental health and morality to viewing them as signs of an independent people group and culture to be celebrated." Furthermore, they note, "this psychiatric identity was replaced over time by a political identity, which ultimately became a public identity."[16] This politicization is no doubt what led the American Association of Pediatricians (AAP) to reject an "outdated watchful waiting" approach with children and youth and instead "facilitate exploration of complicated emotions and gender-diverse expressions while allowing questions and concerns to be raised in a supportive environment."[17] But many theorists question the AAP's approach because of significant numbers of adolescents who desist in their gender identity crisis and resolve to their physiological sex identity. Clinical psychologist James Cantor takes issue with the AAP policy, noting that it overlooks eleven major studies of children with gender dysphoria, in which the majority in every study "ceased to want to transition."[18] This and other research indicates how politicized the issue has become, and frequently what passes as "pure science" is biased ideological constructs.

So given the realities of today, how do we assess gender dysphoria and the transgender movement from a creational-paradigm framework? I find it helpful in such matters (and this would include all LGBTQ discussions)

15. Mark Yarhouse and Julia Sadusky, *Emerging Gender Identities: Understanding the Diverse Experiences of Today's Youth* (Grand Rapids: Brazos, 2020), 7–10.

16. Yarhouse and Sadusky, *Emerging Gender Identities*, 5, 14.

17. Jason Rafferty, "Ensuring Comprehensive Care and Support for Transgender and Gender-Diverse Children and Adolescents," *Pediatrics* 142, no. 4 (2018): 4.

18. James Cantor, "American Academy of Pediatrics Policy and Trans-kids: Fact-Checking," *Sexology Today*, October 17, 2018, 1.

to distinguish three elements that are frequently confused: Christian ethics, pastoral care, and public policy. Christian ethics is the designs of God for all ethical issues, rooted in a Christian worldview, and dependent on biblical authority. It is a high and holy calling for believers, and in the matter of sexuality a Christian ethic affirms what the creation story and Jesus uphold—God "created them male and female" (Mark 10:6 NASB).

But second, there is pastoral care—the love, understanding, empathy, and care for persons limping toward and struggling with God's designs. Here the brokenness of a fallen world meets face-to-face with the creation ethic. Because intersex conditions and gender dysphoria reflect the "groaning" (Rom. 8:22) of creation in a fallen world—much like addiction issues, depression, and anger management—we recognize that attaining God's designs may not be easy. Full healing awaits the eschaton. But we ought not reduce Christian ethics to pastoral care and ought not reduce pastoral care to Christian ethics, though the two must be in constant dialogue. Perhaps persons who struggle with chronic depression can serve as a helpful analogy, though not a perfect one. People experiencing chronic depression frequently struggle to reach consistent joy, a fruit of the Spirit (Gal. 5:22). But the struggle doesn't negate the norm of joy as a fruit of the Spirit, and the person can know by God's grace the full assurance of forgiveness, looking forward to the ultimate healing when God's creation is finally and fully restored in the eschaton. Struggles in sexuality are somewhat similar. And this calls the church to deep love, empathy, and understanding, while simultaneously embracing the ethical norm rooted in creation.

Third, there is public policy—the laws and policies of a society or community that attempt to ensure rights and responsibilities. Here we recognize a clear difference between a Christian ethic and what can be achieved in a society, particularly a pluralistic one. Christians, based on God's creation of humans in his image, must affirm the dignity and therefore the rights of all humans, whatever their sexual identity or orientation. But we should recognize there is a difference between a right to do something and the right thing to do. When protecting the rights of transgender individuals, schools and communities also need to protect the rights of all individuals who might be impacted.[19] And it must be remembered that protecting rights always includes some limitations and responsibilities.

Despite the fallenness and struggles of our broken world, God's design remains clear and is the paradigm for engaging our struggles: "In the image of God he created them; male and female he created them" (Gen. 1:27 NRSV).

19. Here the matter of bathrooms and locker rooms come to mind, as it would no doubt create great harm to have an eleven-year-old transgender female with a penis shower with the other adolescent girls. In this area some transgender radicals push for policies and practices that could endanger others. But there are wise solutions that can protect the rights of all, such as distinct bathrooms for transgender individuals.

Marriage

After creating humans male and female and in his image, God establishes marriage, which serves as the bedrock for the social institution of the family. Genesis 1 hints at marriage with the command to "be fruitful and multiply" (v. 28 NRSV), but it is further elucidated in Genesis 2. Sensing that it is not good for the man to be alone (2:18), and noticing that "no suitable helper was found" (v. 20) among the animals,

> the LORD God caused a deep sleep to fall upon the man, and he slept; then he took one of his ribs and closed up its place with flesh. And the rib that the LORD God had taken from the man he made into a woman and brought her to the man. Then the man said,
>
> "This at last is bone of my bones
> and flesh of my flesh;
> this one shall be called Woman,
> for out of Man this one was taken."
>
> Therefore a man leaves his father and his mother and clings to his wife, and they become one flesh. (vv. 21–24 NRSV)

"The creation of the woman out of the rib of the man should not be taken literally. It indicates, rather, just how closely the man and the woman belong together."[20] Moreover, the term "helper" (Heb. *'ezer*) in v. 18 cannot be taken to designate some sign of inferiority or subservience. It is often translated something like "suitable helper," but as Walter Kaiser notes, "the Hebrew word *ʿēzer* appears twenty-one times in the Old Testament, often in parallelism with words denoting 'strength' or 'power.'" He shows that the word is sometimes even used for God as our helper or strength (i.e., Deut. 33:26, 29). Thus, "what God had intended was to make her a 'power' or 'strength,' who would in every respect 'correspond to' the man, that is to be 'his equal.'"[21]

Adam is ecstatic with God's creation of his new corresponding "strength" and declares that she is bone of his bones (v. 23). What follows is then the closest we have to a definition of marriage in the Bible: "Therefore a man leaves his father and his mother and clings to his wife, and they become one flesh" (v. 24 NRSV). Essentially what is given here is a universal definition of marriage that has three elements: a change of status, a unique commitment, and sexual union, which sets the relationship apart from all others and

20. Bruce Riley Ashford and Craig G. Bartholomew, *The Doctrine of Creation: A Constructive Kuyperian Approach* (Downers Grove, IL: IVP Academic, 2020), 197.

21. Walter C. Kaiser Jr., "Correcting Caricatures: The Biblical Teaching on Women," Walter C. Kaiser Jr. (website), accessed October 12, 2021, http://www.walterckaiserjr.com/women.html. Kaiser also contends that this helps to give a different rendering to 1 Cor. 11:10, regarding the woman covering her head. It is best read, "For this reason a woman ought to have power or authority on her head."

continues human life in this world. Other biblical texts reiterate and provide greater depth to this universal definition, but this provides the overarching paradigm of the essence of marriage. This paradigmatic nature of marriage from creation is affirmed by other biblical texts, ranging from Malachi to Jesus to Paul (e.g., Mal. 2:10–16; Matt. 19:5–6; 1 Cor. 6:16; Eph. 5:31).

Change of Status

First, there is a change of status—"A man leaves his father and his mother." This does not imply a matrilocal system in which the man goes to the wife's family, for ancient Hebrew culture was patrilocal and patriarchal. Rather, the essence of the statement is that a new relationship has been established that is now recognized by families, friends, and society. The man and the woman are now in a new status together, called marriage. Their relational priorities have changed, for "beforehand his first obligations are to his parents: afterwards they are to his wife. In modern Western societies where filial duties are often ignored, this may seem a minor point to make, but in traditional societies like Israel where honoring parents is the highest human obligation next to honoring God, this remark about forsaking them is very striking."[22] Moreover, "for the husband to 'leave' was revolutionary. In effect, the force of this statement is that both are to leave—to cut loose from the ties that would encroach upon the independence and freedom of the relationship."[23] The man and the woman now form a new reality.

A change of status for the man and woman has been universal throughout history, even though it gets worked out in varying ways in particular cultures. It entails differing patterns not only for the couple but also in how parents, other family members, and the community now relate to them. Usually this has been accompanied by some sort of celebration or ritual, which marks the beginning of this new reality. Though the Christian church likely did not perform specific rituals of marriage until around the seventh or eighth centuries, the church always recognized this unique relationship and placed its blessing upon it.[24] Marriage celebrations and rituals signify that something new and important has now been established. In addition to celebrations, most societies would eventually add a legal component that recognized privileges and responsibilities (to both children and each other) in this new status.

22. Gordon J. Wenham, *Genesis 1–15*, Word Biblical Commentary 1 (Waco: Word, 1987), 71.

23. Richard M. Davidson, *Flame of Yahweh: Sexuality in the Old Testament* (Peabody, MA: Hendrickson, 2007), 44.

24. Philip Lyndon Reynolds, *Marriage in the Western Church: The Christianization of Marriage during the Patristic and Early Medieval Periods*, Supplements to Vigiliae Christianae 24 (Leiden: Brill, 2001), 318–23, 362–85. Before specific Christian marriage rituals, cultural patterns of celebration were followed with specific Christian prayers of blessing.

Commitment or Covenant

Second, marriage involves a commitment—"cleaving" (see Gen. 2:24 KJV), which essentially means "sticking to one's spouse." The ESV renders the word here as "hold fast." Marriage has always involved commitment between spouses, and in more communal cultures there is sometimes also a commitment between parents or extended family. Just as the Hebrew believers are to "be united" or "hold fast" to Yahweh (Deut. 10:20; 11:22; Josh. 23:8), so the man and woman in marriage are to hold fast to each other, connoting an abiding commitment and permanence in their relationship. In the language of traditional marriage vows, "I take you to be my wife [or husband], to have and to hold from this day forward, for better, for worse, for richer, for poorer, in sickness and in health, to love and to cherish till death us do part."

Later in Scripture this commitment is termed a *covenant*, mirroring the binding agreement God makes with his people and his people with him. When the prophet Malachi in the fifth century BC denounces both the spiritual and marital unfaithfulness of the people, he appeals to covenant: "Did not one God create us? Why do we profane the covenant of our ancestors by being unfaithful to one another? Judah has been unfaithful. . . . The LORD is the witness between you and the wife of your youth. You have been unfaithful to her, though she is your partner, the wife of your marriage covenant" (Mal. 2:10, 14). Though the language of covenant is not used, Ruth reflects that same binding agreement with her mother-in-law, Naomi, following her husband's death: "Where you go, I will go; where you lodge, I will lodge; your people shall be my people, and your God my God" (Ruth 1:16 NRSV). Ruth had made a covenant promise to her husband; in a communal culture, that frequently included the extended family.

Marriage licenses are contracts seeking to protect marriage partners and to ensure responsibility for offspring. They are, however, quite different from the biblical concept of covenant, for a contract protects one's own interests, while a covenant enables and protects the mutuality of the marital dyad. Similarly, the contemporary language of partnership connotes a contractual or cooperative relationship to achieve a mutual goal, whereas covenant is a binding promise of the heart and mind, which embodies a "holding fast" to the other that can only be broken by radical actions such as unfaithfulness, physical or emotional abuse, or desertion (Matt. 19:9; 1 Cor. 7:15).[25] Public ceremonies in which family, friends, or church members witness the vows of commitment serve as a mechanism of accountability for the couple and their

25. For a defense of abuse as a grounds for divorce, I am drawing on Wayne Grudem, "Grounds for Divorce: An Argument for Including Abuse in the Phrase 'In Such Cases' in 1 Cor. 7:15" (paper presented at the Annual Meeting of the Evangelical Theological Society, San Diego, CA, November 21, 2019). Grudem makes a convincing argument on the basis of grammar and extrabiblical sources that "in such cases" can include situations of harm and self-protection.

commitment. This "implies a devotion and an unshakable faith between humans; it connotes a permanent attraction which transcends genital union."[26]

Physical Union

The third element in marriage is the physical union consummating the other elements—"and they become one flesh" (Gen. 2:24 NRSV). The language of "one flesh" picks up on the previous verse—"bone of my bones and flesh of my flesh" (v. 23 NRSV)—and points not only to a unique kinship bond but to a sexual union that sets this relationship apart from all other relationships. Traditionally, in numerous contexts (e.g., in the USA), a marriage was not a marriage until it was consummated in the physical union of the man and the woman. An annulment could and still can in some jurisdictions be granted if there is no consummation.

Though the term "one flesh" certainly points beyond the physical union to emotional and spiritual oneness, these other elements are encapsuled and symbolized by the sexual union. Thus, when the prophet Malachi challenges the marital and spiritual unfaithfulness of the Hebrew people, he writes, "Has not the one God made you? You belong to him in body and spirit" (Mal. 2:15). Paul uses the phrase "one flesh" explicitly in relationship to sexual intercourse when speaking of a man going to a prostitute: "Do you not know that whoever is united to a prostitute becomes one body with her? For it is said, 'The two shall be one flesh'" (1 Cor. 6:16 NRSV). Thus, when a person engages in sexual intercourse outside of marriage, they have engaged in a life-uniting act without life-uniting intent, for physical intimacy unites two into one. It is the crowning act of the marriage. Therefore, the ongoing physical intimacy of the husband and wife in marriage is a continual sign and reminder to each other of their set-apart relationship, into which no one else may enter in the same manner.

The Significance of Marriage

The significance of marriage is evidenced by its centrality within the creation narrative. It is also affirmed by Jesus in both action and teaching. Jesus chooses to perform his first miracle, turning water into wine, at a wedding, thereby giving his blessing to this creational design. John writes, "This, the first of his signs, Jesus did at Cana in Galilee, and manifested his glory. And his disciples believed in him" (John 2:11 ESV). As to his teaching, Jesus is one day asked by the Pharisees about his take on divorce. Rather than first responding to the divorce question on their terms, Jesus affirms the significance of marriage by quoting from both Genesis 1 and 2: "Because of your hardness

26. Raymond F. Collins, "The Bible and Sexuality," *Biblical Theology Bulletin* 7, no. 4 (1977): 153.

of heart [Moses] wrote this commandment [regarding divorce] for you. But from the beginning of creation, 'God made them male and female.' 'For this reason a man shall leave his father and mother and be joined to his wife, and the two shall become one flesh.' So they are no longer two, but one flesh. Therefore what God has joined together, let no one separate" (Mark 10:5–9 NRSV; cf. Matt. 19:1–9). In addition to quoting the creation paradigm, Jesus uses marriage and wedding language to describe his mission and kingdom. "Jesus comes as the 'bridegroom' to seek his 'bride' (Mark 2:19–20; John 3:29); Jesus calls us to quickly accept the invitation to, and come prepared in proper clothing for, his 'wedding banquet' (Matt. 22:1–14); Jesus admonishes us to eagerly anticipate and vigilantly await his coming as the 'bridegroom' to his 'wedding banquet' (Matt. 25:1–13)."[27]

Other New Testament writings utilize similar language, giving significance to marriage. Paul compares the union of Christ and his church with marriage between a man and a woman and quotes Genesis 2:24 in doing so: "We are members of his body. For this reason a man will leave his father and mother and be joined to his wife, and the two will become one flesh" (Eph. 5:30–31 NRSV). And the book of Revelation portrays the final union of believers with the triune God as a joyous, royal wedding: "'Let us rejoice and exult and give him the glory, for the marriage of the Lamb has come, and his Bride has made herself ready; it was granted her to clothe herself with fine linen, bright and pure'—for the fine linen is the righteous deeds of the saints. . . . 'Blessed are those who are invited to the marriage supper of the Lamb'" (19:7–9 ESV). In the following chapters, the nuptial imagery continues as John, conveying his vision, writes, "I saw the holy city, new Jerusalem, coming down out of heaven from God, prepared as a bride adorned for her husband" (21:2 ESV).

It is precisely texts like these that help explain Jesus's statement that in the coming kingdom the saints "will neither marry nor be given in marriage" (Luke 20:35). Marriage is a wonderful and significant gift of God for this age, but it pales in comparison to the marriage of the Lamb and the union of believers with the triune God, of which marriage is a sign pointing to the ultimate union. Moreover, one significant aspect of marriage—namely, procreation—will no longer then be needed, as death will be wiped away.

Even though marriage of human beings will no longer transpire in the new heaven and the new earth, marriage remains an essential and significant union in this world. As Snyder Belousek puts it, "God ordained and blessed marriage to serve God's purpose in creation and covenant: marriage is for the companionship . . . of man and woman to generate, nurture, and instruct children, rule creation, cultivate virtue, solidify society, and remedy sin. And God designated marriage to signify God's promise of salvation."[28] The glory and significance of marriage in no way denigrates those who are single. Drawing

27. Snyder Belousek, *Marriage, Scripture, and the Church*, 44.
28. Snyder Belousek, *Marriage, Scripture, and the Church*, 31.

on various biblical texts and theological themes related to redemption, Barry Danylak argues that "Christianity is distinctive from its monotheistic sibling faiths of Judaism, Islam, and Mormonism in its affirmation of singleness. While on the one hand Christianity, like the others, affirms a high view of marriage and family and a high sexual ethic, . . . it differs from the others in distinctly affirming both singleness and marriage as something good within the new family of God."[29]

In the past, some churches have had such a focus on family and married people that singles felt left out and spiritually abandoned. But it may be that we are living in a time when we need to give even greater emphasis to marriage and families. Increasingly, Americans are turning away from marriage, for "we have put our confidence in sex but lost our faith in marriage."[30] A Pew study found that in 1990 67 percent of adults aged 25–54 were married, but by 2019 only 53 percent were married, and the numbers are shrinking around the world.[31] The birthrate in the United States has now declined for a number of years in a row, and in 2021, when "women between the ages of 18 to 49 and men between 18 and 59 who said they are not parents were asked the question . . . 'How likely is it that you will have children someday?'" only "26 percent of them said it is very likely, a six-point drop from 2018." And when asked a reason for not having children, 56 percent said, "It's because [we] just don't want them."[32] This is not only leading to severe labor shortages and strains on pension plans, but in places like Japan it is leading to significant loneliness, especially in the face of aging and death. In addition it is exacerbating selfishness since people are not having to learn to share and give of themselves to others, something children naturally require of parents.

Moreover, in the United States 40 percent of children are born outside of marriage.[33] In the Netherlands, Denmark, Sweden, and Portugal more than half of births are outside of marriage, and in France the number is 60 percent.[34]

29. Barry Danylak, *Redeeming Singleness: How the Storyline of Scripture Affirms the Single Life* (Wheaton: Crossway, 2010), 213.

30. Jonathan Grant, *Divine Sex: A Compelling Vision for Christian Relationships in a Hypersexualized Age* (Grand Rapids: Brazos, 2015), 16.

31. Richard Fry and Kim Parker, "Rising Share of U.S. Adults Are Living without a Spouse or Partner," Pew Research Center, October 25, 2021, https://www.pewresearch.org/social-trends/2021/10/05/rising-share-of-u-s-adults-are-living-without-a-spouse-or-partner/.

32. Annabelle Timsit, "More Americans Not Planning to Have a Child," *Charlotte Observer*, November 22, 2021, 6A.

33. Elizabeth Wildsmith, Jennifer Manlove, and Elizabeth Cook, "Dramatic Increase in the Proportion of Births Outside of Marriage in the United States from 1990 to 2016," Child Trends, August 8, 2018, https://www.childtrends.org/publications/dramatic-increase-in-percentage-of-births-outside-marriage-among-whites-hispanics-and-women-with-higher-education-levels.

34. Steve Doughty, "More Babies Are Now Born Outside Wedlock than to Married Couples in Eight EU Countries, Figures Reveal," *Daily Mail*, last updated August 10, 2018, https://www.dailymail.co.uk/news/article-6049223/More-babies-born-outside-wedlock-married-couples-EU-figures-reveal.html.

This frequently leads to single-parent situations, which have dire impacts on the flourishing of children and hence upon society as a whole. "Children are significantly more likely to avoid poverty and prison, and graduate from college, if they are raised in an intact two-parent family."[35]

Some revisionists seek to affirm alternatives to the creation paradigm of marriage by arguing that in Scripture God sometimes accommodates variant patterns, such as polygamy, divorce, levirate marriages, and near-kin marriages. Thus goes the argument: we should be open to accommodating variants today, such as same-sex marriage or even polyamorous relationships (having intimate relations with more than one partner with mutual consent). In some cases in the Old Testament, there are case laws to adjudicate existing situations (e.g., Exod. 21:2–11) and stipulations to control the results of living contrary to God's designs, such as with a certificate of divorce (Deut. 24:1–4). But as Jesus notes, this is because of the hardness of the Hebrew people's hearts, and it deviates from the creation paradigm (Mark 10:5–9). "Some cultural variations in marriage appear neutral with respect to the creational pattern. Whether marrying involves a wife joining her husband's household, or a husband joining his wife's household, or husband and wife establishing an independent household, each practice may be compatible with the creational pattern." Moreover, we can, I believe, affirm that "egalitarian marriage, as a variety of man-woman monogamy, aligns with the creational pattern; but same-sex union, by its very constitution, deviates from the creational pattern."[36]

God's design in creation, affirmed by Jesus, is that marriage between a man and a woman is not only the Christian ethical norm but the best means for human procreation, socialization, and growth into a flourishing adulthood.

Physical Intimacy (Sex)

In creation God designs that physical intimacy be lodged in a very particular relationship, marriage between two persons of the opposite sex.

35. W. Bradford Wilcox, Wendy Wang, and Ian Rowe, "Less Poverty, Less Prison, More College: What Two Parents Mean for Black and White Children," Institute for Family Studies, June 17, 2021, https://ifstudies.org/blog/less-poverty-less-prison-more-college-what-two-parents-mean-for-black-and-white-children. Some critics argue that family structure is less consequential for Black children, but this study shows that while there are differences in the ratios in poverty, college graduation, and incarceration with Black children, growing up with two biological parents is a major factor in avoiding poverty and incarceration and graduating from college for Blacks and whites alike. For example, "black children in homes headed by single parents are about 3.5 times more likely to be living in poverty compared to black children living with two parents in a first marriage" (under "Family Structure and Black Child Outcomes").

36. Snyder Belousek, *Marriage, Scripture, and the Church*, 172, 173.

> So God created humankind in his image,
> in the image of God he created them;
> male and female he created them.
>
> God blessed them, and God said to them, "Be fruitful and multiply." (Gen. 1:27–28 NRSV)

> And they become one flesh. And the man and his wife were both naked, and were not ashamed. (2:24–25 NRSV)

> [Jesus] answered, "Have you not read that the one who made them at the beginning 'made them male and female,' and said, 'For this reason a man shall leave his father and mother and be joined to his wife, and the two shall become one flesh'? So they are no longer two, but one flesh." (Matt. 19:4–6 NRSV)

This is the creational paradigm for physical intimacy.

As we saw in chapter 2, the physical union between man and woman in marriage is one of the realities pronounced good by the Creator. Contrary to misleading cultural influences that have denigrated the physical and embodied realm in Christian history, God gives a positive affirmation to sex, marriage, and the begetting of children: "God saw everything that he had made, and behold, it was very good" (Gen. 1:31 ESV). But the goodness of this gift is frequently isolated from a divine telos, or very specific purposes, which define the meaning of sex. An ethically legitimate sexual relationship is in the context of five primary purposes of this good gift.[37]

Consummation of a Marriage

First, as noted above, sex is given to consummate a marriage, as the two people become one flesh. Sex completes the other elements of a marriage, thereby setting this relationship apart from all other relationships. Spouses may share various activities and resources with friends and colleagues, including time, money, and wisdom. But only in the marriage covenant are spouses to share their bodies. The consummation of the marriage through sexual intercourse brings together not just the couple's bodies but the whole of their being. Authentic sex incorporates the whole person. The contemporary reduction of sex to a mere physical or emotional act belies the biblical meaning of the one-flesh union. "'One body' union denotes something more than the temporary union of two physical bodies in sexual intercourse. It refers to a real and ontological corporate reality created by the sexual union of two unified persons."[38]

37. For a more detailed analysis of these purposes, see Dennis P. Hollinger, *The Meaning of Sex: Christian Ethics and the Moral Life* (Grand Rapids: Baker Academic, 2009), 93–115.

38. S. Aaron Son, "Implications of Paul's 'One Flesh' Concept for His Understanding of the Nature of Man," *Bulletin for Biblical Research* 11, no. 1 (2001): 119.

While the language of "one flesh" is from Scripture, humans intuitively sense that physical intimacy has a profound effect on themselves and a relationship. When even secularists speak of their "partner" having sex with someone else, they frequently say, "They cheated on me." This reflects the natural understanding of the profundity of the physical union in setting a relationship apart from all other relationships. This is reinforced by physical dimensions in that the release of hormones in sexual intercourse is a bonding agent that demonstrates the natural reality of being one flesh. As ethicist Lewis Smedes once put it, "It is the final physical intimacy. Two bodies are never closer: penetration has the mystique of union, and the orgasmic finale is the exploding climax of one person's abandonment to another, the most fierce and yet most sensitive experience of trust."[39] Every sexual act after the initial consummation is an ongoing affirmation of the couple's oneness and set-apartness. This physical oneness is also affirmed by the language of "knowing," used at times in Scripture to convey sexual intercourse (Gen. 4:1, 17; 1 Sam. 1:19). This is not a factual knowing but a deeply personal, emotional, and even spiritual knowing that makes a couple's relationship distinct from all other human interactions. Sex consummates the marriage and is then a continual reminder of the couple's complete bond.

Procreation

The second purpose of God's good gift of sex is procreation: "God blessed them. And God said to them, 'Be fruitful and multiply'" (Gen. 1:28 ESV). Scripture continually affirms the good gift of children, for as the psalmist puts it, "Children are a heritage from the LORD, offspring a reward from him" (Ps. 127:3). Proverbs 17:6 states, "Children's children are a crown to the aged, and parents are the pride of their children." Jesus strongly affirms children when, in contrast to his disciples, he places hands on them and prays for them and says, "Let the little children come to me, and do not hinder them, for the kingdom of heaven belongs to such as these" (Matt. 19:14). If the creation mandate regarding procreation is not merely descriptive of what frequently happens or a command to just Adam and Eve but is paradigmatic, then we must understand procreation as an intrinsic part of sexual relationships. Does this mean that every sexual act must intend to procreate or that every couple must have children?

We can say several things to guide us ethically about the necessity of procreation. First, a legitimate sexual act is one that is in the context of procreation, meaning that the act by its nature is procreative, thus precluding same-sex unions, which by their very nature are nonprocreative. Some may argue, "But isn't sexual intercourse with an infertile couple or a couple past childbearing

39. Lewis B. Smedes, *Sex for Christians: The Limits and Liberties of Sexual Living*, rev. ed. (Grand Rapids: Eerdmans, 1994), 112.

age nonprocreative?" It is true that in these situations procreation will not result from their physical intimacy, but the very nature of their sexual act is procreative in that it is between a man and a woman, which is the only way procreation occurs. "A same-sex couple, even were the partners desiring of children, could not enter marriage aiming to generate offspring by their sexual union, because same-sex intercourse is inherently unfit to that end."[40] Some who affirm same-sex relations argue that the Genesis 2 account of marriage does not include procreation and that Jesus never mentions procreation per se, and thus procreation is incidental to marriage.[41] But it needs to be noted that Jesus, in his discussion of marriage (Matt. 19:4–6), quotes from both Genesis 1 ("made them male and female") and Genesis 2, thus implying the procreative element. Moreover, arguments from silence can be dangerous, for Jesus never addresses many issues we deem important, and "all parties to the marriage debates of Jesus' day, on account of Genesis, would have agreed that marriage and procreation go hand in hand."[42] If Jesus affirmed sex as nonprocreative or affirmed same-sex unions, he would have had to explicitly go against the Jewish consensus of his day. As for the Genesis 2 account not including procreation, some scholars have argued that the assertion that "no suitable helper was found" (v. 20) actually implies a physiological complementarity that could produce offspring.[43]

Second, sex in the context of procreation means that only couples who have married and thus are ready to assume the responsibility of children can morally engage sexually. And even if a married couple in their physical intimacy is not aiming to have children, they must be willing to assume the potential fruit that can come from the act. In this sense their sexual intercourse is in the context of procreation, meaning they are in a position to bear the potential responsibility that is inherent within sexual intimacy, even if not intending to have children. Most unmarried couples having sex are usually not in a position to assume the potential fruit inherent in sexual intercourse.

Third, being married and thus in the context of procreation, couples may wisely use family planning, including ethically legitimate contraceptives, to steward their marital resources and calling. I personally agree with the official stance of the Roman Catholic Church that sex is inherently procreative. But I believe that contraceptives can be utilized within a framework that accepts the procreative nature of sex. Contraceptives that do not destroy nascent life or harm the mother or the relationship can be affirmed as a stewardship of

40. Snyder Belousek, *Marriage, Scripture, and the Church*, 127.

41. See, for example, the arguments of Robert Song, *Covenant and Calling: Towards a Theology of Same-Sex Relationships* (London: SCM, 2014), 27–28, 49; and James V. Brownson, *Bible, Gender, Sexuality: Reframing the Church's Debate on Same-Sex Relationships* (Grand Rapids: Eerdmans, 2013), 110–26.

42. Snyder Belousek, *Marriage, Scripture, and the Church*, 129.

43. See, for example, Brian Neil Patterson, "Does Genesis 2 Support Same-Sex Marriage? An Evangelical Response," *Journal of the Evangelical Theological Society* 60, no. 4 (2017): 681–96.

the couple's life together. After all, the creation mandate, "Be fruitful and multiply" (Gen. 1:28 ESV), is given in the context of stewarding the rest of God's natural creation, implying some intervention and control relative to nature. The Roman Catholic Church allows for natural means in family planning, just not contraceptives. But just as contraception is making a human decision to steward and control, so family planning methods are making a human decision to steward and control. The ethical defense of contraceptives is further bolstered by the multiple purposes of sex, as I am outlining.[44]

Fourth, the procreation mandate can allow for the use of some assisted reproductive technologies within the context and confines of a couple's one-flesh union. With approximately 10–15 percent of all American couples experiencing challenges of infertility,[45] the market for these technologies is quite significant. They include artificial insemination (by the husband or by a donor), in vitro fertilization (bringing the sperm and ovum together in a petri dish), surrogate arrangements, and potentially cloning. There are two primary ethical principles to guide. First, the gametes must be from the husband and the wife, thus keeping procreation, marriage, and the one-flesh relationship together as a whole. Artificial insemination with a donor, surrogacy, cloning, and at times in vitro fertilization all separate procreation from the one-flesh covenant bond. Ethicist Gil Meilaender puts it well: "A child who is . . . begotten, not made, embodies the union of his father and mother. They have not simply reproduced themselves, nor are they merely a cause of which the child is an effect. Rather, the power of their mutual love has given rise to another who . . . manifests in his person the love that unites them."[46] The second ethical principle to guide in reproductive technologies is the preservation of human life. With in vitro fertilization, clinics frequently produce far more embryos than will be implanted in the mother's uterus, leading to either a freezing of those embryos or a destruction of them. My advice to couples contemplating the use of this technique is to find clinics and doctors who will work with them in protecting human life by fertilizing fewer embryos and then utilizing all of them, even if it lessens the potential of pregnancy. There is sometimes a cost to faithful, ethical discipleship.

An Expression of Love

The third purpose of sex is an expression of love between the marriage partners. Even in eras when institutional marriages prevailed over companionship

44. For an in-depth discussion of these arguments, see Dennis P. Hollinger, "The Ethics of Contraception: A Theological Assessment," *Journal of the Evangelical Theological Society* 56, no. 4 (2013): 683–96.

45. "Infertility," Mayo Clinic, September 1, 2021, https://www.mayoclinic.org/diseases-conditions/infertility/symptoms-causes/syc-20354317.

46. Gilbert Meilaender, *Bioethics: A Primer for Christians*, 3rd ed. (Grand Rapids: Eerdmans, 2013), 15.

marriages, love was present. And even where marriages are arranged by family or friends rather than couples falling in love and getting married, love can and should develop and grow over time. In marriage, couples show love to each other in myriad ways: listening, caring, spending time, giving gifts, showing patience, and performing gestures that are welcomed by the marital partner. But deep love between husband and wife yearns to show that love and covenant commitment physically. Though love is not mentioned in the Genesis accounts, it is quite prevalent in other parts of Scripture, including one whole book in the Old Testament, the Song of Songs.

We tend to think of Christian love as primarily *agapē* love, an unselfish love that seeks the good of the other rather than the good of self, and that is frequently set over against *erōs* love. But "the Bible does not teach that *agapē* supplants erotic love. But it does teach . . . that the erotic finds fulfillment only in the context of *agapē*. So the test of love in marriage, according to Paul, is the *agapē* relationship between Christ and the church (Eph. 5:22–23). While *erōs* responds to something lovable, *agapē* creates and sustains lovableness."[47] Thus, sexual love in a marriage is part of unselfish *agapē* love. While there have been varying interpretations of the Song of Songs, clearly it exudes with sensual love, which, to be consistent with the rest of Scripture, must be marital love.

> As an apple tree among the trees of the forest,
> so is my beloved among the young men.
> With great delight I sat in his shadow,
> and his fruit was sweet to my taste.
> He brought me to the banqueting house,
> and his banner over me was love.
> Sustain me with raisins;
> refresh me with apples,
> for I am sick with love.
> His left hand is under my head,
> and his right hand embraces me! (2:3–6 ESV)
>
> Set me as a seal upon your heart,
> as a seal upon your arm,
> for love is strong as death,
> jealousy is fierce as the grave. . . .
> Many waters cannot quench love,
> neither can floods drown it. (8:6–7 ESV)

In God's good gift of sex, a married couple is mutually saying to each other, "I love you."

47. David H. Field, "Sexuality," in *New Dictionary of Theology*, ed. Sinclair B. Ferguson, David F. Wright, and J. I. Packer (Downers Grove, IL: IVP Academic, 1988), 639.

Pleasure

For some it may seem odd to include pleasure as part of the divine telos of sex, for it is frequently portrayed as antithetical to Christian holiness. But pleasure is not the invention of the devil, and as C. S. Lewis in *Screwtape Letters* has one of the demons put it in describing God, "He's a hedonist at heart. . . . At His right hand are 'pleasures for ever more.'"[48] As we've noted earlier, God's pronouncement of goodness in the creation story is primarily about material and physical realities, including many that bring pleasure to the eye or the body: trees, plants, fruit, sun, moon, seas, animals, and marital partners with sexuality. Whereas the eternal pleasures—those rooted in a transcendent God—are ultimate, the other pleasures are good gifts of God that point to the ultimate and eternal pleasures. The apostle Paul tells early believers in the face of false teachers who denied such pleasure, "They forbid people to marry and order them to abstain from certain foods, which God created to be received with thanksgiving by those who believe and who know the truth. For everything God created is good, and nothing is to be rejected if it is received with thanksgiving" (1 Tim. 4:3–4). Physical intimacy is among those good gifts, including its pleasure dimension.

In the Song of Songs, the man says to his lover,

> How delightful is your love, my sister, my bride!
>   How much more pleasing is your love than wine,
> and the fragrance of your perfume
>   more than any spice!
> Your lips drop sweetness as the honeycomb, my bride;
>   milk and honey are under your tongue.
> The fragrance of your garments
>   is like the fragrance of Lebanon.
> You are a garden locked up, my sister, my bride;
>   you are a spring enclosed, a sealed fountain.
> Your plants are an orchard of pomegranates
>   with choice fruits,
>   with henna and nard,
>   nard and saffron,
>   calamus and cinnamon. (4:10–14)

And the woman, finding pleasure with her lover, says,

> His cheeks are like beds of spice
>   yielding perfume.
> His lips are like lilies
>   dripping with myrrh. . . .

48. C. S. Lewis, *The Screwtape Letters* (New York: MacMillan, 1962), 101.

His mouth is sweetness itself;
he is altogether lovely.
This is my beloved, this is my friend. (5:13, 16)

Proverbs 5 warns of the dangers of adultery and enticements to unfaithfulness. When encouraging sexual fidelity, the wise teacher says, "May your fountain be blessed, and may you rejoice in the wife of your youth. A loving doe, a graceful deer—may her breasts satisfy you always, may you ever be intoxicated with her love" (vv. 18–19). In addition to these biblical affirmations, we also know that God has created the male and female with bodily parts that serve no other function than pleasure in physical intimacy—for the male the glans penis and for the female the clitoris. Pleasure is indeed part of God's plan, though it is never to be isolated from the other divine purposes.

A Spiritual Sign and Nurturant

While sex is an intensely physical act, it is also a spiritual act, pointing to God's love for us, flowing from the divine love within the Holy Trinity. When a married couple is sharing together in physical intimacy, it should for Christian believers be an act of spiritual intimacy that nurtures and deepens their relationship with God. "God made us as sexual beings—as men and women with a desire for union—precisely to tell the story of his love for us. In the biblical view, the fulfillment of love between the sexes is a great foreshadowing of . . . the infinite bliss and ecstasy that awaits us in heaven."[49] While the first four purposes of sex can be understood by all humans apart from special revelation, this purpose is part of an explicitly Christian understanding, perceived only through Scripture and realized through the work of the Holy Spirit.

In Ephesians 5 Paul makes explicit the link between marital one-flesh love and Christ's love and care for the church. The text begins with an admonition to mutual submission: "Submit to one another out of reverence for Christ" (v. 21). He then guides husbands and wives in living out this mutual submission in light of specific needs and challenges of each: wives submitting to their husbands (v. 22) and husbands loving their wives as Christ loved the church (vv. 25–27) and as they love their own bodies (vv. 28–29). In verse 31 Paul then moves to the creation paradigm of Genesis 2:24: "Therefore a man shall leave his father and mother and hold fast to his wife, and the two shall become one flesh" (ESV). He ends this section with the link between marital love and Christ's love: "This is a profound mystery—but I am talking about Christ and the church" (v. 32). Thus, the physical love in marriage is a sign of Christ's love for the church.

49. Christopher West, *Fill These Hearts: God, Sex, and the Universal Longing* (New York: Image, 2012), 11. West's writings are attempts to make accessible Pope John Paul II's material on the theology of the body.

By implication the marital physical union that points to our ultimate union with the triune God is a spiritual nurturant. If it points to and embodies in human form God's love for us, it means that our own love for God can and should be enriched through physical intimacy in a marriage.

These five purposes of physical intimacy are intended by God to be held together and not isolated from each other. This can only happen in a marriage between a man and a woman.

Family

The result of sexuality, marriage, and physical intimacy is the bedrock institution of society, the family. While other social institutions, as we will observe in the next chapter, are essential to human flourishing and our life together, the family is the foundation. Jesus expands the notion of family to fellow believers, as the church becomes a new family. One day, when Jesus is speaking to a crowd, his mother and siblings are outside, desiring to speak to him. Informed of this, he replies, "'Who is my mother, and who are my brothers?' And stretching out his hand toward his disciples, he said, 'Here are my mother and my brothers! For whoever does the will of my Father in heaven is my brother and sister and mother'" (Matt. 12:48–50 ESV). Jesus is in no way denigrating or downplaying the significance of his family, for even at the cross he acknowledges his mother's significance and ensures her future care. "Near the cross of Jesus stood his mother. . . . When Jesus saw his mother there, and the disciple whom he loved [i.e., John] standing nearby, he said to her, 'Woman, here is your son,' and to the disciple, 'Here is your mother.' From that time on, this disciple took her into his home" (John 19:25–27). Jesus expands the notion of family, but without minimizing the significance and role of our natural families, which the triune Godhead designed at creation.

In the creation account of Genesis, God ordains marriage, and we see the outcome in the following chapters as the first marital dyad turns into a family with children. "Adam made love to his wife Eve, and she became pregnant and gave birth to Cain. She said, 'With the help of the Lord I have brought forth a man.' Later she gave birth to his brother Abel" (4:1–2). As a result of the fall in chapter 3, this initial family becomes conflictual, and Cain kills Abel. But this is not the fault of the family as an institution. Rather, it is the fault of human sin that too often leads to disharmony and dysfunctional families. Perhaps a sign that families are significant is the lengthy genealogies we have both in the Old Testament and in the Gospel accounts with reference to Jesus. These genealogies have a covenantal significance in paving the way to the Messiah, but they also undergird the significance of families for individual socialization, spiritual development, and societal stability. As Herman Bavinck puts it, "A person is the product of a community and does not exist alone but has been in relation to others since even before birth. Without the mutual relationship between others we would not have existed. We are born *out of*, *in*, *with*, and *toward* various relationships. This *one* relationship of family is germinal and is the type of all the others. From the household family and its relationships stem all the others in variegated complexity."[50]

When the Hebrew people are about to enter the promised land, Moses instructs them on the spiritual significance of the family: "These are the commands, decrees and laws the LORD your God directed me to teach you to observe in the land that you are crossing the Jordan to possess, so that you, your children and their children after them may fear the LORD your God" (Deut. 6:1–2). After giving promises of the results of this family responsibility, we have the famous Shema with more detailed instruction for family spiritual development: "Hear, O Israel: The LORD our God, the LORD is one. Love the LORD your God with all your heart and with all your soul and with all your strength. These commandments that I give you today are to be on your hearts. Impress them on your children. Talk about them when you sit at home and when you walk along the road, when you lie down and when you get up" (vv. 4–7).

Though this text comprises special instruction for the covenant people, it implies a significance of the family for socialization, physical development, emotional stability, and the good of society. Without solid family units, crime runs rampant, humans lose their way, human flourishing is thwarted, and emotional and cultural chaos ensues. Even from a natural standpoint, without the spiritual element, families are central to personal development and societal stability. And God designed it that way at creation. Yuval Levin, a Jewish cultural analyst, puts it well: "The family is our first and most important institution, not only from the perspective of the history of humanity, but also . . . in the life of every individual. It is where we enter the world, literally where we alight when we depart the womb. It gives us our first impression of the world."[51]

Conclusion

Creatures made in God's image are the crown of his creation. And immediately the Creator gives these creatures, made as male and female, the task of not only caring for the earth but also establishing a cherished institution

50. Herman Bavinck, *Reformed Ethics: Created, Fallen, and Converted Humanity*, ed. John Bolt with Jessica Joustra, Nelson D. Kloosterman, Antoine Therin, and Dirk van Keulen (Grand Rapids: Baker Academic, 2019), 1:60.

51. Yuval Levin, *A Time to Build: From Family and Community to Congress and the Campus, How Recommitting to Our Institutions Can Revive the American Dream* (New York: Basic Books, 2020), 139.

that is paradigmatic for all time. The male and female, as God's design, are bonded together in a unique relationship—marriage. And one of the significant dimensions of marriage is physical intimacy—a good gift with very specific purposes, including procreation. And from that emerges family—the foundational institution for life in society. Without families, marriages, sex, and sexuality, there are no people. These gifts are skewed badly in our broken world, and many have lost trust in marriage and the family. But they are central in God's designs, and they are essential for healthy, stable, and just societies and individuals.

6

Created for Relationship (2)

Major Institutions of Society

"The LORD God said, 'It is not good for the man to be alone'" (Gen. 2:18). God created us for relationship, and our relationality is manifested in numerous social realities we term *institutions*. In the last chapter, we explored the first and foundational institution of society, the family, built from sexuality, marriage, and sex. "The institution of the family helps us see that institutions in general take shape around our needs and, if they are well shaped, can help turn those needs into capacities. They literally make virtues of necessities and forge our weaknesses and vulnerabilities into strengths and capabilities."[1] In addition to being created with relationality, we also see that social institutions are necessitated by the Creator's mandate to steward the resources of his creation, "to work it and take care of it" (Gen. 2:15). Frequently termed the *cultural mandate*, this implies that humans made in God's image are "called by God to develop all the potentialities found in nature and in humankind as a whole. [They] must seek to develop not only agriculture, horticulture, and animal husbandry, but also science, technology, and art . . . to develop a God-glorifying culture."[2] We recognize, of course, that since the fall these institutions have mostly not been God glorifying, but nonetheless they play a role in social stability and enablement as gifts of God's common grace.

1. Yuval Levin, *A Time to Build: From Family and Community to Congress and the Campus, How Recommitting to Our Institutions Can Revive the American Dream* (New York: Basic Books, 2020), 140.

2. Anthony A. Hoekema, *Created in God's Image* (Grand Rapids: Eerdmans, 1994), 14.

In this chapter we expand our created relationality beyond the family to explore various other institutions in society that can serve to enable human flourishing, even if in a fallen, broken world they can also at times be agents of oppression, injustice, and unrighteousness. We will seek to show how major social institutions can enable human virtue, societal stability, and justice and guard against their abuses, even if they fall far short of their original creational design and do not offer salvation, which comes only through Christ.

There have been numerous definitions of social institutions set forth by social scientists. Typically, "contemporary sociologists use the term to refer to complex social forms that reproduce themselves such as governments, the family, human languages, universities, hospitals, business corporations, and legal systems."[3] Jonathan Turner describes social institutions as "a complex of positions, roles, norms and values lodged in particular types of social structures and organizing relatively stable patterns of human activity with respect to fundamental problems in producing life-sustaining resources, in reproducing individuals, and in sustaining viable societal structures within a given environment."[4] An early anthropologist, Bronislaw Malinowski, focused primarily on the ways institutions function to meet critical necessities, noting universal elements such as personnel, charters (i.e., goals), norms, activities, and functions.[5] More recently Yuval Levin has defined institutions as "the durable forms of our common life. They are the frameworks and structures of what we do together."[6] Traditionally, social scientists described five major social institutions: government, economy, education, religion, and family. In recent years others have been added to the list, such as media, entertainment (including sports and arts), and sometimes health care. In this chapter we will briefly discuss most of these, contending that some institutions are directly implied in Scripture and others more indirectly. But all of them emanate from the relational dimension of our created selves.

Before exploring these social institutions and their ethical implications, we must note that institutions, particularly in the West, are highly suspect and, as some would contend, are even in crisis. Part of this stems from the expressive individualism we discussed in the last chapter. As Carl Trueman describes today's world, "We think of it much more as a case of raw material that we can manipulate by our own power to our own purposes. . . . Self-creation is a routine part of our modern social imaginary."[7] The human self

3. Seumas Miller, "Social Institutions," Stanford Encyclopedia of Philosophy, last modified April 9, 2019, https://plato.stanford.edu/entries/social-institutions/.

4. Jonathan H. Turner, *The Institutional Order: Economy, Kinship, Religion, Polity, Law, and Education in Evolutionary and Comparative Perspective* (New York: Longman, 1997), 6.

5. Bronislaw Malinowski, *A Scientific Theory of Culture, and Other Essays* (Chapel Hill: University of North Carolina Press, 1944), 71–125.

6. Levin, *Time to Build*, 17.

7. Carl R. Trueman, *The Rise and Triumph of the Modern Self: Cultural Amnesia, Expressive Individualism, and the Road to Sexual Revolution* (Wheaton: Crossway, 2020), 40, 41.

stands alone, autonomous, owing only to itself and defining itself in terms of inner impulses and imaginations. In such a world, social institutions are met with skepticism, and sometimes with outright hostility and a populist sense that the autonomous individual knows best. Levin writes, "Our age combines a populism that insists all of our institutions are rigged against the people with an identity politics that rejects institutional commitments and a celebrity culture that chafes against all structure and constraint."[8] He points to Gallup studies to bolster his claim:

- In the 1970s, 80 percent of Americans had quite favorable confidence in doctors and hospitals, but by 2018 only 36 percent did.
- In 1970, 65 percent of Americans had a "great deal" or "quite a lot" of confidence in organized religion, but it dropped to 38 percent in 2018.
- In the early 1970s, 60 percent had confidence in public schools, but by 2018 only 29 percent did.
- In 1975, shortly after Watergate, 52 percent had confidence in the presidency, but by 2018 only a third of Americans did.
- In the 1970s, 42 percent had confidence in Congress, but by 2018 only 11 percent did.
- Only the military was more trusted in 2018 than in the 1970s, up from 58 percent to 74 percent.[9]

Levin believes that the loss of confidence in our institutions and their ability to be formative in shaping character and virtue is at the heart of our current social crisis. The mood of today in public life "presents itself in bitter divisions, intractable frustrations, and an explosion of populist anger that crosses many demographic and partisan categories and seems to paralyze our system of government even as it energizes our politics."[10] Our institutions, not just politics, have moved from being formative to being performative, with autonomous individuals attempting to gain attention and power largely through an unvetted system of social media. The demise of our institutions comes from both the ideological Right and Left:

> Some, mostly on the Right, have suggested that at the core of the crisis is a collapse of family and religion—and that without these preconditions for individual flourishing we are uprooted and adrift. This would suggest our social crisis is a breakdown of tradition and moral order. Others, largely on the Left, have argued that, although simple economic measures of well-being cannot show us what is wrong, the trouble is still fundamentally material—that

8. Levin, *Time to Build*, 22–23.
9. Levin, *Time to Build*, 28–29.
10. Levin, *Time to Build*, 11.

> contemporary capitalism elevated the interests of the wealthiest above the rest, exacerbating inequality to the point that it becomes impossible for people to feel and function like equal parts of a greater whole.

As Levin sees it, these reigning diagnoses reflect the individualism of our time, failing to attend to the "structure of social life: a way to give shape, place, and purpose to the things we do together."[11]

As we reflect on our relationality in terms of social institutions from a creation-ethics standpoint, we recognize a marked difference between the kingdom of God and the kingdoms of this world. Yet if the kingdoms of this world emanate from the way God created this world and humans in it, we need to reflect on the role they play in the world and the contributions that believers as salt and light can make in various social institutions. But simultaneously we must always recognize the difference between these current realities in our fallen world and the fullness of Christ's kingdom, rooted in the designs of creation.

Religion: The Church

Along with the family, the church universal and local churches in given societies are the most important institutions to which we belong as Christians. Social scientists attend to religion as providing a framework for values, morals, and rituals that enables identity and grounding for life in society and the other social institutions. Embedded in the declaration "It is not good for the man to be alone" (Gen. 2:18) is the framework and grounding for the people of God in the Old Testament and the church since Christ. God certainly calls out individuals, like Abraham, but it is always with a view toward gathering a people under Yahweh's name and blessing the whole world in Christ: "I will make of you a great nation, and I will bless you. . . . And in you all the families of the earth shall be blessed" (12:2–3 ESV). God calls Moses to be the leader of a people who are a corporate reality, not merely a collection of autonomous individuals: "Now therefore, if you will indeed obey my voice and keep my covenant, you shall be my treasured possession among all peoples, for all the earth is mine; and you shall be to me a kingdom of priests and a holy nation" (Exod. 19:5–6 ESV). As the people are about to enter the promised land after years of wandering in the wilderness, God reminds them of his call and their identity as a people: "It was not because you were more numerous than any other people that the Lord set his heart on you and chose you—for you were the fewest of all peoples. It was because the Lord loved you and kept the oath that he swore to your ancestors, that the Lord has brought

11. Levin, *Time to Build*, 16, 17.

you out with a mighty hand, and redeemed you from . . . slavery" (Deut. 7:7–8 NRSV). Throughout the Old Testament, they are referred to as a "people."

Jesus, stating part of his mission, says, "I will build my church, and the gates of hell shall not prevail against it" (Matt. 16:18 ESV). He was calling individuals to be his disciples, but they became a community—his church. In the Great Commission, Jesus gives this mandate to his followers: "Go therefore and make disciples of all nations, baptizing them in the name of the Father and of the Son and of the Holy Spirit, teaching them to observe all that I have commanded you" (Matt. 28:19–20 ESV). This would surely incorporate institutional dimensions, such as "durable forms of our common life" and "frameworks and structures of what we do together."[12] While individuals go and make disciples, there are social forms and guidelines for how we do this, though their meaning and direction are ultimately rooted in Holy Scripture and guided by the Holy Spirit. The church is more than a mere collection of individuals, for, as Peter says, "you are a chosen people, a royal priesthood, a holy nation, God's special possession, that you may declare the praises of him who called you out of darkness into his wonderful light. Once you were not a people, but now you are the people of God" (1 Pet. 2:9–10). Under divine direction the early church appointed various leaders under the titles of elders (or bishops) and deacons and designated various gifts for the church, such as pastor-teachers. Each of these gifts carries various roles with specific qualifications, thus denoting the communal and institutional dimensions of the church.

The relational significance of the church and churches is demonstrated in the familial language used in Scripture: "brother," "sister," "children of God," "his household" (e.g., Eph. 2:19–22; 1 John 3:1). This does not nullify our biological or socializing families but is an addition to them and at times a replacement for them. In some contexts believers have been ostracized from their natural families because of their faith, and the church community fulfills many of the functions of the socializing family. In other situations believers have lost family members, or in dysfunctional families significant familial virtues and functions are absent, and the church steps in. But in all cases, the church family is to be a place of refuge, hope, comfort, and instruction for spiritual and ethical living in our world. The apostle Paul speaks of the "God of all comfort, who comforts us in all our affliction, so that we may be able to comfort those who are in any affliction, with the comfort with which we ourselves are comforted by God" (2 Cor. 1:3–4 ESV). And at the Lord's table, we not only participate with the "blood of Christ" and the "body of Christ," but "because there is one loaf, we, who are many, are one body, for we all share the one loaf" (1 Cor. 10:16–17). It is in the church, along with a believing family, that we learn the doctrines of the Christian faith, but also

12. Levin, *Time to Build*, 17.

the virtues, values, and lifestyles we are to exemplify. Moreover, it is in the church that Christian beliefs and virtues are to be embodied as both a means of spiritual development for believers and as a witness to the world around them. Furthermore, as Luke Bretherton notes, corporate "worship itself can be a means of pursuing the peace of the earthly city and mitigating its unjust and unstable social order."[13]

It is in the church community (and, yes, institution), even with all its flaws (for the church too is a fallen institution), that we learn how to navigate our way in relation to other social institutions. While these social institutions play an important societal and cultural role, they do not define the core of a Christian's life. At times economics, the state, the media, education, or entertainment can conflict with and challenge Christian patterns and beliefs. It is in the church that believers will gain knowledge, courage, and support for living out a creational-kingdom ethic that may stand in direct contrast to the mores of those institutions. It is here that they will discern with other believers the challenging task of being salt and light (Matt. 5:13–16) in a complex, fallen world. Every historical epoch and cultural context carries opposition and challenge to the Christian way of life, rooted in God's designs from creation and Christ's kingdom. Believers never discern their way or live out the path by themselves but do so only in the context of the community called the church. All of this is carried out within a community and will take on institutional characteristics for both guarding and embodying God's designs. There are, however, differences from other social institutions. "All other institutions serve good and honorable purposes at present, but they await termination at the day of Christ's return. The church, in contrast, awaits Christ's return as a day of consummation, when as the bride of Christ she will take her place at the wedding banquet of the Lamb."[14]

Education

All societies have some forms of education, which can be understood as the transmission of knowledge, values, and skills for living within a society. Education normally entails formal structures for enabling the transition from childhood to adulthood and, accordingly, includes norms about what that transition requires and how the final product should look. Beyond the primary and high school institutions are, of course, higher education institutions, including colleges, universities, and specialized vocational schools.

While formal education as a social institution is not directly addressed in Scripture, the creation paradigms provide the foundational elements that

13. Luke Bretherton, *Christ and the Common Life: Political Theology and the Case for Democracy* (Grand Rapids: Eerdmans, 2019), 225.

14. David VanDrunen, *Living in God's Two Kingdoms: A Biblical Vision for Christianity and Culture* (Wheaton: Crossway, 2010), 131.

would eventually breed and support it. Thus, by the end of the second century, Christian leaders had begun their own educational institutions in major cities such as Rome, Alexandria, and Carthage. "The schools not only were functional in forming potential leaders in the church. They were also the primary settings in which intellectual vitality was generated and influence in the culture was exerted."[15] There are a number of theological underpinnings for education. Divine revelation, as we discussed in chapter 1, assumes an ability to comprehend and reflect on God's self-disclosure, thus requiring some form of education. Being created in the image of God entails responsibilities in relation to God, others, and nature. The mandates to "fill the earth and subdue it" (Gen. 1:28 NRSV) and "to work it and take care of it" (2:15) require knowledge and skills for being faithful stewards in God's good world. Moral knowledge in keeping with God's designs as reflected in his instructions to Adam and Eve (vv. 8–17) assumes a level of reflection and discernment that is nurtured not in isolation but in relation to others and in relation to social mechanisms.

After the fall this moral discernment becomes even more significant. For believers the primary locus of moral and spiritual education is the family and the church. But as a gift of common grace to all humans, educational institutions provide knowledge for living together in society, discerning one's role in that society, and developing vocational skills. A society cannot exist without some forms of education to sustain and enrich it, whether these be traditional or alternative models. Even though educational assumptions in many cultures conflict with biblical understandings and virtues, education still plays a significant role that partially reflects the creational designs from which education emerged. Albert Wolters describes it this way: "A human being after the fall, though a travesty of humanity, is still a human being, not an animal. A humanistic school is still a school. . . . Muddled thinking is still thinking. In each case, what something in fallen creation 'still is' points to the enduring goodness of creation."[16] Or as Cornelius Plantinga Jr. puts it in describing varying forms of thought, "Some non-Christians want to care for the earth only because they tend toward materialist pantheism. Christians and Jews say, 'the earth is the Lord's.' Materialist pantheists say, 'the earth is Lord.' But ever the master of irony, God uses even the idolatrous philosophy of people who oppose him to get excellent earthkeeping out of them."[17]

But it is also this wide variety of sentiments in contemporary educational culture that sometimes raise serious quandaries and challenges for Christians.

15. James Davison Hunter, *To Change the World: The Irony, Tragedy, and Possibility of Christianity in the Late Modern World* (New York: Oxford University Press, 2010), 52.

16. Albert M. Wolters, *Creation Regained: Biblical Basics for a Reformational Worldview*, 2nd ed. (Grand Rapids: Eerdmans, 2005), 58.

17. Cornelius Plantinga Jr., *Engaging God's World: A Christian Vision of Faith, Learning, and Living* (Grand Rapids: Eerdmans, 2002), 111.

Educational institutions at all levels, especially secular ones (both public and private), are frequently inhospitable to Christian worldviews, values, and lifestyles. And some academic disciplines are at times antithetical to a Christian view of reality. For example, sociologist Christian Smith writes, "American sociology as a collective enterprise is at heart committed to the visionary project of *realizing the emancipation, equality, and moral affirmation of all human beings as autonomous, self-directing individual agents (who should be) out to live their lives as they personally so desire, by constructing their own favored identities, entering and exiting relationships as they choose, and equally enjoying the gratification of experimental, material, and bodily pleasures.*"[18] While this construal may at times be more implicit than explicit, it raises hard questions for Christians navigating their way in education. Staying in a secular or non-Christian environment holds out the possibility of deepening one's faith amid challenge and also being salt, light, and leaven in that world. At the same time, such a context can undermine deeply held beliefs and commitments, causing significant intellectual and spiritual crises. In response to this, some Christians have opted for the development of Christian institutions or home schooling at the primary and high school levels. These alternatives potentially provide an integration of faith and academics, along with more disciplined models of education, which can actually enhance learning. The downside of Christian educational institutions and home schooling is their potential separation from the world, which can then restrain fruitful patterns of life within society. Moreover, some schools and home-schooling attempts have been fueled by spurious motives, such as racism, fear, and conspiracy theories.

While contemporary educational institutions can raise hard dilemmas for believers, they also face deep divisions and major crises within. Thus, this social institution, which should enable a society to flourish, may undermine its civility, wisdom, and pursuit of true freedom. Historically universities have had three primary visions: professional development, moral activism, and a liberal education to pursue truth. These three visions are typically at odds with each other, and today's moral-activism culture tends to hold sway over the others, with an identity politics that too often renders the pursuit of truth as oppressive. "Its intensity and the aggressiveness with which it is at times enforced are distinct features of university culture at this point and contribute to the sense that the university is becoming a monoculture, closed off to some of the traditional norms and goals of academic life."[19] For the good of society, all three visions should be pursued with a healthy, creative tension. Hopefully Christians with a commitment to all three visions, fueled

18. Christian Smith, *The Sacred Project of American Sociology* (Oxford: Oxford University Press, 2014), 7–8.

19. Levin, *Time to Build*, 95.

by a deeper commitment beyond these academic cultures, can play a role in healing the divisiveness of education that contributes to societal discord.

The Media

The media is the social institution that communicates knowledge, information, and values to a broad audience outside of a formal education process. Though the term *media* did not emerge until the twentieth century, "media history takes account of the period at least from the advent of the handpress in the fifteenth century, and some interpretations include the scriptoria, oral traditions, and wall paintings of medieval times, delving occasionally into ancient and prehistory as well."[20] In the twentieth century, the media primarily consisted of newspapers, magazines, radio, and eventually television. With the decline of print media in our current world, social media has now become a driving force in the dissemination of knowledge, information, and values.

Though this social institution is essential for individuals and society, again there are biblical and theological foundations (including creational designs) for it. As we saw earlier, the phrase "and God said," which occurs throughout Genesis 1, is evidence that God communicates and speaks and, thus, knowledge and information for everyday life is essential. Human dignity stemming from creation in God's image can only be upheld with information about when and where dignity is thwarted and how we best protect dignity and justice in our world. By virtue of God's placement of Adam and Eve in the garden with a choice to obey or disobey their Maker, there is the implication that humans are decision makers and that decisions require a certain level of knowledge, though not from "the tree of the knowledge of good and evil" (Gen. 2:17; cf. 3:2–7). From a rational standpoint, in the contemporary world democracy and the rights of humans can only be maintained when there are sources of knowledge and information to enable citizens to carry out civic responsibilities such as voting and the expression of public sentiment. In a world where we purchase and sell items, making informed decisions based on advertising in the media is part of what it means to be a good steward. Some forms of media and the dissemination of information, knowledge, and values are essential to full humanity within a larger society; and the Christian brings both an affirmation of and additions to that reality.

The media have long faced challenges and ethical dilemmas. In the eighteenth century, Benjamin Franklin wrote an anonymous piece raising concerns about the power of those controlling the press. "[The press] may receive and promulgate accusations of all kinds against all persons and characters

20. Brandon Dooley, "Media and History," in *International Encyclopedia of the Social and Behavioral Sciences*, ed. Neil J. Smelser and Paul B. Baltes, 2nd ed. (Cambridge: Elsevier, 2015), 15:11.

among the citizens of the State . . . and may judge, sentence, and condemn to infamy, not only private individuals but public bodies, etc., with or without inquiry or hearing, at the court's direction."[21] At the core of the press's problems was a lack of standards and the full liberty of its writers. Freedom of the press was deemed a problem. But in the twentieth century, as World War II was coming to an end, a number of publishers and thinkers believed that the freedom of the press was being threatened and that this was a danger to democracy and an informed citizenry. A designated group was formed, and the result was the Hutchins Commission (officially known as the Commission on Freedom of the Press). Members of the commission recognized both the power of the press, with its concentration of power in large media corporations, and its potential misuse. But it rejected a breaking up of vast networks of communication as if they were corporate monopolies, for, in its own words, "the risk is considerable that the freedom of the press will be imperiled through the application of political pressure by that department."[22]

By the 1960s and following, larger media issues were recognized as coming from the use of new technologies. In 1964 Canadian communication theorist Marshall McLuhan coined the phrase "The medium is the message." He argued that the communication medium itself carried significant messages that were often greater than the intended message.[23] A classic example was from the 1960 presidential debates between Richard Nixon and John F. Kennedy. Most of those who listened to the debate by radio thought that Nixon won the debate, but most of those who watched it on television thought Kennedy, with his facial calmness and demeanor, had won the debate. Two decades later Neil Postman, an education and media theorist and cultural critic, lamented that communication technologies rather than information were shaping society and not for the better. In *Amusing Ourselves to Death*, Postman contended that ideas expressed through visual imagery were reducing the media, news, and politics to entertainment.[24] With the onslaught of social media, many critics worry that information, news, and ideas are being distorted by cheap branding, platform expression, conspiracy theories, and politicization. Google, Facebook, and Twitter "possess the ability to filter our information through complex algorithms

21. Benjamin Franklin, *The Writing of Benjamin Franklin*, ed. Albert Henry Smyth (New York: Macmillan, 1905), 10:36–40, quoted in Levin, *Time to Build*, 77.

22. Commission on Freedom of the Press, *A Free and Responsible Press: A General Report on Mass Communication; Newspapers, Radio, Motion Pictures, Magazines, and Books*, ed. Robert D. Leigh (Chicago: University of Chicago Press, 1947), 5.

23. Marshall McLuhan and Quentin Fiore, *The Medium Is the Message: An Inventory of Effects* (London: Penguin, 1967).

24. Neil Postman, *Amusing Ourselves to Death: Public Discourse in the Age of Show Business* (New York: Viking Penguin, 1985).

that can exercise enormous influence over what reaches us and under what circumstances."[25]

While newspapers historically were slanted toward a particular political party, the emergence of social media and round-the-clock news, which is extremely ideological, means that people are more isolated than ever in homogenous groups that never objectively hear the other side. From my perspective, Fox, CNN, and MSNBC should not be considered news stations; they constitute highly biased political commentary integrated into the news. And as veteran journalist Ted Koppel puts it, speaking of major national newspapers, "I think opinion belongs on the opinion page. That's why they call it the op-ed section. That's where the opinion pieces are, the columns, that's where the editorials are and that's where it belongs. I don't like seeing opinion being expressed on the front page of a great newspaper."[26] Moreover, pressure to be the first to publish a news piece has led to distortions from lack of all the facts and contexts. Upon his retirement one reporter recently lamented that trend, and a colleague has said this of him: "He will find out what happened and why it matters. More importantly, not only will he be first, he will be right."[27]

Christians in the media have a significant opportunity to shape authentic information because of their commitment to truth. Followers of Christ are committed to the truth of Scripture and the truth of the gospel, for Jesus says, "I am the way, and the truth, and the life" (John 14:6 NRSV), and "You will know the truth, and the truth will make you free" (8:32 NRSV). As those committed to the truth of the gospel, Scripture, and the truthful designs of creation, believers have the resources to bring to the media an authenticity formed not by divisive politicization but by a commitment to truth in all facets of life. Such authenticity is essential for living in a democracy but, more significantly, is a reflection of the created, relational reality in which the triune God created us.

Entertainment, Recreation, and Leisure

We tend not to think of entertainment, recreation, and leisure activities as a social institution, but when we explore the time, money, and effort put into these spheres of life, as well as their influence on humans and society, we see that they qualify. In the United States, people spend on average 5.5 hours

25. Levin, *Time to Build*, 76.

26. Ted Koppel, interview by Dan Abrams, *Dan Abrams Live*, NewsNation, January 14, 2022, https://www.newsnationnow.com/video/ted-koppel-terribly-concerned-about-modern-media-dan-abrams-live/7305564/, quoted in Rosemary Rossi, "Ted Koppel Blasts News Media for Bias against Trump: 'I Think Opinion Belongs on the Opinion Page,'" TheWrap, Yahoo Entertainment, January 15, 2022, https://www.yahoo.com/entertainment/ted-koppel-blasts-news-media-201219470.html.

27. Theoden James, "Longtime WSOC Reporter Becker Announces Retirement," *Charlotte Observer*, January 13, 2022, 5A.

per day in leisure or entertainment. The most popular daily leisure activities include the following:

- Watching TV—3.05 hours per day
- Playing games and computer use for leisure—0.62 hours
- Socializing and communicating with friends—0.54 hours
- Relaxing and thinking—0.44 hours
- Sports, exercise, and recreation—0.37 hours
- Reading—0.34 hours
- Other leisure and sports activities—0.16 hours[28]

Leisure activities vary significantly by gender, age, and country. In the United States, men spend 0.6 hours more per day in leisure than women. By age, adults over seventy-five spend the most time in leisure, and thirty-five-to-forty-four-year-olds spend the least.[29] As for European countries, Belgium leads the way with 369 minutes per day spent in leisure, followed by Norway at 368, Greece at 353, and Germany at 331.[30] Leisure, recreation, and entertainment are obviously related to economic status, and currently traditional forms of entertainment, such as festivals, drama, and music, are giving way to modern technology. Even in poor countries these days, "most villagers have access to DVDs and videos. Most small towns and large villages have video or DVD rental shops or video rooms with scheduled video shows. Even in small, remote villages without electricity, people can watch videos in a friend's house on a VCR or DVD player powered by a generator or car battery."[31]

Though the worldwide COVID-19 pandemic hit leisure tourism industries hard in 2020, $2.3 trillion was spent that year in leisure tourism, which was down 47 percent from the previous year.[32] When we turn to Hollywood economics, in 2020 the total earnings at the box office in the United States

28. "Time Spent in Leisure and Sports Activities Increased by 32 Minutes per Day in 2020," The Economics Daily, U.S. Bureau of Labor Statistics, October 1, 2021, https://www.bls.gov/opub/ted/2021/time-spent-in-leisure-and-sports-activities-increased-by-32-minutes-per-day-in-2020.htm.

29. "Men Spent 5.5 Hours per Day in Leisure Activities, Women 4.9 Hours, in 2019," The Economics Daily, U.S. Bureau of Labor Statistics, July 2, 2020, https://www.bls.gov/opub/ted/2020/men-spent-5-point-5-hours-per-day-in-leisure-activities-women-4-point-9-hours-in-2019.htm.

30. Joyce Chepkemoi, "OECD Countries That Spent the Most Time on Leisure Activities," WorldAtlas, November 14, 2018, https://www.worldatlas.com/articles/oecd-countries-that-spent-the-most-time-on-leisure-activities.html.

31. "Culture, Media, Sports and Entertainment in the Developing World," Facts and Details, last updated January 2012, https://factsanddetails.com/world/cat57/sub379/item2166.html.

32. "Leisure Tourism Spending Worldwide from 2019 to 2021," Statista, January 5, 2022, https://www.statista.com/statistics/1093335/leisure-travel-spending-worldwide/.

and Canada were $4.48 billion. In 2018 they had been $11.38 billion.[33] When we come to arts and cultural events, $1.39 billion was allotted from federal, state, and local public funding in 2019; all of this was separate from private-sector funding.[34]

In the United States, professional sports expenditures and revenues continue to increase substantially every year, often limiting access for middle- and lower-class Americans. In 2018, for example, Major League Baseball teams averaged $330 million per team in revenue, whereas player costs were $157 million per team.[35] The average National Basketball Association team is worth $1.9 billion, with the New York Knicks at the top, worth $4 billion.[36] Beyond expenditures in professional entertainment are local sports, arts, and entertainment venues. Thus, given the hours and money spent and the powerful influence this investment has on individuals and society, all of this qualifies as "durable forms of our common life" and "frameworks and structures of what we do together."[37]

There have been long debates going back to the ancient world about the definition and significance of *leisure*, which in turn usually embodied normative sentiments. Aristotle, for example, argued that leisure is not the same as play, for the latter, like occupation (i.e., work), inevitably requires exertion. "Leisure is a different matter: we think of it as having in itself intrinsic pleasure, intrinsic happiness, intrinsic felicity. Happiness of that order does not belong to those who are engaged in occupation: it belongs to those who have leisure."[38] For both Aristotle and Plato, leisure was superior to work and was essential for human flourishing and true virtue. The Western medieval world, highly influenced by the Christian church, saw leisure not as idleness or sloth (one of the seven deadly sins from which other corruptions came). Rather, as Josef Pieper affirmingly puts it, "Leisure . . . is a mental and spiritual attitude—it is not simply the result of external factors, it is not the inevitable result of spare time, a holiday, a week-end or a vacation. It is in the first place

33. "Box Office Revenue in the United States and Canada from 1980 to 2021," Statista, January 13, 2022, https://www.statista.com/statistics/187069/north-american-box-office-gross-revenue-since-1980/.

34. Ryan Stubbs and Patricia Mullaney-Loss, "Public Funding for Arts and Culture in 2019," Grantmakers in the Arts, March 2020, https://www.giarts.org/public-funding-arts-and-culture-2019.

35. Mike Ozanian and Kurt Badenhausen, "Baseball Team Values 2019: Yankees Lead League at $4.6 Billion," *Forbes*, April 10, 2019, https://www.forbes.com/sites/mikeozanian/2019/04/10/baseball-team-values-2019-yankees-lead-league-at-46-billion/?sh=4ec071e869b2.

36. Kurt Badenhausen, "NBA Team Values 2019: Knicks on Top at $4 Billion," *Forbes*, February 6, 2019, https://www.forbes.com/sites/kurtbadenhausen/2019/02/06/nba-team-values-2019-knicks-on-top-at-4-billion/?sh=3b677c5ee667.

37. Levin, *Time to Build*, 17.

38. Aristotle, *The Politics*, trans. Ernest Barker (London: Oxford University Press, 1958), 8.3, p. 336.

an attitude of mind, a condition of the soul." This, says Pieper, contrasts with work as activity, toil, or social function, for leisure is a "form of silence," a festival or celebration that is best understood as divine worship.[39]

All of this is a long way from the modern notions of leisure, recreation, and entertainment, which are typically viewed as free time from work, domestic chores, or education. It is deemed a pursuit of freedom but is more likely a form of bondage given the money, time, and exertion we put into it. As Gordon Dahl notes, "We worship our work, work at our play, and play at our worship."[40] In this world leisure is not true recreation, which should mean re-creation. It is a social institution that binds us together in stadiums, concert halls, exercise gyms, and hobby venues but tends to distort the true meaning of work and does not embody the rhythm of life God intended.

We must be clear, however, in the critiques of our times that leisure, recreation, and entertainment arise from our creation givens. In sports and bodily exercise, we affirm the creation paradigm "it is good," for as we saw, what is pronounced good is primarily material and physical. When using our bodies to play, sing, or act, we reflect the reality that we have been created "embodied souls" or "ensouled bodies" (see chap. 10), meaning that our bodies and nonbodily forms merge together as divine gifts. Moreover, when God rests on the seventh day of creation, our Maker develops a rhythm of life calling for a balance of work, play, and worship that unfolds in the biblical story with authenticity of each. The Sabbath, as we will see in chapter 8, is in part self-care, which can and should include a proper balance of work and leisure that is truly renewing of the human person. When Jesus, as a young man, grew "in wisdom and stature, and in favor with God and [people]" (Luke 2:52), we can assume that it included recreation and leisure, for he was the relational and physical being par excellence.

Economics

The economy is generally understood as the social institution that enables the production, distribution, and consumption of goods and services in a society. Throughout history there have been varying forms of economic development, ranging from hunting-gathering societies, agricultural societies, industrial societies, and now service or information societies. In some of the earlier forms, economic exchange was done through bartering, "an act of trading goods or services between two or more parties without the use of money—or a monetary medium, such as a credit card. In essence, bartering involves the

39. Josef Pieper, *Leisure: The Basis of Culture*, trans. Alexander Dru (New York: Random House, 1963), 40, 41.

40. Gordon Dahl, *Work, Play, and Worship in a Leisure-Oriented Society* (Minneapolis: Augsburg, 1972), 12.

provision of one good or service by one party in return for another good or service from another party."[41] Today, however, most economic exchange is expedited through money. In contemporary service or information societies, there is still a production and distribution of goods, but increasingly the focus is on producing and distributing services such as professional services, transportation services, investment services, health care, and media and leisure activities, as discussed above.

Early in history humans recognized that they could not produce everything needed to exist, and so they moved into a division of labor in which they depended on others for part of their existence. This was made possible by forms of trade and a market in which goods and services were broadly distributed. As time went on, this form of trade in the marketplace became even more necessary because not just individuals but whole people groups or nations needed to depend on others due to their geography or natural resources. Today, for example, "the English trade their wool to obtain Portuguese wine because England does not have a suitable climate for vineyards, and Portugal is not a good place to raise sheep."[42] Unfortunately, as markets and trade developed, some economically powerful societies recognized a shortage of human capital to do their work, and enslavement developed, which turned human beings into economic objects.

The two primary forms of economics today are market economies and controlled or command economies. "The activity in a market economy is unplanned; it is not organized by any central authority but is determined by the supply and demand of goods and services." In contrast "a command economy is organized by a centralized government that owns most, if not all, businesses and whose officials direct all the factors of production. China, North Korea, and the former Soviet Union are all examples of command economies."[43] In reality no form is exclusively one or the other, for all market economies include some form of government ownership (such as vast acres of land and national parks in the US) and intervention, and command economies increasingly include some private ownership, as exemplified by China in recent years. All forms of economy face technical and ethical challenges related to producing and distributing sufficiently—and with some semblance of freedom and justice.

Though economics has sometimes been dubbed the "dismal science" because of its challenges, its roots go back to creation design, including our being

41. Will Kenton, "Barter (or Bartering) Definition, Uses, and Example," Investopedia, last updated February 26, 2021, https://www.investopedia.com/terms/b/barter.asp.

42. Brent Waters, *Just Capitalism: A Christian Ethic of Economic Globalization* (Louisville: Westminster John Knox, 2016), 8–9.

43. Leslie Kramer, "Market Economy vs. Command Economy: What's the Difference?," Investopedia, May 29, 2021, https://www.investopedia.com/ask/answers/100314/whats-difference-between-market-economy-and-command-economy.asp.

created for relationship. The phrase "It is not good for the man to be alone" (Gen. 2:18) is clearly evident in the world of economics, for no human being can be self-sufficient in meeting the material and even many of the nonmaterial needs of life. Humans are by nature interdependent when it comes to the production, distribution, and consumption of goods and services. As we saw in chapter 2, the material realities that form economic life (e.g., land, water, vegetation, seasons, and human beings) are all pronounced good and thus have a clear creational affirmation. Ken Barnes writes, "In addition to establishing the critical nature of work, the creation narratives also anticipate the creation of wealth and the development of economic systems, including the use of money as a means of exchange."[44] In creation God gives humans the task of stewarding and using the natural resources of his good world, stating, "I give you every seed-bearing plant on the face of the whole earth and every tree that has fruit with seed in it. They will be yours for food" (1:29). Embedded in this use and care are the realities of economics: production, distribution, consumption, and servicing.

Economic realities are mentioned at various places throughout Scripture. In the garden of Eden, precious resources that could be used in economic exchange are noted: gold, bdellium, and onyx stone (Gen. 2:12). Abram is described as "very wealthy in livestock and in silver and gold" (13:2), and the Old Testament makes numerous references to traders and merchants. The eighth commandment in the Decalogue, "You shall not steal" (Exod. 20:15), implies the ownership of private property. The "wife of noble character" in Proverbs 31 is a woman engaged in significant economic activity and yet with high character and ethics. "First and foremost, she seeks to do that which is good (vv. 11–12); she works hard (v. 13), provides for those under her care (vv. 14–15), invests in the future (v. 16), and makes a profit (vv. 17–19). But then her concern turns immediately to the poor and the needy (v. 20)."[45] The writer of Ecclesiastes endorses work and economic activity: "What gain have the workers from their toil? I have seen the business that God has given to everyone to be busy with. He has made everything suitable for its time. . . . I know that there is nothing better for them than to be happy and enjoy themselves as long as they live; moreover, it is God's gift that all should eat and drink and take pleasure in all their toil" (3:9–13 NRSV). Despite affirming economic activity, the Old Testament continually warns against the abuse of wealth in idolatry, injustice, and apathy for the poor.

When we come to the teachings of Jesus, we find the same tension between affirming economic activity and possessions, on the one hand, while strongly condemning the misuse of wealth, on the other hand. For example, in Luke 12 Jesus tells a story of a successful farmer who, upon having an

44. Kenneth J. Barnes, *Redeeming Capitalism* (Grand Rapids: Eerdmans, 2018), 93.
45. Barnes, *Redeeming Capitalism*, 94.

abundant harvest, decides to build bigger barns to glory in it. "But God said to him, 'You fool! This very night your life will be demanded from you. Then who will get what you have prepared for yourself?'" (v. 20). But later in the chapter, Jesus tells another parable about a faithful and wise manager, who makes good use of a master's wealth. Jesus then affirmingly says, "From everyone who has been given much, much will be demanded; and from the one who has been entrusted with much, much more will be asked" (v. 48). In Matthew 25 Jesus tells the parable of talents or bags of gold, in which one servant is given five bags, another two, and another one. The servants with five bags and two bags invest and gain double the original, but the man with one bag digs a hole in the ground and hides the money. When the master returns, the two who have invested are highly applauded: "Well done, good and faithful servant. You have been faithful over a little; I will set you over much. Enter into the joy of your master" (v. 21 ESV). The unfaithful servant is strongly judged for his lack of investment (vv. 26–29). But along with these various affirmations of activity, including his own work as a carpenter, Jesus recognizes the perils of wealth and warns repeatedly of the potential undermining of justice and righteousness. Apostolic teachings follow the same pattern.

Thus, we can affirm the economic social institution, but with the recognition of its great dangers such as Paul described: "Godliness with contentment is great gain. . . . But those who desire to be rich fall into temptation, into a snare, into many senseless and harmful desires that plunge people into ruin and destruction. For the love of money is a root of all kinds of evils" (1 Tim. 6:6, 9–10 ESV). So how should we think about and respond to this social institution in our world? First, we must note that the economic forms in biblical times were quite different from our own, thus making simplistic moves from then to now fraught with problems. Brent Waters puts it this way: "The teachings of the New Testament reproving wealth and property . . . were made in the context of an economy based predominantly on the natural fecundity of the land. . . . When wealth is based on the land the resulting economy is a zero-sum game, for the amount of land is limited: the easiest way to increase one's wealth is to acquire someone else's land." Thus, the strong biblical injunctions should be read against that backdrop. "Late modern economy, however, is not a zero-sum game, for wealth is derived primarily through the production of goods and services, and through subsequent trading and commercial transactions." Thus, argues Waters, "increased productivity thereby increases wealth. . . . Through increased productivity, commerce, and employment, both rich and poor ideally benefit even though an expanding income gap often results."[46] If Waters is right, then attempting to directly apply the teachings of Scripture such as radical wealth distribution, prohibiting interest

46. Waters, *Just Capitalism*, 34, 35.

on loans (usury), and giving up all of one's wealth, would likely harm the poor rather than help.

A second observation is that Scripture does not give us an economic system, and in a fallen world both command economics and market economics bear the marks of the fall. Some theologians and ethicists, such as the Social Gospel thinkers of the nineteenth century and liberation theologians in the twentieth, have tried to argue that a socialist government (command economics) is more in line with biblical principles than capitalism, or market economics.[47] But historically these approaches have not eradicated poverty and have frequently been accompanied by totalitarian forms of government. Does this then mean that a market economy is the biblical form? No, but what we might say is that even with all its flaws, it's the least fallen alternative we have. Believers need to recognize that in modern and postmodern market economies, greed flourishes, corruption abounds, and social responsibility for the common good frequently gives way to unbounded self-interest. At the same time, we must note that there are believers who bring Christian virtues into their engagement in the marketplace and not only maintain Christian integrity but are salt and light amid this social institution.[48] When analyzing market economies structurally, we should note that the gap between rich and poor widens; but even so, the poor get wealthier. In the past several decades, "it is estimated that nearly a billion people have escaped abject poverty, and income has risen steadily."[49] This did not happen through command economies.

Being created as relational creatures in a material world pronounced good—and given the task of caring for "Eden"—leads naturally to the creation of this social institution called economics. It simultaneously provides jobs, goods, and services for God's image bearers and raises for us some of the hardest ethical quandaries of our time. Christians will likely differ on the best policies and technical solutions to complex economic realities, but we humbly bring transcendent norms into this creational social institution.

47. See, for example, Walter Rauschenbusch, *Christianizing the Social Order* (New York: Macmillan, 1913). He contends that "socialism . . . has laid hold of the industrial working class with the grip of destiny. It promises these propertyless men that they shall once more own the tools of their work, share in the profit of their toil, take part in the management of their shop" (394). He believes that socialism's ideas are "the most thorough and consistent economic elaboration of the Christian social ideal" (397).

48. This is the summons of Barnes in *Redeeming Capitalism*, contending that not only Christians but also non-Christians through common grace can bring the cardinal virtues into a market economy. See also Austin Hill and Scott Rae, *The Virtues of Capitalism: A Moral Case for Free Markets* (Chicago: Northfield, 2010). Hill and Rae argue that the Bible does not focus on specific policies but general principles and that, utilizing those general principles, "capitalism provides opportunities for the poor to help themselves out of poverty and to uphold their dignity" (37).

49. Waters, *Just Capitalism*, 3.

Government

Government "is the political system by which a country or community is administered and regulated."[50] It is the social institution that has the power to make and enforce laws and to maintain order, and thus it typically has the greatest explicit amount of power in a society. Historically this social institution has taken various forms, including monarchy (single, individual rule often by a monarch), oligarchy (rule by a few, typically by the wealthy or an elite group), and democracy (rule by the people through elected representatives). Within each of these, there have been wide variations and subtypes. In early tribal societies (including hunting-gathering societies), the governmental structure was quite informal and sometimes involved shared decision-making. But as history moved toward agricultural and then industrial societies, the government took on greater spheres of responsibility and greater power to facilitate the needs of growing, complex jurisdictions. As a result more and more power around the globe is lodged in government, with totalitarian governments being the most invasive into other spheres of life.

Many Christians, including professional theologians, assume that government is not rooted in creation but rather that it emerged after the fall to control the fallen conditions of humanity and the world. Saint Augustine described two "cities" that exist within the world, each defined by their ultimate loves. The city of God is rooted in love for God and is oriented toward the glory of God and service in charity, whereas "in the city of the world both the rulers themselves and the people they dominate are dominated by the lust of domination."[51] Augustine's two contrasting cities are not the same as Luther's two kingdoms, in which the kingdom of this world is nearly equivalent to the sphere of government. Nonetheless, from his descriptions of the political sphere and the city of humans, Augustine implies that government is a result of the fall, not a mandate of creation. Thus, the state is ordained by God, not from creation in accordance with our relational nature but rather to curb and control the sinful impulses of humanity and society. In the twentieth century, Gordon Clark argued that prior to the fall "there was no provision for civil government," which was ordained primarily because "sinful man needs to be restrained."[52]

The late Anabaptist theologian John Howard Yoder, commenting on Romans 13, states, "God is not said to create or institute or ordain the powers that be, but only to order them, to put them in order, sovereignly to tell them where

50. Hugh Brogan, "Government," Britannica, last updated August 7, 2019, https://www.britannica.com/topic/government.

51. Augustine, *The City of God*, trans. Gerald G. Walsh, Demetrius B. Zema, Grace Monahan, and Daniel J. Honan, abridged ed. (New York: Image Books, 1958), 14.28, p. 321.

52. Gordon H. Clark, *A Christian View of Men and Things* (Grand Rapids: Eerdmans, 1952), 138.

they belong, what is their place." He strongly rejects the idea of a "divine institution of government as a part of God's good creation." Furthermore, "New Testament exegesis has long since abandoned such a simple concept of divine institution in the order of creation."[53] Yoder is no doubt exaggerating the consensus of New Testament exegesis, but he is also reducing government per se to the use of violence to maintain order.

It is clear that "if humans had not sinned, there would be no need for police forces, criminal courts, and penal systems, but those responsibilities are not the only ones that belong to the government of a political community, and they do not define the original, underlying meaning of political life."[54] In the beginning God established relational realities ("It is not good for the man to be alone," Gen. 2:18) and gave to humans the task of stewarding his good creation. Such realities and tasks would inevitably call for some forms of structure, procedures, and power. For example, in carrying out the cultural mandate, without the fall, there would eventually be a need for allocating responsibilities; roads would be needed to transport food and supplies; and some form of taxation would likely be necessary to pay for these various functions. Forms of decision-making and allocation of goods and responsibilities are not results of human sin but simply the result of being relational creatures. Richard Mouw rightly notes that civil government is not directly mentioned in the Genesis creation account, but "it could be asked why there could not be intermediate groupings—say, some families coming together for a pooling of resources under a common decision-making procedure, which would allow for political structures that functioned between the rule of God and the rule of the basic family unit."[55]

In Colossians 1:15–16 Paul writes regarding Christ, "He is the image of the invisible God, the firstborn of all creation; for in him all things in heaven and on earth were created, things visible and invisible, whether thrones or dominions or rulers or powers—all things have been created through him and for him" (NRSV). Though the thrones, powers, rulers, and authorities would eventually stand over against the paths of Christ and be disarmed by him through the cross (Col. 2:15), this text affirms that they are part of creation.[56]

53. John Howard Yoder, *The Politics of Jesus: Vicit Agnus Noster*, 2nd ed. (Grand Rapids: Eerdmans, 1994), 201, 194, 193, respectively.

54. James W. Skillen, *The Good of Politics: A Biblical, Historical, and Contemporary Introduction*, Engaging Culture (Grand Rapids: Baker Academic, 2019), xix.

55. Richard J. Mouw, *Politics and the Biblical Drama* (Grand Rapids: Eerdmans, 1976), 35.

56. Discussion about the powers has elicited much scholarly discussion, with some saying they are angels and others the structures (particularly political structures) within society. For a balanced perspective, see Hendrik Berkhof, *Christ and the Powers*, trans. John H. Yoder (Scottdale, PA: Mennonite Publishing House, 1962). Berkhof speaks of "these powers which unify men, but separate them from God. The state, politics, class, social struggle, national interest, . . . these give unity and direction to thousands of lives. Yet precisely by giving unity and direction they separate these many lives from the true God" (25). He goes on to contend, "They are still the framework of creation" (26).

Clearly the fall brought new realities into the world, which civil government is now tasked by God to address: coercion, disorder, crime, and injustices. Sadly, in its fallen state, civil government itself begins to abuse those functions by misusing coercion and violence and being the harbinger of crime and injustices. Thus, ethical issues surrounding the state have been among the most challenging, precisely because the state has ultimate power in society.

Moreover, we must acknowledge that we face difficult biblical-hermeneutical issues when discerning government's tasks and orientation. For example, Richard Bauckham notes clear differences between the Old Testament and New Testament in political matters, which in part are differences of context. "Much of the Old Testament is addressed to a people of God which was a political entity and . . . is therefore directly concerned with the ordering of Israel's political life. . . . The New Testament is addressed to a politically powerless minority in the Roman Empire." Moreover, the New Testament makes a distinction, which can and has been misused, "between the ethical principles which apply to immediate personal relations and those which apply to political institutions and activities." In addition our biblical interpretation must consider the differences between biblical cultures and our own. So, Bauckham notes, "to argue, for example, that since education in biblical times was not a government responsibility it should nowadays be left purely to parental responsibility, as it was then, makes no more sense than to argue that in accordance with biblical precedent governments should not legislate for road safety."[57]

So how can Scripture and theology inform our views of government, public policy, and Christian political engagement? First, we should make clear that the kingdom of God and the kingdoms of this world can never be equated. As Jesus is facing the government official Pilate following his arrest, he declares, "My kingdom is not from this world. If my kingdom were from this world, my followers would be fighting to keep me from being handed over to the Jews. But as it is, my kingdom is not from here" (John 18:36 NRSV). Jesus is not rejecting the government but making a clear distinction between his kingdom, over which he reigns, and other kingdoms. From Constantine on, one of the grave errors of Christians and the church is to equate these two kingdoms, which ends up denying the lordship of Christ. Frequently, equating the two kingdoms has led to an unbridled nationalism that is not only heretical but a determent to civility and peace.[58]

Furthermore, we should affirm that the Bible gives both positive and negative views of civil government, which we might call "the Romans 13 view" and "the Revelation 13 view," respectively. In Romans 13 governing authorities

57. Richard Bauckham, *The Bible in Politics: How to Read the Bible Politically* (London: SPCK, 1989), 3, 7, 10.

58. Paul D. Miller, *The Religion of American Greatness: What's Wrong with Christian Nationalism* (Downers Grove, IL: IVP Academic, 2022).

are described as having been established by God (v. 1) and as God's servants for good, even as they bear the sword (v. 4). Subjection, taxes, respect, and honor are to be accorded these authorities (vv. 1, 5, 7). This positive view is also affirmed in Jesus's statement "Give to the emperor the things that are the emperor's, and to God the things that are God's" (Mark 12:17 NRSV). But Scripture also gives a negative view of government, as Revelation 13 portrays the state as a beast whom people worship (v. 4) and who blasphemes God (vv. 5–6) and wages war against God's holy people (v. 7). This negative view is also evidenced when the early apostles reject the governing authorities' edict to stop evangelizing: "We must obey God rather than any human authority" (Acts 5:29 NRSV). And when King Herod threatens Jesus's life and ministry, Jesus replies with a derogatory term for the government official: "Go tell that fox, 'I will keep on driving out demons and healing people today and tomorrow'" (Luke 13:32). What do we make of this? Even Paul's Romans 13 statement, in a time when Rome was perhaps less threatening to early believers, does not give carte blanche to government leaders. As John Stott puts it, this "cannot be taken to mean that all the Caligulas, Herods, Neros and Domitians of the New Testament times were personally appointed by God, that God is responsible for their behavior, or that their authority is in no circumstances to be resisted."[59] We can say that though government is a social institution rooted in creation, in their fallen state all governments are at times servant and at times beast, with some being far more one than the other.

A further reflection is that Christian engagement with government depends in part on the context in which believers find themselves. In free democracies Christians have opportunity to influence government through voting, persuasion, holding office, and even at times civil disobedience. In totalitarian societies or theocracies of another religion, such as Islamic countries, these modes of influence are significantly limited. But even in those situations, believers can have an influence by embodying Christian virtues significant for public life. This finds biblical support in God's message through Jeremiah to the Jewish exiles carried off to a foreign land with false gods and unethical practices. The response was not to be one of defiance or pure compliance:

> Thus says the Lord of hosts, the God of Israel, to all the exiles whom I have sent into exile from Jerusalem to Babylon: Build houses and live in them; plant gardens and eat their produce. Take wives and have sons and daughters; take wives for your sons, and give your daughters in marriage, that they may bear sons and daughters; multiply there, and do not decrease. But seek the welfare of the city where I have sent you into exile, and pray to the Lord on its behalf, for in its welfare you will find your welfare. . . . Do not let your prophets and your diviners who are among you deceive you. (Jer. 29:4–8 ESV)

59. John R. W. Stott, *Romans: God's Good News for the World*, Bible Speaks Today (Downers Grove, IL: InterVarsity, 1994), 340.

The people of God would be salt and light by their prayers, everyday routines, living within the community, growing in number, and not conforming to the sinful patterns around them. In whatever contexts Christians find themselves today, they will always need to prayerfully seek God's wisdom for relating to governing authorities.

It is possible, based on Scripture and theology, to understand the basic functions of government. As we've already noted on the basis of creation foundations, government provides the social function of civil administration. It provides a coordinating role for society, inclusive of developing and administering modes of transportation, providing mechanisms for education, establishing and enforcing taxation, and providing overall structures by which humans can carry on their social lives, such as local governments, state or provincial governments, and federal governments. None of these in themselves are results of the fall; rather, they are important functions by which humans and societies exist. But beyond these foundational functions, three functions take on a particular expression in light of sin, though they still reflect their creational intent: order, freedom, and justice. Whereas political theories and systems have historically tended toward one of these realities over the others, I suggest that a wise and healthy system holds them together in creative tension.[60]

The function of order we have already noted in the Romans 13 passage: "Rulers hold no terror for those who do right, but for those who do wrong. . . . If you do wrong, be afraid, for rulers do not bear the sword for no reason. They are God's servants, agents of wrath to bring punishment on the wrongdoer" (vv. 3–4). Order is also at the heart of Peter's statement, "Submit yourselves for the Lord's sake to every human authority: whether to the emperor, as the supreme authority, or to governors, who are sent by him to punish those who do wrong and to commend those who do right" (1 Pet. 2:13–14). In context Peter has recognized that Christians live in the empire as "foreigners and exiles" (v. 11), and he admonishes them to "live such good lives among the pagans that, though they accuse you of doing wrong, they may see your good deeds and glorify God on the day he visits us" (v. 12). This is in a context of opposition in which believers have limited social influence, but nonetheless the government still has a function of maintaining order, even if it misuses it in persecuting Christians. Governments maintain order in two ways: by the enactment of laws and by the enforcement of those laws through coercion. In addition Paul's reference to "the sword" is symbolic of all mechanisms of order, including the necessity of sometimes engaging in just wars to defend the people of a country. When Christian thinkers have hammered out ethical principles for going to and engaging in war, it has been viewed not as a

60. For a more detailed analysis of the functions of government in relation to the contemporary issue of immigration, see Dennis P. Hollinger, "The Role of Government and the Immigration Issue: A Christian Ethics Perspective," *Journal of the Evangelical Theological Society* 63, no. 4 (2020): 759–71.

nationalist mode of expansion[61] or a method of terrorism over others but rather as a mechanism of justice and peace.

Throughout history various thinkers, such as Machiavelli and Hobbes, and certainly numerous political leaders have accentuated order to the neglect of freedom and justice. But a society focused only on order will become despotic and totalitarian, abusing basic human rights and the dignity of all humans, who have been created in God's image. It is precisely because government has ultimate power lodged in police and the military that it can so easily misuse the power of coercion. While order through coercion is essential in a fallen world, Andy Crouch has noted that it is far more than a negative element in society: "Coercion is needed to protect the possibility of creation. . . . The legitimate role of coercion is to make room for flourishing, especially by restraining whatever fundamentally threatens the integrity of God's creative image bearers."[62] This is a long way from the order of violence so prevalent in our world today.

A further function of government is the protection of freedom. Though many versions of freedom are far removed from Christian understandings, a biblical-theological case can be made for the importance of freedom in human life, which the state has the power to maintain. First, the very existence of the church, distinct from the state, establishes a social reality that limits the state and thus implies freedom. "The fact that God has ordained other dimensions of human existence (i.e., family, church, work, or economy) points to a limitation of the state, and this reality implies concepts of human freedom that the state ought to protect."[63] Second, freedom is implied in humanity's creation in the image of God. The dignity of humans means that human choices should be civilly protected, even though those choices may go contrary to God's designs. And third, freedom is grounded in the biblical story of the exodus, the great civil freedom divinely granted to the Hebrew people.

Though the protection of freedom is an essential function of government, this does not include the freedom to harm others. Moreover, this freedom is never isolated from order and justice, for freedom without order is anarchy, and freedom without justice is injustice for many.

A final function of government is the establishment of justice, mechanisms, and laws that render to people what is due them. *Retributive justice* is giving what is due when wrong has been done, and thus it falls somewhat within the function of order. But retributive justice must be done fairly, without partiality according to race, gender, creed, or class. *Distributive justice* is giving

61. For a helpful work on the difference between an unbridled nationalism and a proper patriotism, see Richard J. Mouw, *How to Be a Patriotic Christian: Love of Country as Love of Neighbor* (Downers Grove, IL: InterVarsity, 2022).

62. Andy Crouch, *Playing God: Redeeming the Gift of Power* (Downers Grove, IL: IVP Books, 2013), 147.

63. Hollinger, "Role of Government," 765.

people their due in the various rights, goods, opportunities, and services of a society. Justice in this realm does not mean equal results but equal opportunities in the other institutions of society, such as economics and education. Justice finds significant biblical support throughout Scripture. Fairness in judicial proceeding is set forth in Leviticus 19:15: "You shall not render an unjust judgment; you shall not be partial to the poor or defer to the great: with justice you shall judge your neighbor" (NRSV). God's commitment to and command for justice is prominent: "I know that the LORD maintains the cause of the needy, and executes justice for the poor" (Ps. 140:12 NRSV). And Jesus strongly repudiates the legalistic patterns of the Pharisees, who tithe meticulously but neglect the weightier matters of the law—namely, "justice and mercy and faithfulness" (Matt. 23:23 ESV). In chapter 8 below, we will explore the theme of justice in greater detail, noting that one of the complexities in executing justice is varying definitions of what is owed people. While justice is imperative for government, it is not the only virtue. For justice without freedom is oppression, and justice without order is anarchy. Order, freedom, and justice must always be held together.

Within the social institution of government, it is not always easy to find the wisest public policies and the best mechanisms for a balance of political power with other social institutions, such as economics, education, and the media. Mary Ann Glendon puts it well: "There's a growing recognition that human beings do not flourish if the conditions under which we work and raise our families are entirely subject either to the play of market forces or to the will of distant bureaucrats."[64] And as Michael Gerson and Peter Wehner note, "Scripture simply does not offer detailed guidance on . . . trade; education; welfare; crime; health care; affirmative action; immigration; foreign aid; legal reform; . . . climate change; and much else."[65] As a result Christians need much wisdom in their political reflections within the parameters of their broader biblical-theological understandings, with clear comprehension of the issues at hand and the pros and cons of various technical solutions.

Conclusion

Though social institutions are highly suspect in a populist culture, they play an important role in societies and in the lives of human beings. Even though they are deeply flawed in a fallen world and frequently work against human good, they are reflections of the fact that we are created as social beings. And they are essential to prevent the social chaos that would ensue without them.

64. Mary Ann Glendon, "Beyond the Simple Market-State Dichotomy," *Origins*, May 9, 1996, 797.

65. Michael Gerson and Peter Wehner, *City of Man: Religion and Politics in a New Era* (Chicago: Moody, 2010), 36.

Contrary to Aristotle, who argues that "the state is by nature clearly prior to the family and to the individual,"[66] the foundational social institutions for Christians are the family and the church, as they ground and socialize us in the things most essential for flourishing as human beings as God intended. But other social institutions—including ones not treated in this chapter, such as health care—play a role in our sociality as humans and cultures. They all need Christians in them who will not seek to turn them into the church or the kingdom of God but will prudentially engage them for the glory of God and the common good of the social order, informed by a creational ethic and the kingdom of God.

Particular stances within given institutions are frequently complex. Wisdom, prayer, and conversation with fellow believers are essential for navigating our way as social beings—rooted in creation. The very way we engage others, including ardent secularists, anti-Christians, and social institutions, is part of being salt, light, and leaven in a broken world.

66. Aristotle, *Politics*, trans. Benjamin Jowett, in *Aristotle on Man in the Universe*, Classics Club (Roslyn, NY: Walter Black, 1943), 1.2, p. 250.

7

Created to Work

Connecting Sunday to Monday

"It's the bane of human existence!" "It's the glory and goal of human existence!" Throughout the ages these have been among the many and varied perspectives on human work. As one philosopher describes the contrasting views, "In the aristocratic [ancient] world-view, work was considered a defect, a servile activity—literally reserved for slaves. In the modern world-view, it becomes an arena for self-realization, a means . . . of fulfillment. . . . Work becomes the defining activity of man. . . . His aim is to create himself by remaking the world."[1] But the creational paradigm, affirmed throughout the rest of Scripture and by Christ the Creator-Redeemer, has a different perspective with different parameters and goals.

The key texts from the Genesis creation story are as follows:

> In the beginning God created the heavens and the earth. (1:1)
>
> Then God said, "Let us make humankind in our image, according to our likeness; and let them have dominion over the fish of the sea, and over the birds of the air, and over the cattle, and over all the wild animals of the earth, and over every creeping thing that creeps upon the earth." . . . "Be fruitful and multiply, and fill the earth and subdue it; and have dominion over the fish of the sea and over the birds of the air and over every living thing that moves upon the earth." God said, "See, I have given you every plant yielding seed that is upon the face

1. Luc Ferry, *A Brief History of Thought: A Philosophical Guide to Living*, trans. Theo Cuffe (New York: Harper Perennial, 2011), 126.

> of all the earth, and every tree with seed in its fruit; you shall have them for food." (vv. 26, 28–29 NRSV)

> And on the seventh day God finished his work that he had done, and he rested on the seventh day from all his work that he had done. So God blessed the seventh day and made it holy, because on it God rested from all his work that he had done in creation. (2:2–3 ESV)

> Now no shrub had yet appeared on the earth and no plant had yet sprung up, for the Lord God had not sent rain on the earth and there was no one to work the ground. (v. 5)

> The Lord God took the man and put him in the Garden of Eden to work it and take care of it. (v. 15)

> Now out of the ground the Lord God had formed every beast of the field and every bird of the heavens and brought them to the man to see what he would call them. And whatever the man called every living creature, that was its name. The man gave names to all livestock and to the birds of the heavens and to every beast of the field. (vv. 19–20 ESV)

These texts form the foundational paradigm for understanding work, the human as worker, and thus the larger framework for approaching the many ethical issues that surround work. We can best appreciate this paradigm by first understanding the many other philosophies of work that have existed throughout history. But before that, we need to define the term itself.

When people think of work, they tend to think of their job or career, which is essential to provide a livelihood. But work is not defined only as productivity to receive remuneration. Many people do not have jobs outside the home but do much work related to childcare, upkeep of their home, and voluntary work without pay in their communities. People like myself who are retired frequently note they are almost as busy as before retirement with voluntary work associated with their churches, voluntary organizations, and extended families. One writer gives this helpful definition: "Work, in sociology, is defined as the carrying out of tasks, which involves the expenditure of mental and physical effort, and its objective is the production of goods and services that cater to human needs."[2] What is helpful about this definition is its distinction between work and an occupation or job. We actually work at many things not associated with salary. For example, we noted in the last chapter that many people work hard at leisure and in such a way that the exertion of energy differs little from their work within a job. As Witold Rybczynski notes, "The word 'weekend' started life as 'week-end' but lost

2. Ashley Crossman, "Sociology of Work and Industry," ThoughtCo., last updated March 3, 2019, https://www.thoughtco.com/sociology-of-work-3026289.

its hyphen somewhere along the way, ceasing to be merely the end of the week and acquiring, instead, an autonomous and sovereign existence. . . . People used to 'play' tennis; now they 'work' on their backhand."[3] Thus, while some people work in order to get to leisure, the demarcation between the two has clearly dwindled. Scripture views work as our everyday activities and tasks that require a deep involvement of ourselves, in such a way that it is our calling in life. It will quite typically be a means to meeting our needs—but also the needs of others and the work of God's kingdom, whether or not there is pay.

Historic Views of Work

The creation story, as we've noted throughout this book, stands in contrast to the many competing worldviews that have existed throughout history; and the same is true for work. For example, the Sumerian creation myths of the ancient Near East (written in the mid- to late second millennium BC) assert that humanity was formed for the sake of the gods, to alleviate their work. Work was deemed beneath the gods and their status. In Enuma Elish the god Marduk creates humans "first, in order to release the gods from their burdensome menial labors, and second, to provide a continuous source of food and drink to temples," to service the gods.[4] This is a long way from the Creator of Genesis, whose creation is defined as work and who ordains humans to be colaborers in the garden he has created. And the verdict? "It was very good" (1:31 ESV).

In the ancient Greek world, "work is important chiefly because it makes possible leisure."[5] Hesiod, the Greek poet, says that in the golden age of the Greeks, humans lived like gods, and the gods did not engage in work. "For the gods keep hidden from men the means of life. Else you would easily do work enough in a day to supply you for a full year even without working."[6] For both Plato and Aristotle, physical work may be necessary but is demeaning and fit primarily for slaves. In Plato's utopian *Republic*, there are three kinds of workers: laborers or the mercantile class, those who keep the peace and defend the city, and the ruling class of philosopher-kings, who are freed from physical work for leisure and thinking, which are inimical to physical labor. In similar fashion Aristotle argues "that leisure is higher than

3. Witold Rybczynski, "Waiting for the Weekend," *Atlantic Monthly*, August 1991, 35, 36.

4. Ira Spar, "Mesopotamian Creation Myths," Heilbrunn Timeline of Art History, Metropolitan Museum of Art, April 2009, https://www.metmuseum.org/toah/hd/epic/hd_epic.htm.

5. Gilbert C. Meilaender, introduction to *Working: Its Meaning and Its Limits*, ed. Gilbert C. Meilaender, Ethics of Everyday Life (Notre Dame, IN: University of Notre Dame Press, 2000), 5.

6. Hesiod, "Works and Days," in *The Homeric Hymns and Homerica*, trans. Hugh Evelyn-White, rev. ed., Loeb Classical Library (London: William Heinemann, 1982), 5.

occupation, and is the end to which occupation is directed."[7] Work had no intrinsic good for the Greeks, and those sentiments carried over to the Romans, who also structured work around a slave class, freeing the aristocracy from physical labor.

In medieval Europe the highest form of dedication to God was the monastic life, which entailed leaving the institutions of marriage and work for a higher calling. Whereas some early ascetic monks eschewed any work for a life of total prayer and contemplation, later monastic reformers incorporated work into the vocational calling of monks and nuns. For example, Benedict in his *Rule* (sixth century) rejects the "individualism and wild asceticism of the earlier solitaries," but "the ascetic craving for simplicity . . . and for freedom from the corrupting entanglements of the secular world was continued and nurtured as a true pattern of Christian life." Nonetheless, Benedict's *Rule* "expressly enjoins at least seven hours of manual labor in each day except the Sunday of Rest."[8] Thus, work in this epoch had a mixed profile. It is with the Protestant Reformation, as we will note later, that vocation is extended to all believers into whatever calling God leads.

Nonetheless, in Europe suspicion persisted regarding work, for "in many European languages the word for 'labor' is closely associated with pain—as in the Greek *panos*, the French *travail*, and the German *Arbeit*."[9] And even Jacques Ellul, the French lay theologian and sociologist, has a purely utilitarian view of work. Ellul asserts that in the Bible "work is not presented as the service of God. It has to be done, and the Bible is realistic enough not to overlay this necessity with superfluous spiritual ornamentation. Moreover, the Bible displays no essential interest in the situation of work. Work is the painful lot of all men, but it is not particularly important." Ellul goes on to state, "I am not saying that work is bad. What I am saying is that its value is purely utilitarian and that it is one of the necessities of life."[10] The portrayal of work in this chapter is at significant odds with Ellul's sentiments.

At the other end of the spectrum was Karl Marx portraying the human person as defined essentially by work. The problem for Marx is that capitalism has alienated humans from the product of their work and thus from one's true self. In his utopian dreams of a classless society, Marx writes, "In communist society, where nobody has one exclusive sphere of activity, but each can become accomplished in any branch he wishes, society regulates the general production and thus makes it possible for me to do one thing today and another

7. Aristotle, *The Politics*, trans. Ernest Barker (London: Oxford University Press, 1958), 8.3, p. 335.

8. Robert L. Calhoun, "Work and Vocation in Christian History," in *Work and Vocation: A Christian Discussion*, ed. John Oliver Nelson (New York: Harper & Brothers, 1954), 93.

9. Meilaender, introduction, 7.

10. Jacques Ellul, *The Ethics of Freedom*, trans. Geoffrey W. Bromiley (Grand Rapids: Eerdmans, 1976), 495, 496.

tomorrow."[11] The workers themselves will own and control the process and outcome of their experiment and thus end oppression in the world.

When we move outside the Western world, we find a broad array of views primarily focused on what workers bring to their jobs but not so much on the meaning of work. For example, "traditional Confucian thought . . . embraces hard work, perseverance, the maintenance of professional relations, and identification with organizational values."[12] In Hinduism one contemporary writer describes work as a duty in life and states, "We work through the karma [actions with cause and effect] we created in the past and create new karma to be faced in the future. With this in mind, we can see that our daily work contributes to our spiritual progress just as much as attending pujas in the temple, worshiping in our home shrine, going on pilgrimage," and so forth. And as Yogaswami, writing in the first part of the twentieth century, puts it, "All work must be done with the aim of reaching God."[13] In classical Hinduism the type of work one did was determined by a set caste system, with a social hierarchy moving from intellectual and spiritual leaders at the top down to unskilled laborers at the bottom, with the Dalit group, or "untouchables," below the caste system.

Work and the Creation Story

When we come to the creation account in Genesis, we find a rather different perspective on work, with the creation itself being God's work and then work being ordained by God for human beings. Work is good and part of human nature, but it is not the defining point of humanity, nor is it the ultimate end of humans' role in this world.

God the Worker in Creation

In the opening chapter of the Bible, God is at work and finds great joy in the fruit of his labors. God is not only fashioning reality without preexisting material but is taking what he has created and forming and shaping it into the designs of the universe. In Genesis 2:2–3 the word "work" is actually used for the triune God's creation activity, for "on the seventh day he rested from all his work. Then God blessed the seventh day and made it holy, because on it he rested from all the work of creating that he had done." Thus, in creation "every glimpse of God shows Him as a mighty worker who brings new things

11. Karl Marx, "The German Ideology," in *Marx and Engels: Basic Writings on Politics and Philosophy*, ed. Lewis S. Feuer (Garden City, NY: Doubleday Anchor, 1959), 254.

12. Michael Cholbi, "Philosophical Approaches to Work and Labor," Stanford Encyclopedia of Philosophy, January 11, 2022, https://plato.stanford.edu/entries/work-labor/.

13. "Work Is Worship," *Hinduism Today*, July 1, 2004, https://www.hinduismtoday.com/magazine/july-august-september-2004/2004-07-work-is-worship/.

into existence and untiringly oversees all the enterprises in His vast domain. In accomplishing His greatest work, God sends a carpenter to construct a city into which men will bring the fruits of all their labors."[14] The Creator puts his image bearers into the garden to care for and work it and demonstrates his providential care over the works of his hands. "God's own work in Genesis 1 and 2 is 'manual' labor, as he shapes us out of the dust of the earth, deliberately putting a spirit in a physical body, and as he plants a garden."[15]

God the worker in Genesis is a long way from the Greek gods who would never stoop to work, especially to do manual labor. In fact, we can safely say that the first thing we know about God in Scripture is that God is a worker—the Creator. Pope John Paul II describes it this way:

> The Church finds in the very first pages of the Book of Genesis the source of her conviction that work is a fundamental dimension of human existence on earth. . . . [This truth is] decisive for man from the very beginning, and at the same time [it traces] out the main lines of his earthly existence, both in the state of original justice and also after the breaking, caused by sin, of the creator's original covenant with creation in man. . . . Every human being reflects the very action of the creator of the universe.[16]

If work is not beneath the dignity of the triune God, it is not beneath the dignity of humanity made in his image.

God Institutes Work for Humans

God makes humans in his image so that (in part) they might work: "Then God said, 'Let us make [humanity] in our image, in our likeness, so that they may rule over the fish in the sea and the birds in the sky, over the livestock and all the wild animals, and over all the creatures that move along the ground'" (1:26). God then gives the command that will involve the work of parenting and the work of creation care and cultural development: "Be fruitful and increase in number; fill the earth and subdue it. Rule over the fish in the sea and the birds in the sky and over every living creature that moves on the ground" (v. 28). God then grants to the man and the woman the right to eat food from the earth (v. 29), which will involve work to cultivate, harvest, and preserve. All of God's work and the commission for human work receives an acclamation: "God saw all that he had made, and it was very good" (v. 31).

In Genesis 2 we have a fuller expression of the overview of Genesis 1, and work receives a positive portrayal. In verse 5 we are told that "there was no one

14. Paul S. Minear, "Work and Vocation in Scripture," in Nelson, *Work and Vocation*, 33.

15. Timothy Keller, *Every Good Endeavor: Connecting Your Work to God's Work*, with Katherine Leary Alsdorf (New York: Dutton, 2012), 49.

16. John Paul II, *On Human Work: Laborem Exercens* (Washington, DC: United States Catholic Conference, 1981), 9–10.

to work the ground," but after forming *'adam*, the human, "the LORD God took the man and put him in the Garden of Eden to work it and take care of it" (v. 15). The Hebrew word for "work" in both verses is *'avad*, sometimes translated "work," sometimes "serve," and sometimes even "worship." Tom Nelson describes the breadth and significance of the noun form, *'avodah*: "*Avodah* is used to describe the back-breaking hard work of God's covenant people making bricks as slaves in Egypt (Ex. 1:14), the artisans building the tabernacle (Ex. 35:24), and the fine craftsmanship of linen workers (1 Chron. 4:21)." In the dedication of the temple, Solomon uses the word with regard to worship under the leadership of the priests and Levites (2 Chron. 8:14). Thus, "though there are distinct nuances to *avodah*, a common thread of meaning emerges where work, worship, and service are inextricably linked and intricately connected." This tells us "that God's original design and desire is that our work and our worship would be a seamless way of living."[17] It is also significant that the two words for "work" and "take care of" are used in Numbers (3:7–8; 18:7) to describe the priesthood and their work in the tabernacle. The work in the garden of Eden is holy and is paradigmatic for all human work.

Later in Genesis 2, Adam takes on the scientific work of classification. God brings all the animals "to the man to see what he would call them. And whatever the man called every living creature, that was its name" (2:19 ESV). All of this from Genesis 1–2, taken together, provides a broad view of the nature of work. "Humans would 'work the garden' not only by cultivating plant life but also by cultivating art, architecture, music, liturgy, clothing, sport, and entertainment and by forming domestic, religious, social, and political institutions. God did not merely give humanity the *capacity* to make culture; he in fact *commanded* us to use those capacities."[18] In work we are taking what God made and developing it further. Tim Keller beautifully puts it this way:

> [Work] is rearranging the raw material of God's creation in such a way that it helps the world in general, and people in particular, thrive and flourish. This pattern is found in all kinds of work. Farming takes the physical material of soil and seed and produces food. Music takes the physics of sound and rearranges it into something beautiful and thrilling. . . . When we take fabric and make a piece of clothing, when we push a broom and clean up a room, when we use technology to harness the forces of electricity, when we take an unformed, naïve human mind and teach it a subject, when we teach a couple how to resolve their relational disputes, when we take simple materials and turn them into a poignant work of art—we are continuing God's work of forming, filling, and subduing.[19]

17. Tom Nelson, *Work Matters: Connecting Sunday Worship to Monday Work* (Wheaton: Crossway, 2011), 26–27.

18. Bruce Riley Ashford and Craig G. Bartholomew, *The Doctrine of Creation: A Constructive Kuyperian Approach* (Downers Grove, IL: IVP Academic, 2020), 253.

19. Keller, *Every Good Endeavor*, 59.

We are by nature workers who take the works of God and extend them not only to meet our own needs or even the needs of others but also for the glory of the Creator.

All of this leads Dorothy Sayers to say, "Work is not, primarily, a thing one does to live, but the thing one lives to do. It is, or it should be, the full expression of the worker's faculties, the thing in which he finds spiritual, mental, and bodily satisfaction, and the medium in which he offers himself to God." Thus, work should not be viewed "as a necessary drudgery to be undergone for the purpose of making money, but as a way of life in which the nature of man should find its proper exercise and delight and so fulfill itself to the glory of God."[20] When a person cannot work through no fault of their own or will not work through their own volition, something in their very nature is lost. But all of this must be balanced with something else in the creation story, the institution of the Sabbath.

Work Is Not the Essence or End of Human Life

In a fallen world, there is a tendency to think that our work is everything. Thus, humans tend toward a works righteousness in the pursuit of salvation, assuming that all their good works will bring them to God. Moreover, there is a tendency in everyday life to make work (and money from it) a god, seeking to find our ultimate identity and satisfaction in what we do and how much we make. Thus, in the creation story and before the fall, God builds a rhythm of life that will combine worship, work, and leisure. All of this is to get life right in its orientation and a balance that prevents us from making work ultimate. "On the seventh day God finished his work that he had done, and he rested on the seventh day from all his work that he had done. So God blessed the seventh day and made it holy, because on it God rested from all his work that he had done in creation" (Gen. 2:2–3 ESV).

In the next chapter, we will explore the *shabbat* more fully, but a few observations for the context of work are appropriate here. God doesn't need to rest in the sense that he is tired from his work. Rather, God is putting into place a pattern of life that humans need to fully flourish and faithfully follow their Maker. Thus, what God institutes at creation becomes the fourth commandment in the Decalogue: "Remember the sabbath day, and keep it holy. Six days you shall labor and do all your work. But the seventh day is a sabbath to the LORD your God; you shall not do any work—you, your son or your daughter, your male or female slave, your livestock, or the alien resident in your towns. For in six days the LORD made heaven and earth, the sea, and all that is in them, but rested the seventh day; therefore the LORD blessed the sabbath day and consecrated it" (Exod. 20:8–11 NRSV). Here

20. Dorothy L. Sayers, *Why Work?* (1947; repr., McLean, VA: Trinity Forum, 2011), 18, 15.

the very rationale for obeying the Sabbath command is God's action of rest in creation. In Deuteronomy 5 Moses reiterates the Decalogue some years after giving the law, as the Hebrews are about to enter the promised land. Here the rationale for obeying the Sabbath is this: "Remember that you were slaves in Egypt and that the LORD your God brought you out of there with a mighty hand and an outstretched arm. Therefore the LORD your God has commanded you to observe the Sabbath day" (v. 15). The two rationales for keeping the Sabbath demonstrate that creation and liberation or redemption are unified. What God designs at creation is then explicitly commanded in the Decalogue and is reinforced by God's emancipation of his people from slavery.

The rhythm of life instituted in creation and commanded by God in the Decalogue demonstrates that while work is highly significant and part of our human nature, it is not the essence of life or the end and apex of human existence. "Since God rested after his creation, we must also rest after ours," for it is "part of our created nature. Overwork or underwork violates that nature and leads to breakdown. . . . To violate the rhythm of work and rest (in either direction) leads to chaos in our life and in the world around us. Sabbath is therefore a celebration of our design."[21]

Work in the Rest of the Biblical Story

The creation paradigm of work is reaffirmed throughout the rest of Scripture, including in the life and teachings of Jesus of Nazareth, the "carpenter" and Creator.

The Old Testament and Work

The Old Testament makes various references to work both in a positive vein and through the lens of the fall, which we will address more fully in a separate section. In an account of Adam's offspring, we find early references to various forms of work: "Lamech married two women, one named Adah and the other Zillah. Adah gave birth to Jabal; he was the father of those who live in tents and raise livestock. His brother's name was Jubal; he was the father of all who play stringed instruments and pipes. Zillah also had a son, Tubal-Cain, who forged all kinds of tools out of bronze and iron" (Gen. 4:19–22). This family exhibits various gifts and skills, including nomadic agriculture, music makers, and toolmakers. While these vocational gifts are lauded, Derek Kidner wisely notes, "At the same time we are saved from over-valuing these skills; the family of Lamech could handle its environment but not itself. The attempt to improve on God's marriage ordinance (v. 19;

21. Keller, *Every Good Endeavor*, 235.

cf. 2:24) set a disastrous precedent, on which the rest of Genesis is comment enough; and the immediate conversion of metal-working to weapon-making is equally ominous." Kidner goes on to observe, "Cain's family is a microcosm: its pattern of technical prowess and moral failure is that of humanity."[22]

After the exodus God gives instructions to build the tabernacle, the place of sacrifices and worship for the Hebrew people. A creational perspective on work—its value, glory, and creativity—is provided in the project: "Then the LORD said to Moses, 'See, I have chosen Bezalel son of Uri . . . of the tribe of Judah, and I have filled him with the Spirit of God, with wisdom, with understanding, with knowledge and with all kinds of skills—to make artistic designs for work in gold, silver and bronze, to cut and set stones, to work in wood, and to engage in all kinds of crafts. Moreover, I have appointed Oholiab . . . to help him'" (Exod. 31:1–6). What is significant here is that skills, artistic creativity, knowledge, wisdom, and the work of God's Spirit are all intertwined in work—and not just because the people are building a sacred place. These elements of work are evident throughout Scripture.

In the sixth century BC, exiles returned to Jerusalem from captivity in Babylon. One of the first tasks for the people was the work of building the wall for security, under the leadership of Nehemiah. There was opposition from both internal and external sources, but in the end the work was successfully completed in fifty-two days. When recounting the work, Nehemiah writes, "When all our enemies heard about this, all the surrounding nations were afraid and lost their self-confidence, because they realized that this work had been done with the help of our God" (Neh. 6:16). Though humans carried out the work ordinance from creation, God was also at work in and through them, a reminder needed for all human work by believers in all times. Thus, the psalmist can write, "Let your work be manifest to your servants, and your glorious power to their children. Let the favor of the Lord our God be upon us, and prosper for us the work of our hands—O prosper the work of our hands!" (Ps. 90:16–17 NRSV).

As God restores his people back to their homeland, he uses a diversity of workers, and we have three different books of the Bible describing their work:

> First, the book of Ezra is about a minister, a teacher of the word. The Jews needed to be reacquainted with the Bible so their lives could be shaped by what God said. Second, the book of Nehemiah is about an urban planner and developer who used his management skills to rebuild the wall of Jerusalem and reinstate stability so that economic and civic life could begin to flourish again.

22. Derek Kidner, *Genesis: An Introduction and Commentary*, Tyndale Old Testament Commentaries (Downers Grove, IL: InterVarsity, 1972), 78.

> Last, the book of Esther is about a woman with power in the civil government working against racial injustice. Here you have male and female, lay and clergy. You have people working for spiritual maturity, economic flourishing, and better public policy, in cultures that defined and valued these ideas differently from the Jews. And God is using them all.[23]

Even while in exile in a foreign land, the Lord through the prophet Jeremiah instructs the people to get to work: "Build houses and settle down; plant gardens and eat what they produce. . . . Seek the peace and prosperity of the city to which I have carried you into exile. Pray to the LORD for it, because if it prospers, you too will prosper" (Jer. 29:5, 7).

In the prophet Isaiah's eschatological portrayal of a new heavens and new earth, work is extolled: "[God's people] will build houses and inhabit them; they will plant vineyards and eat their fruit. . . . My chosen shall long enjoy the work of their hands. They shall not labor in vain" (Isa. 65:21–23 NRSV). But Isaiah says that even before that day when the creation paradigm is consummated, God guides people in the natural processes of work:

> Listen and hear my voice;
> pay attention and hear what I say.
> When a farmer plows for planting, does he plow continually?
> Does he keep on breaking up and working the soil?
> When he has leveled the surface,
> does he not sow caraway and scatter cumin?
> Does he not plant wheat in its place,
> barley in its plot,
> and spelt in its field?
> His God instructs him
> and teaches him the right way. . . .
>
> Grain must be ground to make bread;
> so one does not go on threshing it forever. . . .
> All this also comes from the LORD Almighty,
> whose plan is wonderful,
> whose wisdom is magnificent. (28:23–26, 28–29)

Though much of the book of Ecclesiastes portrays life without God, including its impact on work (as we will note later), there are glimpses of the creation paradigm: "I know that there is nothing better for people than to be happy and to do good while they live. That each of them may eat and drink, and find satisfaction in all their toil—this is the gift of God" (Eccles. 3:12–13).

23. The quote is from Keller, *Every Good Endeavor*, 120, summarizing Raymond J. Bakke, *A Theology as Big as the City* (Downers Grove, IL: InterVarsity, 1997), 105–12.

Proverbs 31 paints a powerful portrait of a woman of high character who is an industrious, successful businesswoman, combined with a faithful wife and mother:

> She selects wool and flax
> and works with eager hands.
> She is like the merchant ships,
> bringing her food from afar.
> She gets up while it is still night;
> she provides food for her family
> and portions for her female servants.
> She considers a field and buys it;
> out of her earnings she plants a vineyard.
> She sets about her work vigorously;
> her arms are strong for her tasks.
> She sees that her trading is profitable,
> and her lamp does not go out at night. . . .
> She opens her arms to the poor
> and extends her hands to the needy.
> When it snows, she has no fear for her household;
> for all of them are clothed in scarlet.
> She makes coverings for her bed;
> she is clothed in fine linen and purple. . . .
> She makes linen garments and sells them,
> and supplies the merchants with sashes.
> She is clothed with strength and dignity;
> she can laugh at the days to come.
> She speaks with wisdom,
> and faithful instruction is on her tongue.
> She watches over the affairs of her household
> and does not eat the bread of idleness. . . .
> Honor her for all that her hands have done,
> and let her works bring her praise at the city gate.
> (vv. 13–18, 20–22, 24–27, 31)

This is superwoman, whose work, family care, and reputation are almost beyond comprehension. But what is esteemed here is work in all its forms, mixed with the highest of ethical character. The woman models the principle of the psalmist: "Blessed is everyone who fears the Lord, who walks in his ways! You shall eat the fruit of the labor of your hands; you shall be blessed, and it shall be well with you" (Ps. 128:1–2 ESV).

Jesus the Worker

In his home community, before he was recognized as the Messiah, Jesus was known as a carpenter. In the early days of his ministry, Jesus was in his hometown of Nazareth on the Sabbath. "He began to teach in the synagogue, and many who heard him were amazed. 'Where did this man get these things? . . . What are these remarkable miracles he is performing? Isn't this the carpenter? Isn't this Mary's son and the brother of James, Joseph, Judas and Simon? Aren't his sisters here with us?' And they took offense at him" (Mark 6:2–3). The hometown folks couldn't imagine that a working-class person—a carpenter and the son of a carpenter—could be the Savior of the world, let alone its Creator. Recent linguistic, textual, and cultural analysis suggest that *tektōn*, the word frequently translated "carpenter," is best rendered "builder," likely referring to a builder who works with stone. Thus, Jesus the "stone mason" is likely the best rendition, and this fits with his frequent use of stone and rock metaphors.[24] Nonetheless, the carpentry image makes the point of Jesus as laborer: "The One who had masterfully fashioned humans from the dust of the earth was making chairs for people to sit on in their houses. No doubt Jesus had strong, well-worn, callused hands. It is all too easy for us to overlook the fact that Jesus knew what it meant to get up and go to work every day."[25]

Jesus not only knew the pain and suffering of the cross. He knew the pain, stress, conflicts, and misunderstandings of the workplace. Phillip Jensen and Tony Payne eloquently describe it this way: "If God came into the world, what would he be like? For the ancient Greeks, he might have been a philosopher-king. The ancient Romans might have looked for a just and noble statesman. But how does the God of the Hebrews come into the world? As a carpenter."[26] Thus, as the writer of the Epistle to the Hebrews puts it, "We do not have a high priest who is unable to sympathize with our weaknesses, but one who in every respect has been tempted as we are, yet without sin" (Heb. 4:15 ESV). Work is one of the most rewarding of human experiences, but also one of the most trying for finite, fallen humans. But there is great consolation in knowing not only that the Christ was part of the work in creation but that, while on earth, he had a job like the rest of us. He empathizes with us in the daily grind of work—and in its rich rewards.

That Jesus was a worker gives dignity to human work. It affirms that part of our created nature is to take our divine image-bearing qualities and work to meet personal needs, the needs of others, and the needs of the kingdom, and to reflect God's calling for humanity. Jesus refers to his own ministry as work, in the same way the Father works in providentially upholding his creation: "My Father is always at his work to this very day, and I too am working" (John 5:17). The dignity and significance of human work is also

24. See Jordan K. Monson, "The Stonemason the Builders Rejected," *Christianity Today*, December 2021, 38–43.

25. Nelson, *Work Matters*, 90.

26. Phillip D. Jensen and Tony Payne, *Beginnings: Eden and Beyond*, Faith Walk Bible Studies (Wheaton: Crossway, 1999), 15.

supported by Jesus's many references to work and workers in his teaching. "His discourses are full of illustrations from the work of vinedressers, builders, farmers, woodworkers, shepherds, stewards, magistrates, harvest hands, and . . . other common occupations."[27] That God was a worker in creation and the Savior a worker in the incarnation is confirmation that we were made to work, but not to allow work to become our god.

Work in the Rest of the New Testament

Throughout the New Testament and particularly in Paul's Epistles, work receives considerable attention, with three primary considerations: the responsibility to work, work as a calling for the glory of God, and the rewards of work.

On the responsibility of work, with several rationales for committing to it, are these texts:

- "Anyone who has been stealing must steal no longer, but must work, doing something useful with their own hands, that they may have something to share with those in need" (Eph. 4:28).
- "Aspire to live quietly, to mind your own affairs, and to work with your hands, . . . so that you may behave properly toward outsiders and be dependent on no one" (1 Thess. 4:11–12 NRSV).
- "Anyone who does not provide for their relatives, and especially for their own household, has denied the faith and is worse than an unbeliever" (1 Tim. 5:8).
- "Even when we were with you, we gave you this command: Anyone unwilling to work should not eat" (2 Thess. 3:10 NRSV). This follows Paul expressing his own pattern of not being a burden while with the church in Thessalonica but working to cover his own expenses. Following the rule, he refers to some among them who are idle and busybodies, and he commands them to "settle down and earn the food they eat. . . . Never tire of doing what is good" (vv. 12, 13).

Second are texts describing work as a calling and done for God's glory:

- "Bondservants, obey in everything those who are your earthly masters, not by way of eye-service, as people-pleasers, but with sincerity of heart, fearing the Lord. Whatever you do, work heartily, as for the Lord and not for [humans]. . . . You are serving the Lord Christ" (Col. 3:22–24 ESV). This text cannot be used as a rationale for chattel slavery, which was practiced in the Western world for several centuries. Instead, it is

27. Calhoun, "Work and Vocation," 86.

no doubt referring to a person in a form of debt slavery (hence "bond-servant" in the ESV), in which a person was not owned by a master but was working to pay off a debt.

- "Each person should live as a believer in whatever situation the Lord has assigned to them, just as God has called them" (1 Cor. 7:17).
- "So, whether you eat or drink, or whatever you do, do all to the glory of God" (10:31 ESV).

Third are several texts pointing to the rewards of work:

- "The hardworking farmer should be the first to receive a share of the crops" (2 Tim. 2:6).
- "The worker deserves his wages" (1 Tim. 5:18). The same wording is used in Luke 10:7.
- "Whoever plows and threshes should be able to do so in the hope of sharing in the harvest" (1 Cor. 9:10).

Thus, the New Testament affirms the creation paradigm that humans are created to work, there is dignity in work, and humans have a responsibility to work. Being a worker, with its rich rewards for self, others, and God's kingdom, is part of what it means to be a human being created in the image of God.

Work in a Fallen World

Though work is a good gift of God and filled with dignity, the fall has had a powerful impact on work in all its forms. Adam and Eve are put into the garden to "work it and take care of it" (Gen. 2:15), but they give in to the tempter, perceiving they have a better angle on life than their Maker. The results of the fall are ubiquitous, impacting every realm of life, including work on the job, in the home, and even our voluntary work. "I will make your pains in childbearing very severe; with painful labor you will give birth to children. . . . Cursed is the ground because of you; through painful toil you will eat food from it all the days of your life. It will produce thorns and thistles for you, and you will eat the plants of the field. By the sweat of your brow you will eat your food until you return to the ground, since from it you were taken; for dust you are and to dust you will return" (Gen. 3:16–19). "Work is not itself a curse, but it now lies with all other aspects of human life under the curse of sin."[28] "Thorns and thistles," literally and metaphorically, are present in various dimensions of work.

28. Keller, *Every Good Endeavor*, 89.

Stress in Work

Stress has been part of the "thorns and thistles" of work since the fall. "In language after language the same word is used for toil and child-bearing, e.g. 'labor' and 'travail.'"[29] In blue-collar jobs, stress tends to be physical in nature, while in white-collar jobs it tends to be more mental and emotional in nature. Humans devise technologies to curb the stress of work, but the technologies themselves become sources of stress. The National Institute for Occupational Safety and Health states, "Job stress can be defined as the harmful physical and emotional responses that occur when the requirements of the job do not match the capabilities, resources, or needs of the worker. Job stress can lead to poor health and even injury."[30]

Forty percent of all workers in America report that their job is "very or extremely stressful," while 25 percent report that their jobs are the number one stressor in their lives. Despite all the mechanisms to make work more palatable, 75 percent of employees believe that work has more stress today than a generation ago.[31] Thus, while work is a good gift of God from creation and filled with dignity and moral good, since the fall, humanity has experienced strains in work that then impact their health, relationships, and even spiritual lives. Stress is one of the fallen realities in the workplace.

Meaninglessness

Another part of the "thorns and thistles" of work is failing to find some meaning in work or failing to perceive one's work as meaningful. Some work at jobs simply because they believe they have no alternative and will seek to find meaning in other realms of life. In the book of Ecclesiastes, Qoheleth, the writer (teacher), is seeking to find meaning in life. First, he pursues wisdom and knowledge (1:12–18; cf. 2:12–16); second, he turns to pleasure (2:1–3); third, he pursues wealth (vv. 4–11); and fourth, he turns to work (vv. 17–26). His verdict? "Meaningless! Meaningless! . . . Everything is meaningless" (1:2). With regard to work, he describes it this way:

> So I hated life, because the work that is done under the sun was grievous to me. All of it is meaningless, a chasing after the wind. I hated all the things I had toiled for under the sun, because I must leave them to the one who comes after me. And who knows whether that person will be wise or foolish? Yet they will have control over all the fruit of my toil into which I have poured my effort and

29. W. R. Forrester, *Christian Vocation: Studies in Faith and Work* (New York: Scribner, 1953), 129.

30. Steven Sauter et al., "Stress . . . at Work," National Institute for Occupational Safety and Health, Centers for Disease Control and Prevention, accessed March 6, 2022, https://www.cdc.gov/niosh/docs/99-101/default.html.

31. Sauter et al., "Stress . . . at Work."

> skill under the sun. This too is meaningless. So my heart began to despair over all my toilsome labor under the sun. . . . All their days their work is grief and pain; even at night their minds do not rest. This too is meaningless. (2:17–20, 23)

Many people do find meaning in their work, but substantial numbers do not. One study at MIT reports, "We were anticipating that our data would show that the meaningfulness experienced by employees in relation to their work was clearly associated with actions taken by managers. . . . Instead, our research showed that quality of leadership received virtually no mention when people described meaningful moments at work, but poor management was the top destroyer of meaningfulness." The study describes the "seven deadly sins" causing meaninglessness at work: disconnecting people from their values, taking employees for granted, giving people pointless work to do, treating people unfairly, overriding people's better judgment, disconnecting people from supportive relationships, and putting people at risk of physical or emotional harm.[32] In a survey of 12,000 professionals by the Harvard Business Review, "half said they felt their job had no 'meaning and significance,' and an equal number were unable to relate to their company's mission, while another poll among 230,000 employees in 142 countries showed that only 13% of workers actually like their job."[33] Clearly then, rather than finding a sense of calling and service, many do experience work as meaningless, one of the "thorns and thistles" of the fall.

Idolatry

Because work is part of human nature and an essential means to personal and family livelihood, it is understandable that in a fallen world, work could become a god. The opening command of the Decalogue is definitive: "You shall have no other gods before me" (Exod. 20:3). We typically think of idolatry impacting only our relationship with God, but it also impacts our total self and others. Kathryn Butler describes her obsession with work during her surgical residency, along with an accident on a snowy morning at 4:00 a.m. on her way to work: "My obsession with work so enslaved me that I barreled through catastrophe to feed my fragile sense of self-importance. I risked lives in the process—first on the road, then through my befuddled meanderings in the hospital. My actions that day were reckless, dangerous, and stupid." Her perseverance, even in the face of harm to self and others, earned her the name "Mighty Mouse" as others applauded her passionate drive. "To someone scrambling for worth in the dark, the accolades were

32. Catherine Bailey and Adrian Madden, "What Makes Work Meaningful—or Meaningless," *MIT Sloan Management Review*, June 1, 2016, https://sloanreview.mit.edu/article/what-makes-work-meaningful-or-meaningless/.

33. Reported in Bailey and Madden, "What Makes Work Meaningful."

intoxicating. I soon guarded my professional identity as if it were a crust of bread during famine."[34]

The prophet Isaiah continually challenges the idolatry of God's people in the sixth century BC, including its links to work. At times Isaiah sees injustice and idolatry in the workplace (e.g., Isa. 5:9–13), and in one place he challenges those who are making gods:

> All who fashion idols are nothing, and the things they delight in do not profit. Their witnesses neither see nor know, that they may be put to shame. Who fashions a god or casts an idol that is profitable for nothing? Behold, all his companions shall be put to shame, and the craftsmen are only human. . . . The ironsmith takes a cutting tool and works it over the coals. He fashions it with hammers and works it with his strong arm. He becomes hungry, and his strength fails; he drinks no water and is faint. The carpenter stretches a line; he marks it out with a pencil. . . . He shapes it into the figure of a man, with the beauty of a man, to dwell in a house. . . . Also he makes a god and worships it; he makes it an idol and falls down before it. . . . He prays to it and says, "Deliver me, for you are my god!" They know not, nor do they discern, for he has shut their eyes, so that they cannot see, and their hearts, so that they cannot understand. . . . A deluded heart has led him astray. (Isa. 44:9–13, 15, 17–18, 20 ESV)

Here we see a mix of the good and the bad—work used to meet human need and express creativity yet mingled with idolatry. Similarly, in the workplace today many seek to define themselves through what they do and the money they make.

Sloth

At the other extreme from turning work into a god is sloth, laziness, and indifference toward one's job. It can take the form of refusing to work and so to carry out life's responsibilities or doing one's job poorly with apathy or indifference. Sloth is considered one of the seven deadly sins, which seriously impact relationship with God and limit human flourishing.[35] Various proverbs point to sloth as a vice, utilizing several different terms. Here is a sampling of the many proverbs on sloth and laziness:

> Go to the ant, O sluggard; consider her ways, and be wise. Without having any chief, officer, or ruler, she prepares her bread in summer and gathers her food in harvest. How long will you lie there, O sluggard? When will you arise from

34. Kathryn Butler, "Idolatry at the Office: Confessions of a Workaholic," Desiring God, October 16, 2017, https://www.desiringgod.org/articles/idolatry-at-the-office.

35. See, for example, Rebecca Konyndyk DeYoung, *Glittering Vices: A New Look at the Seven Deadly Sins and Their Remedies*, 2nd ed. (Grand Rapids: Brazos, 2020).

> your sleep? A little sleep, a little slumber, a little folding of the hands to rest, and poverty will come upon you like a robber. (Prov. 6:6–11 ESV)

> The way of the sluggard is blocked with thorns, but the path of the upright is a highway. (15:19)

> Slothfulness casts into a deep sleep, and an idle person will suffer hunger. . . . Whoever is generous to the poor lends to the LORD, and he will repay him for his deed. (19:15, 17 ESV)

> Sluggards do not plow in season; so at harvest time they look but find nothing. (20:4)

Sloth is understood in these proverbs not just as inaction but as a negative character trait that thwarts the kind of person God designed us to be. In the New Testament, the character focus continues and is related to the life of faith: "We do not want you to become lazy, but to imitate those who through faith and patience inherit what has been promised" (Heb. 6:12). And "do not be slothful in zeal, be fervent in spirit, serve the Lord. . . . Contribute to the needs of the saints and seek to show hospitality" (Rom. 12:11, 13 ESV). And in Jesus's parable of the talents, the master says to the man who failed to invest what he received, "You wicked and slothful servant! You knew that I reap where I have not sown and gather where I scattered no seed? Then you ought to have invested my money with the bankers, and at my coming I should have received what was my own with interest" (Matt. 25:26–27 ESV).

Sloth is a problem because it runs counter to the essential creation paradigm that a person is created to work. The failure to work or the inability to work goes against our very nature as human beings. This is why Christians must favor public policies that encourage and enable work, in order not just to meet needs but to be the kind of people God created us to be.

Injustice

Another result of the fall in the workplace is injustice, the failure to grant to others what they are owed by virtue of their work or simply being human. In Ecclesiastes Qoheleth sees frequent injustice, which adds to his own sense of meaninglessness in work: "If you see the poor oppressed in a district, and justice and rights denied, do not be surprised at such things; for one official is eyed by a higher one, and over them both are others higher still. The increase from the land is taken by all; the king himself profits from the fields" (5:8–9). And what was the cause of this injustice? "Whoever loves money never has enough; whoever loves wealth is never satisfied with their income. . . . As goods increase, so do those who consume them. And what benefit are they to the owners except to feast their eyes on them" (vv. 10–11). In similar fashion

Amos addresses injustices in the marketplace: "Hear this, you who trample the needy and do away with the poor of the land, saying, 'When will the New Moon be over that we may sell grain, and the Sabbath be ended that we may market wheat?'—skimping on the measure, boosting the price and cheating with dishonest scales" (Amos 8:4–5).

Injustices have been prevalent in the marketplace since the fall, but during the industrial revolution of the eighteenth and nineteenth centuries, they became more pronounced and menacing. People began moving to towns and cities for jobs, and when they arrived, "they experienced conditions that were nothing short of appalling. Factories and living quarters were virtually on top of each other, creating dangerously unhealthy situations. People, including children, worked for exceedingly long hours, seven days per week, often in cramped, uncomfortable, and dangerous environments."[36] This was the context that particularly stimulated Karl Marx to describe the alienations workers experienced, as well as their "exploitation, veiled by religious and political illusions."[37] Fortunately, Christians like Lord Shaftesbury in England also saw the abuses and led the way toward social reforms regarding child-labor laws and working conditions. Amid workplace injustices in the world today, some Christians are silent, but others, like those working with the International Justice Mission, are actively working to bring justice amid new forms of slavery and oppression.

Theological Foundations to Shape an Ethic for Work

We have looked at the creation paradigm on work and the rest of Scripture supporting that paradigm, including the work and teaching of Jesus. Before we come to the ethical virtues and principles needed in the workplace, especially in light of the fall, it will be helpful to pull together the theological foundations from what we have covered.

Work as a Good Gift of God Has Dignity

God's work in creation, the creational mandate to work, and Jesus's affirmation of work demonstrate that work is a good gift of God. After mandating work in caring for his creation, "God saw everything that he had made, and indeed, it was very good" (Gen. 1:31 NRSV). Though work since the fall has various "thorns and thistles," it remains a good gift of God. And thus, when we work, it is an act of dignity that has inherent worth and brings self-worth to the worker. When humans are working, and when they bring biblical under-

36. Kenneth J. Barnes, *Redeeming Capitalism* (Grand Rapids: Eerdmans, 2018), 49–50.

37. Karl Marx, *The Communist Manifesto*, trans. Samuel Moore (Chicago: Henry Regnery, 1965), 19.

standings into their work, they experience meaning, vitality, and purpose, even in the less desirable aspects of their labor. Moreover, because human work as finite creatures mirrors in small measure the creative work of the infinite Creator, workers should seek to bring creativity into their work.

The dignity of labor means that workers should bring a particular perspective to their work, and owners and leaders in the marketplace should ensure that even among the "thorns and thistles" some form of dignity can be experienced. Dignity in the workplace is captured well by Martin Luther King Jr. when he writes, "If it falls to you to be a street sweeper, sweep the streets like Michelangelo painted pictures, like Shakespeare wrote poetry, like Beethoven composed music; sweep streets so well that all the host of heaven and earth will have to pause and say, 'Here lived a great street sweeper, who swept his job well.'"[38]

Humans Are by Nature Workers

The Creator not only gives humans a mandate to work but creates us in such a way that we are wired to work. Part of what it means to be human is to exert physical or mental energy in taking God's good creation and developing it not only to meet the needs of self and others but also to express something of our own humanness. If God created humans in his image so that they would care for and develop the garden (Gen. 1:26; 2:15), it only follows that work is intrinsic to who we are—thus the New Testament mandates on work (2 Thess. 3:10; 1 Tim. 5:8).

Some have predicted that robots will eventually replace humans in the workplace, and it will be a glorious transition to a life of doing what we want to do whenever we want to do it. Carl Frey and Michael Osborne of Oxford University have argued that 47 percent of US jobs are threatened by automation,[39] and as Jean-Philippe Deranty notes, "Some progressive thinkers advocate jettisoning our work ethic and building a world without work." But Deranty rightly argues that "work is tied to our constitution as a species."[40] Thus there is concern that seven million American men between the ages of twenty-five and fifty-four are intentionally not working or seeking

38. Martin Luther King Jr., "Facing the Challenge of a New Age," in *A Testament of Hope: The Essential Writings and Speeches of Martin Luther King, Jr.*, ed. James Melvin Washington (New York: HarperSanFrancisco, 1986), 139.

39. Carl Benedikt Frey and Michael A. Osborne, "The Future of Employment: How Susceptible Are Jobs to Computerisation?," September 7, 2013, https://www.oxfordmartin.ox.ac.uk/downloads/academic/The_Future_of_Employment.pdf.

40. Jean-Philippe Deranty, "Work Is a Fundamental Part of Being Human. Robots Won't Stop Us Doing It," The Conversation, December 9, 2019, https://theconversation.com/work-is-a-fundamental-part-of-being-human-robots-wont-stop-us-doing-it-127925. Deranty argues that work is part of human nature on the grounds of evolutionary development, in which humans are set apart from other animals.

employment. As one economist notes, "What is striking . . . is how little of this enormous dividend of extra free time is devoted to activities that would be of help to others in the family . . . or others in the community."[41] We should remember that work isn't just our jobs for which we receive pay, but it is the physical and emotional energy we bring into any type of service that meets the needs of self, others, and society. Thus, when a segment of society is not doing employment work, house work, child care, or voluntary work, it runs counter to the designs of creation.

Work Is a Calling of God

As noted earlier, the idea of vocation as a calling from God was reserved for life in the monastery during the medieval period. One of the themes of the Protestant Reformation was that every person has a vocation, a calling of God through which God works in a person's everyday life. This Reformational idea of all human work as calling is partially rooted in Paul's injunction that "each person should live as a believer in whatever situation the Lord has assigned to them, just as God has called them" (1 Cor. 7:17). But it is also rooted in work's importance in Scripture and the general idea of being called as a believer. This then meant that "the only way of living acceptably to God was not to surpass worldly morality in monastic asceticism, but solely through the fulfilment of the obligations imposed upon the individual by his position in the world. That was his calling."[42] Thus, at the Reformation the whole world now became a monastery and every person a monk.

Work therefore becomes a sacred space and calling that impacts the way one carries out their daily labors, whether on the job, in the home, or in voluntary endeavors. This repudiates any hierarchy in modes of work, for as the English Reformer William Tyndale puts it, "There is no work better than another to please God; to pour water, to wash dishes, to be a souter [cobbler], or an apostle, all is one; to wash dishes and to preach is all one . . . to please God."[43] With work as a calling from God, there is a direct connection between worship on Sunday and vocation on Monday. In the words of Luther, "If you are a manual laborer, you find that the Bible has been put into your workshop, into your hand, into your heart."[44]

41. Nicholas Eberstadt, "Men without Work," American Enterprise Institute, January 30, 2018, https://www.aei.org/articles/men-without-work-2/.

42. Max Weber, *The Protestant Ethic and the Spirit of Capitalism*, trans. Talcott Parsons (New York: Scribner, 1958), 80.

43. William Tyndale, "A Parable of the Wicked Mammon," in *Doctrinal Treatises and Portions of Holy Scripture*, ed. Henry Walter (Cambridge: Parker Society, 1848), 98.

44. Martin Luther, *The Sermon on the Mount*, trans. Jaroslav Pelikan, in *Luther's Works*, vol. 21, *The Sermon on the Mount and the Magnificat*, ed. Jaroslav Pelikan (St. Louis: Concordia, 1955), 237.

Work as Love of Neighbor

When we work, we are actually loving our neighbor by providing resources and services that they could not garner on their own. Luther observes, "God gives the wool, but not without our labor. If it is on the sheep, it makes no garment."[45] Thus humans must shear and card the wool. There is thus a division of labor in work in which one individual's specialization and gifts enable others without those specializations to flourish. No one individual has all the economic capabilities to exist. This means that in work we are neighbor to others, even though the neighbor may be invisible to us. We care for others simply by being part of the workforce, whether that be jobs for pay or voluntary work.

Jesus says the second great commandment is to "love your neighbor as yourself" (Mark 12:31, quoting Lev. 19:18). Through our work we are loving our neighbors in the same way that we are loving ourselves in meeting our own needs and the needs of our immediate family. There is a proper kind of self-love that is inherent in neighbor love when we work. When one willfully refuses to work or when one is unable to work due to lack of jobs, it actually impacts their ability to carry out the neighbor-love command. Job creation is, then, one means by which neighbor love is achieved, while simultaneously enabling a proper kind of self-love. And when humans recognize their work as love of neighbor and service to society, they carry out their work as a true vocation, a calling from God. Furthermore, human work for pay enables us to advance the work of the church and God's kingdom through the stewardship of giving.

Ethical Principles and Virtues for Work

Given its biblical and theological foundations, this creation paradigm has implications for ethics in the workplace. Our Christian ethics flows out of the designs of God in creation, even when the creation story may not have spelled them out explicitly or in detail. They arise from the whole of Scripture but are rooted in the creational design of the triune God.

Integrity

Integrity means truthfulness, but it also embodies a wholeness or completeness in our human activity. This means that human work should be whole, authentic, and a reflection of the truthfulness our character is to

45. Martin Luther, *Lectures on Isaiah*, in *Luther's Works*, vol. 17, *Lectures on Isaiah: Chapters 40–66*, ed. Hilton C. Oswald, trans. Herbert J. A. Bouman (Saint Louis: Concordia, 1972), 418, quoted in Gustaf Wingren, *Luther on Vocation*, trans. Carl C. Rasmussen (1957; repr., Eugene, OR: Wipf & Stock, 2004), 8–9.

reflect. Dorothy Sayers captures this well when she writes, "The Church's approach to an intelligent carpenter is usually confined to exhorting him not to be drunk and disorderly in his leisure hours, and to come to church on Sundays. What the Church should be telling him is this: that the very first demand that his religion makes upon him is that he should make good tables. . . . No piety in the worker will compensate for work that is not true to itself; for any work that is untrue to its own technique is living a lie."[46] Taking shortcuts in our work or failing to carry out the responsibilities of our calling is really a matter of integrity, a lack of wholeness and truthfulness in our work.

Integrity also has implications for those who work in marketing and management roles. Marketing is intended to inform the public of a product or service's value for given spheres of life. Some marketing is performed by individuals within a particular company, but today many business entities utilize marketing agencies to both form and deliver a company's advertising. From a Christian-ethics perspective, sexual appeals in marketing are contrary to a Christian understanding of God's good gift and frequently objectify women (and increasingly today men as well). Such allures are primarily selling a sex appeal rather than a product. Another problem is marketing that makes claims for a product or service that are simply false. Because truth in advertising has become such a major problem today, the Federal Trade Commission has had to set high legal standards that only further bureaucratize the marketing process.

Another area in which integrity is significant for those in management roles is honesty in financial reports. *Cooking the books* "is a slang term for using accounting tricks to make a company's financial results look better than they really are. Typically, cooking the books involves manipulating financial data to inflate a company's revenue and deflate its expenses in order to pump up its earnings or profit." Companies may do this because "banks often lend, in part, based on the value of a company's accounts receivables and can fall victim to lending off false receivables."[47] Companies may also cook the books to lower their tax liability, as evidenced by the fact that in 2020 fifty-five Fortune 500 companies paid no income taxes, though many simply use legal tax loopholes that raise serious justice issues.[48] Standing against corporate policies with ethical conscience is certainly not easy, but Christian ethics rooted in creation often leads us to stand against the tide of the world around us, even when we may have to pay a price for it.

46. Sayers, *Why Work?*, 22.

47. Will Kenton, "What It Means to 'Cook the Books' Plus Examples," Investopedia, last updated March 31, 2021, https://www.investopedia.com/terms/c/cookthebooks.asp.

48. Geoff Colvin, "Last Year 55 Fortune 500 Companies Paid No U.S. Income Tax: How Can They Get Away with That?," Fortune, June 7, 2021, https://fortune.com/2021/06/07/last-year-55-fortune-500-companies-paid-no-u-s-income-tax-how-can-they-get-away-with-that/.

Human Dignity

As we have seen throughout this book, human dignity is rooted in humanity's creation in God's image. In the workplace we always have a responsibility to treat our fellow workers with dignity and worth. Here we must distinguish between the intrinsic worth of a human being and a person's value to the company or institution. Obviously, there are times when a person may need to be let go due to their performance or because of a company's change in direction or need to make cuts. But even when a person or their job is terminated, their human value and dignity must be protected by the company and the manager, and even within one's own self-perception.

I've talked to Christian corporate leaders who have said the hardest thing ethically in their jobs is figuring out how to fire someone "Christianly." Sometimes a person facing termination is simply not a good fit for the task or the company, and in such cases managers can attempt to guide the worker into a career path more suited to their gifts and proclivities. Caring in severance is an ethical imperative. But it's not only the responsibility of those at executive and managerial levels to treat others with dignity. Some today hold a deep resentment and hatred toward those in leadership roles, but they, too, should be treated with dignity. Mutual respect and affirmation at all levels of a company or institution go a long way in creating an atmosphere of enjoyment and fairness, because they reflect the creational design of human dignity.

Justice (Fairness)

We've noted already that injustice is one of the major results of the fall in the workplace. In the next chapter, we will unpack justice as a major biblical commitment in general and sort through the varying definitions and spheres of justice, but here a few words about justice related to work are appropriate. As we've seen, injustices are a major focus of the Old Testament prophets, particularly in work and economic life. But in a positive vein, justice is a much-needed principle in the workplace. Isaiah, writing in the eighth century BC, says to the Hebrew people, "Learn to do good; seek justice, rescue the oppressed, defend the orphan, plead for the widow" (Isa. 1:17 NRSV). And the Levitical law defines justice as a form of fairness: "You shall not render an unjust judgment; you shall not be partial to the poor or defer to the great: with justice you shall judge your neighbor" (Lev. 19:15 NRSV). Throughout Scripture justice is linked with both a commitment to fairness and a commitment to the special needs of the poor and marginalized in society. Thus, the two need to be held together. In the workplace fairness should be implemented in several arenas.

First, there should be fairness in pay. External qualities, such as gender, race, or religion, should never be factors in what a person is paid. Pay scales are generally developed on the basis of market rates and demand, and within that, pay then is based on expertise, years of experience, and the diligence one brings to the job. But even though the market usually determines the overarching pay scales, we must ask whether it is truly fair that significant numbers of people in wealthy societies work incredibly hard, bringing their best to the job, and yet cannot make ends meet, even sometimes working multiple jobs. Though market economies best alleviate poverty and enhance human dignity, we still must ask if it is just and fair when the average mean salary in the United States in 2022 was $53,490,[49] while some CEOs and professional athletes are making well over $40,000,000 per year. I recognize that there is strong competition for these CEOs and athletes and, thus, that high pay is needed to procure their services, but perhaps it's time for those at the highest end to voluntarily take cuts to enable those at the bottom.

Second, there should be fairness in hiring and promotions. In the workplace it's important to disassociate personal likes and dislikes when it comes to hiring. Certainly Jim Collins's *Good to Great* mandate of "getting the right people on the bus" and "the right people in the right seat on the bus" has validity.[50] But there needs to be a fairness in how this is made operational. Nepotism, hiring a friend or family member, is not illegal in the private sector, but corporate law requires disclosure of potential conflicts of interest. Usually nepotism has come back to haunt company and hirer, even if conflict of interest has been disclosed. It's hard to release a close friend or family member for underperforming, and if done, it brings significant conflict to the relationship. Family businesses have frequently faced this conundrum.

Third, there should be fairness in the contracting of suppliers. Here again conflicts of interest need to be indicated, and a breach of contract can do severe damage to personal relationships. In this and other areas, federal and state (or provincial) laws keep expanding to protect against these injustices, placing further burdens on institutions and corporations.

Justice as fairness is a vital Christian principle that needs to be implemented with integrity and care. Unfair treatment of workers and potential servicing entities frequently reaps negative results and causes disarray in the marketplace as well as in society. At the same time, we must recognize that justice for the worker does not negate the personal responsibility of the worker.

Profit without Idolatry

Profit is essential for companies. Companies without bottom-line profit become ex-companies that then are unable to provide jobs to meet the needs of individuals and society. Of course, these profits must come with integrity

49. "Average Salary in the U.S. (2022)," Jobted, accessed September 26, 2022, https://www.jobted.com/salary.

50. Jim Collins, *Good to Great: Why Some Companies Make the Leap . . . and Others Don't* (New York: HarperBusiness, 2001).

and justice, but because profits are essential to the personal, corporate, and societal good, profits themselves can be viewed as a moral good.

But we must not idolize profits. When profit becomes our god, it engenders unethical behaviors at the individual and corporate levels. It is not money that is the root of evil; rather, as Paul puts it, "Those who want to get rich fall into temptation and a trap and into many foolish and harmful desires that plunge people into ruin and destruction. For the *love of money* is a root of all kinds of evil. Some people, eager for money, have wandered from the faith and pierced themselves with many griefs" (1 Tim. 6:9–10, emphasis added). Paul here is not condemning profits or even a prosperous salary; rather, he is saying that if these are motivated by greed, they lead to unethical behaviors, which then frequently cause a lack of trust for both workers and consumers.

Profit can never stand alone, as it apparently does in Milton Friedman's famous doctrine that the primary responsibility of a corporate executive is "to make as much money as possible while conforming to the basic rules of the society, both those embodied in law and those embodied in ethical custom."[51] The problem with just obeying the basic rules of society embodied in law or custom is that it "does not guarantee responsible behavior."[52] Many companies and individuals have made profit their god, and the consequences can be disastrous, as Lehman Brothers learned in the infamous crash of 2008. Today the company no longer exists.[53]

The Social Responsibility of Job Creation

If work is part of human nature and a good gift of God for humanity, it only follows that we should do everything we can to facilitate job creation. When people are unable to work, something of their created nature is thwarted. Creativity, personal responsibility, and care for others—all part of the nature of work—are hindered in the absence of work. When people are unable to work, they feel inferior, incomplete, and lost. Moreover, work is the best way out of poverty, as long as it is accompanied by just compensation for the work that is done.

This principle has two major implications for our lives within a given society. First, when people can develop businesses and institutions that create jobs and not do harm to other responsibilities in life, they should take the opportunity. Dennis Bakke—who was the cofounder and then president of AES, an energy company based in northern Virginia—guided his company to develop core values that included social responsibility. Part of that social

51. Milton Friedman, "A Friedman Doctrine—The Social Responsibility of Business Is to Increase Its Profits," *New York Times*, September 13, 1970, https://www.nytimes.com/1970/09/13/archives/a-friedman-doctrine-the-social-responsibility-of-business-is-to.html.

52. Barnes, *Redeeming Capitalism*, 9, 10.

53. See Barnes, *Redeeming Capitalism*, 3–14.

responsibility, which encompassed safe, clean, and affordable electricity, was job creation. "In Leflore County, Oklahoma, unemployment fell from 13.6% to 4% after AES built a 320-megawatt plant there."[54] Job creation is a social responsibility. Second, we should favor public policies that help to enable jobs as opposed to destroying jobs. There are, of course, significant debates as to how we best do this and how best to alleviate poverty, but clearly a steady job is a remedy for personal economic deprivation, while also meeting a need that is part of one's created nature as a human being. Moreover, job creation is highly significant in enabling poor countries to move out of poverty and dependence. This is easier said than done, but it ought to be one of our significant operating ethical principles in the world of work and economics as Christians.

Conclusion

Work is part of our created nature. It is rooted in God as worker in creation and the commands to work in the Genesis account. Thus, work as a creational paradigm stands in stark contrast to work in many other creation stories and worldviews. The creation account of work is reinforced throughout the rest of Scripture and most visibly evidenced by Jesus Christ, our Creator-Redeemer coming into the world as a worker.

As a result, work is a good and dignified gift of God, a calling of God, and a way humans carry out the second-most-salient command, to love our neighbors as we love ourselves. Despite the impact of the fall, humans are by nature workers, and thus when they cannot or will not work, it goes contrary to their created nature. From all of this flows ethical principles for work: integrity, dignity, justice, profit without idolatry, and the social responsibility of job creation.

But work is not the end of human existence. For on the seventh day of creation, our Creator rested from all his work. And it is to that Sabbath paradigm that we now turn.

54. Dennis W. Bakke, *Joy at Work: A Revolutionary Approach to Fun on the Job* (Seattle: PVG, 2005), 30.

8

Sabbath

God Institutes a Rhythm of Life for Worship, Self-Care, and Justice

After God works in creation and institutes work for humanity, there is a pause in the action. God institutes a rhythm of life both to get our perspectives aright and to ensure that our work does not become abusive spiritually or morally. "By the seventh day God had finished the work he had been doing; so on the seventh day he rested from all his work. Then God blessed the seventh day and made it holy, because on it he rested from all the work of creating that he had done" (Gen. 2:2–3).

Throughout Jewish and Christian history, the Sabbath has been a source of strength, identity, and hope but also a source of great conflict, debate, and dour sentiments—especially in the Christian church. Much of the debate has centered on what one can and cannot do on the Sabbath, whether the Sabbath is still operative in the church, and if so, whether the day has changed from the seventh day of the week to the first day of the week. In all these discussions, what is lost is the ultimate meaning of the Sabbath. What I will attempt to argue in this chapter is that the Sabbath is establishing a rhythm of life to balance our worship, work, and rest or leisure. The issue is not the specific day but the principles inherent in this rhythm—namely, worship, self-care, and justice. As Jewish writer Samuel Dresner puts it, "The Sabbath has taught us how to sanctify time and bring a dimension of holiness into the profane rhythm of life; how to unite a way of thinking with a way of living."[1]

1. Samuel H. Dresner, *The Sabbath* (New York: Burning Bush, 1970), 15.

When God rests from all of his work at creation, it is not because he is tired. Rather, our Creator is putting in place a paradigm for living that produces holiness, love of neighbor (hence justice), and loving self in a proper way. After all, Jesus says we are to love our neighbors as we love ourselves (Matt. 22:39). God puts in place a rhythm of life that is affirmed in the Decalogue and the rest of the Old Testament. It is also affirmed by Jesus, who attempts to correct its misguided understandings and practices, and by other New Testament voices, inclusive of its final fullness in the eschaton. As a creation paradigm, the primary focus is not the specific day, though that is strongly stipulated and regulated in the Old Testament, but a pattern of life needed in order to be fully human. Creation's framework of a seven-day week with one special day has been affirmed and practiced not only by Jews and Christians but by other religions and cultures. Attempts to move away from the pattern have been met with resistance, because something about the rhythm rings true to human nature and experience. If this rhythm of life is part of created human nature, it's only natural that we find expressions of it in some manner throughout the world.

But there is something unique about this creational paradigm as echoed throughout Scripture. According to Richard Lowery, "Mesopotamian culture had market days tied to the lunar cycle, but Israel's seventh-day sabbath is unparalleled in the ancient world" when it comes to its meaning and significance.[2] "It was not only among the Hebrew people that the number seven had special significance. Indeed, it was seen as evil throughout the vast region from Canaan to Mesopotamia. . . . Since the seventh day was evil, one was expected to abstain from all labor or any other activity that might lead to harm or accidents." Thus, the meaning and motive for many ancients resting on the seventh day was not positive ethics, "and the day itself was not joyful."[3] In contrast, the biblical portrait of Sabbath is one of joy, adoration of the Creator, and a framework of protection for self and others. Work as instituted by God at creation is essential to human life and part of human nature. But "to violate the rhythm of work and rest (in either direction) leads to chaos in our life and in the world around us. Sabbath is therefore a celebration of our design."[4] And it is highly significant that it is instituted by God in creation. It is a day made holy by the Creator, meaning it is set apart from all other periods of time. With Israel and the giving of the law, it is a sign of the covenant between God and the people that they, too, may be holy as God is holy. Ezekiel the prophet puts it this way: "I [the Lord] gave them

2. Richard H. Lowery, *Sabbath and Jubilee*, Understanding Biblical Themes (St. Louis: Chalice, 2000), 4.

3. Justo L. González, *A Brief History of Sunday: From the New Testament to the New Creation* (Grand Rapids: Eerdmans, 2017), 4–5.

4. Timothy Keller, *Every Good Endeavor: Connecting Your Work to God's Work*, with Katherine Leary Alsdorf (New York: Dutton, 2012), 235.

my Sabbaths as a sign between us, so they would know that I the LORD made them holy" (Ezek. 20:12; cf. v. 20). Our practice of Sabbath principles today also engenders ethical holiness.

Sabbath and the Decalogue

The fourth commandment is to keep the Sabbath, and it reinforces and gives rationale and further direction for this creation paradigm. The commandment serves as a bridge between the first table of the law, focused on honoring God, and the second table of the law, focused on responsibilities to and protections of our fellow humans. Immediately this gives us a clue as to the meaning of the Sabbath, with its focus on God, self, and others. The Decalogue occurs in two places: Exodus 20, with the giving of the law at Mount Sinai, and Deuteronomy 5, as the Hebrew people are about to enter the promised land after years of wandering (which is both physical and spiritual).

The Exodus version is as follows: "Remember the sabbath day, and keep it holy. Six days you shall labor and do all your work. But the seventh day is a sabbath to the LORD your God; you shall not do any work—you, your son or your daughter, your male or female slave, your livestock, or the alien resident in your towns. For in six days the LORD made heaven and earth, the sea, and all that is in them, but rested on the seventh day; therefore the LORD blessed the sabbath day and consecrated it" (Exod. 20:8–11 NRSV). This is by far the longest of the Ten Commandments, no doubt showing its significance and relationship to many of the other commandments. The commandment and the whole Decalogue come between two great building projects, which Ellen Davis describes this way:

> Exodus is setting before us two lengthy, vivid pictures. In the first thirteen chapters, we see Israel enslaved in Egypt, trapped in "that iron furnace" (Deut. 4:20), the great industrial killing machine of Pharaonic Egypt. There Israel builds store cities for a king so deluded he thinks he is a god. Then at the other end of the book, thirteen chapters portray Israel's first concerted activity in freedom. Israel's first "public work" is to build a sanctuary for her God, who is of course the real God. These two long narratives at beginning and end are a sort of unmatched pair, designed to contrast absolutely. They are, respectively, perverted work, designed by Pharoah to destroy God's people, and divinely mandated work, designed to bring together God and God's people in the closest proximity possible in this life.[5]

In the middle of these building projects—one devoted to injustice and oppression and the other to worship and holiness—comes a command that

5. Ellen F. Davis, "Slaves or Sabbath-Keepers? A Biblical Perspective on Human Work," *Anglican Theological Review* 83, no. 1 (2001): 30–31.

brings together worship, self-care, and justice. The stipulations include cessation from work for oneself, family, workers, immigrants, and even animals. The rationale in the Exodus version is God's own action in creation: "For in six days the LORD made heaven and earth, the sea, and all that is in them, but rested on the seventh day" (v. 11 NRSV). God makes this day holy, set apart from the rush and pressures of everyday life, much of which stems from God's good but now fallen gifts, such as work. But "on the Sabbath we are at peace with nature. Six days a week we compete with the natural world—building, subduing, struggling to overcome lest we be overcome. . . . On the Seventh Day we withdraw, moving from creation to Creator, . . . from nature to the Lord of all nature."[6]

The Deuteronomic version has some slight but significant differences in its rendering, as the people are now in a context different from Mount Sinai and its surroundings.

> Observe the sabbath day and keep it holy, as the LORD your God commanded you. Six days you shall labor and do all your work. But the seventh day is a sabbath to the LORD your God; you shall not do any work—you, or your son or your daughter, or your male or female slave, or your ox or your donkey, or any of your livestock, or the resident alien in your towns, so that your male and female slave may rest as well as you. Remember that you were a slave in the land of Egypt, and the LORD your God brought you out from there with a mighty hand and an outstretched arm; therefore the LORD your God commanded you to keep the sabbath day. (Deut. 5:12–15 NRSV)

In this version the command is initially to "observe" rather than "remember," and the list of entities to experience the day of rest includes oxen and donkeys, which are the animals commonly used in agricultural pursuits once they settle into the promised land.

But the biggest difference in this version is the rationale for keeping the Sabbath: "Remember that you were a slave in the land of Egypt, and the LORD your God brought you out from there with a mighty hand and an outstretched arm" (5:15 NRSV). The two rationales for the Sabbath in the two versions demonstrate that creation and liberation (or redemption) are complimentary and go hand in hand. But in the Deuteronomic rationale, focusing on liberation from bondage in Egypt, God's people are reminded that they are freed "from a condition in which they were not human beings, but simply units of capacity in Pharaoh's brick production system. Anyone who cannot obey God's command to observe the Sabbath is a slave, even a self-imposed one." Thus, the people then and God's people today are to remember that the Sabbath is "a declaration of our freedom. It means you are not a slave—not to your culture's expectations, your family's hope, . . . not even to your own

6. Dresner, *Sabbath*, 37–38.

insecurities."[7] As we view these two rationales for the Sabbath, we see that "the God who rests [in creation] is the God who emancipates from slavery."[8]

Some have argued that the Sabbath command does not involve worship but primarily a rest from one's labors. But in Exodus 31, just after the Lord's instruction on building the tabernacle (the place of sacrifice and worship), the text moves immediately to the Sabbath, thus suggesting that Sabbath does involve worship. "Then the LORD said to Moses, 'Say to the Israelites, "You must observe my Sabbaths. This will be a sign between me and you for the generations to come, so you may know that I am the LORD, who makes you holy. Observe the Sabbath, because it is holy to you"'" (vv. 12–14). Certainly Israel would know the Lord and his holiness not simply by resting but also by serious reflection on God and the meaning of the covenant relationship. Leviticus 23 lays out significant festivals, sacred assemblies, and gatherings of celebration and begins with the Sabbath. It explicitly states, "The seventh day is a day of sabbath rest, a day of sacred assembly" (v. 3). And Psalm 92 has the title "A psalm. A song. For the Sabbath day." It is clearly focused on worship and begins, "It is good to praise the LORD and make music to your name, O Most High" (v. 1). The Sabbath in the commandment is, after all, a "sabbath to the LORD your God" (Exod. 20:10). A focus on God is central to its meaning, along with the other dimensions.

The Sabbath from creation and the Decalogue is wholistic in focus. Dennis Olson sums it up well: "The biblical theme of the Sabbath offers rich resources for fundamentally reshaping our view of time as it integrates and balances the way we relate to all of our primary connections in life—our relationship with God, with other humans, with nonhuman creation, and even with ourselves."[9]

The Old Testament and Sabbath

Sabbath is mentioned more than one hundred times throughout the Old Testament. Not only is there affirmation of the Sabbath day, but the concept gets extended to include established years and longer periods of time. Caring for others by providing rest, which is explicit in the Decalogue, gets extended to larger justice issues, showing that the creation paradigm and the fourth commandment are pregnant with deeper applications than might first meet the eye.

In the above section, we mentioned Exodus 31 coming after the instructions on building the tabernacle. That chapter involves extended description of the

7. Keller, *Every Good Endeavor*, 236.

8. Walter Brueggemann, *Sabbath as Resistance: Saying No to the Culture of Now*, rev. ed. (Louisville: Westminster John Knox, 2017), 2.

9. Dennis T. Olson, "Sacred Time: The Sabbath and Christian Worship," in *Sunday, Sabbath, and the Weekend: Managing Time in a Global Culture*, ed. Edward O'Flaherty and Rodney L. Petersen, with Timothy A. Norton (Grand Rapids: Eerdmans, 2010), 44.

Israelites' responsibilities, including severe consequences for nonobservance. "Anyone who desecrates [the Sabbath] is to be put to death; those who do any work on that day must be cut off from their people. For six days work is to be done, but the seventh day is a day of sabbath rest, holy to the LORD" (vv. 14–15; cf. 35:2). This severe penalty shows how significant the Sabbath was for the Hebrew people and its close association with holiness. But the section begins by alluding to plural Sabbaths: "You must observe my Sabbaths" (31:13). This is no doubt a recognition that the Sabbath laws extend to the seventh-year stipulations and the Jubilee year, which are clearly focused on mechanisms of justice and care for all people in their midst. The text goes on to command that the people are "to observe the Sabbath, celebrating it for the generations to come as a lasting covenant. It will be a sign between me and the Israelites forever, for in six days the LORD made the heavens and the earth, and on the seventh day he rested and was refreshed" (vv. 16–17). In Exodus 34:21 the Sabbath command is again stated and applied "even during the plowing season and harvest."

The Hebrew prophets not only remind the people of their duty to keep the Sabbath but also warn of failures related to the Sabbath. Isaiah links justice and Sabbath keeping: "Maintain justice, and do what is right. . . . Happy is the mortal who does this, the one who holds it fast, who keeps the sabbath, not profaning it, and refrains from doing any evil" (Isa. 56:1–2 NRSV). He also speaks of the great rewards and joy that come from keeping the Sabbath, upon the people's return from captivity: "If you turn back your foot from the Sabbath, from doing your pleasure on my holy day, and call the Sabbath a delight and the holy day of the LORD honorable; . . . then you shall take delight in the LORD, and I will make you ride on the heights of the earth" (58:13–14 ESV). But Isaiah also calls the people to account for practicing sacrifices and Sabbath keeping as a cover-up for their own idolatry and unrighteousness (1:12–13). The prophet Amos similarly calls out the people's religious practices, including Sabbath keeping, which they saw as limiting their unethical practices: "Hear this, you who trample the needy and do away with the poor of the land, saying, 'When will the New Moon be over that we may sell grain, and the Sabbath be ended that we may market wheat?'—skimping on the measure, boosting the price and cheating with dishonest scales" (Amos 8:4–5; cf. Hosea 2:10–11).

Speaking to his fellow Israelites exiled in Babylon in the sixth century BC, Ezekiel reminds the people of their ancestors' unfaithfulness to God in the wilderness. He begins with the Lord saying, "I gave them my Sabbaths as a sign between us, so they would know that I the LORD made them holy" (Ezek. 20:12). But the Lord reminds them of how their ancestors "desecrated my Sabbaths" and "rejected my laws" (vv. 13, 16) because "their hearts were devoted to their idols" (v. 16). Still, God kept his end of the covenant and did not destroy the ancestors in the wilderness, and he will not destroy the exiles in captivity. Thus, the Lord admonishes the people to keep following his decrees and designs and to "keep my Sabbaths holy, that they may be a sign between us. Then you will know that I am the LORD your God" (v. 20). After the people return to Jerusalem from exile, they are reminded of God's law and creation paradigm regarding the Sabbath (Neh. 9:14), and the people make a binding agreement that "when the neighboring peoples bring merchandise or grain to sell on the Sabbath, we will not buy from them on the Sabbath or on any holy day. Every seventh year we will forgo working the land and will cancel all debts" (10:31). But like God's people before them, and even after years of captivity in Babylon, they quickly go back to their old patterns and those of neighboring peoples, desecrating the Sabbath and seeking economic gain over Sabbath worship, rest, and justice (13:15–22).

The Old Testament teaching on Sabbath is not only focused on the seventh day of the week but extended to a Sabbath year, on the seventh year, and then a Jubilee year after seven Sabbath years—that is, on the fiftieth year. These are clearly mechanisms to achieve justice in Israel.

Exodus 23 puts the seventh-day rest (v. 12) and the seventh-year rest together: "For six years you shall sow your land and gather in its yield, but the seventh year you shall let it rest and lie fallow" (vv. 10–11a ESV). What was the reason for this practice in an agricultural society? "That the poor of your people may eat; and what they leave the beasts of the field may eat. You shall do likewise with your vineyard, and with your olive orchard" (v. 11b ESV). The next verse then reiterates the command for the seventh day. It is significant that provision is made not only for the poor but also for another segment of God's good creation, the wild animals. Exodus 21 adds to the seventh year a provision for freeing slaves, who were likely indentured servants who served to pay off debt. "If you buy a Hebrew servant, he is to serve you for six years. But in the seventh year, he shall go free, without paying anything" (v. 2).

In Deuteronomy 15 the seventh year also includes debt cancellation as a means of addressing poverty. "At the end of every seven years you must cancel debts. . . . Every creditor shall cancel any loan they have made to a fellow Israelite. They shall not require payment from anyone among their own people, because the LORD's time for canceling debts has been proclaimed" (vv. 1–2). The result and rationale of this action is that "there need be no poor people among you, for in the land the LORD your God is giving you to possess as your inheritance, he will richly bless you" (v. 4). The text goes on to call for openhandedness, generosity, and integrity in carrying out the law (vv. 7–11). Leviticus 25 specifically employs the language of a Sabbath for the land:

> When you come into the land that I give you, the land shall keep a Sabbath to the LORD. For six years you shall sow your field, and for six years you shall prune your vineyard and gather in its fruits, but in the seventh year there shall be a Sabbath of solemn rest for the land, a Sabbath to the LORD. You shall not

> sow your field or prune your vineyard. You shall not reap what grows of itself in your harvest, or gather the grapes of your undressed vine. It shall be a year of solemn rest for the land. The Sabbath of the land shall provide food for you, for yourself and for your male and female slaves and for your hired worker and the sojourner who lives with you, and for your cattle and for the wild animals that are in your land. (vv. 2–7 ESV)

Here not only is there provision for people and animals, but even consideration of the land, for as we saw in chapter 4, creation care is a mandate for creation itself. "Today, of course, we know that there are good agricultural reasons for letting fields 'rest,' and even in biblical times there must have been some inkling that a fallow year would allow nutrients to be replenished and ecological diversity to be maintained."[10]

Leviticus 25 goes on to lay out another Sabbath-related mandate, the Jubilee year. "Count off seven sabbath years—seven times seven years—so that the seven sabbath years amount to a period of forty-nine years. . . . Consecrate the fiftieth year and proclaim liberty throughout the land to all its inhabitants" (vv. 8, 10). The stipulations not only prohibit sowing and reaping crops on this Jubilee year; they also prescribe a return of land to original owners (v. 13), along with stipulations about selling and buying land proportionate to the timing of the Jubilee year (vv. 14–17). The upshot of this law, which as far as we know was never actually put into practice, is to prevent a land monopoly that would permanently keep people in poverty. "No one family or group could permanently amass unduly large tracts of land for itself on the one hand, or be forced into permanent poverty on the other. Every family was periodically to gain access again to their fair portion of the economic pie."[11] The rationale is quite simple: "The land must not be sold permanently, because the land is mine and you reside in my land as foreigners and strangers" (v. 23).

The extension of the Sabbath day to the Sabbath year and the year of Jubilee clearly shows that this creation paradigm is broader than just rest or worship. In the Decalogue the care for self, others, and animals is explicit, but in the Sabbath year and Jubilee, it is explicitly related to issues of justice, what is owed people in the various spheres of life. The stipulations are, of course, clearly established for an agrarian culture, with a zero-sum economic framework focused mostly on the land. In a zero-sum situation, one individual's gain means another person's loss. Most of us today don't live in agrarian cultures, and in market economies a zero-sum approach is naive and self-defeating. Thus, we have to think about how we might apply these justice principles to our contemporary settings. We will explore this later in the chapter, but we must clearly affirm that the Sabbath paradigm, including

10. Andy Crouch, *Playing God: Redeeming the Gift of Power* (Downers Grove, IL: IVP Books, 2013), 258.

11. Olson, "Sacred Time," 60.

the Sabbath-year and Jubilee-year principles, are still normative for us today. Though Jubilee was likely not practiced in ancient Israel, Andy Crouch points out that it was never forgotten. "The true God never gave up on his people and the flourishing that his image bearers were meant to bring. When Jesus began his ministry, he found the place in the scroll where Isaiah revived the hope of the Jubilee year and read it aloud (Luke 4). Wherever Jesus went there were foretastes of Jubilee."[12]

Jesus and the Sabbath

Jesus both practiced the Sabbath and critiqued contemporary misunderstandings and applications of it. Jesus and his disciples were Jews, and they thus practiced the creation paradigm. For example, Mark 1 tells us that "they went into Capernaum, and immediately on the Sabbath [Jesus] entered the synagogue and was teaching. And they were astonished at his teaching, for he taught them as one who had authority, and not as the scribes" (vv. 21–22 ESV). In several other places in the Gospel accounts, Jesus and his disciples go to the synagogue on the Sabbath, and he is usually engaged in teaching (e.g., Luke 13:10; John 6:59).

But Jesus and his disciples run into problems with religious authorities because of some of their actions on the Sabbath. On one occasion "Jesus went through the grainfields on the sabbath; his disciples were hungry, and they began to pluck heads of grain and to eat. When the Pharisees saw it, they said to him, 'Look, your disciples are doing what is not lawful to do on the sabbath'" (Matt. 12:1–2 NRSV). Jesus responds with Old Testament stories that involve actions of eating to meet human need, including the stories of David and his companions eating the consecrated bread reserved for priests in the house of God (vv. 3–4) and of the priests on Sabbath duty in the temple breaking the Sabbath and yet remaining innocent (v. 5). Jesus then makes two vital points about himself in relation to the Sabbath. First, referring to himself, he says, "I tell you, something greater than the temple is here" (v. 6 NRSV). And then he adds, "The Son of Man is lord of the sabbath" (v. 8 NRSV), no doubt referring to the fact that, as part of the triune Godhead, he was there at creation in establishing the creation paradigm. In Mark's Gospel Jesus adds, "The sabbath was made for humankind, and not humankind for the sabbath" (2:27 NRSV), attempting to get beyond the legalistic laws added to the Sabbath to get to the real reason for God establishing the paradigm in creation.

In Luke 13 Jesus heals a woman who had been "crippled by a spirit for eighteen years. She was bent over and could not straighten up at all" (v. 11). Jesus puts his hands on her, freeing her from her infirmity, and she immediately

12. Crouch, *Playing God*, 264.

straightens up. The local synagogue leaders are indignant, saying there are six other days to do healing work. Jesus responds, "You hypocrites! Doesn't each of you on the Sabbath untie your ox or donkey from the stall and lead it out to give it water? Then should not this woman, a daughter of Abraham, whom Satan has kept bound for eighteen long years, be set free on the Sabbath day from what bound her?" (vv. 15–16). Here Jesus is getting to the heart of the Sabbath principles, for it's not about the day per se but about a rhythm of life that incorporates worship, self-care, and care for others. Freeing a woman from both spiritual and physical bondage is an act of care commensurate with the teaching of the fourth commandment, which seeks to protect self, family, servants, and animals.

In John 5 Jesus on a Sabbath goes to a pool in Jerusalem that is popularly known for its healing powers. There Jesus encounters a man who has been an invalid for thirty-eight years and who complains to Jesus that he has no one to help him get into the pool when the waters stir.[13] "Jesus said to him, 'Get up! Pick up your mat and walk.' At once the man was cured; he picked up his mat and walked" (vv. 8–9). The Jewish leaders get upset because this occurs on the Sabbath, and they begin to persecute him. A similar event in John 9 occurs when, on a Sabbath, Jesus heals a man born blind from birth. The Pharisees complain, "This man is not from God, for he does not keep the Sabbath" (v. 16).

Clearly in these and other incidents, Jesus is acting contrary to the thirty-nine types of labors that the Mishnah prohibits on the Sabbath. The Old Testament spells out some specific regulations, but many more were added to the list by the time of Jesus. William Barclay writes, "Principles became regulations, and law became legalism. There was a reason for this. Centuries of subjection to greater nations robbed the Jews of all possibilities of outward expansion, and as it were, drove the nation in upon itself. Their scholars and experts and theologians began to study their own laws under a microscope."[14] For example, the law forbids work on the Sabbath, but the religious leaders expanded the concept with a vast delineation of types of work. One type of work was carrying a burden, but that precipitated the question, "What is a burden? So it comes to be argued whether or not a man may lift his child on the Sabbath. Yes, he may, but not if the child has a stone in his hand, for the stone is a burden even if the child is not. Then there comes the inevitable question. What is a stone?"[15]

13. Some ancient manuscripts, though likely not original texts, give further explanation about the healing waters. The tradition was "that a periodic disturbance of the waters was due to an angel. The first to enter the pool at such a time, they thought, would be healed." Leon Morris, *The Gospel according to John*, New International Commentary on the New Testament (Grand Rapids: Eerdmans, 1971), 302.

14. William Barclay, *The Ten Commandments for Today* (Grand Rapids: Eerdmans, 1977), 32.

15. Barclay, *Ten Commandments*, 32–33.

Jesus is clearly in the bounds of the Jewish tradition by healing on the Sabbath, for the "Talmud and interpreters of the Talmud are unanimous in affirming the principle that saving a life supersedes the Sabbath."[16] But the religious leaders of Jesus's day and especially those opposed to him had developed such legalistic stances that they essentially went against their own tradition and against the intent and scope of creation, the fourth commandment, and the teachings of the Hebrew Scriptures. Christ the Redeemer is also Creator and, thus, partakes in resting "from all the work of creating that he had done" (Gen. 2:3). The Son of God was part of the authoring of the Decalogue, with its Sabbath law designed to enable humans to truly worship God, care for themselves, and care for others. Christ, the eternal author of Sabbath and the one who will bring about the final Sabbath rest, was in his actions on this earth demonstrating the full meaning of the Sabbath, which was made for humanity—and not the other way around.

The New Testament and Sabbath

When we come to the rest of the New Testament, we must note that Sabbath is not a major theme. That doesn't mean the principles inherent in the Sabbath paradigm go away, but rather the focus on the particular day seems to be of less concern. From the book of Acts, it appears that initially believers observed the Sabbath by attending synagogue worship services in which they actually taught about Christ (Acts 13:14–16; 17:1–3). We then have two texts that indicate that Christ followers were beginning to gather for worship and teaching on the first day of the week (Sunday), no doubt in honor of the resurrection of Christ. Acts 20:7 states, "On the first day of the week we came together to break bread. Paul spoke to the people." In 1 Corinthians 16:1–2, Paul writes, "Now about the collection for the Lord's people: Do what I told the Galatian churches to do. On the first day of every week, each one of you should set aside a sum of money in keeping with your income." The term "the Lord's Day," which came to eventually be utilized as the Christian day of worship and rest (Sunday), appears just once in the New Testament, in John's apocalypse: "On the Lord's Day I was in the Spirit, and I heard behind me a loud voice like a trumpet, which said: 'Write on a scroll what you see and send it to the seven churches'" (Rev. 1:10–11).

The evidence that the day itself was not primary is seen in two texts. In Colossians 2:16–17 Paul writes, "Therefore let no one pass judgment on you in questions of food and drink, or with regard to a festival or a new moon or a Sabbath. These are a shadow of the things to come, but the substance belongs to Christ" (ESV). Similarly, in Galatians Paul admonishes the believers

16. Lowery, *Sabbath and Jubilee*, 143.

to not be enslaved again to legalistic patterns, such as patterns concerning "special days and months and seasons and years" (4:10). This would seem to indicate that the early church leaders were not throwing out the laws of God as ethical requirements but attempting to focus on the underlying commitments and principles inherent in the commands, rather than the forms in which those commitments are expressed. In this case the specific day, which over the years had come to sometimes be more important than God, was not the crucial point. Rather, the creation paradigm—with its principles of worship, self-care, and care for others, or justice (as spelled out in the fourth commandment and the rest of Scripture)—was the abiding commitment and true essence of Sabbath.

Moreover, the writer to the Hebrews brings an eschatological dimension to Sabbath rest in contrast to the people's ancestors, who failed to experience rest due to their disobedience. He links this rest to God's own rest from all his works on the seventh day (4:4) and states, "There remains a Sabbath rest for the people of God, for whoever has entered God's rest has also rested from his works as God did from his. Let us therefore strive to enter that rest, so that no one may fall by the same sort of disobedience" (vv. 9–11 ESV). This eschatological Sabbath does not negate the Sabbath paradigm in this world, but it does remind us that here "we have no lasting city, but we seek the city that is to come" (13:14 ESV). Saint Augustine closes his monumental work, *The City of God*, by pointing to the eschatological Sabbath, not as an escape from this world but as a framework in which we carry on our work and rest in this world. "This . . . will be that ultimate Sabbath that has no evening and which the Lord foreshadowed in the account of His creation. . . . On that day we shall rest and see, see and love, love and praise—for this is to be the end without the end of all our living, that Kingdom without end, the real goal of our present life."[17]

The Sabbath in Christian History

We must acknowledge that throughout Christian history there has not been unanimity regarding the Sabbath. Questions have abounded:

- Were the Old Testament Sabbath and its requirements (including the seventh day) abolished with the coming of Christ?
- Will the real Sabbath rest be fulfilled in the eschaton?
- Is Sunday a replacement for the seventh day in observing the Sabbath?

17. Augustine, *The City of God: Books XVII–XXII*, trans. Gerald G. Walsh and Daniel J. Honan, Fathers of the Church (Washington, DC: Catholic University of America Press, 1954), 22.30.

- If Sunday is the new day of rest, what can and cannot be done on this day?
- Is Sabbath universal (applicable to all people) or only for believers?

Clearly there has been much variation in interpretations, but I believe that is largely because the focus has been on the day or on restrictions rather than the paradigm and underlying principles.

It seems clear that early Christians, beginning in the New Testament, were setting aside the first day of the week for special observance. The Didache, from around 100 AD, urges its readers, "On the Lord's Day come together, break bread, and give thanks,"[18] and Ignatius, writing in the early second century, contends that the Sabbath of the old covenant is no longer binding for Christians, for they are "no longer keeping the Sabbath but living in accordance with the Lord's day."[19] Historian Justo González argues that there is evidence "that at least as late as the fourth century, some or perhaps even most Christians observed the Sabbath, and then the Lord's day on the following day. In other words, the Lord's Day . . . was not a substitution for the Sabbath, but a separate celebration of the resurrection of Jesus."[20] In this account Sunday was not a day of rest as the Sabbath had been. It was with Constantine in the fourth century that Sunday came to be more closely associated with the Sabbath, though with greater flexibility than the Jewish practices. Throughout the medieval period, the church set forth a number of decrees with restrictive measures regarding the Lord's Day, which increasingly was called the Sabbath.[21]

In the Protestant Reformation, there was no unanimity on equating Sabbath with the Lord's Day, and many interpreted the fourth commandment to be ceremonial in nature rather than moral. John Calvin argued that though the seventh day, with the ceremonial part of the fourth commandment, has been abolished, there are abiding elements for Christians: "first, that during our whole lives we may aim at a constant rest from our own works . . . ; secondly, . . . that all may observe the legitimate order appointed by the church, for the hearing of the word, the administration of the sacraments, and public prayer: and, thirdly, that we may avoid oppressing those who are subject to us."[22] Calvin makes clear, and I believe rightly so, that the primary issue is not the day on which we attend to these. A century later the Puritans would go much further in England and the colonies by enacting laws that prevented the

18. Didache, in *The Apostolic Fathers: Greek Texts and English Translations*, ed. and trans. Michael W. Holmes, 3rd ed. (Grand Rapids: Baker Academic, 2007), 14.1, p. 365.

19. Ignatius, *To the Magnesians*, in Holmes, *The Apostolic Fathers*, 9.1, p. 209.

20. González, *Brief History of Sunday*, 23.

21. González, *Brief History of Sunday*, 83–96.

22. John Calvin, *Institutes of the Christian Religion*, trans. Henry Beveridge, rev. ed. (Peabody, MA: Hendrickson, 2008), 2.8.34.

sale of merchandise and food and limited travel and work on Sundays. This Puritan view was clearly established in the Westminster Confession of 1647, which equated Sabbath and the Lord's Day: "This Sabbath is then kept holy unto the Lord, when men, after a due preparing of their hearts, and ordering of their common affairs beforehand, do not only observe an holy rest all the day from their own works, words, and thoughts about their worldly employments and recreations, but also . . . worship."[23] These directives then found expression in Sunday blue laws in the United States and Europe, banning certain business and recreational enterprises.

In the past century, Sabbath restrictions have been lifted with a secularization process that has, in the public mind, overturned even nonreligious rationales for such laws. The church itself has experienced much laxity regarding Lord's Day restrictions, and many churches have offered services at other times than Sunday. At the same time in recent years, there has been a resurgence of interest in Sabbath rest, particularly as a spiritual discipline that brings balance to life and draws one more deeply to God.

Ethical Implications of the Sabbath Creation Paradigm for Today

As I have argued throughout this chapter, the Sabbath paradigm rooted in God's rest in creation establishes a rhythm of life to balance work, worship, and leisure. As we observed, in the teaching of the Decalogue, the application in the Old Testament, and the examples from Jesus and the early church, the primary issue is not about the particular day or even restrictions on a given day. Rather, the rhythm finds its application in the principles of worship, self-care, and care for others (justice). Based on tradition most believers have participated in public worship primarily on Sundays in honor of Christ's resurrection, and they also experience a change of pace on that day. However, there are some cultures in which Sunday worship is not feasible due to cultural patterns, and for some professions, including the ministry, Sunday is hardly a day of rest. The key is that we follow a rhythm of life in which worship, self-care, and justice can be incorporated into the very fabric of our lives. This is best done with devoted times each week, especially for worship and self-care. But the legalisms that have sometimes developed throughout Christian history were frequently far removed from the paradigm.

Worship

For some it may seem strange to include worship in a book and section on ethics, but the worship of the triune God must be at the heart of and the

23. Westminster Confession, in *Westminster Confession of Faith* (Glasgow: Free Presbyterian Publications, 1994), 21.8, p. 95.

motivation for the Christian moral life. For one day (or period) a week, we stop making the world in order to recognize that God already made it and, hence, conform our lives to the designs of our Maker. "In ancient Rome, the days on which there were no religious festivals or public games were called *dies vacantes*, 'empty days.'"[24] But Gilbert Meilaender wisely points out that, in contrast, "Sunday for Christians, like the Sabbath for Jews, should be full—filled with shared celebration and marked by trust that we are free from the need to secure our own life through the things we possess."[25]

As we noted earlier, the Sabbath command in the Decalogue is a bridge between responsibilities to God and responsibilities to others amid life in family, community, and society. The Decalogue begins with the first commandment—"You shall have no other gods before me" (Exod. 20:3)—followed by two commands to protect the holiness and rightful place of God in our lives—no idols or images of the transcendent God (vv. 4–6) and no misuse of God's name for our own self-centered purposes (v. 7). Then comes the Sabbath command, incorporating a day of rest that includes worship of this God. As Karl Barth once noted regarding the first commandment, "All the laws of Israel and all the concrete demands addressed by God to individual men in Israel are simply developments and specific forms of this one law, demands not to withhold from the God of the covenant the thanks which is His due, but to render it with a whole heart."[26] Hence, we daily give allegiance to God, but at least one time a week we gather with fellow believers to acknowledge our Creator-Redeemer-Sustainer, to not only give him what is due his name but also to set our lives and thinking in right perspective for life in this good but now fallen world. It is in worship that we recognize that "the good things of our world [such as the natural world, family, and work] are good precisely because they participate in the goodness of the Creator."[27]

While the Decalogue does not explicitly spell out worship as part of the special day, it is "a sabbath to the LORD your God" (Exod. 20:10), implying that the day is directed to God and hence a day involving special acts of worship. Exodus 31 puts the tabernacle (hence worship) and Sabbath together, and Leviticus 23:3 is explicit: "The seventh day is a day of sabbath rest, a day of sacred assembly." The Sabbath worship of the Hebrew people "likely involved the use of the full range of psalms from lament to praise, from prayers of confession to songs of thanksgiving. One important biblical text brings together the Sabbath and worship as it offers an ideal and distant future vision

24. Michael Walzer, *Spheres of Justice: A Defense of Pluralism and Equality* (New York: Basic Books, 1983), 194.

25. Gilbert Meilaender, *Thy Will Be Done: The Ten Commandments and the Christian Life* (Grand Rapids: Baker Academic, 2020), 92.

26. Karl Barth, *Church Dogmatics*, vol. IV/1, *The Doctrine of Reconciliation*, trans. G. W. Bromiley, ed. G. W. Bromiley and T. F. Torrance (Edinburgh: T&T Clark, 1956), 42–43.

27. Meilaender, *Thy Will Be Done*, 115.

of all humanity gathered together before God: 'from Sabbath to Sabbath, all flesh shall come to worship before me, says the LORD' (Isa. 66:23)."[28] Though they were free from bondage, "extracting the Israelites out of the Egyptian economy was one thing; extracting the Egyptian economy out of the Israelites was another thing entirely."[29] If the people were to forge an identity as God's people and live faithful to his designs, regular times together to reflect on and adore the God who made them and redeemed them were essential. And so it is for the Christian church today.

Personal devotional and worship times with God are essential for believers, but being part of the body of Christ, the collective gathering, encourages and reinforces a life rooted in the triune God. All of life in one sense is an act of worship to God, but as James K. A. Smith notes, "If all of life is going to be worship, the sanctuary is the place where we learn how."[30] And we learn how to worship not merely through cognitive learning via preaching and teaching, but also through the use of all our senses in experiencing the reality of God, reinforced by fellow believers engaged in the same act. Giving praise and honor to our God continually points us to the source of our ethical life, including self-care and care for others (justice). It regularly reminds us that while work is a good gift of God to meet our needs and the needs of others and to utilize our personal gifts in God's good world, there is the continual temptation for work to become a god and the vehicle of injustice and self-centeredness. In a book on work and worship, Matthew Kaemingk and Cory Willson write: "Worship gathers workers in from a wide variety of careers and callings. From all over the city they come. Worship gathers workers so that they might offer their working lives to God and so that God might offer his work to them. . . . It sends them out with a great work that must be extended into the city. Worship scatters workers, transformed by the work and Word of the Lord, throughout the city to be salt and light wherever they have been called."[31]

Interestingly the Bible does not give us a detailed description of how we honor the Sabbath in worship, leading us to understand that the forms are contextual. But clearly it should include praise to God that is usually though not exclusively done in music; prayers of a wide variety, though utilizing the structure of the Lord's Prayer (with praise, confession, and petition) is most useful; and hearing the Word of God both read and preached or taught. While the structure and forms of music and liturgy will vary according to context, Psalm 150 can be a useful guide. We analyze it under the following four categories:

28. Olson, "Sacred Time," 51.

29. Matthew Kaemingk and Cory B. Willson, *Work and Worship: Connecting Our Labor and Liturgy* (Grand Rapids: Baker Academic, 2020), 68.

30. James K. A. Smith, "Sanctification for Ordinary Life," *Reformed Worship*, March 2012, www.reformed-worship.org/article/march-2012/sanctification-ordinary-life.

31. Kaemingk and Willson, *Work and Worship*, 18.

- The object of worship: "Praise the LORD" (v. 1a). God alone is the object of our worship.
- The location of our worship: "Praise God in his sanctuary; praise him in his mighty heavens" (v. 1b). Praise can take place in the beauty of his creation, but it must also take place in the sanctuary, the gathering of God's people.
- The reason for our worship: "Praise him for his acts of power; praise him for his surpassing greatness" (v. 2). We don't praise our Maker because it makes us feel good or satisfies an aesthetic need within; rather, it's the only adequate response to a God of power and greatness.
- The means of worship: "Praise him with the sounding of the trumpet, praise him with the harp and lyre, praise him with timbrel and dancing, praise him with the strings and pipe, praise him with the clash of cymbals, praise him with resounding cymbals. Let everything that has breath praise the LORD" (vv. 3–6). The point is to use every available, culturally appropriate vehicle that will lead us into the presence and praise of God.

So the first principle in the Sabbath rhythm of life, established by God in creation, is worship. Worship is essential to our spirituality, but it is also essential for our ethics, our life within the world, for it centers our life on the one who designed the good, right, and just.

Self-Care

We were created to work, and work is part of both creation care and the cultural mandate to develop the good resources of the world. But work, both paid and unpaid, can easily become an idol and can be a physical and emotional burden that harms us and harms our various responsibilities in life: family, church, community, workplace, and society. Thus, the fourth commandment is explicit about care for oneself: "Remember the Sabbath day by keeping it holy. . . . On it you shall not do any work" (Exod. 20:8, 10). The Old Testament spells out some specific restrictions about the rest to enable the Hebrew people to truly put this into practice. But with the fuller revelation in Jesus and the New Testament, it is not the restrictions about rest but rather the principles underlying the command that are salient. As Jesus puts it, "The sabbath was made for humankind, and not humankind for the sabbath; so the Son of Man is lord even of the sabbath" (Mark 2:27 NRSV).

The self-care inherent in the Sabbath principle is evident in Jesus's command to "love your neighbor as yourself" (Mark 12:31). Here Jesus seems to be asserting a legitimate and important place for a proper self-love. This does not mean narcissism or self-absorption, in which we are so caught up in ourselves that we cannot step outside of ourselves to care for another. Rather, it means a care for ourselves that then enables us to love and care for our neighbor, including the "other" who is not quite like us. We only can truly express *agapē* love to our neighbor when we have cared for ourselves physically, emotionally, and spiritually. Brent Waters wisely writes, "Appropriate self-care does not diminish loving and serving one's neighbors. Neighbors cannot be loved properly if one is impaired by self-loathing."[32] The Sabbath rest, or change of pace from our work life and other daily grinds, is given for our good, to enable wholistic human flourishing. "We need time and activities that restore our energies, quiet our anxious minds, and regenerate our troubled spirits. Regular Sabbath rest enables our work and service to God and neighbor to continue in healthy and productive ways."[33]

Numerous studies show that stress among broad age groups is higher than ever, and this is not just related to the stress of the COVID pandemic. In a study commissioned by the American Psychological Association, one-third of Americans say they have been so stressed that they have difficulty in making basic daily decisions as to what to eat and what to wear. "49% said that the Coronavirus pandemic has made planning for the future feel impossible."[34] The National Institute for Occupational Safety and Health reports, "Problems at work are more strongly associated with health complaints than are any other life stressor—more so than even financial problems or family problems." One-fourth of workers in America view their job as the number one stressor in their lives, and three-quarters believe that stress on the job is greater than it was a generation ago.[35] Numerous studies are finding that our technology devices, such as smart phones, are major causes of anxiety, in part because of what they are doing to our brains and in part because the boundary between work and home is no longer clear.

Amid such stress and anxiety, the need for Sabbath rest and self-care is greater than ever. Sabbath rest and self-care will take on various forms from one person to the next. The biblical mandate of one day in seven is the wisest form of self-care because it fits with human nature, though clearly some professions might mandate a different format. For some, self-care will be leisure activities, including exercise and recreation, though, interestingly, legalistic renditions of the Sabbath, such as among the Puritans, forbade any such leisure on the Lord's Day. But we also need to note that for many people

32. Brent Waters, *Common Callings and Ordinary Virtues: Christian Ethics for Everyday Life* (Grand Rapids: Baker Academic, 2022), 29.

33. Olson, "Sacred Time," 64.

34. "Stress and Decision-Making during the Pandemic," American Psychological Association, October 26, 2021, https://www.apa.org/news/press/releases/stress/2021/october-decision-making.

35. Steven Sauter et al., "Stress . . . at Work," National Institute for Occupational Safety and Health, Centers for Disease Control and Prevention, accessed May 6, 2022, https://www.cdc.gov/niosh/docs/99-101/default.html.

their leisure and recreation have become work and not a true re-creation that rejuvenates the mind, body, and spirit. For some, self-care may be reading or listening to music, whereas for others it may include a walk in the woods or the park. For some, it will incorporate genuine bodily rest after a busy week that has left them physically tired. Numerous people are taking a true rest from their technology devices—doing no emails or text messages and not engaging in any web searches one day a week. Others find that special time with family and friends, engaging in constructive conversation, is the best form of rest and self-care. Perhaps the best rule of thumb is to ask what truly brings emotional, physical, and spiritual renewal, not just to enable us to go back out to another hard week of stress but rather to be the kind of people God wants us to be. Sabbath self-care should be wholistic in nature because we are whole beings.

We tend to think that Sabbath rest and self-care will curb our productivity and render us less competitive in the economic marketplace or the social arenas. But Andy Crouch has pointed out that "the successful electronics retailer B&H, owned by Orthodox Jews, not only closes its massive . . . Ninth Avenue store in Manhattan every Saturday in order to keep the Sabbath, but turns away orders on its website for those twenty-four hours as well." Something similar can be said about the "restaurant chain Chick-fil-A, which is closed every Sunday in consistently profitable defiance of retail wisdom."[36] Both have been highly successful economically. I have sometimes asked workers in Chick-fil-A restaurants how they feel about the Sunday closing, and inevitably they say they love it and feel rejuvenated. They also perceive less turnover in their stores than their competitors.

The cycle of one day in seven fits with the way God has made us. Though historically there have been various week frameworks, the seven-day week was normative in the Western world for several centuries. In the modern world, there have been occasional attempts to circumvent this cycle, usually as a reaction against the Judeo-Christian heritage. For example, after the French Revolution there was for a period of time a ten-day week, and the Soviet Union experimented with a five- and then a six-day week (but with continual cycles of industry). In both cases there was strong pushback and eventually a change back to the seven-day week, perhaps in part because the rhythm of seven days with one day of rest fits with our physical and mental design.

Our Creator knows that our human enterprises, such as work and familial responsibilities—though good gifts of creation—tend to dominate our lives and bring stress and anxiety. After the fall, with the "thorns and thistles," they only intensify. Thus, God rests on the seventh day to put in place a paradigm for human good and flourishing. To carry out this rhythm of life is not only a physical and emotional good—it is an ethical good. And it is especially

36. Crouch, *Playing God*, 256.

needed in a time when "we worship our work, work at our play, and play at our worship."[37]

Justice / Care for Others

Justice has generally been defined as what we owe people in the various spheres of life and society. The fourth commandment is explicit in extending Sabbath rest to care for others, including key portions of capital—land (an implication of the command) and animals. "Six days you shall labor and do all your work, but the seventh day is a sabbath to the LORD your God. On it you shall not do any work, neither you, nor your son or daughter, nor your male or female servant, nor your animals, nor any foreigner residing in your towns" (Exod. 20:9–10). There is particularly a justice appeal in the rationale given in Deuteronomy: "Remember that you were slaves in Egypt and that the LORD your God brought you out of there with a mighty hand and an outstretched arm. Therefore the LORD you God has commanded you to observe the Sabbath day" (5:15). Just as God redeemed the people from oppressive slavery, so God's freed people were now to put into practice a mechanism that would care for people and help to forestall any oppression in daily work and the various contours of society.

The justice commitment inherent in Sabbath is further evidenced in the Sabbath year and the Jubilee year. As we saw, particular stipulations of justice were put into place to protect other human beings, particularly the most vulnerable. Most of the stipulations center on practices germane to an agricultural society, so the task for us today is to find application of the principles of justice to an urban, pluralistic, and market-oriented society. Christian care for others always incorporates both love and justice. Historically, love and justice have frequently been seen as quite distinct from each other and, for some, even at odds with each other in their focus. Justice is seen as being institutional and structural in nature and love as being personal in nature. But they can never be pulled too far apart, for as philosopher Nicholas Wolterstorff writes, "Love for another seeks to secure that she be treated justly by oneself and others—that her rights be honored, that she be treated in a way that befits her worth."[38]

Discerning the best strategies for implementing justice in contemporary societies is not easy. For starters we must differentiate between spheres of justice: *retributive justice*, which is discerning what is owed when wrong has been done to another person or to society; *distributive justice*, which is distributing rights, goods, and services to people in society; and some today add

37. Gordon Dahl, *Work, Play, and Worship in a Leisure-Oriented Society* (Minneapolis: Augsburg, 1972), 12.

38. Nicholas Wolterstorff, *Justice in Love*, Emory University Studies in Law and Religion (Grand Rapids: Eerdmans, 2011), 93.

restorative justice, which "seeks to examine the harmful impact of a crime and then determines what can be done to repair that harm while holding the person who caused it accountable for his or her actions."[39] I personally see restorative justice as a creative and wise subset of retributive justice. But beyond the spheres of justice are varying definitions of *justice*. Essentially, they can be boiled down to three primary definitions, especially in the sphere of distributive justice: merit, equality, and need. Many of the struggles over justice today stem from differing definitions of how we determine what is owed a person.

Merit justice asserts that what is owed a person is based on their merit related to particular efforts and actions in given spheres of society or an institution. Here the focus of justice is not on actual outcomes but on an impartiality in discerning what individuals have earned by virtue of what they have done.[40] *Egalitarian justice* asserts that what is owed a person is defined by a principle of equality. Some in this camp have emphasized equal outcomes,[41] but the most popular version stresses equal access. In this version we should ensure that all persons have an equal opportunity in rights, housing, pay, jobs, and other opportunities.[42] Third is *need justice*, which defines just acts as determined by the needs of individuals and collectives in particular spheres of life. This view particularly emphasizes that equality of opportunity doesn't always address past wrongs and harms, and thus forms of redress must be put in place in light of specific needs of individuals and groups.[43]

One can make a biblical case for each of these definitions, which suggests that particular spheres of life call for different definitions. Merit justice is inferred in Jesus's parable of the talents in Matthew 25:14–30, in which those who have stewarded their rewards well are rewarded and those who have not are rebuked. It's also implied in 2 Thessalonians 3:10: "If anyone is not

39. "About Restorative Justice," Law School, University of Wisconsin–Madison, accessed May 31, 2022, https://law.wisc.edu/fjr/rjp/justice.html. See also Daniel Philpott, *Just and Unjust Peace: An Ethic of Political Reconciliation*, Studies in Strategic Peacebuilding (New York: Oxford University Press, 2012).

40. The most widely recognized advocate of merit justice is Robert Nozick, *Anarchy, State, and Utopia* (New York: Basic Books, 1974).

41. A good contemporary example of equal-outcomes justice is implied by Ibram X. Kendi, *How to Be an Antiracist* (New York: One World, 2019). He writes, "Racial inequity is when two or more racial groups are not standing on approximately equal footing. . . . An example of racial equity would be if there were relatively equitable percentages of all three racial groups [white, Black, and Latinx] living in owner-occupied homes" (18).

42. Here the classic statement is set forth by John Rawls, *A Theory of Justice* (Cambridge, MA: Harvard University Press, 1971).

43. This view is echoed in Karl Marx's famous words "From each according to his ability to each according to his need" (*Critique of the Gotha Programme* [Peking: Foreign Language, 1972], 18). Rawls also includes this view, along with his egalitarian commitments, when he writes, "Social and economic inequalities . . . are just only if they result in compensating benefits for everyone, and in particular for the least advantaged member of society" (*Theory of Justice*, 302).

willing to work, let him not eat" (ESV). Egalitarian justice is clearly stated in Leviticus 19:15—"Do not pervert justice; do not show partiality to the poor or favoritism to the great, but judge your neighbor fairly"—and is implied in Jesus's statement about God's allocation of natural resources: "He makes his sun rise on the evil and on the good, and sends rain on the just and on the unjust" (Matt. 5:45 ESV). And need justice is frequently implied in the Psalms with God's special care for the poor and downtrodden: "The LORD works righteousness and justice for all who are oppressed" (103:6 ESV), and "I know that the LORD will maintain the cause of the afflicted, and will execute justice for the needy" (140:12 ESV). It is also captured in Mary's Magnificat: "He has scattered the proud in the thoughts of their hearts; he has brought down the mighty from their thrones and exalted those of humble estate; he has filled the hungry with good things, and the rich he has sent away empty" (Luke 1:51–53 ESV).

It takes great wisdom to discern which definition of the term *justice* is appropriate for specific situations. Part of the problem is that we frequently have differing renditions of the situation being analyzed. Our factual or empirical judgments about given situations have a significant bearing on where we land in ethics, and this is particularly true when it comes to justice. Our ideologies, vested interests, and personality proclivities often tilt us toward rather biased judgments. Justice calls us to a significant mix of objectivity, personal responsibility, moving outside our comfort zones, and seeking the deep care of other humans, especially the most vulnerable. The Sabbath rest of justice seeks to stop our frantic efforts at self-centered power in order to seek the same kind of care for humans reflected in the Holy Trinity's creation, providence, redemption, and final restoration. Justice for the Christian is not a secular agenda but a divine mandate and perspective amid the complexities of a fallen, broken, prejudiced, self-oriented world. Moreover, justice as care for others does not negate personal responsibility in the recipients of justice.

Isaiah 58 brings together justice and Sabbath keeping in the face of religious practices used to justify the people's injustice and immorality. To the people's complaints that they have humbled themselves but God has taken no notice (v. 3a), the Lord, speaking through the prophet, says, "Yet on the day of your fasting, you do as you please and exploit all your workers. Your fasting ends in quarreling and strife" (vv. 3b–4). In place of such misaligned religiosity, the Lord says to his people:

> Is not this the kind of fasting I have chosen:
> to loose the chains of injustice
>   and untie the cords of the yoke,
> to set the oppressed free
>   and break every yoke?
> Is it not to share your food with the hungry
>   and to provide the poor wanderer with shelter—

> when you see the naked, to clothe them,
> and not to turn away from your own flesh and blood?
> Then your light will break forth like the dawn,
> and your healing will quickly appear;
> then your righteousness will go before you,
> and the glory of the LORD will be you rear guard. (vv. 6–8)

Later in the chapter, the prophecy turns to the Sabbath: "If you keep your feet from breaking the Sabbath and from doing as you please on my holy day, if you call the Sabbath a delight and the LORD's holy day honorable, and if you honor it by not going your own way and not doing as you please . . . , then you will find your joy in the LORD" (vv. 13–14).

Conclusion

The Sabbath has not gone away with the coming of Christ, with Pentecost, or with the formation of the Christian church. What God established in creation is a paradigm for all time—buttressed by the Decalogue, expanded throughout the Old Testament, and made clear in the ministry and teachings of our Lord. God established a rhythm of life that is essential to true faith and the Christian moral life.

At the heart of the Sabbath are three principles that are timelier than ever amid our harried, self-centered world: worship, self-care, and justice / care for others. We tend not to view these as correlates, but in God's economy they go together. We desperately need Sabbath. The church does, and so does our world.

9

Limited and Dependent

The Ethics of Human Finitude

When Christians reflect on human limitations, they typically think of human sinfulness. But there is another limitation, separate from human fallenness, and it is the way God made and intended us, part of the Creator's good design. It is human finitude. Kelly Kapic, in his book *You're Only Human*, argues that "being dependent creatures is a constructive gift, not a deficiency." We too often assume that we are in control and can conquer all barriers and alleviate all challenges. But "denying our finitude cripples us in ways we don't realize. It distorts our view of God and what Christian spirituality should look like."[1] It also distorts our view of ethics and leads to serious moral problems. With all our technology and human progress, much of which is to be welcomed, we have been deluded into thinking that we can transcend human limitations and even sin. "We are more than conquerors through all we are and have achieved," goes the modern and postmodern mantra. But such a view is not only self-defeating; it is harmful to self, others, and society. After all, "as creatures, humans have the limitations that go with being finite. Only the Creator is infinite."[2]

Reinhold Niebuhr once noted that the "Christian view of man is sharply distinguished from all alternative views by the manner in which it interprets and relates three aspects of human existence to each other." First is "the

1. Kelly M. Kapic, *You're Only Human: How Your Limits Reflect God's Design and Why That's Good News* (Grand Rapids: Brazos, 2022), 10, 5.

2. Millard J. Erickson, *Christian Theology*, 3rd ed. (Grand Rapids: Baker Academic, 2013), 454.

height of self-transcendence," coming from creation in God's image. Second is human "weakness, dependence, and finiteness," stemming from "involvement in the necessities and contingencies of the natural world, without, however, regarding this finiteness as . . . a source of evil in man." And third is human sin as a result of a person's "unwillingness to acknowledge his dependence, to accept his finiteness."[3] Christian theology (and ethics as well) has focused most clearly on creation in God's image and on human sin resulting from the fall. But finitude has been missing in most Christian theologies, and the neglect is to our detriment. For as Dietrich Bonhoeffer writes, "*The human being's limit is at the center of human existence*, not on the margin."[4]

What is human finitude? It essentially means that we are limited, dependent, temporal, and bounded creatures. Finitude means that we cannot transcend certain givens of human nature and that the attempts to do so have significant reverberations—morally, spiritually, emotionally, and physically. "On the one hand our finitude prevents us from being able to think of anything, including the whole of reality, as truly infinite. On the other hand it also prevents us from being able to think of anything finite . . . as the whole of reality,"[5] though we constantly try to do so. Only God is infinite, with no limitations on his power and presence, though God, of course, is limited by his character of perfect holiness. In contrast to divine infinity, Peter, quoting the prophet Isaiah, describes human finitude this way: "All people are like grass, and all their glory is like the flowers of the field; the grass withers and the flowers fall, but the word of the Lord endures forever" (1 Pet. 1:24–25; cf. Isa. 40:6–8). The personal, practical implication of our finitude is that "we need to stop asking (or feeling that we should ask) for God's forgiveness when we can't do everything, and we need to ask forgiveness for ever imagining we could."[6] Our finitude stems from creation and is clearly evident in the creation story and then throughout the rest of Scripture, including teaching from the Infinite One who took on finite flesh in the incarnation—Christ our Savior and Lord.

Finitude in Creation

When God creates humans in his image, he creates them to be limited, dependent creatures. The finite dimension is implicit in a number of elements within the creation narrative.

3. Reinhold Niebuhr, *The Nature and Destiny of Man*, vol. 1, *Human Nature* (New York: Scribner, 1941), 150.

4. Dietrich Bonhoeffer, *Creation and Fall: A Theological Exposition of Genesis 1–3*, ed. John W. de Gruchy, trans. Douglas Stephen Bax, Dietrich Bonhoeffer Works 3 (Minneapolis: Fortress, 1997), 86.

5. A. W. Moore, "Infinity," *Routledge Encyclopedia of Philosophy*, accessed June 8, 2022, https://www.rep.routledge.com/articles/thematic/infinity/v-1/sections//human-finitude.

6. Kapic, *You're Only Human*, 14.

Creatures, not Creator

In the creation story, creatures of various sorts are created on the fifth and sixth days, with humans on the sixth day as well. On the sixth day, God creates creatures of the land with the statement "Let the land produce living creatures according to their kinds" (Gen. 1:24). On that same day, God makes humans in his image, and like the animals, humans are formed "from the dust of the ground" (2:7; cf. 2:19). This, as we've noted before, may not be a literal scientific designation, but it is clearly a theological one. It demonstrates that though humans are set apart from the rest of creation by bearing the image of God, they are still creatures, limited and dependent—akin to animals but far beyond them in capacity and responsibility.

Being made in God's image, humans are given the unique task of stewarding the rest of creation: "Then God said, 'Let us make [humanity] in our image, in our likeness, so that they may rule over the fish in the sea . . . , over the livestock and all the wild animals, and over all the creatures that move along the ground'" (1:26). The elevation of humans to reflect the glory of their Maker by caring, managing, and developing God's good creation does not elevate them to be minigods. They are still creatures—limited, dependent, and bounded. The Genesis account is clear that though all of creation has implicit power in its own sphere and though humans have a power of stewardship over that creation, they are still creatures, not God. Only the triune Creator designs, speaks things into being, and does so on the basis of the eternal love inherent in the Holy Trinity. The creaturely dimension of humans will be reflected in their creativity, showing that they bear the image of their Creator, though in a finite way. But these living human organisms, like the other living organisms with whom they share some DNA (and in some cases much DNA), are still creatures from the dust of the ground. Finitude in nonhuman creatures is suggested by the boundedness in the various spheres of creation, indicated by the reoccurring phrase "according to their kinds."[7] Throughout the creation story, God is Creator and infinite; humans made in God's image are minicreators, but like other creatures, they are finite.

Dependence on Nature

Another way in which the creation story portrays human finitude is by depicting humanity's dependence on nature. Though he gives them the unique task of stewarding nature, God says to the first humans, "I give you every seed-bearing plant on the face of the whole earth and every tree that has fruit

7. Katherine Sonderegger, "Finitude and Death," in *T&T Clark Companion to the Doctrine of Sin*, ed. Keith L. Johnson and David Lauber (New York: Bloomsbury T&T Clark, 2016), 392. It should be noted, however, that whereas the rest of creation is created "according to their kinds," humans are created according to God's kind, in his image.

with seed in it. They will be yours for food" (1:29). This human dependence on nature for their existence is later extended in God's covenant to Noah to include animals: "Everything that lives and moves about will be food for you. Just as I gave you the green plants, I now give you everything"; but there is a qualification: "You must not eat meat that has its lifeblood still in it" (9:3, 4). This reference to blood no doubt is pointing to the sacrificial system that would be put in place as atonement for sin and, beyond that, to the ultimate sacrifice of Christ's blood atoning for human sin, once for all.

Animals, too, participate in this dependence on other aspects of nature for their livelihood. "And to all the beasts of the earth and all the birds in the sky and all the creatures that move along the ground—everything that has the breath of life in it—I give every green plant for food" (1:30). The plant life that produces food for humans and animals is made with the capacity of continual reproduction: "'Let the land produce vegetation: seed-bearing plants and trees on the land that bear fruit with seed in it, according to their various kinds.' . . . The land produced vegetation: plants bearing seed according to their kinds and trees bearing fruit with seed in it" (vv. 11–12). The creation narrative points to an interaction and interdependence among the various parts of creation. The vegetation, nonhuman creatures, and human creatures are not independent of each other but need each other in their given spheres of the created order. This interdependence demonstrates that nature, animals, and human beings are all finite, needing each other for their own existence. It is precisely this interrelationship that calls for humans to be good stewards in their creation care. "Everything is connected. We live, like it or not, in a single, interconnected biosphere. . . . We owe our existence to a Creator, and we exist as part of—not apart from—the thing we call creation."[8]

The Limitations of Our Bodies

The human body has long been a source of questioning and frustration for Christians. As we saw in chapter 2, early on in Christian history there were thinkers and leaders who saw the body as problematic and adopted Gnostic tendencies that eulogized the soul and denigrated the body. Some radical Gnostics even posited two separate creations and creators. But the human body plays a significant role in the creation story and is affirmed as good by the Creator. Though this body is good, it is finite and limited by both the inherent confines of physical existence and the God-ordained boundaries placed on human creatures.

The first indication of bodily existence is when God creates humans in his image with the indication "Male and female he created them" (1:27). That in itself points to a physiological boundedness, which is then furthered by the

8. Douglas J. Moo and Jonathan A. Moo, *Creation Care: A Biblical Theology of the Natural World*, Biblical Theology for Life (Grand Rapids: Zondervan, 2018), 181.

command "Be fruitful and increase in number" (v. 28). The man cannot reproduce by himself, and the woman cannot reproduce by herself. With sexually distinct bodies, they are limited beings. Only in their becoming "one flesh" (vv. 23–24), bodily and together, can reproduction occur. The embodiment of the man and the woman, as distinct sexes, means they are interdependent and hence finite. Only cloning can bypass this interdependence of two distinct bodies, and attempts at human reproductive cloning up to this point have failed—even with all of our scientific knowledge.[9] This indicates our finitude and points to a moral line that ought not to be transgressed.

With their bodies humans eat, work, procreate, care for creation, and engage in creative arts and the sciences. Though they continually discover, create new objects and technologies, and overcome physical and medical obstacles, they remain bodies that are dependent. These bodies, though finite and limited, are nonetheless highly significant in theological understanding, for "a theology of the body means that we understand the body as not merely a biological category but supremely as a theological category, designed for God's revelatory and saving purposes. In short, the body makes the invisible mysteries of God's nature and redemption manifest and visible."[10] This meaning of the body stands in stark contrast to social critic Camille Paglia's statement that "fate, not God, has given us this flesh. We have absolute claim to our bodies and may do with them as we see fit."[11] To the contrary it is precisely because our bodies are finite and dependent that they require a meaning from beyond the impulses of our bodies; and that meaning and design comes from the Infinite One, who does have ultimate claim over our bodies because he created them.

Dependent on Others

Another way in which the creation story points to human finitude is by highlighting our dependence on other human beings. We are not created as "lone rangers" but as social beings who need others and who find our greatest temporal satisfactions in relation to others. When God creates humans in his image, as male and female, it implies a relational mode of existence. Just as the divine Trinity exists in an eternal relationship of love, so humans have a unique capacity of love toward others, made possible by divine love and grace. Love of neighbor has become a hallmark of Christian responsibility, after

9. Artificial insemination and in vitro fertilization also bypass two bodies coming together for reproduction, but they still involve two gametes from two distinct bodies. Other ethical issues are related to these modes of human reproduction, as noted in chap. 5.

10. Timothy C. Tennent, *For the Body: Recovering a Theology of Gender, Sexuality, and the Human Body* (Grand Rapids: Zondervan Reflective, 2020), 13. It was John Paul II who really gave the theology of the body momentum.

11. Camille Paglia, *Vamps and Tramps: New Essays* (New York: Vintage, 1994), 71.

the highest hallmark of love for God (Matt. 22:37–40). The most intimate and socially significant kind of love is instituted by God in the relationship of marriage: "That is why a man leaves his father and mother and is united to his wife, and they become one flesh" (Gen. 2:24). This institution clearly demonstrates that humans would only come into earthly existence and then be socialized in this interdependent bond of marriage and family. Humans are not capable of birth or socialization solitarily, but only through a bond between others. Hence, from the beginning of our lives we are dependent and thus finite.

Before the institution of marriage in Genesis 2, we have the statement "It is not good for the man to be alone. I will make a helper suitable for him" (v. 18). Humans, especially in their fallen state, frequently tend to go it alone, assuming that self-sufficiency is the ideal. In fact, it hinders all forms of development: emotional, moral, and spiritual. We achieve a genuine self-actualization not as isolated selves but as relational selves, engaged with other finite humans. To best flourish and be authentically human, we engage with others in work, play, church, community, and society. A society can never function with isolated, entirely self-sufficient creatures. Nor can the church. And in this mutual dependence on others, we discover not only more of our true selves but the beauty and significance of others, including the "other," who is not like us. As Kapic notes, "A healthy Christian view of human limits and differences encourages mutual delight, an awareness of our dependence on others, the integrity of relationships. . . . We can and should value our particularity while seeing this as related to our communities, culture, and history, rather than simply my own self-choosing."[12] To attempt to negate or overcome our relational dependency is a negation of our true selves as finite creatures. And it is in relational dependence that we finite creatures live out our ethical responsibilities in this world as designed in creation.

Dependent on God

Though human interdependence is essential to authentic humanness, our greatest need for dependence is on the One who made us, best knows us, and can redeem us. A creature's dependence on a Creator is only logical, but the dependence is made explicit in the creation story. The Lord God places the man in the garden full of bountiful vegetation to meet the needs of finite humans: "The Lord God made all kinds of trees grow out of the ground—trees that were pleasing to the eye and good for food. In the middle of the garden were the tree of life and the tree of the knowledge of good and evil" (2:9). These trees are morally and spiritually significant, for they represent either dependence on the One who made them or dependence on self as one seeks to

12. Kapic, *You're Only Human*, 72.

transcend that dependence and finitude, defining reality and morals on one's own terms. "And the LORD God commanded the man, 'You may freely eat of every tree of the garden; but of the tree of the knowledge of good and evil you shall not eat, for in the day that you eat of it you shall die'" (vv. 16–17 NRSV).

There has been much exegetical and theological discussion as to the meaning of the trees and why God establishes this particular test. But Calvin is certainly right when he asserts, "The prohibition to touch the tree of the knowledge of good and evil was a trial of obedience, that Adam, by observing it, might prove his willing submission to the command of God. For the very term shows the end of the precept to have been to keep him contented with his lot, and not allow him arrogantly to aspire beyond it."[13] The tree itself is not evil, but the prohibition surrounding the tree gives humans the opportunity to either follow the true wisdom of God as finite creatures or attempt to transcend their limited, dependent knowledge and patterns of life. "The Biblical view is that the finiteness, dependence and the insufficiency of man's mortal life are facts which belong to God's plan of creation and must be accepted with reverence and humility."[14] Humans, made in the image of God, are created with the possibilities of creativity, ingenuity, and growth in various realms of life, but all of those possibilities are to take place within the limitations of God's designs and in dependence on their Maker. To turn their creativity, ingenuity, and growth into a transcendent stance is to seek to be infinite and hence to follow the path of the tree of the knowledge of good and evil. Yes, they would know good from their own reason and frameworks, but in so doing they would encounter and know the forces of evil spiritually, morally, and even physically. To remain finite and dependent is to embody the most authentic form of humanness as God intends.

Finitude throughout the Rest of Scripture

The finite, dependent stance of humanity is not only found in the creation story but is explicit throughout the rest of Scripture. The very fact that God gives laws, principles, paradigms, and various forms of guidance to humans assumes that human beings are dependent. They are bounded by designs that are rooted outside of themselves. Job, after defending his own innocence, comes to see his own creaturely status in the face of an infinite God. The Lord asks him, "Where were you when I laid the earth's foundation? Tell me, if you understand. Who marked off its dimensions? Surely you know! Who stretched a measuring line across it?" (Job 38:4–5). In this and the grand tour of God's creation, Job "is confronted with the limits of human understanding and

13. John Calvin, *Institutes of the Christian Religion*, trans. Henry Beveridge, rev. ed. (Peabody, MA: Hendrickson, 2008), 2.1.4.

14. Niebuhr, *Nature and Destiny of Man*, 1:167.

power. Yet these limits are not cause for sorrow or despair; on the contrary, they are a cause for celebration. They mean that Job can neither save himself (40:14), nor need he."[15]

Human finitude manifested in relational dependence is beautifully echoed in Ecclesiastes 4:9–12:

> Two are better than one,
> because they have a good return for their labor:
> If either of them falls down,
> one can help the other up.
> But pity anyone who falls
> and has no one to help them up.
> Also, if two lie down together, they will keep warm.
> But how can one keep warm alone?
> Though one may be overpowered,
> two can defend themselves.
> A cord of three strands is not quickly broken.

The psalmists frequently note the temporality and limitedness of human life. "You have made my days a mere handbreadth; the span of my years is as nothing before you. Everyone is but a breath, even those who seem secure" (Ps. 39:5). Amid life's trials and divine resources, a psalm of David reminds us, "He knows how we are formed, he remembers that we are dust. The life of mortals is like grass, they flourish like a flower of the field; the wind blows over it and it is gone, and its place remembers it no more." But then comes the promise to finite humanity: "From everlasting to everlasting the LORD's love is with those who fear him, and his righteousness with their children's children" (103:14–17).

The prophet Isaiah is no doubt combining human finitude and sin when he writes in the context of a messianic prophecy, "All people are like grass, and all their faithfulness is like the flowers of the field. The grass withers and the flowers fall, because the breath of the LORD blows on them. Surely the people are grass. The grass withers and the flowers fall, but the word of our God endures forever" (Isa. 40:6–8). Later in Isaiah 40, human limitedness is implicitly contrasted to the infinity of humanity's Maker:

> Who has measured the waters in the hollow of his hand,
> or with the breadth of his hand marked off the heavens?
> Who has held the dust of the earth in a basket,
> or weighed the mountains on the scales
> and the hills in a balance? . . .
> Whom did the Lord consult to enlighten him,
> and who taught him the right way?

15. Moo and Moo, *Creation Care*, 63.

> Who was it that taught him knowledge,
>   or showed him the path of understanding?
>
> Surely the nations are like a drop in a bucket. . . .
>
> With whom, then, will you compare God? (vv. 12, 14–15, 18)

At the end of the chapter, this finitude leads not to despair but hope, for this infinite God "gives strength to the weary and increases the power of the weak. . . . Those who hope in the LORD will renew their strength. They will soar on wings like eagles; they will run and not grow weary, they will walk and not be faint" (vv. 29, 31). But they do so as dependent beings.

Throughout his teachings, Jesus is calling people not to a life of self-sufficiency but to a life of dependence made possible by divine grace. In a discussion on the futility of worry, he reminds his disciples of their limitations when he asks, "Can any one of you by worrying add a single hour to your life?" (Matt. 6:27). In similar fashion James states, "Now listen, you who say, 'Today or tomorrow we will go to this or that city, spend a year there, carry on business and make money.' Why, you do not even know what will happen tomorrow. What is your life? You are a mist that appears for a little while and then vanishes" (James 4:13–14). In contrast to a person's grandiose sense that they are in control and can transcend all human contours and limitations, believers are called to "seek first his kingdom and his righteousness, and all these things will be given to you as well" (Matt. 6:33). Many of these biblical texts assume both human finitude and fallenness, but the two are not the same. Nonetheless, humans are continually reminded of their created nature; they are limited, temporal, and dependent. To transcend their finitude brings divine judgment.

The Fall: A Rejection of Finitude

Being made in the image of God, humans have a sense of their own grandeur and dignity. They can think, make decisions, devise, and implement. It is only natural that those inherent attributes could be turned in baser directions, which is exactly what happens in the fall. As noted, only one prohibition is given to the humans—to abstain from the tree of the knowledge of good and evil. When Satan comes to the woman in the garden through the serpent, he challenges God's authenticity and veracity: "Did God really say, 'You must not eat from any tree in the garden'?" (Gen. 3:1). The woman replies, "We may eat fruit from the trees in the garden, but God did say, 'You must not eat fruit from the tree that is in the middle of the garden, and you must not touch it, or you will die'" (vv. 2–3). The serpent responds, "You will not certainly die. . . . For God knows that when you eat from it your eyes will be opened, and you will be like God, knowing good and evil" (vv. 4–5). The serpent is challenging the finite, dependent nature of God's creation. Thus, "when the woman saw that the fruit of the tree was good for food and pleasing to the eye, and also desirable for gaining wisdom, she took some and ate it. She also gave some to her husband, who was with her, and he ate it" (v. 6).

Following Augustine, many have suggested that this first sin is pride, but I believe it is preferable to term it as a rejection of their finitude, their dependent and limited nature. The serpent is promising that they will have deeper knowledge and wisdom and will actually become like God in this knowledge and wisdom. In other words the finite creatures will ascend to infinity in this deceptive promise. The first couple believes this will grant them greater wisdom and a more pleasing state than they have in their finite, dependent state. And hence they eat, rendering them fallen, and the whole world has never been the same since. As John Milton puts it in the opening lines of *Paradise Lost*:

> Of man's first disobedience, and the fruit
> Of that forbidden tree whose mortal taste
> Brought death into the world, and all our woe,
> With loss of Eden, till one greater Man
> Restore us, and regain the blissful seat.[16]

Throughout history humans have tended to think of themselves more highly than they ought (cf. Prov. 3:7; Rom. 12:3). This is the grasping after an infinity in knowledge and actions, which is contrary to their created nature, rendered even more beyond their grasp after the fall. Niebuhr writes, "Man is ignorant and involved in the limitations of a finite mind; but he pretends that he is not limited. He assumes that he can gradually transcend finite limitations until his mind becomes identical with universal mind." What is the heart of this temptation? "Is it not the fact that man is a finite spirit, lacking identity with the whole, but yet a spirit capable in some sense of envisaging the whole, so that he easily commits the error of imagining himself the whole which he envisages?"[17] And hence we imagine greater knowledge than we really have, greater wisdom than we could ever attain, and greater moral heights than is possible as finite, fallen creatures.

This, of course, is not the first fall that emanates from grasping after infinity. In at least two places in Scripture, the fall of Satan is described in this manner:

> How you have fallen from heaven,
> morning star ["Lucifer" in KJV], son of the dawn!
> You have been cast down to the earth,
> you who once laid low the nations!

16. John Milton, "Paradise Lost, Book I," in *The Norton Anthology of English Literature*, ed. M. H. Adams, rev. ed. (New York: Norton, 1968), 1:597.
17. Niebuhr, *Nature and Destiny of Man*, 1:178–79, 181.

> You said in your heart,
> "I will ascend to the heavens;
> I will raise my throne
> above the stars of God;
> I will sit enthroned on the mount of assembly,
> on the utmost heights of Mount Zaphon.
> I will ascend above the tops of the clouds;
> I will make myself like the Most High."
> But you are brought down to the realm of the dead,
> to the depths of the pit. (Isa. 14:12–15)

In similar fashion Ezekiel's prophecy against the king of Tyre appears to move beyond the earthly king to Satan.

> You were the seal of perfection,
> full of wisdom and perfect in beauty.
> You were in Eden,
> the garden of God; . . .
> You were anointed as a guardian cherub,
> for so I ordained you.
> You were on the holy mount of God; . . .
> You were blameless in your ways
> from the day you were created
> till wickedness was found in you. . . .
> Your heart became proud
> on account of your beauty,
> and you corrupted your wisdom
> because of your splendor.
> So I threw you to the earth;
> I made a spectacle of you before kings. . . .
> So I made a fire come out from you,
> and it consumed you,
> and I reduced you to ashes on the ground. . . .
> All the nations who knew you
> are appalled at you;
> you have come to a horrible end
> and will be no more. (Ezek. 28:12–15, 17–19)

Satan's downfall was the same as Adam and Eve's—a failure to recognize that only God is infinite, while striving after their own infinity in thought and action.

After the fall recorded in Genesis 3, we have a story in Genesis 11 in which people in the plain of Shinar attempt to build a society that transcends all known limitations. They say, "Come, let us build ourselves a city, with a tower that reaches to the heavens, so that we may make a name for ourselves; otherwise we will be scattered over the face of the whole earth" (v. 4). The

Infinite One intervenes with judgment into their aspirations of hegemony: "'If as one people speaking the same language they have begun to do this, then nothing they plan to do will be impossible for them. Come, let us go down and confuse their language so they will not understand each other.' So the LORD scattered them from there over all the earth" (vv. 6–8).

The Meaning of Human Finitude for Ethics

As we explore the ethical implications of human finitude, it is helpful first to discern what it does not imply. It does not mean the status quo. It does not mean that we must maintain human physical conditions as they were at creation, throughout biblical times, or one hundred years ago. Finitude does not preclude scientific and technological discoveries that have lessened the burdens of physical life, including the burdens of the fall. Diseases are a result of the cosmic fall, but that does not mean we must forever live with specific diseases and do nothing to prevent, overcome, or ameliorate their impact. Human finitude does not imply a negative stance toward intellectual and scientific advancements. We are grateful for the insights that come from psychology, history, philosophy, sociology, and the arts. Physical and emotional life is frequently less burdensome because of these advances, which are divine gifts of common grace—though not saving grace.

Human advances in all realms of life stem from the cultural mandate at creation to rule, fill, increase, and be fruitful. "This would mean managing all of [creation's] creatures and resources for good purposes: to allow their beauty to flourish, to use them wisely and kindly, and to promote well-being for all."[18] As Bill Edgar puts it, "Embedded in this human activity is (at least in germ form) the development of agriculture, the arts, economics, family dynamics, and everything that contributes to human flourishing, to the glory of God."[19] But all of this is to transpire within the boundedness of God's creational paradigms and in dependence on God. Our posture in developing good things in this world and growing in the various domains of life is to always be from a framework that we are limited, finite creatures. Kapic notes that various early church thinkers saw creation not as an end but rather as "a trajectory, a movement, a process." But that trajectory does not negate the designs of God given in creation, enunciated throughout Scripture, and affirmed and lived out in Jesus Christ. "Creation is not described to us as a static picture, but as a living story. God designed us to live and to grow in love and wonder. . . . Salvation in Christ by the Spirit does not undermine God's

18. C. John Collins, *Genesis 1–4: A Linguistic, Literary, and Theological Commentary* (Phillipsburg, NJ: P&R, 2006), 69.

19. William Edgar, *Created and Creating: A Biblical Theology of Culture* (Downers Grove, IL: IVP Academic, 2016), 142.

original creation but puts us back into the trajectory of life and love, within the warmth of the divine embrace." Thus, God's people have been "beckoned to a love and communion with God for which they were originally created, a call that was not meant to take them beyond being fully human, but rather to the heart of it. Growth and development were not a way to cease nor surpass finite creature existence, but to accomplish God's perfectly humane expectation."[20]

But within all the good human activities in this world, there are limits and boundary markers that unfortunately have frequently been transgressed in human history. There have been attempts to build our towers of Babel and deny our finitude. While many of these endeavors have been touted as human progress, as we will see they have had negative impacts on human beings and society. The attempts at human infinity have resulted in the natural and direct judgments of our Creator.

Utopias

Throughout history philosophers, political theorists, and "people on the street" have debated whether societies can reach an ideal utopian dream or, in contrast, maintain a realism in human pursuits of justice and the common good.[21] A *utopia* is an ideal community or commonwealth either as a literary proposal or an established community built on utopian premises. Usually it has assumed that a perfect or near-perfect reality can be constructed here on earth. It envisions a world without sin and one that can transcend the finite limitations that have been evident in humanity and societies throughout history.

Plato's *Republic* is usually thought to be the first literary political utopia, though there have been varying interpretations of Plato's work, including some that reject the portrayal of a utopian republic. One critic of the utopian-society view says, "The republic inside him [i.e., inside Glaucon, a key figure in the *Republic*] is of greater importance than any city."[22] Nonetheless, there do appear in this work to be notions of both individual and societal perfection. Book 4 of the *Republic* argues that the ideal leader for a state will be the philosopher-king, who best combines virtues and knowledge to lead a society. "Neither cities nor states nor individuals will ever attain perfection until the small class of philosophers whom we termed useless but not corrupt are providentially compelled . . . to take care of the State, and until a like necessity be laid on the State to obey them." Such will be a small class of

20. Kapic, *You're Only Human*, 150, 152.

21. See, for example, Michael Weber and Kevin Vallier, eds., *Political Utopias: Contemporary Debates* (New York: Oxford University Press, 2017).

22. Alfred Geier, "Plato's Republic: A Utopia for the Individual," *Philosophy Now*, accessed July 1, 2022, https://philosophynow.org/issues/70/Platos_Republic_A_Utopia_For_The_Individual.

people "whose mind is fixed upon true being" and whose "eye is ever directed towards things fixed and immutable . . . , all in order moving according to reason."[23] Plato seems to assume a malleable human nature that can transcend human limitations to reach a form of perfection without blemish or finitude.

Sir Thomas More was actually the first to use the term in his fictional, sociopolitical satire, *Utopia*, published in 1516. He not only critiques some of Europe's social ills at that time but, through a correspondence mode of writing, sets forth what an ideal and perfect society would look like. It is a communalistic society in which private property is eradicated, hospitals are free, and premarital sex and adultery are severely punished, but euthanasia is permitted. He writes, "Now I have declared and described unto you . . . the form and order of that commonwealth, which verily in my judgment is not only the best, but also that which alone of good right may claim and take upon itself the name of commonwealth or public weal. . . . And though no man owns anything, yet every man is rich. For what can be more rich than to live joyfully and merrily, without grief and worry, not concerned for his own living."[24] Though More claims that the common good and good of individuals is paramount, he envisions slavery as part of utopian life, with every household having two slaves, coming from prisoners of war, poverty, or criminality. More's work was the harbinger for many other utopias and dystopias that would be written in ensuing centuries. Among these, though not formally called a utopia, are the writings of Karl Marx and Friedrich Engels with their portrayal of a classless society, which, they argue, would eradicate most societal ills and lead to a world of pure justice and peace.

In nineteenth-century America, various utopian, communitarian groups formed to achieve human and societal perfection. Some, like the Shakers, were rooted in religious ideals, following "the principles of simplicity, celibacy, common property, equal labor and reward espoused by their founder Mother Ann Lee."[25] At one time in the 1830s, they had attracted six thousand members, but they essentially became defunct within several decades. Robert Owen in 1825 founded New Harmony in Indiana, not on religious principles but on secular political and equality principles. The utopian cooperative fell apart after only two years. The Oneida Community, founded by John Humphrey Noyes in upstate New York, was committed to "group marriage, communal child rearing, group discipline, and attempts to improve the genetic composition of their offspring."[26] The utopian dream lasted just over three decades and was rife with internal conflict. The Brook Farm in Massachusetts was built

23. Plato, *The Republic*, trans. B. Jowett, Classics Club (Roslyn, NY: Walter Black, 1942), 384, 385.

24. Thomas More, *The Utopia*, Classics Club (Roslyn, NY: Walter Black, 1947), 169.

25. "Experiments with Utopia," U.S. History, Independence Hall Association, accessed July 6, 2022, https://www.ushistory.org/us/26b.asp.

26. "Experiments with Utopia."

on transcendental ideals of self-reliance and a rejection of external authority and cultural traditions. "It was supposed to bestow the highest benefits of intellectual, physical, and moral education to its members. . . . Those who joined the fellowship . . . were supposed to understand and live in social harmony, free of government, free to perfect themselves."[27] The farm was the subject of numerous critiques by those who were part of or near to it, and it dissolved after six years.

One might respond to these utopian writings and endeavors as merely attempts at social reform to address existing injustices and societal ills. But the fact that the communal utopias were short lived is no doubt evidence that they were contrary to both the finitude of human nature and its sinfulness—hence, unattainable. Moreover, many utopian efforts, such as Marxist states, actually ended up being oppressive and the very opposite of their justice dreams. Australian philosopher John Passmore, in a book on perfectibility, argues that such attempts are not benign. "Perfectibilism is dehumanizing. To achieve perfection . . . it would first be necessary to cease to be human, to become godlike, to rise above the human condition." Looking at the history of utopian dreams, he warns that "to attempt, in the quest for perfection, to raise men above that level is to court disaster."[28] And Niebuhr, critiquing the utopians of the modern world, writes, "They thought that these ultimate possibilities of human freedom transcending all history were not only simple possibilities of history but that they were actualities of nature as given." He notes that "the combined influence of religious and secular utopianism has brought confusion into the whole problem of justice in the modern . . . world."[29]

Eugenics

Eugenics literally means "good genes" and is the attempt through natural, technological, and even forced means to achieve a desired gene pool among a given group of people. Positive eugenics seeks to breed in "good" genes, and negative eugenics seeks to breed out perceived "bad" genes. This, too, is an example of seeking to overcome finitude, for as award-winning journalist Edwin Black writes in *War against the Weak*, "Mankind's quest for perfection has always turned dark. Man has always existed in perpetual chaos. Continuously catapulted from misery to exhilaration and back, humanity has repeatedly struggled to overcome vulnerability and improve upon its sense of strength. The instinct is to 'play God' or at least mediate His providence." And what is the result of these eugenic attempts at infinity? "Too

27. "Experiments with Utopia."

28. John Passmore, *The Perfectibility of Man*, 3rd ed. (Indianapolis: Liberty Fund, 2000), 511, 512.

29. Niebuhr, *Nature and Destiny of Man*, 1:298.

often, this impulse is not just to improve, but to repress, and even destroy those deemed inferior."[30]

The idea goes way back in history as Plato espoused in the *Republic* that the fittest men and women mate to produce a superior class, while the Spartans, Romans, and Athenians practiced exposure, allowing infants deemed inferior to die. But it was with Francis Galton, Charles Darwin's cousin, that the modern eugenics movement developed. He argued that human "natural abilities are derived by inheritance, under exactly the same limitations as are the form and physical features of the organic world. Consequently, as it is easy . . . to obtain by careful selection a permanent breed of dogs or horses gifted with peculiar powers of running, . . . so it would be quite practicable to produce a highly gifted race of men by judicious marriages during several consecutive generations."[31] Soon Galton's ideas for developing noble people with keen intellect—and limiting those without—spread throughout Europe and the United States. Inherent in his ideas is the notion that certain nationalities and races are inferior to others, with white Europeans being superior.

In the United States, "during the first few decades of the twentieth century, eugenics flourished in the liberal Protestant, Catholic, and Jewish mainstream; clerics, rabbis, and lay leaders wrote books and articles about eugenics, joined eugenics organizations, and lobbied for eugenics legislation. They . . . adopted eugenic solutions to the social problems that beset their communities."[32] Even the Social Gospel movement, with some of its key leaders like Josiah Strong and Walter Rauschenbusch, was caught up in the movement. Christine Rosen points out that it is easy to see why this progressive reform movement embraced eugenics. "The two movements shared certain assumptions. Salvation for Social Gospelers was a social matter; social redemption was as much a part of salvation as one's own personal redemption. In a similar vein, eugenicists argued that heredity should be a social matter, . . . [with] reform to guarantee the preservation of the race."[33] Eugenics was mainstream in America and supported by various leaders, including the presidents of Harvard and Stanford, several US presidents, Alexander Graham Bell, sociologist William Graham Sumner, and Margaret Sanger, founder of Planned Parenthood.

These leaders espoused limitations on immigration for certain nations and secured legislation in a number of states to sterilize criminals and the "feeble minded" and to prevent marriages between certain groups of people. In 1927 the United States Supreme Court in *Buck v. Bell* concluded that the

30. Edwin Black, *War against the Weak: Eugenics and America's Campaign to Create a Master Race* (New York: Avalon, 2003), 9.

31. Francis Galton, *Hereditary Genius: An Inquiry into Its Laws and Consequences* (London: Macmillan, 1869), 1.

32. Christine Rosen, *Preaching Eugenics: Religious Leaders and the American Eugenics Movement* (New York: Oxford University Press, 2004), 4.

33. Rosen, *Preaching Eugenics*, 16.

state of Virginia was legitimate in their forced sterilization policy. The ruling was written by Oliver Wendell Holmes Jr., who argued that the interest of public welfare was greater than that of individuals and concluded with his infamous statement, "Three generations of imbeciles are enough."[34] Fourteen years earlier President Theodore Roosevelt stated, "Society has no business to permit degenerates to reproduce their kind. . . . Some day, we will realize that the prime duty, the inescapable duty, of the good citizen of the right type, is to leave his or her blood behind him in the world; and that we have no business to permit the perpetuation of citizens of the wrong type."[35]

The most notorious experiment in eugenics occurred in Nazi Germany under the leadership of Adolf Hitler. Many of the Nazi Party's initial ideas were actually borrowed from the American eugenics movement, and it was not until the horrors of the Holocaust fully came to light that the American experiments and interest began to wane, after initial support of the German programs. The first eugenics law to be passed in Germany was mass compulsory sterilization in 1933. It included numerous categories of "defectives" identified for sterilization, including those afflicted by manic depression, epilepsy, deafness, homosexuality, hereditary blindness, and alcoholism. Four hundred thousand Germans were subject to sterilization.[36] In addition the extermination of millions of Jews and others deemed a threat to national purity was rooted in eugenics ideals. There was a positive eugenics program, the Nordic breeding program *Lebensborn*, which encouraged those with Aryan characteristics to come together and have many children to achieve a pure race.

When the German atrocities were revealed, eugenics support around the world began to wane for a period of time. But in recent decades, with new technologies it has again emerged, though often without the "eugenics" nomenclature. One form this can take is gamete donation, with people advertising for eggs or sperm to get a gifted offspring. Here is an ad that appeared in college newspapers throughout the United States in the 1990s: "Egg Donor Needed / large financial incentive / intelligent, athletic egg donor needed / for loving family / You must be at least 5'10" / Have a 1400+ SAT score / Possess no major family medical issues / $50,000 / Free Medical Screening / All Expenses Paid."[37] Utilizing in vitro fertilization or artificial insemination, some eugenics selectivity is used to get the "right child." Preimplantation genetic diagnosis can be selective of embryos utilizing in vitro fertilization, and amniocentesis can determine genetic makeup of a child in the womb, possibly leading to an abortion. This is significantly impacting the number of children born with Down syndrome each year in Europe and the United

34. Buck v. Bell, 274 U.S. 200 (1927).

35. Letter to Charles Davenport, January 3, 1913, quoted in Black, *War against the Weak*, 99.

36. Black, *War against the Weak*, 299.

37. Reprinted in "Superior People," *Commonweal*, March 26, 1999, 5–6, https://www.commonwealmagazine.org/superior-people.

States. A study in the *European Journal of Human Genetics* found that "the growth of prenatal screening in Europe has reduced the number of babies being born per year with Down syndrome (DS) by an average of 54%," and "the same team found that 33% fewer babies with DS per year were born in the United States as a result of pregnancy terminations."[38] In Iceland, Down syndrome has almost totally disappeared. With the development of the latest technology in genetic engineering, CRISPR, there is the possibility of making genetic changes that could significantly alter one's own genetic makeup as well as that of future offspring. And there are numerous scientists who are supporting these new forms of eugenics. There appears to be "a growing consensus . . . developing that children with a disability should not be brought into existence. . . . Of course, coercive policies are generally absent, but . . . eugenic ideologies have just returned under the compassionate guise of 'therapeutic genetic selection.'"[39]

From an ethical standpoint, eugenics tends to be racist and sexist, has been involved in murder, and is contrary to the dignity of human beings. But underlying the eugenics agenda of developing superior people is a more fundamental issue—the drive for perfection that is unwilling to accept human finitude. "Perfection requires manipulation and elimination—a kind of purificationist imperative is at work here, aiming to weed out the flawed and recognizing only the perfect and fit." Moreover, it is "wrapped up in a quest for control, immersed in the images and rhetoric of choice and self-possession."[40] This does not mean that we don't seek to eradicate diseases and viruses, but we ought not to change human nature in the process nor do away with humans who "don't fit the mold." There are givens and boundaries in the very nature of being a human being, and one of those boundaries is that we are finite and limited. We are not capable of reaching perfection, and striving for it leads to dire results for human beings and for society.

Transhumanism

A variant of the new eugenics, but one that deserves separate treatment, is transhumanism and its near kin, posthumanism. Nick Bostrom, an Oxford

38. Massachusetts General Hospital, "Prenatal Testing Has Halved the Number of Babies Born with Down Syndrome in Europe, Study Finds," ScienceDaily, December 18, 2020, https://www.sciencedaily.com/releases/2020/12/201218131911.htm, reporting on Gert de Graaf, Frank Buckley, and Brian G. Skotko, "Estimation of the Number of People with Down Syndrome in Europe," *European Journal of Human Genetics* 29 (2021): 402–10, http://dx.doi.org/10.1038/s41431-020-00748-y.

39. Calum MacKellar, *Christianity and the New Eugenics: Should We Choose to Have Only Healthy or Enhanced Children?* (London: Inter-Varsity, 2020), 219.

40. C. Ben Mitchell, Edmund D. Pellegrino, Jean Bethke Elshtain, John F. Kilner, and Scott B. Rae, *Biotechnology and the Human Good* (Washington, DC: Georgetown University Press, 2007), 107.

University philosopher who has been one of the primary advocates of the diverse movement, says transhumanism is "a way of thinking about the future that is based on the premise that the human species in its current form does not represent the end of our development but rather a comparatively early phase." Transhumanism, he states, "affirms the possibility and desirability of fundamentally improving the human condition through applied reason, especially by developing and making widely available technologies to eliminate aging and to greatly enhance human intellectual, physical, and psychological capacities."[41] But this commitment goes far beyond the historic end of medicine, healing, to an enhancement in which humans as we have known them throughout history will be radically changed. This, suggests Bostrom, may well lead us into a future of the "posthuman."

What might this look like? Bostrom paints a scenario:

> Let us make a leap into an imaginary future posthuman world, in which technology has reached its logical limits. The superintelligent inhabitants of this world are *autopotent*, meaning that they have complete power over and operational understanding of themselves, so that they are able to remold themselves at will and assume any internal state they choose. An autopotent being could, for example, easily transform itself into the shape of a woman, a man, or a tree. Such a being could also easily enter any subjective state it wants to be in, such as a state of pleasure or indignation, or a state of experiencing the visual and tactile sensations of a dolphin swimming in the sea. We can also assume that these posthumans have thorough control over their environment, so that they can make molecularly exact copies of objects and implement any physical design for which they have conceived of a detailed blueprint. . . . They would have the same kind of control of physical reality as programmers and designers today have over virtual reality.[42]

There are various emphases and advocates in the movement. Ray Kurzweil, a former MIT professor whose research enabled face-recognition technology, speaks of a point of singularity in which a human being will be as much machine as biological human. "The Singularity will allow us to transcend . . . limitations of our biological bodies and brains. We will gain power over our fates. Our mortality will be in our own hands. We will be able to live as long as we want." Kurzweil believes that "by the end of this century, the nonbiological portion of our intelligence will be trillions of trillions of times more

41. Nick Bostrom, *The Transhumanist FAQ: A General Introduction*, version 2.1 (N.p.: World Transhumanist Association, 2003), 4, https://nickbostrom.com/views/transhumanist.pdf.

42. Nick Bostrom, "Dignity and Enhancement," in *Human Dignity and Bioethics: Essays Commissioned by the President's Council on Bioethics* (Washington, DC: The President's Council on Bioethics, 2008), https://bioethicsarchive.georgetown.edu/pcbe/reports/human_dignity/chapter8.html.

powerful than unaided human intelligence."[43] Aubrey de Grey, a biogerontologist, believes that through medical technology we will be able to control the aging process and live hundreds of years in good health. "We will be in possession of indefinite youth. We will die only from the sort of causes that young people die of today—accidents, suicide, homicide, and so on—but not of the age-related diseases that account for the vast majority of deaths in the industrialized world today."[44] Despite the diversity within the movement, "transhumanists . . . share the common objective of shifting from being submitted to natural evolution to a chosen technological evolution, thanks to technoscientific and biomedical advances. The transhumanists indeed seek to transcend human biological boundaries since, they feel, humans do not in any way have a prescribed essence."[45]

Among the transhumanist advocates, there is usually a strong antireligious sentiment believing that religion, especially Christianity, inhibits technological advancement to enhance human progress. As one advocate puts it, "The greatest threat to humanity's continuing evolution is theistic opposition to Superbiology in the name of a belief system based on blind faith in the absence of evidence."[46] While most transhumanists aim to improve life and society in general through technologies, Julian Savulescu, also at Oxford, believes we have a moral imperative to permanently improve the genetic lot of future humanity through genetic engineering. "The next stage of human evolution will be rational evolution, where we select children who not only have the greatest chance of surviving, reproducing, and being free of disease, but who have the greatest opportunities to have the best lives in their likely environment."[47] While Savulescu rejects the term *eugenics* for his philosophy, he is clearly moving in the direction of eugenics.

From a Christian perspective, numerous critiques can be made of transhumanism. While both Christianity and transhumanism want transformation in this world, they have different approaches for getting there and, hence,

43. Ray Kurzweil, *The Singularity Is Near: When Humans Transcend Biology* (New York: Penguin Books, 2005), 9. See also Max Borders, *The Social Singularity: A Decentralist Manifesto* (Austin: Social Evolution, 2018).

44. Aubrey de Grey, "Foreword: Forever Young," in *Religion and the Implications of Radical Life Extension*, ed. Derek F. Maher and Calvin Mercer (New York: Seabury, 2010), 9. See also a conversation with de Grey in Douglas Lain, *Advancing Conversations: Aubrey de Grey* (Croydon, UK: Zero Books, 2016).

45. Nicholas Le Dévédec, "Unfit for the Future? The Depoliticization of Human Perfectibility, from the Enlightenment to Transhumanism," *European Journal of Social Theory* 21, no. 4 (2018): 491.

46. Simon Young, *Designer Evolution: A Transhumanist Manifesto* (Amherst, NY: Prometheus Books, 2006), 324.

47. Julian Savulescu, "Genetic Interventions and the Ethics of Enhancement of Human Beings," in *Readings in the Philosophy of Technology*, ed. David M. Kaplan, 2nd ed. (Lanham, MD: Rowman & Littlefield, 2009), 427.

vastly different eschatologies. Long before the emergence of transhumanism, theologian Carl Braaten once described the difference between futurology and Christian eschatology this way: "The future of secular futurology is reached by a process of the world's *becoming*. The future in Christian eschatology *arrives* by the *coming* of God's kingdom. The one is *becoming* and the other a *coming*."[48] The one is God's doing with human stewardship involved; the other is achieved solely by humans who take on an aura of infinity. In addition, Christianity gives a strong affirmation of the physical body in contrast to a loathing of the existing human body by transhumanism. Brent Waters argues that we must affirm "what it means to take mortal and finite bodies seriously, since they have been affirmed, vindicated, and redeemed by God in Christ, the Word made flesh, particularly in light of current attempts to overcome the limits of finitude and mortality." As Waters sees it, the attempts to overcome natural limits are "initiating a new age of Manichean disdain for the body, Gnostic search for immortality, and Pelagian quest for perfection."[49] With transhumanist ideals there will likely be greater injustices, with a condescension toward those who are unable to achieve their posthuman standards of what is now a truly valued being. Sympathy, mercy, and empathy for the sick, mentally challenged, disabled, and even the poor would likely wane in a transhumanist utopia.

Above all, transhumanism fails humans and society because it cannot accept human dependence, limitation, and finitude, along with human fallenness. "The project . . . is based on the false assumption that freedom is expanded by overcoming all finite and temporal limits. . . . The posthuman project is actually enslaving."[50] And as Michael Sandel puts it, "Changing our nature to fit the world, rather than the other way around, is actually the deepest form of disempowerment. It distracts us from reflecting critically on the world, and deadens the impulse to social and political improvement."[51]

Nonacceptance of Mortality at the End of Life

As we saw in chapter 3, humans sometimes take life into their own hands and play God through medical assistance in dying, or euthanasia, as it was called historically. But there is another way in which we might fail to accept our finitude: the refusal to accept death when our mortality is upon us. Given medical technologies such as ventilators, feeding tubes, or even cancer treatments, the natural processes leading to death can be significantly extended. Here we are talking not about brain death but rather about futility of treat-

48. Carl E. Braaten, *The Future of God: The Revolutionary Dynamics of Hope* (New York: Harper & Row, 1969), 29.

49. Brent Waters, *This Mortal Flesh: Incarnation and Bioethics* (Grand Rapids: Brazos, 2009), 9.

50. Waters, *This Mortal Flesh*, 161.

51. Michael J. Sandel, *The Case against Perfection: Ethics in the Age of Genetic Engineering* (Cambridge, MA: Harvard University Press, 2007), 97.

ments for a dying patient. Hippocrates long ago stated that we should "refuse to treat those who are overmastered by their disease, realizing that in such cases medicine is powerless."[52] Medicine is powerful and a wonderful gift of God. But it, too, is finite.

There are those, often out of misplaced Christian convictions, who refuse to accept their own mortality in the face of impending death and resort to a medical vitalism that unnecessarily elongates the dying process. In part medical vitalism is a result of the "Baconian project," which, following the philosophy of Francis Bacon in the sixteenth and seventeenth centuries, believed that science and technology could overcome all human limitations. "The most noble end of medicine was regarded as the preservation of life. In pursuit of that end, no patient would be regarded as 'overmastered' by disease. . . . Death was the great enemy to be defeated by the greater powers of medicine. The best hope against suffering, disease, and death was thought to be scientific knowledge and technology."[53] In contrast to this project of control, Dr. L. S. Dugdale reminds us that "our human life span is exceedingly short when juxtaposed with the existence of the universe. We are finite creatures in finite bodies. Yet, paradoxically, we cannot seem to fathom our own mortality." She then asks, "Can we die well if we refuse to acknowledge our finitude? . . . We must be prepared to say, 'Yes, I am human and therefore mortal. One day I will die.'"[54]

A Christian theology of death should affirm that death is both friend and foe. Death is clearly foe in that "the last enemy to be destroyed is death" (1 Cor. 15:26), and it is linked to the fall of humanity (Rom. 5:12), even if theologians debate exactly how physical death and the fall intersect. In Scripture death is associated with despair (Ps. 88:15), anguish (2 Sam. 22:5–7; Ps. 116:3), fear (Heb. 2:15), and a valley of shadow (Ps. 23:4). But for believers death is also friend, for "precious in the sight of the Lord is the death of his faithful servants" (116:15), and the apostle Paul, feeling torn between going into the presence of his Maker and carrying out God's mission on earth, says, "For to me, to live is Christ and to die is gain" (Phil. 1:21). Death in Scripture is also portrayed in this present, fallen world as the natural end of life, as it is being "gathered to my people" (Gen. 49:29; cf. 25:8; 49:33), the destiny of every person (Eccles. 7:2; Heb. 9:27), and a returning to the ground, for "dust you are and to dust you will return" (Gen. 3:19; cf. Eccles. 3:20).

Though in the future resurrection with and through Christ the "sting of death" is overcome (1 Cor. 15:55–57), in this world we are mortal, finite beings.

52. Hippocrates, *Decorum* 16, quoted in Thomas W. Laqueur, "When Medicine Is Powerless," Virtual Mentor, *AMA Journal of Ethics*, December 15, 2013, https://journalofethics.ama-assn.org/article/when-medicine-powerless/2013-12.

53. Allen Verhey, *The Christian Art of Dying: Learning from Jesus* (Grand Rapids: Eerdmans, 2011), 38.

54. L. S. Dugdale, *The Lost Art of Dying: Reviving Forgotten Wisdom* (New York: HarperOne, 2020), 27.

Death as both friend and foe precludes both a medical vitalism that refuses to stop burdensome, futile treatment when death is calling and medical assistance in dying (i.e., euthanasia) when suffering is making our mortal lives difficult. We are finite, limited creatures who must accept our mortality, rather than playing God by either course of action. For believers in Christ, there is hope, not because we take death and life into our own hands but because we can declare with Paul, "Thanks be to God! He gives us the victory through our Lord Jesus Christ" (v. 57).

Accepting Our Finitude

In the face of our finitude, dependence, and mortality, it is imperative that we refuse the temptations that led to the fall of Satan and the first humans. This starts with a recognition that only God is infinite, which "means not only that God is unlimited but that he is illimitable. In this respect, God is unlike anything we experience."[55] God is limited only by his character. Part of our problem in theology and ethics is attempting to think about God in human categories and to think about humanity in divine categories. We need to affirm the words of Paul in Athens: "The God who made the world and everything in it is the Lord of heaven and earth and does not live in temples built by human hands. And he is not served by human hands, as if he needed anything. Rather, he himself gives everyone life and breath and everything else" (Acts 17:24–25). God is the Infinite One; we are not.

Part of our motivation and model for accepting finitude is that the Infinite One from all eternity has entered into our time-bound limitations through the Incarnate One, Jesus Christ. "Wrapped in finitude—within the limits of the creaturely experience—the Son paradoxically comes as the divine embrace of the creation. He comes to draw near and renew. In this coming we discover the heart of God. And his coming links human flourishing to our creaturely limits."[56] In the apostle Paul's admonition to humility among the Philippian believers, he appeals to Jesus's incarnation as a taking on of finitude, while maintaining his divinity:

> Have the same mindset as Christ Jesus:
> Who, being in very nature God,
> did not consider equality with God something to be used to his own advantage;
> rather, he made himself nothing
> by taking the very nature of a servant,
> being made in human likeness.

55. Erickson, *Christian Theology*, 243.
56. Kapic, *You're Only Human*, 50.

> And being found in appearance as a man,
> he humbled himself
> by becoming obedient to death—even death on a cross!
> (Phil. 2:5–8)

Jesus, our Savior and Lord, knows what it means to live as a mortal, limited being in this world because he has entered into the limitations of our world. And this is the heart of Paul's appeal to not think of ourselves more highly than we ought as finite creatures.

Humility is one of the most significant virtues for finite humans, especially in their endeavors both to understand the world and to shape it. As we seek justice and goodness in this temporal world, we are tempted toward an arrogance that presumes we fully and absolutely know what it will look like in a complex world. Niebuhr wisely writes, "Man is tempted to deny the limited character of his knowledge, and the finiteness of his perspective. He pretends to have achieved a degree of knowledge which is beyond the limit of finite life. This is the 'ideological taint' in which all human knowledge is involved and which is always something more than mere human ignorance."[57] It is one thing to rightly believe there is truth and be committed to the truth. It is another thing to believe we have fully grasped it, as if we were beyond the limits of finitude. As humans, and especially as believing humans, we need to mimic the posture of Proverbs 11:2: "When pride comes, then comes disgrace, but with humility comes wisdom."

Humility comes from the Latin *humo acclinis*, literally meaning "bent toward the ground." This is a reminder that we are "dust and ashes," which is part of our limited, mortal nature. Kapic writes, "Instead of starting with sin, we must ground our theology of humility in the goodness of *creation*. Humility is a distinctly biblical virtue *because it begins with the knowledge that there is a good Creator Lord and we are the finite creatures he made to live in fellowship with him*." He goes on to state (rightly, I believe), "Humility consists in a recognition of (and a rejoicing in) the good limitations that God has given us; it is not a regrettable necessity, nor simply a later addition responding to sinful disorders."[58] To accept our finitude in all spheres of life is a virtue. When we don't accept our finitude, we transgress the created nature of ourselves and the created nature of our neighbor and our world.

Conclusion

We are limited, dependent human beings because God in his infinite wisdom made us that way. The creation story and the rest of God's written Word are

57. Niebuhr, *Nature and Destiny of Man*, 1:182.
58. Kapic, *You're Only Human*, 103.

clear about our finitude and its necessary acceptance for life in this world. Humanity's fall and Satan's fall resulted from attempts to transcend finitude and to somehow be in essence and knowledge like God. Sin is the negative limitation in our lives resulting from the fall, but finitude is the creational limitation, which is significant for wisely, justly, and righteously carrying out the cultural mandate to be stewards of God's good creation in this world. Finitude does not mean acceptance of the status quo, nor does it prevent attempts to curb illness, scarcity, and wrong. But we carry out our image-bearing mandates within the confines of God's designs.

Unfortunately, history has been full of experiments to transcend finitude, including utopias, eugenics, transhumanism, and playing God at the end of life by not accepting our mortality. They are all self-defeating, harmful to others, unjust, and incur divine judgment. Why? Because finite is how the Infinite One made us. We are called as Christians to follow the model of the Infinite One who became incarnate, tasting of our finitude and bearing our sins. As finite beings we are called to a life of humility, "bent to the ground" in our journey in this world but awaiting the day when we will be transformed fully into God's designs, as his limited, dependent children—though then without death. But even in the eschaton, we will still be finite creatures, for only God is infinite.

10

Embodied Souls or Ensouled Bodies

The Meaning and Implications of Being Whole Beings

At least four times in Scripture, the writers ask, "What are human beings that you are mindful of them . . . ?" (Ps. 8:4 NRSV; cf. Job 7:17; Ps. 144:3; Heb. 2:6). Thus far in our journey, we have seen that humans are divine image bearers, stewards of creation, relational creatures, workers, and finite. But inevitably we get around to the question, What is the constitution of a person? What constitutes the different dimensions of a human being, considering the fact that we have bodies but engage in activities that seem to transcend the body, such as thinking, desiring, moral deliberation, feeling, and spiritual quests? As we will see in this chapter, this is not just a theoretical philosophical or theological question but has significant practical and ethical implications.

Historically there have been a number of views about human nature in terms of its essential, constituent parts. In the Christian church, the debate was often between a trichotomous view—in which humans are thought to consist of body, soul, and spirit, frequently with each deemed to be a discrete part with very different functions—and the dichotomous view, which sees spirit and soul as one but with a significant separation between body and soul. The split between the two was expanded by the philosopher René Descartes and the Cartesian dualism that followed him. But for Descartes the soul was essentially the mind, and the philosophical issue was a mind-body relationship rather than the soul-body relationship.

Observing the contemporary scene, Joel Green notes four major views, encompassing both religious and secular viewpoints. First is *reductive materialism*, in which "emotional, moral, and religious experiences will ultimately and decisively be explained by the natural sciences." There is nothing in humans but the product of organic chemistry. Second is *radical dualism*, "the view that the soul (or mind) is separable from the body, having no necessary relation to the body, with the human person identified with the soul."[1] A third view is *wholistic dualism* (also called *substance dualism*), in which body and soul are distinct but seen as corollaries working together in unity. Moreland and Rae, advocating a unity of the self, argue that there is only one substance, and that "one substance is the soul, and the body is an ensouled biological and physical structure that depends on the soul for its existence."[2] Fourth is *monism* or *nonreductive materialism*, in which human mental actions are recognized to be part of the physical world but cannot be reduced to natural, physical causes alone. Advocate Nancey Murphy writes, "We are bodies—there is no additional metaphysical element such as the mind or soul or spirit." This does "not deny that we are intelligent, moral, and spiritual. We are, at our best, complex physical organisms, imbued with the legacy of thousands of years of culture, and most importantly, blown by the Breath of God's Spirit; we are *Spirited bodies*."[3]

Today in the intellectual Christian world, the debate is primarily between wholistic or substance dualism and monism or nonreductive materialism, both attempting to assert a wholistic view of humans. At a popular level, a more radical dualism is no doubt still prevalent. I am not going to resolve those philosophical and theological debates; rather, I simply affirm that a creational paradigm must assert a unity of the human person in which the bodily and nonbodily elements are held closely together. They are so closely intertwined that what happens in the body affects the nonbodily dimensions, and vice versa. Hence, we are either embodied souls or ensouled bodies, and this unity of the self has important implications for our life in this world—for ethics. I do personally believe that we must maintain in our philosophical or theological stance an understanding that physical death is not the end of a person, even though "dust [we] are, and to dust [we] will return" (Gen. 3:19).

1. Joel B. Green, *Body, Soul, and Human Life: The Nature of Humanity in the Bible*, Studies in Theological Interpretation (Grand Rapids: Baker Academic, 2008), 30, 31.

2. J. P. Moreland and Scott B. Rae, *Body and Soul: Human Nature and the Crisis in Ethics* (Downers Grove, IL: InterVarsity, 2000), 201.

3. Nancey Murphy, *Bodies and Souls, or Spirited Bodies?*, Current Issues in Theology (Cambridge: Cambridge University Press, 2006), ix.

Creation and Embodied Souls or Ensouled Bodies

When thinking of the topic at hand, some might be prone to start with Genesis 2:7: "Then the Lord God formed a man from the dust of the ground and breathed into his nostrils the breath of life, and man became a living being [or "soul" in some translations]." Traditionally this text was frequently employed to posit a body-soul dualism that, along with the *imago Dei*, set humans apart. The Hebrew word for "living being" or "soul" is *nephesh*, and interestingly it is used four times before this text with reference to animals: Genesis 1:20, 21, 24, and 30. Moreover, *nephesh* has various meanings depending on the context and can be translated "soul," "living being," "person," "mind," "breath," "desire," "self," and even "throat." Genesis 2:7 is theologically rich, but it's very difficult to draw from it an extreme body-soul dualism or a clear distinction between humans who have souls and animals who do not. Rather, "Genesis 2:7 intentionally unites in one verse both the fashioning of the human body and the breathing of God's spirit into us. . . . With its bright, glorious, unifying vision of who we are, this one stunning verse sweeps away all the fragmenting, dichotomizing divisions between body and spirit that have plagued the human race."[4]

In the creation story, human beings are portrayed with bodily dimensions, nonbodily dimensions, and a unity between them—what I am terming "ensouled bodies" or "embodied souls."

The Bodily Dimension in Creation

As we saw in chapter 2, God gives a pronouncement of goodness after each day of creation, and what is good is primarily physical or material in nature. After God creates humans in his image, with bodily form, we read, "God saw all that he had made, and it was very good" (Gen. 1:31). Within that good creation is a physiological distinction: "In the image of God he created them; male and female he created them" (v. 27). While gender expressions may take on various cultural expressions, God's design is that bodily dimensions of sexuality, male and female, would both continue life on earth and also provide identity for humans. In a fallen world, there are biological anomalies (intersex conditions) and psychological anomalies (gender dysphoria), but the normative structure of God's design is male and female. (See chap. 5 for more details on these anomalies.) Amid the fallen conditions of humanity, this is the goal toward which we must work medically, psychologically, and spiritually—recognizing that this is not always easy or simple, especially in a pluralistic society.

Having created humans with significant bodies, the very first command God gives to humans is to "be fruitful and increase in number" (Gen. 1:28).

4. Timothy C. Tennent, *For the Body: Recovering a Theology of Gender, Sexuality, and the Human Body* (Grand Rapids: Zondervan Reflective, 2020), 15.

Procreation with unique (male and female) sexuality is the means by which not only human life on earth continues, but all of life. When God creates vegetation and plants, they have seeds "according to their kinds," which enable reproduction in the natural world (vv. 11–13). Animal life, too, is given the mandate to "be fruitful and increase in number" (v. 22), and the phrase "according to its kind" (v. 24) is employed with them as well. This should not be taken to nullify biological mutations and evolutionary processes in the animal world but rather to point toward the bodily, reproductive dimension of all creation, including humans. Without this bodily dimension of procreation, human life ceases. "The sexual act has the potential to produce new life, even as the intimate communion within the Trinity is fruitful in producing life."[5] Moreover, the bodily, reproductive dimension is a sign of the spiritual reproduction, when by faith in the Savior humans can come into a personal relationship with the God who created them.

The bodily dimension of humans is further explicated in Genesis 2 in the institution of marriage. After no "suitable partner" is found (v. 20), the text tells us that "the LORD God made a woman from the rib he had taken out of the man, and he brought her to the man. The man said, 'This is now bone of my bones and flesh of my flesh; she shall be called "woman," for she was taken out of man'" (vv. 22–23). In a way similar to God's creation of the man from physical stuff—that is, the ground (v. 7)—so, too, the woman is formed with physical stuff from the man. The language of "bone of my bones and flesh of my flesh" exudes with bodily dimensions so that the two experience a physical unity, not just an emotional one. This is further emphasized in verse 24: "That is why a man leaves his father and mother and is united to his wife, and they become one flesh." As we saw earlier, the "one flesh" is a deep organic unity that involves the bodies of two who are unalike, male and female, and from the physical union comes the possibility of new physical life. Adam and Eve were at home with their physicality to the point that they "were both naked, and they felt no shame" (v. 25). In the creation of sexuality, reproduction, and marriage, the body is integral, and it is all pronounced good by the Creator.

In addition the bodily dimensions of human life are front and center in the Creator's mandate to work and to care for the garden—creation care. When God gives to his image bearers the responsibility of ruling over the animal world (1:28) and harvesting the seed-bearing plants (v. 29), it is assumed that physicality would be involved. Humans would need strength, vitality, and various physical traits to carry out the stewardship task of caring for and developing further God's good world. Without the human body and its physical features, this stewardship task could never be accomplished. Inherent in this care and in the command to work and care for the garden of Eden (2:15) is the institution of work in all its forms. Work is far more than physical

5. Tennent, *For the Body*, 53.

exertion, but work is impossible without the body, its molecules, chemical makeup, and functioning organs. Whereas the Gnostics and other extreme dualists try to downplay physicality and materiality, the Genesis record is clear in its emphasis on the body as essential for life functioning and relationships. From this it would only make sense that the body is never far removed from spirituality and our relationship with God. As Marc Cortez notes, there is frequently "an inappropriate reduction of the human person to the spiritual dimension alone, resulting in a denigration of the body as having merely instrumental value in spiritual formation."[6]

The Nonbodily Dimensions in Creation

While the human body is front and center in the creation account, it is also clear that if we reduce all elements of humanness to the physical body, we have misread the opening chapters of the Bible. Marriage is a highly physical relationship, but entailed in the procreation of children and the one-flesh relationship are planning, emotions, love, and a spiritual awareness that this relationship will be an ensouled-body relationship. The very act of faithfulness entails a physical discreetness in relationships with others, but also a will to refrain from entering into other inappropriate acts with someone other than one's spouse. Adultery is a physical act, but as Jesus points out, it is first an act of the heart (Matt. 5:27–30) and, thus, a whole-person act. Moreover, "one could avoid committing adultery yet nonetheless be unfaithful to one's spouse . . . by withholding physical or emotional intimacy that restricts the one-flesh unity of marriage."[7] For this one-flesh relationship to grow and flourish, it must incorporate commitment, trust, good communication, and patience—virtues and skills that go far beyond human genes and biology. All of this demonstrates that marriage as God intends incorporates bodily and nonbodily dimensions that are deeply intertwined. The creation story of Genesis 1 and 2 presents a wholistic understanding of sexual union between the man and the woman and, within that union, an anthropology in which "a human being does not have a soul, he/she is a soul. A human is a living being, a psychophysical unity."[8]

Marriage and family are, of course, just one part of our human relationality. When the Lord God says, "It is not good for the man to be alone," this is not only a pathway to marriage but also a declaration that we are relational creatures

6. Marc Cortez, "Beyond Imitation: The Image of God as a Vision for Spiritual Formation," in *Tending Soul, Mind, and Body: The Art and Science of Spiritual Formation*, ed. Gerald Hiestand and Todd Wilson (Downers Grove, IL: IVP Academic, 2019), 29.

7. Brent Waters, *Common Callings and Ordinary Virtues: Christian Ethics for Everyday Life* (Grand Rapids: Baker Academic, 2022), 107.

8. Richard M. Davidson, *Flame of Yahweh: Sexuality in the Old Testament* (Peabody, MA: Hendrickson, 2007), 36.

who will encounter others bodily, including neighbors, friends, coworkers, and fellow members of society with whom we will need understanding, love, and some of the internal virtues that are essential to a marriage. As Brent Waters puts it, "We are not intended to be alone. . . . To be always alone would make one less than fully human. Humans are creatures who flourish in the company of others. . . . Without these bonds, we become, in effect, free-floating specters rather than the embodied and finite creatures we were created to be."[9] We never encounter others fully in disembodied forms, for our bodies speak, care, and convey meaning. But relationality always requires something more than the body to "love your neighbor as yourself" (Matt. 22:39).

Work, stewarding creation, and carrying out the cultural mandates from God will always incorporate the body, but also far more than just the body. To work and steward creation entails organization, planning, responsibility, and ethical judgments and sensitivities. Our work in this world should never be as robots mechanically going through the motions, but as we explored in our chapter on work, it is a calling from God in which spiritual life and disciplines are deeply intertwined. In one of Adam's first tasks, he engages in the scientific enterprise of classification, naming the animals. This was a mental task that would call for precision and creativity, incorporating physical seeing with careful analysis and likely lighthearted play in his ingenious naming. Work, creation care, and the development of cultural realities within this world will always require the best of embodied souls or ensouled bodies. To dislodge one from the other would be an affront to God's calling for humanity.

Further, the creation account introduces a relationship with God that will incorporate the whole self. God designs and speaks realities into being, with an assumption that readers in all times and places will recognize a cognitive role in discerning those designs, through both special revelation and natural revelation. The natural revelation part includes not merely reason, for as Paul says, "since the creation of the world God's invisible qualities—his eternal power and divine nature—have been clearly seen, being understood from what has been made, so that people are without excuse" (Rom. 1:20). Here bodily, sensory mechanisms are combined with cognition and spiritual response.

In the creation story, God speaks directly. God first gives the command to tend the garden (2:15) and then the command to refrain from the tree of the knowledge of good and evil (v. 17); then he asks Adam to name the animals (vv. 19–20). After Adam and Eve choose to go against the command and seek autonomy and infinitude, God speaks to them as they are hiding in the garden (3:8–9), and a conversation on their moral and spiritual choices ensues. In all of this, we see various nonbodily dimensions at work. There is communication, moral responsibility, emotional reactions, and a comprehension of judgment. While the taking of the prohibited fruit is a bodily action, these

9. Waters, *Common Callings*, 64–65.

other dimensions go far beyond mere bodily mechanisms, though not without bodily ramifications. When Adam and Eve engage in blame and experience shame following the fall, surely their emotional and moral responses involve internal bodily responses.[10]

Embodied Souls / Ensouled Bodies in the Rest of Scripture

The unified and interactive dimensions of the human person are evident throughout the whole of the Bible. For starters the many terms used to describe parts of the human being carry a variety of meanings and are often used interchangeably. We've already mentioned this with the word *nephesh*, but similarly, "*bāśār* might be translated with the English terms 'flesh,' 'body,' 'meat,' 'skin,' 'humankind,' or '(the) animal (kingdom).' Translations of *lēb* might include 'heart,' 'mind,' 'conscience,' and 'inner life.' Finally, *rūah* might be taken as a reference to 'wind,' 'breath,' 'seat of cognition and/or volition,' 'disposition,' 'spirit,' or 'point on a compass.'"[11] These terms not only have different meanings in different contexts but are sometimes used either interchangeably or together in a wholistic way. At times they have a more physical or bodily dimension in view, while in other settings they have a very spiritual or nonbodily focus. The same is true of the varied Greek terms. "*Sōma* is capable of translation into English as 'body,' 'physical being,' 'church,' 'slave,' and even 'reality'; *psychē* as 'inner self,' 'life,' and 'person'; *pneuma* as 'spirit,' 'ghost,' 'inner self,' 'way of thinking,' 'wind,' and 'breath'; and *sarx* as 'flesh,' 'body,' 'people,' 'human,' 'nation,' 'human nature,' and, simply, 'life.'"[12] In addition the Greek word *nous* is most often translated "mind" but at times "understanding," and in some contexts it conveys a sense of "the will."

All of this makes it very difficult to divide up the human self into tidy, separate compartments in which the body, soul, spirit, and mind are distinct components of a human being. The broad range of meanings for each term and their interchangeability points to a unified self in which the bodily and nonbodily dimensions are so intricately related that we are best to speak of embodied souls or ensouled bodies.

This unity of the self is evident in numerous biblical texts. For example, the Shema of Deuteronomy 6:4–9 incorporates a wholistic view of a person:

> Hear, O Israel: The Lord our God, the Lord is one. You shall love the Lord your God with all your heart and with all your soul and with all your might. And these words that I command you today shall be on your heart. You shall teach them diligently to your children, and shall talk of them when you sit in your house, and

10. See Curt Thompson, *The Soul of Shame: Retelling the Stories We Believe about Ourselves* (Downers Grove, IL: IVP Books, 2015).

11. Green, *Body, Soul, and Human Life*, 54.

12. Green, *Body, Soul, and Human Life*, 55.

> when you walk by the way, and when you lie down, and when you rise. You shall bind them as a sign on your hand, and they shall be as frontlets between your eyes. You shall write them on the doorposts of your house and on your gates. (ESV)

The text exudes physical and nonphysical dimensions in such a way that they can hardly be separated. "Heart and . . . soul and . . . might" is a way of saying "Love God with every part of your inner being." The reference to talking about God's commands at home, while walking, lying down, and getting up points beyond merely the inner self. And then taking action to bind them as symbols on oneself and in one's home and community signifies physical actions and places for the commands to take root. Here there is no dividing up of soul and body or spiritual and secular; the human self and all of life are intricately tied together in the life of an embodied soul or ensouled body.

Language similar to that of the Shema occurs throughout Scripture, with an interchangeability of terms related to the various dimensions. In the Magnificat Mary says, "My soul magnifies the Lord, and my spirit rejoices in God my Savior" (Luke 1:46–47 ESV). Here the references to soul and spirit are not indicators of two discrete parts of Mary; rather, they are akin to Hebrew parallelism, in which the second term and line just reinforces the first. Jesus, articulating the greatest commandment, exhorts, "Love the Lord your God with all your heart and with all your soul and with all your mind" (Matt. 22:37)—and the account in Mark's Gospel adds "with all your strength" (12:30). Jesus here is not carving up human beings into distinct parts but rather using broad, interchangeable words to speak of a unified love from a unified self. And such love of God and neighbor will always incorporate physical actions.

Paul brings the whole self together in his letter to the church in Thessalonica: "May God himself . . . sanctify you through and through. May your whole spirit, soul and body be kept blameless at the coming of our Lord Jesus Christ" (1 Thess. 5:23). And in Romans 12:1–2, he again uses various terms that embrace the whole person in the process of sanctification: "Offer your bodies [plural of *sōma*] as a living sacrifice, holy and pleasing to God—that is your true and proper worship. Do not conform to the pattern of this world, but be transformed by the renewing of your mind." And the writer to the Hebrews gives clear evidence of an embodied soul / ensouled body when he writes, "For the word of God is alive and active. Sharper than any double-edged sword, it penetrates even to dividing soul and spirit, joints and marrow; it judges the thoughts and attitudes of the heart" (Heb. 4:12).

When we put the creation paradigms, Jesus, and all of Scripture together, we find not a Greek dualism but a unified self in which the nonphysical and physical are working together as a whole. To isolate one at the expense of the other is to denigrate God's creational design of humanity. Thus, "our integrated unity of body, soul, spirit as a whole person is an 'icon' in the world of both the triune nature of God (three persons, one unity) and also of

Christ (two natures united in one person)."[13] Summarizing the biblical view of humans, theologian Millard Erickson wisely notes several main understandings that should be held together:

- The human person is a unity, such that the spiritual condition of a person is not independent of the physical or psychological dimensions. This is evidenced through psychosomatic medicine in which the physical and psychological are intertwined.
- Humans are complex beings, not reducible to single principles or dimensions.
- All aspects of the human person, whether physical or nonphysical, should be attended to.
- Spiritual development is not subjugating one part of human nature to another.[14]

In all of this, we must affirm that at death a nonphysical dimension continues on in some manner, for at the cross Jesus gives hope to the repentant criminal who is about to die: "Truly I tell you, today you will be with me in paradise" (Luke 23:43). And the future eschaton includes a resurrection of the body that will then last throughout all eternity:

> For the trumpet will sound, the dead will be raised imperishable, and we will be changed. For the perishable must clothe itself with the imperishable, and the mortal with immortality. When the perishable has been clothed with the imperishable, and the mortal with immortality, then the saying that is written will come true: "Death has been swallowed up in victory."
>
> "Where, O death, is your victory?
> Where, O death, is your sting?"
>
> . . . But thanks be to God! He gives us the victory through our Lord Jesus Christ. (1 Cor. 15:52–55, 57)

And in that future resurrected state, we will still be embodied souls / ensouled bodies.

Ethical Implications of Embodied Souls / Ensouled Bodies

That humans have this unique unity in which the physical and nonphysical are in continual interaction is not abstract theology or philosophy. It has

13. Tennent, *For the Body*, 16.
14. Millard J. Erickson, *Christian Theology*, 3rd ed. (Grand Rapids: Baker Academic, 2013), 493.

significant ethical implications, to which we now turn. We will explore three issues related to our being embodied souls / ensouled bodies: evangelism and social concern, artificial intelligence and the technicization of humans, and virtual gathering for worship and work. Gender dysphoria and transgender realities could also fit here, but we dealt with them in chapter 5.

Evangelism and Social Concern

One of the clearest implications of our unified constitution as humans is a commitment to both evangelism and social concern. For some it may seem odd to state this as an ethical implication, but if both nonphysical and physical dimensions are at the heart of our being, we must, in the mission of the church and in our personal lives, be attentive to caring both for an individual's personal relationship with God through Christ and for their physical, psychological, and social conditions.

Drawing on biblical exegesis, systematic theology, and analytic philosophy, Christa McKirland contends "that one's understanding of what it means to be human is inseparable from one's understanding of fundamental need, because what causes harm or flourishing for a subject is bound to what kind of being it is." In contrast to an anthropology of absolute autonomy, she argues that our greatest need as human beings is a dependence on the God who made us and shaped us. "Humankind is intended to experience dynamic flourishing in and through personal communion with the very triune life of God. Such communion is possible through the incarnation of the Logos, the firstborn of creation, putting on human form, depending on the Spirit, and giving the Spirit so that all humanity might flourish both now and always."[15] If this is true, then as Christians we have an ethical responsibility to share that good news with fellow humans and to invite them to experience the forgiveness and life-giving reality of Christ, whereby one becomes the kind of person God intends them to be, ensuring their presence with God for all eternity. Yes, evangelism is a moral responsibility.

This will be at odds with an anthropology of reductive materialism, which contends that all our humanness can be reduced to physical forces such as genes and biochemistry, for such a worldview leaves no space for anything beyond the physical realm. But an anthropology of the embodied soul / ensouled body sees something more than physical impulses and recognizes a spiritual dimension to our humanness. This means that humans by nature have an awareness of something beyond themselves, a longing for that something, and an intuitive sense that perhaps that something has shaped us toward certain patterns of life. To fail to give attention to this dimension of the human person is to go contrary to what most humans through the ages have

15. Christa L. McKirland, *God's Provision, Humanity's Need: The Gift of Our Dependence* (Grand Rapids: Baker Academic, 2022), 2, 14.

sensed. And they have sensed this not because of a reductive materialism but because there is a given in the very nature of humanity that propels them to seek for transcendence. As Saint Augustine so powerfully puts it, "You made us for yourself and our hearts find no peace until they rest in you."[16] Certainly humans throughout history have translated this search for transcendence in varying ways, with multiple conceptions of God or the gods and sometimes no god at all, other than the transcendence of humanity itself.

But from a creational perspective, Christians understand this journey to be part of the way God made us. If we are made in the image of God, there will be a yearning to know what that image means and looks like in this world. And if the yearning is best fulfilled in dependence on our Maker, then it is incumbent on those who have experienced that dependence through Christ to share it with others, that they, too, might experience, as Jesus puts it, "life and have it abundantly" (John 10:10 ESV). This ethical responsibility of evangelism stems not just from a theology of creation but also from an understanding of the fall and the means and meaning of salvation. Though we were created to flourish in dependence on the Creator, the entrance of sin into the world means that all human beings are alienated from God, thereby distorting their patterns of life and understandings of reality. God's ultimate solution is through the Son of God, who was with the Father in creation but, for our sakes in love, entered our world not merely to show us true human flourishing in dependence but to die on our behalf. Salvation is not a human initiative to correct our flaws but the very act of God's grace in Christ to do for us what we could not do for ourselves. Thus, "God made him who had no sin to be sin for us, so that in him we might become the righteousness of God" (2 Cor. 5:21). As a result "we are therefore Christ's ambassadors, as though God were making his appeal through us" (v. 20). Coming into a life of dependence on God through Christ implies a personal relationship with God that both transcends our physical being and is always interacting with the physical side of life.

Unfortunately, in some "Christian" quarters, there has been a tendency to either distort the meaning of salvation or downplay its significance. For example, some shrink the gospel by inverting God's love to mean "love is God." "Then a human definition of *love* (nice, tolerant, nonjudgmental) is substituted, and sinners find great comfort in this personification and deification of love."[17] Others opt for a universalism, arguing that all people are in Christ and thus saved. I've talked to individuals who have attended church all their life and never once heard about the need to repent and turn to Christ as Savior and Lord. In such contexts people often like Jesus (or part of Jesus)

16. Augustine, *Confessions*, trans. R. S. Pine-Coffin (New York: Penguin Books, 1961), 1.1.1, p. 21.

17. Will Metzger, *Tell the Truth: The Whole Gospel to the Whole Person by Whole People; A Training Manual on the Message and Method of God-Centered Witnessing to a Grace-Centered Gospel*, 3rd ed. (Downers Grove, IL: InterVarsity, 2002), 39.

but not the meaning of his salvation. As a result they disregard one of his important teachings, enunciated just before he ascended back to the Father: "Go therefore and make disciples of all nations, baptizing them in the name of the Father and of the Son and of the Holy Spirit, and teaching them to obey everything that I have commanded you" (Matt. 28:19–20 NRSV).

If Jesus is "the way and the truth and the life," and if "no one comes to the Father except through [him]" (John 14:6), then believers have an ethical responsibility to share the good news in word and in deed. We explain it but must also live it. Unfortunately, evangelism in word has sometimes been carried out in unethical ways, resulting in significant opposition to evangelism or proselytizing. We must note that some of this opposition has also been fueled by strident secularism, in which secularity itself becomes a worldview, often characterized by intolerance and coercion against Christianity. Elmer John Thiessen in *The Ethics of Evangelism* lays out fifteen criteria by which we can distinguish ethical and unethical proselytizing (his preferred term), and among these are the following:

- The dignity criterion—"ethical proselytizing [EP] is always done in such a way as to protect the dignity and worth of the person . . . being proselytized."
- The care criterion—EP will have concern for the whole person, including physical, social, economic, emotional, and spiritual needs.
- The physical-coercion criterion—EP "will therefore allow persons to make a genuinely free and uncoerced choice with regard to conversion."
- The psychological-coercion criterion—EP avoids both excessive psychological manipulation and exploiting the vulnerabilities of persons.
- The inducement criterion—"proselytizing accompanied by material enticement such as money, gifts or privileges, is immoral."
- The truthfulness criterion—proselytizing must tell the truth about one's own religion and be truthful about other worldviews.
- The humility criterion—rather than being arrogant or condescending, proselytizing must be done in humility.
- The tolerance criterion—EP "treats persons holding beliefs differing from that of the proselytizer with love and respect."
- The cultural-sensitivity criterion—EP values the uniqueness of every culture and is sensitive to the culture of those being proselytized.[18]

Because we are whole beings, Christians have a moral responsibility to share the good news of Christ with others, and to do so in an ethical way.

18. Elmer J. Thiessen, *The Ethics of Evangelism: A Philosophical Defense of Proselytizing and Persuasion* (Downers Grove, IL: IVP Academic, 2011), 234–37.

But humans are not just "spiritual beings" who have a need for dependence on their Creator. As embodied souls or ensouled bodies, they have physical, psychological, and social needs that call for our care, mercy, and justice. Social concern must always be part of the mission of the church, and we have an ethical responsibility to show it. This flows from many themes we have already covered in this book: human dignity from the *imago Dei*, the cultural mandate to care for God's good creation, our relationality as humans, the institution of work to meet human need, and the call to justice in our world. All of this is so important that Jesus says,

> Come, you who are blessed by my Father; take your inheritance, the kingdom prepared for you since the creation of the world. For I was hungry and you gave me something to eat, I was thirsty and you gave me something to drink, I was a stranger and you invited me in, I needed clothes and you clothed me, I was sick and you looked after me, I was in prison and you came to visit me. . . . Truly I tell you, whatever you did for one of the least of these brothers and sisters of mine, you did for me. (Matt. 25:34–36, 40)

In this text Jesus is clear that one's entrance into the kingdom of God is linked to these kinds of actions. Jesus here is not teaching a salvation by works but rather indicating that those who have genuinely embraced him by faith are those who demonstrate it by their actions of care, mercy, and justice.

But the point we are making here, commensurate with the Law, the Psalms, the Prophets, Jesus, Paul, and other apostles, is that our actions of care, mercy, and justice flow from our understanding of the wholeness of human beings. If a person has come to faith in Christ but is hungry, enslaved, or treated violently, they are unable to experience the fullness of what God intends for human beings as embodied souls / ensouled bodies. One's salvation through Christ is never an escape from the perils of a fallen, vengeful, apathetic world but rather a renewal toward a journey of wholeness in which all that God intends them to be can come to fruition. The physical, psychological, and social side of humanity is a result of God's good creation, and its fullness in this fallen world is dependent on the actions of other people. Salvation itself is totally the work of God's grace, but that grace is to be efficacious in Christ followers in such a way that they seek to enable all humans to experience the wholeness in which God created them. And as we've seen, that includes inviting them to Christ as well as seeking to meet their wholistic needs.

If one has experienced salvation in Christ but is undergoing oppression, marginalization, or prejudices in this world, their own discipleship is thwarted. Of course, as the apostle Paul says amid his own persecution and opposition, "we must go through many hardships to enter the kingdom of God" (Acts 14:22). But Paul also sought to overcome those hardships where possible by appealing to his rights as a Roman citizen (16:37–40; 22:26–27), and he asks believers to pray "for kings and all those in authority, that we may live peaceful and quiet lives in all godliness and holiness" (1 Tim. 2:2). Paul's hardships and persecutions were an opportunity for God's sustaining power and for witness to the wider world of divine grace and power. But all of this is not reason for believers to look the other way amid others' oppression, hardships, or poverty. Jesus's second great command is to love one's neighbors (Matt. 22:39), and he defines one's "neighbor" as anyone in need, meaning needs of embodied souls / ensouled bodies. James is also clear about authentic faith being accompanied by deeds: "What good is it, my brothers and sisters, if someone claims to have faith but has no deeds? . . . Suppose a brother or a sister is without clothes and daily food. If one of you says to them, 'Go in peace; keep warm and well fed,' but does nothing about their physical needs, what good is it?" (James 2:14–16). Such inaction, despite all the "spiritual" talk, is dead faith. The physical and social conditions of humans are of vital concern because those dimensions are always interacting with the spiritual, psychological, and cognitive dimensions of a person.

Unfortunately the church has not always done a good job of holding evangelism and social concern together. One study has found four main church types in relating these two. First are those holding that "explicit evangelism is not part of the church's outreach mission. This type of church is committed to serving the needy and advocating for justice in Christ's name but without making an explicit attempt to bring those they serve to Christ." A second type believes that "evangelism is valued and practiced but not in the context of social ministry." Here there is a dual-mission focus, with both present but in separate parallel tracks. In a third type, "little conventional social ministry is present." Here the assumption is that social needs are essentially spiritual in nature and evangelism is the means to social, physical, and psychological change. For the fourth type, "evangelism and social ministry are integrated in various ways. In this type, evangelism and social action are distinguishable but inseparable, like the two sides of a coin."[19] If humans are an integrated whole, then something akin to the fourth type seems most authentic. In such an approach, there should always be a recognition that in the body of Christ there are a variety of gifts, so that not everyone will be involved in the same ministries. Moreover, there will be times when evangelism is done without direct social action and times when ministries of social mercy and justice will not be appropriate for specific evangelism. However, holding these two together means that the church's mission and our individual commitments will embrace the gospel, proclaimed in word and deed.

Of course, strategies vary for carrying out evangelism and social concern, and therein are frequently some of our most significant conflicts. Should

19. Ronald J. Sider, Philip N. Olson, and Heidi Rolland Unruh, *Churches That Make a Difference: Reaching Your Community with Good News and Good Works* (Grand Rapids: Baker Books, 2002), 110–11.

evangelism be en masse or personal? Can it be anonymous, or must it be rooted in friendship? And when it comes to social concern, strategies range from relief to development to structural strategies that seek to change patterns and policies of a society. The latter will frequently engage individuals and the church in broader societal issues, which are sometimes guided more by ideological perspectives than biblically rooted wisdom. There are times when the Christian church will need to speak into the public arena, and we have examples from history in which the church did not sufficiently do so, to its own detriment and to the harm of society—such as the church's failure in slavery, the church's failure in Nazi Germany, and the church's complicity in the 1994 Rwandan massacre. But when the church needs to address structural, societal issues, it needs to be extremely cautious of politicization, identifying Christian faith with a particular political group.

Despite strategic issues and divides, the fact that we are embodied souls / ensouled bodies means that we must be committed to both evangelism and social concern. We must care deeply about a person's eternal destiny and their greatest spiritual need (the need for forgiveness in Christ); at the same time, we must care deeply about the physical, psychological, and social dimensions of their existence.

Artificial Intelligence and the Technicization of Humans

Artificial intelligence (AI) is no longer just part of the futurist predictions of science fiction; rather, it is part of everyday life in our world today. It is a vital part of many forms of current technology, ranging from smart phones and search platforms to social devices and instruments used at home and at work. Artificial intelligence is so interwoven into the fabric of our society that one analyst has projected, "If all of the AI systems decided to go on strike tomorrow, our civilization would be crippled: We couldn't get money from our bank, and . . . communication, transportation, and manufacturing would all grind to a halt."[20]

What is AI? One writer describes it as "an emerging field of technology defined as nonbiological intelligence, where a machine is programmed to accomplish complex goals by applying knowledge to the task at hand."[21] Another writer states, "AI can be defined as intelligence displayed or simulated by code (algorithms) or machines."[22] AI is often linked to or compared with human intelligence and thus is said to be much like human intelligence, though

20. Ray Kurzweil, *How to Create a Mind: The Secret of Human Thought Revealed* (New York: Viking, 2012), 158.

21. Jason Thacker, *The Age of AI: Artificial Intelligence and the Future of Humanity* (Grand Rapids: Zondervan Thrive, 2020), 233–34.

22. Mark Coeckelbergh, *AI Ethics*, MIT Press Essential Knowledge Series (Cambridge, MA: MIT Press, 2020), 64.

that begs the question of the nature of intelligence. Early in the development of AI, the Turing test (named after Alan Turing) determined whether a machine or robot could fool people into believing it was a human. Today "chatbots have . . . become clever and ubiquitous. They are tireless customer service agents, answering questions about the ingredients, store hours, and mysterious error codes at any time of day or night. . . . They are participants in online games, appearing as opponents, and teammates."[23] ChatGPT can respond to sophisticated questions and spit out essays on nearly any topic imaginable in a matter of seconds, with significant accuracy.

AI raises a wide range of ethical issues, including privacy, deception, worker displacement, and built-in biases and hence injustices through the use of algorithms. As philosopher Mark Kingwell puts it, "There is no such thing as a neutral algorithm, any more than there is such a thing as neutral technology. Technology always has inbuilt biases and tendencies."[24] These are all noteworthy issues, but because this is a chapter on embodied souls / ensouled bodies, my focus will be to explore two primary issues: Can we attribute humanness to artificial intelligence, and what does AI do to us as human beings?

Some have suggested that though it's difficult to define *human nature*, AIs perform in ways that evoke humanness, and that, they believe, is to be welcomed. After all, it is noted, AI systems such as face recognition can far outperform the human mind. Ray Kurzweil believes that by 2045 we will reach the point of "Singularity," in which we will be more machine than human, and we will overcome the restrictions of our bodies.[25] Some advocate for AIs to be viewed on par with human beings and believe we can even speak of them having moral agency, perhaps outdoing humans in moral reasoning since they are not carried away by emotions. Some support this view by arguing that the human brain is essentially a biological computer, though inferior to our machines.[26] Indeed, if one works from a materialist worldview, then everything, including thinking and morality, is reduced to matter. The distinction between human and machine is a moot point for a consistent materialist.

All of this is far removed from a Christian conception of the human being as an embodied soul / ensouled body. For starters, Jason Thacker is, I believe, right when he argues, "Computer systems should be called intelligent, albeit artificially, because intelligence doesn't define what it means to be human."

23. Judith Donath, "Ethical Issues in Our Relationship with Artificial Entities," in *The Oxford Handbook of Ethics of AI*, ed. Markus D. Dubber, Frank Pasquale, and Sunit Das (New York: Oxford University Press, 2020), 59.

24. Mark Kingwell, "Are Sentient AIs Persons?" in Dubber, Pasquale, and Das, *Oxford Handbook*, 335.

25. Ray Kurzweil, *The Singularity Is Near: When Humans Transcend Biology* (New York: Penguin Books, 2006).

26. For a helpful overview of these and related views, see Coeckelbergh, *AI Ethics*, 47–94. Coeckelbergh is a philosopher of media and technology at the University of Vienna.

Disembodied intelligence is not human, but "the truth is that we tend to talk about AI in ways that dehumanize us and humanize our machines."[27] Machine learning is a statistical process frequently employing pattern recognition with algorithms to explain data and make predictions about future data.[28] Facial recognition, for example, can determine who a person is based on data patterns, but that is far different from our relationality in which we encounter other humans as bodies with a history, emotions, attachments, moral capacity, and spiritual inclinations. Machines can calculate all options before a person makes an ethical decision and can give some kind of calculation as to the "right choice." But ethical decisions are not data-pattern calculations, for they involve internal virtues within the embodied soul / ensouled body and frequently involve judgments of wisdom amid highly complex dilemmas. And as philosopher Mark Coeckelbergh says to conclude his book *AI Ethics*, "AI is good at recognizing patterns, but wisdom cannot be delegated to machines."[29]

Robots can never have a personal relationship with God, though their designers can script prayers for them. One can program AI to do some good actions, but it can never love in the wholistic sense, bringing together thinking, will, emotions, affections, and actions. It can never experience pain, guilt, or shame from its unjust, unethical, and evil actions. AI can never experience the fruits of the Spirit, which are expressions of a whole self: "But the fruit of the Spirit is love, joy, peace, forbearance, kindness, goodness, faithfulness, gentleness and self-control. . . . Those who belong to Christ Jesus have crucified the flesh with its passions and desires. Since we live by the Spirit, let us keep in step with the Spirit" (Gal. 5:22–25). The spontaneity, sensitivity, and deep spiritual resonance of this life do not characterize the life of algorithms.

One of the most pseudoembodied examples of AI is the sexbot, robots made to look real, speak, and interact sexually with human beings. Made with silicone bodies, they "are highly customizable with upgradable body parts and hyperrealistic features. The dolls are designed so that customers can choose their perfect 'companion.' . . . The company claims that this product provides a form of companionship, a way for men [and now women too] never to be lonely again."[30] Many designers say this can be as fulfilling as sex with a human being. The reality, of course, is that this is masturbation, not sex, and such robots likely only exacerbate the loneliness of their users and sexualize and dehumanize people, especially women, through their stereotypical sexual imagery. As we saw in chapter 5, the creation paradigm for sex is a "one flesh" relationship between a man and a woman that consummates a marriage, brings children into the world, expresses love, provides pleasure, and is a sign to us of Christ's love for and union with his church. Sex in the

27. Thacker, *Age of AI*, 39, 42.
28. Coeckelbergh, *AI Ethics*, 83
29. Coeckelbergh, *AI Ethics*, 202.
30. Thacker, *Age of AI*, 86.

Christian understanding can never be a disembodied act or merely a bodily act, for it is constituted by wholistic humans giving their total selves to the other, for the sake of the other, and to the glory of God. That is a long way from an impersonal sexbot.

The other primary ethical issue for embodied souls / ensouled bodies is to reflect on what our technology and AIs in particular do to us. Technologies of any type are never neutral. This should not lead us to a Luddite position but rather to a discernment about how they impact us and then to wisdom in their use—personally, in our families, in the church, and in the marketplace. Some designers of AI champion "the idea that machines will take over, will master us rather than the other way around."[31] But what would happen to us as human beings if we reached Kurzweil's point of "Singularity" and, as individuals, became more machine than conscious, sentient, wise, emotive human beings? It is hard to imagine that the technicization of human beings will create more just, caring, wise, sensitive, loving people or societies.

One of the primary influences of AI on humans is seen through the impact of personal devices and social media, especially on the iGen age group. Sometimes also called the Z Generation, these young people were born between 1995 and 2012. Some analysts prefer iGen language because the *i* stands for *internet*, which was commercialized the year they were born, and also for *iPhone*, which came out in 2007 as they were early adolescents. AI plays a strategic role with this cohort through smartphones and through their favorite social media platforms: Snapchat, TikTok, and Instagram. Jean Twenge has amassed significant studies on iGen'ers, and she concludes that this group is growing up to be less happy, to have far greater mental health issues, and to be less prepared for adulthood than previous generations, primarily because of the impact of the technology. She found that "iGen high school seniors spent an average of 2¼ hours a day texting on their cell phones, about 2 hours a day on the Internet, 1½ hours a day on electronic gaming, and about a half hour on video chat. . . . That totals to six hours a day with new media—and that's just during their leisure time."[32] What are the results of all this interaction with technology stemming from AI? "The results could not be clearer: teens who spend more time on screen activities . . . are more likely to be unhappy, and those who spend more time on non-screen activities . . . are more likely to be happy." In testing for variables and reverse causation, all of the studies are abundantly clear: this generation is experiencing lower satisfaction, far higher rates of suicide, and higher rates of mental illness than previous generations at the same age. As an example, "46% more teens killed themselves in 2015 than in 2007. The rise occurred

31. Coeckelbergh, *AI Ethics*, 11.

32. Jean M. Twenge, *iGen: Why Today's Super-Connected Kids Are Growing Up Less Rebellious, More Tolerant, Less Happy—and Completely Unprepared for Adulthood* (New York: Atria, 2017), 51.

just as new-media screen time started to increase and in-person social activities began to wane."[33]

As I write, there is much discussion about the nationwide decrease in test scores, during and in the aftermath of COVID-19. During this time many schools have resorted to virtual learning, believing that screen time is innocuous and can even enhance learning. The jury is still out on low test-score causation, but many are beginning to theorize that all our screen exposure and social media engagement—all fueled by AI technologies—are doing something to our brains that we do not yet understand. The answer to all of this is not to turn our backs on AI and its accompanying technologies but rather to utilize much restraint and wisdom for our own personal engagement and that of our children. I'm personally delighted to see the way my own grandchildren and many friends' children are being guided toward traditional and constructive play, loads of personal interactions, lots of reading, and minimal time on devices. After all, our children are embodied souls / ensouled bodies and should not be reduced to machines. We must control our technology rather than letting our technology control us, precisely because of our unique constitution as whole beings made in God's image.

Virtual Gathering for Worship and Work

One of the benefits of our new technologies is the possibility of carrying out various activities virtually, at a distance. This particularly became prominent from 2020 on due to COVID-19 in churches, the workplace, and educational institutions. I want to focus primarily on the ethical viability of virtual activities in worship and work. Though the institutions related to these activities have opened up again as I have written this book, the question has emerged—Is virtual worship and work a good thing? Many approach this query from a pragmatic standpoint, with a view toward its logistical workability or economic implications, but it's important to analyze it ethically and theologically in light of our nature as embodied souls / ensouled bodies.

During the height of COVID-19, 72 percent of Americans who said they are regular churchgoers indicated they had worshiped virtually, and many churches reported they had virtual drop-ins by folks who didn't attend regularly.[34] Thus, they contended, they are able to extend their mission and reach through a virtual platform. Virtual worship was particularly affirmed by elderly and sick people, for whom coming to a physical place was a challenge. But many churches and parishioners have continued to laud it as just another

33. Twenge, *iGen*, 77, 87.

34. Justin Nortey, "More Houses of Worship Are Returning to Normal Operations, but In-person Attendance Is Unchanged Since Fall," Pew Research Center, March 22, 2022, https://www.pewresearch.org/fact-tank/2022/03/22/more-houses-of-worship-are-returning-to-normal-operations-but-in-person-attendance-is-unchanged-since-fall/.

option for people who are used to alternatives in life. In response to this, Anglican priest Tish Harrison Warren contends, "Online church, while it was necessary for a season, diminishes worship and us as people." Why? "We seek to worship wholly—with heart, soul, mind and strength—and embodiment is an irreducible part of that wholeness."[35] Warren's *New York Times* article prompted significant pushback, mostly consisting of pragmatic responses related to historic technology use in general and growth patterns as a result of virtual worship. In one research study of twenty-seven hundred congregations across thirty-eight denominations in the context of the pandemic, the following was reported: "Churches with a hybrid approach—with both in-person and online services—saw reported worship attendance growing by 4.5%. Churches that only met in person saw attendance decline by 15.7%, while those that only met online declined by 7.3%."[36]

So how do we assess all of this? Clearly pragmatic judgments have a place when it comes to reflecting on strategies employed by the church. But this must always be done in the larger context of the nature of the church and, in this case, the nature of worship, which entails theological reflection. Warren is right to appeal to human wholeness in approaching this issue, for the body of Christ is a gathering of Christ's people, who bring their whole selves to the gathering, including their bodily and nonbodily dimensions. It is significant that one of the primary terms for the church in the New Testament is "body of Christ," which implies that just as Christ's own physical body was once visibly present on earth, so now his body continues to be on earth through the people that confess him as Savior and Lord. This implies a physicality in the body of Christ. Moreover, worship is both individual and corporate in nature and employs physical dimensions (singing, kneeling, reciting, partaking in the sacraments, and hearing) as well as nonphysical elements, such as the heart and the mind. One cannot think of church as disembodied members, and one cannot regularly worship as a disembodied self.

Still, circumstances might call for virtual ministries and strategies. The church has long found ways of ministering to the elderly or ill and administering the Lord's Supper for them. Moreover, we might even contend that Paul and the apostles in the early church employed a form of virtual ministry in writing epistles to the churches when physical presence was not possible. But in these cases, Paul and the apostles were clear in their intent to come and

35. Tish Harrison Warren, "Why Churches Should Drop Their Online Services," Opinion, *New York Times*, January 30, 2022, https://www.nytimes.com/2022/01/30/opinion/church-online-services-covid.html, quoted in Bob Smietana and Elizabeth E. Evans, "Streaming Online Has Been a Boon for Churches, a Godsend for Isolated," Religion News Service, February 1, 2022, https://religionnews.com/2022/02/01/streaming-online-has-been-a-boon-for-churches-a-godsend-for-isolated/.

36. Smietana and Evans, "Streaming Online." The study was carried out by the Hartford Institute for Religion Research.

meet them face-to-face—as embodied souls / ensouled bodies (Rom. 15:23–24; 1 Cor. 16:7; Phil. 2:23–24; 1 Thess. 3:10; 2 Tim. 1:4; 2 John 12; 3 John 13–14). Exceptions never define the norm, and thus we can say that we have a theological and ethical responsibility to gather with our fellow believers, making room for exceptions, because God has created us as whole beings who need each other in our wholeness to carry out the ministries and mission of the church of Jesus Christ. Meeting face-to-face with our whole selves is part of what it means to be the church.

Working from home or remotely has been in existence for a while but gained momentum in recent years. A number of pragmatic reasons have been given for virtual work: increased productivity, financial savings, employee retention, minimizing distractions, and delivering results.[37] Malcom Gladwell, a podcaster and a freelance writer with numerous bestsellers, set off a firestorm of response on a podcast hosted by a British entrepreneur. Gladwell was concerned that people working from home can be "socially disconnected from their organization." As the head of Pushkin Industries, a podcast and audiobook company, he noticed that employees who came to the office and connected with others seemed more excited and stayed longer with the company. Being together as human beings engenders more collaborative and creative work.[38] Gladwell was criticized for hypocrisy by those who argue that working virtually is productive, because he frequently works from home or coffee shops.

Arguments have gone back and forth in the corporate world about the pros and cons of virtual work, but I personally think Gladwell is right to raise cautions. If God ordained work in creation and if work is an expression of our whole selves (body, mind, affections, reasons, emotions, and moral and spiritual sensibilities), then work should at least in part include face-to-face encounters. Business people I've talked to have mentioned that while you can obviously have conversations by Zoom, because you can't discern body language—a significant part of our communication—it's often hard to know the deep-seated feelings and viewpoints of colleagues. Many have also said trust is frequently lost without face-to-face encounters, and they see a waning in loyalty to their companies and institutions when everything is virtual. As we explore this as a society, perhaps an ideal, at least for some jobs, is a hybrid in which part is virtual and part is face-to-face. From a Christian theological and ethical standpoint, we should place into the conversation that we are whole people—embodied souls / ensouled bodies—and that is difficult to be

37. Mehul Shah, "Remote Work Ethics: What You Need to Know," Minterapp, November 2, 2021, www.minterapp.com/remote-work-ethics.

38. Quoted in Megan Sauer, "Malcom Gladwell, Addressing Criticism: 'Solitary Work' Can Be Done at Home but for Creative Work, 'Offices Really Do Matter,'" CNBC Make It, last updated August 12, 2022, https://www.cnbc.com/2022/08/12/malcolm-gladwell-on-the-evolution-of-his-working-from-home-stance.html.

expressed if we are always disembodied. To be fully human in the workplace, we need some embodied interactions with each other. Moreover, we should note that virtual work only exacerbates the blue-collar and white-collar divide in society, for it is primarily the latter that don't have to come into the office in virtual work. This then becomes a justice issue.

Conclusion

In God's marvelous creation of humans in his image, the Creator makes us whole beings. Both the material and nonmaterial dimensions are displayed in the creation account and then affirmed throughout the rest of Scripture. The material and nonmaterial parts of humanity are continually interacting with each other in such a way that they can't be isolated from each other. We are embodied souls / ensouled bodies, and this impacts every dimension of our lives, from our spirituality to our relationships to our work.

That we are embodied souls / ensouled bodies has significant implications for ethics, as we have outlined in this chapter. It means that we must affirm and hold together both evangelism and social concern as moral imperatives. It implies that AI and related technologies can be employed with wisdom, that AI does not constitute humanness, and that we should be wary of unbridled technicization of humanity. This good but fallen gift to humanity never encompasses the wholeness of a human being. And in a time when virtual gathering is gaining impetus in worship and work, we should be aware that true worship should always include a physical gathering of Christ's people, and virtual gatherings should only be used for warranted exceptions and emergencies. Finally, work, as ordained by God, calls for us to bring our whole selves into our everyday callings. This need not eliminate some virtual elements, but regular physical interactions are critical to trust and good communication.

Being made whole, we can never revert to a purely material approach to life or a purely "spiritual" approach. We come to God through Christ as embodied souls / ensouled bodies, and we best flourish as God's people when we live commensurate with those wholistic realities in every phase of life.

Conclusion

Living Out a Creation Ethic in a Pluralistic, Complex, Fallen World

The opening lines of Dante's *Divine Comedy* seem highly relevant to our own times:

> Midway this way of life we're bound upon,
> I woke to find myself in a dark wood,
> Where the right road was wholly lost and gone.[1]

Our world today appears to be in a dark wood, having lost its way in both personal and societal life. As Christians seek to live out a creation ethic amid such a world, they too frequently grapple with finding their way through the moral and cultural darkness in terms of expectations for that world and their own journey in it. The right road ethically seems lost and gone.

Because the world is fallen from its creational designs, the Christian moral journey has always proven difficult and challenging. The fundamental assumptions and guiding aspirations of all cultures throughout history have in various ways been at odds with the kind of ethical thinking and commitments we have chronicled in this book. However, the pluralism, secularity, and complexities of our own time bring added challenge to the moral journey. Competing worldviews and moral systems have a way of undermining the kinds of ethical commitments that flow from a creational ethic.

This kind of ethic and its moral commitments stem from a particular worldview that reflects the overarching narrative of the Bible. That story is essentially creation, fall, redemption, and a final restoration. As this book has attempted

1. Dante, *The Comedy of Dante Alighieri the Florentine, Cantica I: Hell*, trans. Dorothy L. Sayers, Penguin Classics (Baltimore: Penguin Books, 1949), 71.

to demonstrate, if we pull out creation, the whole narrative falls apart. Thus, an ethic rooted in creation is an essential part of the whole biblical story. Moreover, creation is a theme throughout the canon of Holy Scripture. As we have demonstrated, it runs through every part of Scripture and in multiple genres of God's written Word. Creation as a foundation for ethics has implications for the doctrine of the Trinity. Many ethicists, theologians, and lay people have attempted to build an ethic from Jesus or the kingdom with a neglect or even outright rejection of creation ethics. But the command of God the Creator and God the Redeemer must be one, or we jettison the unity of the triune Godhead. This is reinforced by the fact that the Son of God was there at creation, and thus all the ethical paradigms flow from the Son as well as the Father and the Holy Spirit.

Final restoration, the eschaton, is a vital part of the Christian narrative, and we've demonstrated continuity between creation and eschaton. The final restoration is precisely that—not a destruction of this good yet fallen world but a restoration to what God intended in "the beginning." Thus, the paradigms and designs of creation will be fulfilled in the new (renewed) heavens and earth. Creation is also important because it includes numerous ethical paradigms and frameworks for the moral life. We have seen the following:

- A loving God designs and speaks, and this love and design are spoken in creation and the whole of the Bible, including in Christ.
- The physical world is pronounced good, including the human body; thus, money, sex, and power are really good gifts of God, a view that contrasts with the various teachings of Gnosticism and asceticism. Though deeply fallen, we should start with the goodness and telos of these gifts.
- Humans and the rest of creation reflect some continuity, but only humans are made in God's image and hence have an inherent dignity—to be guarded in all humans and all phases of life. This has great relevance for ethnocentrism, racism, abortion, and medical assistance in dying.
- God gives humans, as image bearers, a stewardship task of caring for this good physical world. The earth will not be destroyed in the eschaton, so kingdom people should care for it now.
- Humans are created as relational beings, and thus God institutes sexuality (male and female), marriage, physical intimacy, and family as foundational institutions of society, the means of continuing life in this world, and even signs of Christ's love for his church.
- Because humans are relational beings, numerous other institutions emerge from the foundational elements of creation—church, education, media, recreation or entertainment, economics, and the state among them. Though all human institutions are fallen, including family and

church, they all serve a significant role in society, with the church being the place believers discern how to navigate the institutions of society.

- God institutes work as a reflection of his own creation and as a reflection of the incarnate Son of God coming into this world as a worker. Work is a calling of God, mandated at creation, and thus it is to be carried out with commensurate ethical commitments, such as dignity, integrity, justice, and profit without idolatry.
- But work is not the end of human life, and thus God in creation institutes a Sabbath, which calls us to worship as a foundational element of the ethically good life, to self-care, and to care for others with justice.
- Despite the grandeur of being image bearers, God creates humans as finite creatures, meaning they are limited, dependent, and bounded. Distinct from the effects of the fall, our finitude means we can never create actual utopias on earth and are limited in attempts to transcend our humanness or even thwart death.
- Finally, we are embodied souls or ensouled bodies, meaning that we are whole beings with physical and nonphysical dimensions intertwined. Thus, we must care for all dimensions of the human self through evangelism and social concern, and we should never let the human self become a machine or live as disembodied or purely physical beings.

In large part these creational paradigms are understood as part of our Christian worldview and empowered by the work of the Holy Spirit. While unbelievers may partially comprehend the creational paradigms and partially live up to these designs, we can never expect a full expression in thought or life by those outside of Christ. As the writer to the Hebrews notes, "By faith we understand that the universe was formed at God's command, so that what is seen was not made out of what was visible" (Heb. 11:3). Though the visible elements of creation provide pointers to the Creator and creational designs, it is through faith that we grasp the full realities of the paradigms, as revealed to us in Scripture. Thus, we cannot expect those who do not have faith in Christ, the Creator-Redeemer, and do not accept the authority of Scripture, which elucidates the creational norms, to fully embrace or exemplify these norms. And we therefore can hardly expect these norms to be fully manifested in non-Christian social institutions.

All of this, then, raises the question, How should we navigate the turbulent waters of living in a society whose cultural norms are at odds with the creation paradigms and Jesus himself, recalling that all societies and cultures are to varying degrees at odds with the biblical norms? We are called to be salt, light, and leaven in the world, but what does that mean, and how should we carry out that mission as followers of the Creator-Redeemer, Jesus Christ?

Christians frequently make one of two errors in responding to the salt, light, and leaven mandates. Some view the world around them as so far removed from Christian perspectives that they must withdraw from the world (or large portions of it) or primarily defy the world to remain faithful to their Christian calling. Others assume that Christians should dominate the world by gaining social or political control of it.

The withdrawal or defiance approach has various forms of expression, but it essentially reflects what H. Richard Niebuhr in his classic work *Christ and Culture* terms "Christ against culture."[2] Christian ethics is relegated primarily or even only to the life of the church or Christian institutions. Historically this approach has been most frequently associated with the Anabaptist movement, such as John Howard Yoder's writings, or the neo-Anabaptist movement, such as Stanley Hauerwas. Neither calls for a total withdrawal from society, but both emphasize that the Christian ethic is primarily an ethic of the Christian community and, hence, has little guidance for navigating the waters of social institutions. It is primarily an embodiment ethic with a negative stance against the culture and society.

Another modified withdrawal approach is set forth by Rod Dreher in *The Benedict Option*. The essential stance, rooted in the thought and pattern of Saint Benedict in the sixth century, is "to develop creative, communal solutions to help us hold on to our faith and our values in a world growing ever more hostile to them. We would have to choose to make a decisive leap into a truly countercultural way of living Christianity, or we would doom our children and our children's children to assimilation." This approach "foretells a world in which the church will live in small circles of committed believers who live the faith intensely, and who will have to be somewhat cut off from mainstream society for the sake of holding on to the truth."[3] Dreher is not calling for an entire abandonment of the public square, and since he wrote the book, his conservative political alignments have at times pulled him back into the public square, as evidenced by his admiration of Viktor Orbán's right-wing government in Hungary.[4]

None of these thinkers calls for a total withdrawal from society, and their writings are valuable in chronicling the sickness of modern and postmodern societies, the need for faithfulness among Christian believers, and the cultural role that the church and Christian institutions can play by embodying the Christian ethic. But the major question is whether the withdrawal or defiance approach truly captures the meaning of being salt, light, and leaven within

2. H. Richard Niebuhr, *Christ and Culture* (New York: Harper & Row, 1951), 45–82.

3. Rod Dreher, *The Benedict Option: A Strategy for Christians in a Post-Christian Nation* (New York: Sentinel, 2017), 1, 4.

4. Rod Dreher, "'Why Hungary?' The New Yorker Asked Me," *The American Conservative* (blog), September 14, 2021, https://www.theamericanconservative.com/hungary-new-yorker-rod-dreher-viktor-orban-conservatism/.

the world. These are metaphors of influence that likely cannot be carried out in a purely negative fashion that focuses on ecclesial embodiment alone. Adherents to this approach frequently "claim their message is prophetic but in its net effect (that is, in what people both inside and outside of the tradition hear), it is overwhelmingly a message of anger, disparagement, and negation."[5] Moreover, God calls us to live within the world, even with all of its denigration of creation and kingdom ethics, for as the writer to the Hebrews puts it, "The bodies of those animals whose blood is brought into the sanctuary by the high priest as a sacrifice for sin are burned outside the camp. Therefore Jesus also suffered outside the city gate in order to sanctify the people by his own blood. Let us then go to him outside the camp and bear the abuse he endured. For here we have no lasting city, but we are looking for the city that is to come" (Heb. 13:11–14 NRSV). Precisely because we are rooted in an enduring city, we can wisely engage the profane city, not flee from it.

The other error in attempting to be salt, light, and leaven in the world is a pursuit of societal dominance, usually through political means. Here the assumption is that if we elect the right people to governmental office, get the right people into key leadership roles in major social institutions, and hold to the right sociopolitical and legal perspectives, we can most effectively implement the Christian ethic in the social order. Many in this camp look longingly to the medieval world, with its Christendom alliance between church and state, or nostalgically to a "Christian America," even though America never was deeply Christian. Today there are various expressions of the dominance model, and they are usually tied to ideological alliances. Among many theologically progressive or liberal people, there is a strong alliance with progressive social agendas. On the other side are more conservative wings of the church (found among both evangelical and Roman Catholic Christians), who have sometimes made alliance with conservative or even right-wing political movements and ideologies. One example of a dominance model in conservative Roman Catholic circles is the integralist movement that seeks to employ a natural law ethic to give legal and policy privilege to Roman Catholic commitments. Adrian Vermeule, a Harvard Law School professor, "is an integralist in the sense that he sees political authority as ordered to the common good of human life, that rendering God true worship is essential to that common good, and that political authority therefore has the duty of recognizing and promoting the true religion."[6]

Many secularists and progressives see the politicized dominance approach as primarily occurring on the religious and political right, and those alliances have been well chronicled. But sociologists George Yancey and Ashlee Quosigk

5. James Davison Hunter, *To Change the World: The Irony, Tragedy, and Possibility of Christianity in the Late Modern World* (New York: Oxford University Press, 2010), 165.

6. Edmund Waldstein, "What Is Integralism Today?," *Church Life Journal*, October 31, 2018, https://churchlifejournal.nd.edu/articles/what-is-integralism-today/.

argue from their research that there is politicized dominance on both sides, with some interesting twists regarding identities. They found that progressive Christians "emphasize political values relating to social justice issues as they determine who is part of their in-group; they tend to be less concerned about theological agreement. Conservative Christians, however, do not put strong emphasis on political agreement in order to determine if you are one of them—their major concern is whether you agree with them on core theological points."[7] As a result progressive Christians tend to identify more with atheists and Muslims who share their political views than with conservative Christians who don't. This doesn't mean progressives are politicized while conservatives are not, but the two differ in their fundamental identities—the former finding it in social ideology and the latter in theological identity. Yancey and Quosigk therefore claim that the core of progressive religion "is built upon a value set of inclusiveness, tolerance and social justice. Christianity is just one of many paths to achieving a society of inclusion and justice for the marginalized. It is not necessarily a superior path."[8]

Many analysts would argue—rightly, I believe—that both conservative Christians and progressive Christians have too frequently politicized their faith, equating Christianity with particular political parties and ideologies in their attempts to change the world. As Paul Miller puts it in *The Religion of American Greatness*, "Progressives envision a utopian future; nationalists [i.e., the religious right] a romantic past." He goes on to say,

> Progressives want to usher in their promised land of autonomous individuals empowered to express any identity they prefer, with the state responsible for providing primary goods, punishing dissent, and policing identity choices. At the extreme, it has deteriorated into a hectoring, authoritarian movement that seeks to enforce its ideals through legal bullying, speech codes, and "cancel culture." Nationalists want to re-create the imagined culture of American greatness, usually envisioned as the era of 1950s White, middle class, Protestant America—the greatness of America as a "Christian nation." They equate the nation with the majority culture in a way that leaves little room for the diversity of subcultures in America.[9]

7. George Yancey and Ashlee Quosigk, *One Faith No Longer: The Transformation of Christianity in Red and Blue America* (New York: New York University Press, 2021), 4.

8. Yancey and Quosigk, *One Faith No Longer*, 191. John W. Morehead notes that "according to [moral foundations] theory, while human beings share the same moral intuitions, conservatives and liberals emphasize different moral foundations. Liberals tend to draw upon two foundations, care and fairness, whereas conservatives tend to emphasize loyalty, authority, and purity" ("Evangelicals and Gross Religions: Disgust and Fear in Multifaith Engagement," in *A Charitable Orthopathy: Christian Perspectives on Emotions in Multifaith Engagement*, ed. John W. Morehead and Brandon C. Benziger [Eugene, OR: Pickwick, 2020], 64).

9. Paul D. Miller, *The Religion of American Greatness: What's Wrong with Christian Nationalism* (Downers Grove, IL: IVP Academic, 2022), xvi–xvii. It should be noted that Miller sees both the progressive and nationalist agendas as believing government is "responsible for

There are numerous mistakes in both the withdrawal/defiance and dominance approaches. For one they fail to fully comprehend the meaning of salt, light, and leaven; for these are neither metaphors of dominance nor metaphors of withdrawal or defiance, but rather of influence from within. The metaphors assume a distinctiveness of Christian believers (in both thought and action) from the world around them, and this would include social and political ideologies. This then means there is a clear distinction between the kingdom of God and the kingdoms of this world, including their worldviews and ethics. To politicize the faith in any form is to blur the distinction between these two kingdoms and to misconstrue the calling to be salt, light, and leaven.

Jesus's call to be kingdom people and, thus, to be aligned with a creation ethic is not a call away from the world and its major social institutions. It is a call to engage them in a way that stands apart from the conventional sociopolitical ideologies of a given culture. This is quite clear in Jesus's prayer for his disciples during one of his last gatherings with them:

> I have given them your word, and the world has hated them because they are not of the world, just as I am not of the world. I do not ask that you take them out of the world, but that you keep them from the evil one. They are not of the world, just as I am not of the world. Sanctify them in the truth; your word is truth. As you sent me into the world, so I have sent them into the world. And for their sake I consecrate myself, that they also may be sanctified in truth. (John 17:14–19 ESV)

The thrust of Jesus's prayer is contrary to both the withdrawal and dominance responses. It points to a clear presence in the world, but also a distinctive, holy pattern of life within it—a world that hates Christ followers. Exactly how this plays out will vary by context, for obviously the mode of being salt and light will look different in Kenya than it will in China; it will be different in North America and in North Korea, but the distinctive holiness should always remain.

In contrast to either dominance or withdrawal modes, Christian sociologist James Hunter proposes a faithful-presence model. "Faithful presence in the world means that Christians are fully present and committed in their spheres of social influence, whatever they may be: their families, neighborhoods, voluntary activities, and places of work." Such an approach will certainly expect that the major embodiment of a Christian ethic will be in the church and in Christian institutions or organizations. But it will seek to be salt, light, and leaven within the contours of social institutions, without assuming they can be turned into the kingdom of God. It will seek the common good and the

---

bringing about their preferred social and cultural vision. . . . They only differ on the direction of the state's social engineering programs" (xvii). This, of course, is different from the withdrawal or defiance approach to culture.

good of all and, when appropriate, will seek to defend the right of churches and Christian institutions to maintain their convictions in hiring and lifestyle expectations when the larger society seeks to impose its secular will. Rather than merely a negative voice, "within the dialectic between affirmation and antithesis, faithful presence means a constructive resistance that seeks new patterns of social organization that challenge, undermine, and otherwise diminish oppression, injustice, enmity, and corruption and, in turn, encourage harmony, . . . wholeness, beauty, joy, . . . and well-being."[10]

Christopher Watkin observes that "if Christians approach our culture merely with the aim of denouncing or humiliating it, they are unlikely to make any impact, will almost never bring healing, and are more at risk of not recognizing where their own thoughts and instincts are more cultural than biblical." This may be the tendency of the withdrawal/defiance approach. But, says Watkin, "if they approach our culture only with the goal of affirming or even praising it, they are signing up for biblical unfaithfulness and cultural irrelevance."[11]

A faithful-presence model within the world will lead Christians to at times stand with or against particular public policy positions, but to do so without the politicization and ideological commitments that have too often plagued the Christian church. Ideological and politicized approaches usually lead to what James Mumford has called "package-deal ethics," in which it is assumed that if you buy into a given position on one issue, other issues have been bundled together as part of the ideological commitments. As a result "our political factions are simply modern varieties of the tribes human beings have belonged to . . . throughout history. Tribes have their own heroes, saints, villains, stories, scriptures, symbols and colors. They are sites of intense emotional attachment." Our ideological tribes isolate us into factions with predetermined responses to social and ethical issues, and thus "we need to exit the echo chambers of social media and meet each other in person—to engage with rather than demonize our liberal or conservative adversaries."[12]

The creation ethic we have set forth in this work is not package-deal ethics, as it incorporates ethical paradigms and commitments typically not put together in conservative, nationalist, or progressive ideologies. We have denounced racism in its multiple forms (insisting on human dignity for all people) while simultaneously affirming the right of the unborn to live (and human dignity in all phases of life). We have set forth the biblical case for creation care and affirmed that sex is reserved for marriage between a man and a woman. We have upheld the biblical case for justice (rooted in the Sabbath paradigm)

10. Hunter, *To Change the World*, 247, 248.

11. Christopher Watkin, *Biblical Critical Theory: How the Bible's Unfolding Story Makes Sense of Modern Life and Culture* (Grand Rapids: Zondervan Academic, 2022), 27.

12. James Mumford, *Vexed: Ethics beyond Political Tribes* (London: Bloomsbury Continuum, 2020), Kindle loc. 103, 169.

while simultaneously affirming work as a calling of God and material realities, including money, as good gifts of God. Because we are whole beings, we have affirmed a strong commitment to evangelism while also embracing social concern. These and other paradigms defy the tribalistic ideologies of our time. This means that based in a creation ethic, Christians should carry out their role as salt and light in ways that are not expected by the societies in which they live.

As we attempt to be a faithful presence within the world, it is wise to become bilingual in the way we enunciate our ethic within the institutions of society. When I have spoken to secular audiences on ethical issues or served on hospital ethics committees, I have quickly discerned that I will not get much of a hearing if I immediately appeal to the Bible or to theological constructs as I have done in this book. Thus, while rooting our ethics in creation and Scripture, we need to learn to articulate ethical commitments in a broader language in those contexts. For example, Christians root human dignity in humanity's creation in the image of God. But as we noted in chapter 3, the 1948 "Universal Declaration of Human Rights" bases human rights in the dignity of human persons. No religious language is used to support these commitments, for the reality is that all human beings want to be treated with dignity, and thus we can make a strong case that dignity is intrinsic within human beings. This is the kind of argumentation that can be utilized in secular settings (hospitals, government agencies, etc.) when dealing with divisive issues such as abortion and medical assistance in dying. Or let's take the biblical injunction to avoid adultery and remain faithful in marriage, which, of course, the Bible is quite clear on. But one could also follow the example of Søren Kierkegaard, the nineteenth-century philosopher who, in his book *Either/Or*, has an imaginary letter from an older married man to a young bachelor. The married man speaks of a "historical love," with his relationship placed in time, focused not just on the immediate moment but moving into the future together.[13] As Mumford summarizes it, such love is similar to our familiarity with material objects in which true appreciation "involves forgoing immediacy and committing to renewed contact with them. Similarly, with love, only repetition—the experience of the same person afforded by relationships that endure over time—yields a fuller appreciation of his or her beauty."[14]

Appealing to a broader language when enunciating a creation or Christian ethic in pluralistic settings is not hiding our faith but attempting to build a bridge in order to get a hearing. When I have spoken in secular settings in this way, inevitably people come to talk afterward, and the way is open for more

13. Søren Kierkegaard, *Either/Or: A Fragment of Life*, trans. Alastair Hannay (London: Penguin, 2002), 467. See discussion in Mumford, *Vexed*, chap. 3.

14. Mumford, *Vexed*, Kindle loc. 1200.

specifically Christian language and understandings in the personal interactions. One thinks of the apostle Paul in Athens at the Areopagus in Acts 17. He is brought to the marketplace of ideas to talk about "this new teaching" (v. 19), but he begins with points of contact by noting their inscriptions and later quoting their poets. Only after building a bridge to where his hearers are in this eminently non-Christian setting does he get around to the resurrection (vv. 31–32).

Being a faithful presence in our world today means recognizing the pluralism with varying worldviews and ethical systems around us. We enter into this world as Christians with a particular worldview that is not pluralistic in its understanding of ultimate truth and salvation, for Jesus says, "I am the way and the truth and the life. No one comes to the Father except through me" (John 14:6). Jesus calls us to bear witness to that truth, inviting people to come and experience its life-giving salvation. But the metaphors of salt, light, and leaven are not a call to impose this way of life by political edict or ideological mandates. Thus, we can simultaneously embrace a particular ethic and worldview and a pluralistic society—albeit one that hopefully allows for a Christian voice at the table. At times the church may even have to call for its right to exist. John Inazu, professor of law at Washington University and a committed believer, calls for a principled pluralism or a confident pluralism at the societal level:

> Confident pluralism argues that we can, and we must, learn to live with each other in spite of our deep differences. It requires a tolerance for dissent, a skepticism of government orthodoxy, and a willingness to endure strange and even offensive ways of life. Confident pluralism asks that those charged with enforcing our laws do better in preserving and strengthening our constitutional commitments to voluntary groups, public forums, and certain kinds of generally available funding. It also challenges each of us to live out the aspirations of tolerance, humility, and patience in our civic practices.

And for the American context, he adds, "Confident pluralism does not give us the American Dream. But it might help us avoid the American Nightmare."[15]

Living within a fallen, secular, pluralistic world is not easy, for "we live in a culture that lacks a shared understanding of the common good. Beneath our social, religious, and political disagreements lie different understandings of moral authority, human nature, and even perceptions of reality."[16] As a result there are frequent attempts to undermine and malign a Christian ethic, especially one rooted in creation. But we live by faith in Christ, the

15. John D. Inazu, *Confident Pluralism: Surviving and Thriving through Deep Difference* (Chicago: University of Chicago Press, 2015), 121.

16. John Inazu and Timothy Keller, conclusion to *Uncommon Ground: Living Faithfully in a World of Difference*, ed. Timothy Keller and John Inazu (Nashville: Nelson Books, 2020), 193.

Creator-Redeemer who created us in love and redeemed us in love. It is precisely that gracious love that sustains us in the journey. Our world desperately longs for and needs people who maintain a clear commitment to a creation ethic—expressed in love, courage, and humility, even in the most trying situations. Maintaining a commitment to this ethic involves deep biblical and theological commitments, but in a world that rebuts it, it is only sustained by a deep inner spirituality and by the fellowship and encouragement of fellow believers committed to these patterns of life. Ultimately it is the power and presence of the triune God that make it possible to live out of a creation ethic, for it was the triune God who created the paradigms and now calls us to faithful embodiment and witness in Dante's "dark wood, where the right road [seems] lost and gone."

Scripture Index

Old Testament

Genesis

Acts

Romans

1 Corinthians

2 Corinthians

Galatians

Ephesians

Philippians

Colossians

1 Thessalonians

Subject Index